THE CHANGING SOCIAL STRUCTURE

Restructuring Britain

The Economy in Question
edited by John Allen and Doreen Massey

The Changing Social Structure
edited by Chris Hamnett, Linda McDowell and Philip Sarre

Politics in Transition
edited by Allan Cochrane and James Anderson

The following are associated Readers published by Hodder and Stoughton in association with The Open University:

Uneven Re-Development: Cities and Regions in Transition
edited by Doreen Massey and John Allen

Divided Nation: Social and Cultural Change in Britain
edited by Linda McDowell, Philip Sarre and Chris Hamnett

A State of Crisis: The Changing Face of British Politics
edited by James Anderson and Allan Cochrane

Open University Course D314 Restructuring Britain
(Details of this course are available from the Student Enquiries Office, The Open University, PO Box 71, Milton Keynes MK7 6AG)

Restructuring Britain

THE CHANGING SOCIAL
STRUCTURE

edited by
Chris Hamnett, Linda McDowell
and Philip Sarre

SAGE Publications
in association with

The Open
University

First published 1989

 SAGE Publications Ltd
28 Banner Street
London EC1Y 8QE

SAGE Publications Inc
2111 West Hillcrest Drive
Newbury Park, California 91320

SAGE Publications India Pvt Ltd
32, M-Block Market
Greater Kailash – I
New Delhi 110 048

British Library Cataloguing in Publication Data

The Changing social structure. – (Restructuring Britain)
1. Great Britain. Social structure
I. Hamnett, Chris   II. McDowell, Linda
III. Sarre, Philip
305′.0941

ISBN 0–8039–8199–6
ISBN 0–8039–8200–3 Pbk

Library of Congress catalog card number 88–63545

Typeset in Linotron 202 Times by
Fakenham Photosetting Ltd, Fakenham, Norfolk

Printed in Great Britain by Billing and Sons Ltd, Worcester

Contents

Course team

John Allen, Lecturer in Economic Geography
James Anderson, Lecturer in Geography
Chris Brook, Lecturer in Applied Regional Studies
Allan Cochrane, Senior Lecturer in Urban Studies
Chris Hamnett, Senior Lecturer in Geography (Course Team Chair)
Pat Jess, Staff Tutor, Northern Ireland
Linda McDowell, Senior Lecturer in Geography
Doreen Massey, Professor of Geography
Philip Sarre, Senior Lecturer in Geography

Consultants

Patrick Dunleavy, Lecturer in Politics, London School of Economics
Mark Goodwin, Lecturer in Geography, Goldsmiths College, University of London
Laurence Harris, Professor of Economics, The Open University
Richard Meegan, Senior Research Member, CES Ltd, London
Simon Mohun, Lecturer in Economics, Queen Mary College, University of London
Chris Pond, Director, Low Pay Unit
Mike Savage, Lecturer in Sociology, University of Surrey
Peter Taylor, Reader in Political Geography, University of Newcastle upon Tyne
Nigel Thrift, Reader in Geography, University of Bristol

External assessors

John Urry, Professor of Sociology, University of Lancaster (Course Assessor)
Huw Beynon, Professor of Sociology, University of Manchester
Paul Lawless, Principal Lecturer in Urban and Regional Studies, Sheffield
Andrew Sayer, Lecturer in Urban Studies, University of Sussex

Tutor testers

Cliff Hague, Senior Lecturer, Town and Country Planning, Heriot-Watt University, Edinburgh
Mark Hart, Lecturer in Environmental Studies, University of Ulster at Jordanstown
Jill Vincent, Research Fellow, Centre for Research in Social Policy, Loughborough University of Technology

Course support

Melanie Bayley, Editor
Ann Boomer, Secretary
Sarah Gauthier, Secretary
Rob Lyon, Graphic Designer
Ray Munns, Cartographer/Graphic Artist
Carol Oddy, Secretary
Varrie Scott, Course Manager
Jane Tyrell, Secretary
David Wilson, Editor

Restructuring Britain: introduction

The Changing Social Structure is part of a series on the changes which have reshaped the economic, social, political and geographical structure of the UK since the end of the 1950s. Each book is free-standing and can be read on its own, or it can be studied as part of the Open University course *Restructuring Britain*. One book deals with questions about the structure of the economy, production and work; this book deals with changes in social structure and culture, including class, gender, race, income, wealth and consumption; and a third with the reshaping of politics and the role of the state. Together with three associated Readers, the three textbooks form an integrated theoretical and empirical analysis of the changing structure of contemporary Britain.

There have probably been few periods in recent history when change of some sort has not been on the agenda; it is one of the defining characteristics of modern society. Yet the last two or more decades do seem to have been marked by transformations of a very different order, and moreover transformations which in different ways and with different timings have affected a wide range of aspects of society. The place of the UK in the international world has changed: its role in the international economic order has shifted quite dramatically and its political position between Europe and the USA has been renegotiated. Within the economy the shift from manufacturing to services has been reinforced, and with it the whole economic geography of the country. The future of cities and of some regions is at stake; and at national level the question must be whether the economy can survive by exporting services. Such shifts, together with wider changes in the labour process, have transformed the occupational structure of the workforce. While unemployment has risen, the most rapidly growing segment of the population in paid work is that of professionals, managers and administrators. But in the less well-paid parts of the economy, many of the new jobs have been in part-time and increasingly in casualized employment. All these changes in the economy have gone along with changes in the social structure too. There has been talk of 'the end of the working class' – certainly of the old image of the male-dominated kind, working in manufacturing – and of the burgeoning of white-collar middle strata: processes that are mirrored geographically in the counterposition of the recent fortunes of different regions of the country. Has women's lot been improved by all this, or are women now caught in an even more contradictory position? And how important have changes in consumption patterns been in moulding the shifting social structure? There have also been changes at the political level, and attempts, some more successful than others, to break the mould of the old party politics and to end the comfortable old consensus. It has, indeed, been the period when the very term 'restructuring', if not newly invented, has been rehabilitated and put to frequent use.

This series is built around an examination of these changes. Perhaps most fundamentally we wanted to explore the questions: what is the nature of all this change; does it amount to a structural change; are we at some kind of historical turning-point? In order to get to grips with these issues, a number of different threads have been chosen, which run throughout this series. There are three, and they are necessarily intertwined with each other as their investigation develops.

The *first* is simply the empirical changes themselves. *Restructuring Britain* covers a wide range of empirical material, and our aim is to investigate it bearing in mind always the questions: what kinds of change have these been; has there been structural change? One point to make from the start is that we want to consider the material geographically, that is, to take the spatial dimension as integral to our whole concern. Thus, while our key question concerns periodization, an underlying hypothesis is that different eras of history are bound up with distinct forms of uneven development. The argument is not that they merely happen together, but that they are integrally related to each other.

But one cannot examine empirical data for structural change, either social or spatial, without some notion of what structural change might be. So this, too, is an enquiry which runs through the series. How can one characterize distinct historical eras, or spatial formations; how does one assess what are the key relations; or what features can be said to be dominant? Indeed what does 'dominant' mean in this context? This in turn raises questions of the conceptualization of systems, and of structures themselves.

The *second* concern is to investigate the debates which have taken place within the social sciences about the nature of these empirical changes and about their explanation. Some theories and debates span all three books in this series, since their scope itself ranges from economic to political; the nature of the structural change they postulate or debate involves all aspects of society. Other theoretical debates tend to be more confined in their scope relating to perhaps only one or a bundle of the empirical changes we are considering here. Many of them, too, do not have an explicitly geographical element, and in some of these we have tried to inject our own spatial perspective, drawing out from them what are in some cases already implicit geographical implications. This is not appropriate in all cases, of course; but what we are after in the end is to analyse the nature of the reorganization of economic-social-political relations over space, and the impact of that.

Thirdly, we stand back even further from the empirical changes and explore how those debates within the social sciences can themselves be assessed. Here we examine the different questions which distinct approaches may address, even when they appear to be examining 'the same phenomena' and to be engaged in the same debate. The different modes of 'self-evaluation' implied by various theoretical approaches are pointed to, and the varying ways in which they relate to 'evidence' are contrasted. Much of this links back quite directly to, and intertwines with, the issues explored under the first heading – different theories, indeed, have quite distinct notions even about what is structural change.

The structure of the series

The Economy in Question introduces some of the theoretical debates over economic aspects of these issues: the definition and importance of deindustrialization, the nature of the international economic order, the characteristics of post-industrial society, the definition of service employment and its links to manufacturing, the changing organization of the labour process, and the concepts of work and economy. *The Changing Social Structure* introduces the debates over gender relations, race and class structure and changing patterns of consumption. Are we witnessing the end of the working class and the emergence of a predominantly middle-class society, dominated by private home and car ownership and a privatized and individualized social ethos? *Politics in Transition* examines the debates over the changing political role of the UK internationally, and the changing structure of politics and state intervention within the country. It looks at, amongst other things, the changing relationship between central and local government, the arguments regarding class dealignment and consumption in voting behaviour and the UK's position vis-à-vis the USA, the European Community and the Commonwealth.

There are, of course, links between all these issues. The division into three groups of issues, and indeed below that into individual chapters within each book, is made for analytical purposes. Although everything may well be connected to everything else, it is nonetheless necessary to hold things apart at certain stages of work in order to be able to explore in more depth the most salient social processes. But the links and interdependencies are still important. Indeed, one of the recent developments in the social sciences generally has been an increasing recognition of their interdependence. When considering questions of sectoral shifts within the economy, for instance, or questions of the location of industry, it is necessary also to be aware of prerequisite changes in the structure and nature of the potential labour force. And the labour force is not constructed by economic processes alone but also through cultural, political and ideological ones. To take another obvious example, neither the economic nor social changes of recent years, nor the changes in gender relations or consumption patterns can be fully considered outside of the context of quite marked shifts in the political climate. Where it is appropriate we have tried to build some of the more important of these interlinkages into the texts.

One issue which does emerge from a consideration of the whole series together, and which raises again the question of the nature of the connections between the processes discussed in each of them, is the distinct timings of those different social processes. Interesting issues are raised by what seem to be the contrasting periodizations of the transformations of different aspects of British society. It raises yet again the question of what is meant by structural change.

Finally, this is very much a course about questions. By no means all the questions are simply answered. This series of Open Texts, and the associated Readers, are meant to be more guides to an exploration and a stimulus to thought, than a treatise which settles the debate. This is true, too, about questions for the future. There are clearly a number of directions in which British economy and society could go. To explore them would take a parallel series on policy. But we hope that enough light is thrown on possible options to provoke further debate about the possibilities.

Introduction

It is commonplace to argue that the social structure and culture of the UK has changed dramatically over the last 30 years. From a society still characterized by ration books and austerity in the early 1950s, Britain was rapidly transformed during the 1960s 'long boom' and the 'white heat' of Harold Wilson's technological revolution into an affluent consumer society. Growing industrial output, rising productivity and rising real incomes during the 1950s and '60s meant that the working class began to enjoy the fruits of economic prosperity and affluence for the first time.

Television, car and home ownership all expanded rapidly, and the package holiday industry took off as working-class people began to take foreign holidays, and Harold Macmillan told the electorate in 1959 'you never had it so good'. Real incomes and domestic consumption were rising, but interpretations of what was happening differed. Some sociologists began to talk of the *embourgoisement* of the working class, but this was strongly disputed by Goldthorpe and Lockwood (1968, 1969, 1970) in a series of influential studies of what they termed 'the affluent worker': the fact that the working class enjoyed higher living standards did not automatically make them middle class.

But, while the debate raged, the traditional male working class was being rapidly eroded as a result of changes in the structure of economic activity and job opportunities. During the 1950s and 60s women began to enter the paid labour force in large numbers, and labour shortages led to the immigration of West Indian and other New Commonwealth workers. At the same time, growth of the service sector led to an equally rapid expansion of professional, managerial and technical jobs. The occupational structure shifted away from manual and towards non-manual jobs.

The social geography of the UK also changed as a growing number of people moved out, or were forced out, of the inner areas of the large cities into the burgeoning owner occupied suburbs, exurban villages, peripheral council estates and New Towns. In the process, it is frequently argued that old working-class communities were destroyed and replaced by a new, more anonymous, impersonal, materialistic suburban culture.

Since the late 1970s, the pace and direction of change seems to have shifted. First, recession wreaked havoc in the manufacturing industries of the midlands and the north, creating unemployment on a scale not seen since the 1930s. Then, as the recovery began in the mid–1980s, new service jobs were concentrated in the south of England, and part-time jobs for women increased while male full-time jobs declined. In addition, the growth of the welfare state seems to have been halted and reversed. The stress is now on private rather than state provision of housing, education and health care, and a new privatized culture of consumption is said to be emerging, linked to growing inequalities of employment, income and wealth.

These are some of the commonly accepted views of social change in the UK. But are they correct and, if so, what explanations can be put forward to account for them? It is with the analysis of these questions that this book is concerned. In the process we have drawn on a wide range of empirical evidence, but the aim of this text is not to provide a comprehensive descriptive account of social changes in the UK over the last 30 years. Instead, our main aim is to introduce you to some of the important theoretical debates and questions surrounding these changes.

Any aspect of social change involves interpretation and there is no shortage of explanations for the changes mentioned above. Indeed, not only the explanations but also the descriptions of change vary. Some observers assert that Britain is characterized by growing affluence across all social classes, while others argue that the distribution of income and wealth has recently become more, not less, unequal. And, while some commentators argue that the working class is rapidly disappearing as a growing number of people take on the material trappings of middle-class lifestyles (houses, cars and consumer durables), others argue that these similarities in consumption patterns have made little difference to the class structure. Rather than class differences withering away, they suggest that we are seeing a change in their form, and part of the disagreement lies in the different ways in which class is defined. Similar disputes exist regarding the changing place of women and minority racial groups in British society. Some argue that the position of women has greatly improved while others argue that little has changed.

Each of these issues represents an area of theoretical debate. But they are not just 'academic' debates of little or no concrete significance. On the contrary, not only have the changes been of considerable direct importance, but their various interpretations help shape our views of British society and play a major role in political argument and policy formation. It is, therefore, important to examine these interpretations carefully, looking at their assumptions, their logical coherence and the type and validity of the evidence they select and deploy.

Theories are the vehicles through which we attempt to make sense of the changing world around us, and the main focus of this book is on the extent to which different theories can help us interpret and make sense of some of the *structural* social changes which are frequently argued to have taken place in the UK. As the general series introduction pointed out, defining structural change is itself a problematic issue, but the issues included in this book have been chosen because they constitute the key dimensions of social stratification which seem to have undergone radical changes of various kinds over the past 30 years.

The areas chosen for examination are those of class structure and class recomposition, the changing structure of race and gender relations, the distribution of income and wealth, the structure of consumption, and cultural change. The key questions addressed in each chapter are the scale and nature of the changes which have occurred, the extent to which they have been structural in nature, their periodization, spatial dimensions and explanation. These questions are often closely interrelated in practice as different definitions and explanations commonly have different temporal and spatial dimensions. Those who maintain that there has been an intensification of social divisions in Britain during the 1980s and that these have widened the north-south divide will have a different perception and explanation of events from those who maintain that there has been growing homogeneity since the 1950s.

To take one example, in the 1980s, it has been suggested that the decline of Labour voting is linked to the contraction of the working class. But the same point was made in the 1950s when Labour also lost three elections in a row to the Conservatives! If there *has* been a contraction of the working class and a growth of the middle classes defined in occupational terms, this raises questions over whether the changes have occurred continuously since the 1950s, whether they have been discontinuous, or whether different processes have been at work at different times. Each of these possibilities involves different explanations and each may have different geographies. A continuous national process of change is very different from a series of temporally and spatially distinct changes.

Similar problems occur where the growth of home ownership is concerned. Although home ownership has grown steadily from the 1950s onwards, levels of ownership are regionally uneven, with much higher levels in the South East of England than elsewhere. Is this a product of regional differences in occupational class structure, and income and wealth, or is it linked to differences in regional cultures or state intervention? And what is the nature of the relationship between the growth of home ownership and culture? It is often suggested that the changing class structure and the growth of owner occupation have been associated with major cultural changes as individualism and consumerism have grown more important and collective working-class cultures have shrunk in importance.

Culture is often treated as a superstructural manifestation of underlying changes in economic and social structure. This seems excessively deterministic, and cultural changes can be both causes and effects of changes in other spheres. For this reason, we have chosen to begin our treatement of social change in the UK with culture. This is followed, in Chapter 2, by an analysis of changes in the distribution of income, wealth and poverty which forms a springboard for the discussion of class restructuring in Chapter 3. Chapters 4 and 5 extend this discussion to consider the links between class restructuring, race and gender, while Chapter 6 looks at the recent arguments regarding the role of consumption sectors and their relation to class. Finally, Chapter 7 examines the role of regional and local variations in culture and economic activity and asks to what extent the UK is becoming geographically and culturally homogeneous.

Chapter 1 addresses the question of whether there has been a cultural transformation in the UK over the last 20 years and, if so, the form it has taken. This is a difficult question, not least because, the concept of 'culture' is a difficult one to pin down. As Nigel Thrift points out, this is partly because 'culture' is so pervasive and all-embracing. It includes not only material artefacts but, equally importantly, the socially constructed and transmitted meanings, beliefs and attitudes which underpin and give meaning to these and other objects, signs and symbols.

As Thrift stresses, there is not a single British national culture, but a variety of cultures each with its own meanings and attitudes. These cultures are constantly, if impersonally, battling for supremacy in the effort to establish meanings as legitimate or dominant, and Thrift argues that it is possible to identify dominant, emergent and residual cultures. These can take a variety of different forms, from mundane issues (such as the growing dominance of lager drinking) to more abstract economic, social and political conceptions. During the 1980s, for example, the Conservatives have been engaged in a major campaign to reduce what they see as the 'dependency culture' fostered by the welfare state and excessive state intervention, and replace it by an 'enterprise culture' in which individual initiative and self-reliance are given free rein. And, over a much longer period, it can be argued that traditional working-class culture has been eroded and partially replaced by a new consumer culture based on wider affluence and home and consumer durables ownership.

It is this consumer culture which Thrift focuses on. He argues first that it is linked with the rise of the new service class of managers, professionals and technicians, and secondly, that it is laying claim to be a new national culture. This may be true but, as Thrift accepts, its dominance is limited outside the South East, and working-class cultures are still strong in most of the large industrial cities. Within the service class, Thrift argues that there are a number of important cultural 'traditions' and he singles out two for particular attention: the countryside and heritage 'traditions'. His analysis of these traditions is, necessarily, largely symbolic and includes the growth of National Trust membership, the rise of 'country living' colour supplements, Barbour waterproof jackets, Range Rovers, green wellies, country houses and other symbols of the landed gentry which have been appropriated and transformed by the new class.

This is an interesting form of analysis, particularly when the status symbols of enterprise culture are examined – the Porsches, mobile phones, American Express gold cards, Rolex watches and the like. But it poses a number of queries regarding the extent and dominance of different cultures. Are cultural signs and symbols commonly accepted, or do they only have meaning within certain, rather limited groups? As Thrift points out, there are other groups and cultures for whom the symbolic value of Barbours will be largely meaningless or the object of derision. In Brixton, Burnley or Belfast, other values may hold sway which reflect the real differences in employment, occupation and income between different groups and parts of the country. To this extent, cultures may be class, income and area specific, and Chapter 2 considers the distribution of income, wealth and poverty and their links to the labour market and government policy.

Interpretations of the changing distribution of income, wealth and poverty vary sharply. Some observers suggest that the last 30 years have seen rising real incomes for all social classes, while others argue that the structure of social inequalities has stayed largely unchanged. Opinions are also divided over the impact of Thatcherism, some arguing that it has widened wealth distribution (through council house sales and wider share ownership) and others arguing that the concentration of weath has increased rapidly.

It is to these questions that Chris Pond devotes Chapter 2. His approach is primarily empirical in that he first sets out to describe the major trends, and then attempts to explain them. Taking government statistics as his main source of evidence, he shows that, while the distribution of total income became slightly more equal in the 30 years from 1949 to 1979, the inequalities widened from 1979 onwards as the share of the top 10 per cent of incomes has grown. These inequalities have also been reflected in sharp differences both within and between regions.

The key question is why inequality remained stable for most of the post-war period, but grew in the 1980s. Pond suggests that two main explanations can be identified. The first is that of trends in the labour market, and the second points to the role of the state through its manipulation of taxes and social benefits. Pond argues after Le Grand, that the 'strategy of equality', pursued by governments for most of the 1960s and '70s, failed both because of reluctance to intervene in market forces, and the failure to introduce progressive taxation and social security policies. The key cause of the persistence of inequality, he suggests, is found in the labour market and the differences in employment conditions and incomes in different parts of the market and in different areas.

In the 1980s, the strategy of equality has been abandoned by government in favour of the operation of market forces in wage determination. This has been intensified by policies of deregulation, privatization and the removal of 'rigidities', such as minimum wage agreements which prevented wages adjusting downwards to bring supply and demand for labour in equilibrium. Pond also argues that the cumulative impact of the various social security changes has restricted both the level of benefits and the groups entitled to them as well as increasing the amount of means testing.

Pond then examines the extent to which the distribution of wealth inequality has changed over the last 30 years. He shows that, after several decades during which inequality decreased, it increased during the 1980s. Although home ownership has widened the distribution of wealth, the picture is one of stability rather than radical change, and he argues that the rise of privatization and wider share ownership in the 1980s had little or no effect on the concentration of share ownership among wealthy individuals and City institutions, such as insurance companies and pension funds. But, to the extent that the growth of institutional share ownership has broken the link between individual ownership and control, this raises questions about the changing class structure of the UK.

This debate is taken up in Chapter 3 where Philip Sarre examines the arguments regarding the growth of the middle class and the decline of the traditional working class. But, as he points out in his introduction, there is a large gulf between the theoretical discussions of class on the one hand, and the available empirical evidence on the other. Most of the official data on occupational class are collected by the Registrar General, but the categories employed are, at best, only loosely related to those employed by class theorists. The Registrar General's definition of class is largely based on occupational status rather than the distribution of income, wealth and power.

Using census data, Sarre shows that there have indeed been considerable changes in occupational class over the last 30 years which have resulted in large gains for the professional, managerial and technical occupations at the expense of skilled, semi-skilled and unskilled manual occupations. This has occurred as a result of changes in industrial and occupational structure, and it has been reflected in a significant degree of intergenerational upward social mobility. But, as Sarre points out, interpretation of such changes is altogether a more complex and difficult matter. Changes in occupational class structure do not necessarily entail changes in the class structure on other definitions. As he puts it:

> All the major authors would concur that to look at data on occupational change is to focus on surface appearances. To understand and explain changes in the class structure involves analysis of ownership, relation to job markets, social organization of production, political struggles and state intervention, especially as they relate to changes in legal entitlements.

Not only are there major disagreements between the Marxist and Weberian theories of class, there are also major disagreements within them. While traditional Marxist class theory focused on the distinction between the ownership and control of the means of production versus the sale of labour power as the key determinants of class, Weber took a broader view which, although it stressed the ownership and non-ownership of property as the basic determinant of class, was extended to cover a variety of marketable resources including domestic property. He also related this to questions of status and power.

Rather than arguing that the traditional Marxist and Weberian theories are irreconcilable, and arguing for the supremacy of one or the other, Sarre focuses on some of the major recent attempts to reconstruct both theories to take account of contemporary problems. One of the key problems faced by Marxists has been the divorce between ownership and control of the means of production, and the growing number of professional and managerial workers who may control or supervise the means of production without owning them. They occupy what have been termed 'contradictory class locations'. For Weberians, the key problem has been to integrate considerations of class, status and power without losing all explanatory power.

Sarre uses his theoretical discussion of the differentiation of class position and the processes of class formation within the two traditions as a vehicle to look at changes in different parts of the class structure. These are, the divorce between ownership and control, the growth of the service class, the role of the petty bourgeoisie, the proletarianization of the lower-middle class, and the erosion of the working class as a result of both embourgeoisement from above, and the creation of a new underclass of state benefit dependants from below. Finally, he attempts to integrate the theoretical and empirical discussion by identifying a variety of class positions in Britain on the basis of property, credentials and organizational position. But, as he states in conclusion, his analysis of class is necessarily incomplete because it leaves out other crucial social cleavages, notably those of race and gender, and the role played by state intervention in influencing the opportunities for consumption by different social groups. These divisions are discussed in the following three chapters.

The growth of black minorities in the population has been one of the most visible changes in British post-war society, and their disadvantaged position in the labour and housing markets has been well documented. It is possible to raise a number of questions regarding the role and position of these minorities, but the key question addressed in Chapter 4 is how they have fitted into and/or changed the British class structure. In doing so, Sarre focuses on the relations of these minorities to the economy, the state and majority society.

The discussion of race and class is particularly difficult as it involves theoretical disagreements about class, disagreements about the concept of race and disagreements regardings the relative importance and interaction of the two. Sarre suggests that there are three broad positions that can be argued concerning the class position of racial minorities. The first is that class is the key division in British society, race having only secondary effects. The second is that race is primary, with class having secondary effects, and the third is that the two factors are interrelated in complex ways with both having significant effects. In general, Marxists tend to emphasize the dominant role of class, while Weberians emphasize the importance of race. Marxists have thus tended to see minorities as a racialized class fraction or a black underclass, while Weberians tend to see race as a status attribute independent of class. But, recently, Marxist analysts have accepted the importance of race and culture and have sought to integrate this with analysis of the legacy and experience of colonialism and imperialism.

Sarre then looks at some of the major events of the last 40 years in the light of these theoretical perspectives. Examining the relationship between immigrant labour and the class structure, he looks first at the class-based perspectives which see blacks as similar to the 'guestworkers' of other Western European countries – they are part of a reserve army of labour to be called and sent home when needed. But, while black immigrants initially fulfilled this role, many black British have either lived here for a long time or have been born here. The guestworker analogy has broken down, but what has not changed in the 1980s is the concentration of blacks in less skilled and lower paid jobs. He asks how far this is attributable to difference in class, and how far it is attributable to racism and racial discrimination.

While there are sharp occupational class differences between blacks and whites, he suggests that race is of crucial importance, and that, rather than there being one single racialized class fraction, there may be several related fractions across all classes which collectively form a kind of 'geological fault' slicing through the class strata similar to the notion of a status cleavage cutting across class. As with his chapter on class, Sarre's approach is not to opt for one perspective at the expense of others, but to try to show how different theories may have certain common elements which can be related together and used to explain social change. His approach to the study of race and class is one of theoretical complementarity rather than theoretical opposition.

Chapter 5 extends the discussion of economic and social change in Britain by looking at the role of gender relations. These have become increasingly important since the 1960s as a growing number of women have entered the waged labour force and challenged their traditional socially constructed roles of 'wives and homemakers'. Linda McDowell focuses on two main aspects. The first is the impact of economic restructuring on the gender division of labour, both in the workplace and in the home. As she points out, the growing feminization of the labour force has made gender a central issue to the debate about the impact of economic restructuring. She suggests that we may be faced, not with the end of the working class, but its changing gender, and that the gender division of labour is as important as class divisions in Britain today. The second aspect is the growing contradiction since the late 1970s between women's dual role: their position in the paid labour force and their position in the home and community.

Her starting point is the growth of women's waged labour and the nature of the jobs they do. The distinction between sex and gender is fundamental to her approach. While sex is a biological difference between men and women, gender is socially constructed and is crucial to understanding how different jobs become seen as men's or women's jobs. Why, for example, are the great majority of secretaries and nurses women? McDowell distinguishes three major types of explanation. The first is neo-classical economic theory, which argues that women have been drawn into the labour force as a result of changes in the supply and demand for labour. She also looks at a more sophisticated variant – human capital theory – which makes explicit the implicit assumptions of neo-classical supply and demand models about gender divisions in domestic work and the role of childcare and the nuclear family. The second type of theory is a variant of Marxism that extends the concept of a reserve army of labour to women's position in waged work. Finally she looks at theories that integrate an analysis of capitalist and patriarchal relations. She critically assesses the explanatory power of the different theories, their assumptions and arguments, and the nature and type of the empirical evidence deployed. She also suggests that the utility of the reserve army of labour approaches lies in their recognition of the changing links between waged and domestic labour. But, when it comes to explaining why women are concentrated in certain jobs, McDowell suggests that it is necessary to look at the structure of *power relations* between men and women. Studies in this area are divided by a theoretical disagreement as to whether it is necessary to incorporate the concept of *patriarchy* as a set of social relations, analytically distinct from capitalist social relations, and McDowell examines the arguments for and against this position.

There are parallels here with the arguments discussed by Sarre between the proponents of race and class in explaining the position of minorities in the class structure. While Marxists tend to stress the primacy of class, non-Marxists emphasize other social relations as well. In the last part of her chapter McDowell focuses on the contradiction between women's dual role in the waged labour force and their key role in social reproduction. She argues that while this is not new, it has been intensified by the growth of women's waged work, the ideology of domesticity and family life, and by the recession and the 1980s cuts in welfare provision.

The debate between class and other social divisions is taken a stage further in Chapter 6, which examines the growing importance of consumption divisions in contemporary Britain. Chris Hamnett focuses primarily on the work of one theorist – Peter Saunders – which he subjects to close theoretical and empirical critical attention. This approach differs from that of previous chapters where several different theories are critically examined.

Saunders argues that, in recent years, the post-war consensus concerning the continued growth of the welfare state has broken down, partly as a result of its increasing cost. As a result of this and the post-war increase in real income, he suggests that we are witnessing the emergence and growing importance of new privatized forms of consumption in education, housing and health care. These are creating a growing division between those dependent on state provision and those able to gain access to private provision. He argues further that these divisions are independent of class and may be becoming more important than class divisions in terms of the distribution of life changes, income, wealth and politics.

Hamnett examines the theoretical and empirical validity of each of these propositions in turn. First, he looks at the extent to which Britain has seen two important transformations in the structure of consumption since the war, initially with the advent of the welfare state post-war, and then with the growth of private provision. Next he looks at the extent to which consumption is in fact class related. The stronger the links, the weaker Saunders' argument that consumption and class are independent must become. Saunders accepts that consumption and class are related but he argues that class does not determine consumption locations. However, while this is true at the individual level, Hamnett shows that there are still strong aggregate statistical relationships. While it is impossible to say that an individual unskilled worker will be a council tenant rather than an owner, it is possible to say that unskilled workers are several times more likely to be council tenants than professional or managerial workers.

Hamnett then examines Saunders' neo-Weberian argument that housing can be considered a key element of class stratification by virtue of home ownership's potential for capital accumulation. It is shown that while owner occupation does often fulfil this role, it does not resolve the problem of how home-owning manual workers or professional council tenants are to be categorized in class terms. As Sarre showed in Chapter 3, there are a number of different relations of exploitation involved. Saunders attempts to solve this problem by arguing that home ownership is seen as a dimension of social stratification rather than class. But this merely serves to displace rather than resolve the problem.

Finally, Hamnett considers the implications of privatized consumption for ideology and politics. It is frequently argued that home and share ownership gives people a 'stake in the system' and makes them more conservative. While this argument has been criticized theoretically, the empirical evidence tends to support it. This raises some interesting questions regarding the relative weight to be given to theoretical argument and empirical evidence, and the stress accorded to them by different writers.

This point is taken up in Chapter 7 where Mike Savage examines whether Britain is becoming geographically and culturally more homogeneous or more differentiated. There was considerable debate during the 1980s as to whether Britain was divided into two nations of north and south, whether there were increasing differences between the inner cities and the suburbs, and whether local cultures were disappearing. Savage contrasts the arguments of Massey and Warde over economic differentiation and outlines a number of criteria against which these spatial change arguments can be judged. These are: scale, absolute versus relative change, and typicality. He argues that many of the current arguments about the existence of sharp regional differences are over-simplified and the picture is more complex.

How can we conclude our assessment of whether there has been a radical social change in Britain? It is clear that, on a number of dimensions, there have been major changes in social structure over the last 30 years. But these have been neither uniform nor simultaneous. In the case of the restructuring of class, race and gender relations, the processes of change have been going on since the 1950s. The same is true of the rise of owner occupation although the expansion of other forms of privatized consumption are more a product of the 1980s. And, where income distribution was concerned, it can be said that the period up to 1979 was one of minimal change.

But, overlying these long-term developments, the 1980s have seen the advent of a series of new, and more radical, changes in the spheres of class restructuring, the distribution of income and wealth, gender and race relations, the rolling back of the welfare state, the growth of private provision and the emergence of a new enterprise culture. In some cases, developments in the 1980s have reinforced and speeded up the pre-existing processes of change, while in other areas, notably in the labour market, social benefits and consumption, the 1980s have seen the emergence of new processes of change. The periodization, spatial dimensions and explanations of these changes are often rather different from those of earlier years.

So, in some respects, the social structure of Britain has been characterized by continuity rather than radical change, in other respects there has been continuous if gradual change since the Second World War, and, in some areas, the 1980s have seen the advent of radical changes which have reversed or speeded up the changes of the 1950s, '60s and '70s. What is clear is that there has been no single structural transformation of British society, but a series of related changes, some of which have been structural and others not.

1   Images of social change

Nigel Thrift

Contents

1.1   Introduction

From newspaper columnists to social scientists, from politicians to bishops, the message seems clear: since the 1970s British society has undergone a number of dramatic changes. Indeed, for some, the changes are so dramatic, so wide-ranging, that the United Kingdom has become 'a different country . . . You have to blink and rub your eyes' (Jaques, 1987, p.10).

Many of these changes have been cultural, that is they consist of shifts in the way that meanings are generated and circulated in British society. But the mere mention of a term like 'culture' can inspire feelings of unease in some readers. For a start, it seems a nebulous, airy-fairy type of concept, difficult to pin down and difficult to work with. Then again, culture has been represented before now as a subordinate outgrowth of economic and social change, with no independent life of its own, and so requiring no independent analysis.

And yet, the study of British culture is now at a height. This is because it now seems that some of the most important changes going on in the UK *are* cultural. This chapter is devoted to considering some of these changes. Its first task will be to consider what constitutes culture. A second task will be to consider which cultural changes have been most important in British society in the 1970s and '80s. A third task will be to consider some of these changes in more detail, especially those associated with the rise of a service class, made up of managers and professionals. Finally, the chapter considers cultures which may be outside the mainstream, but which make a vital contribution to what British culture is.

As you read through the chapter, you will find it helpful to consider the following issues and questions as a means of evaluating the arguments. In section 1.2, which is on the notion of culture, the argument is quite abstract, but the ideas are essential in considering the other sections. Section 1.3 looks at cultural change in Britain. Here you should consider whether any of the changes mentioned are taking place in your own locality and, if so, in what form? Can you see the signs of shifts in class culture?

Section 1.4 considers two of the dominant cultural traditions of contemporary middle-class life – countryside and heritage – and how they have changed in response to class changes. Here you can do two things. The first is to consider how you relate to these traditions. Do you long for the calm certainties of the countryside? Why? Does it seem important to you to conserve historic buildings? Why? Secondly, you can look for evidence in magazines and newspapers of advertisers using these traditions to appeal to you to buy their products, like the examples in the chapter.

Finally, section 1.5 considers the places and social groups which are to some extent excluded from these dominant traditions. Here you might consider whether it is possible to think of a UK in which there were *no* dominant cultural traditions. What would it feel like? What would it look like? What would it be like to live in?

1.2   What is 'culture'?

Culture is one of those bewildering ideas that, at some time or another in history, seems to have meant all things to all people. It has been hijacked by a succession of artists and academics intent on showing the special sensitivity of the 'high' arts, like opera, fine art or classical music, and, either directly or by implication, the dreadful lack of taste of popular cultural forms like the music-hall, cartoons or rock music. It has been used as a prop for all kinds of racial theorists, providing an heroic Wagnerian past for blue-eyed, blonde-haired Aryanism, or Biggles-like accounts of the British Empire, replete with dashing young subalterns educated on the playing-fields of Eton. It has been used by some anthropologists and geographers simply to refer to 'material culture', that is to the inventory of material objects that make a society unique, from types of stone axe through to Ford Zephyrs and Morris Minors. It has been used to look at ways of life, usually rural and full of folklore and strange rituals.

However, recently, a broad consensus has emerged concerning what culture is, which can give us clues about how to study British culture today. This consensus has four main features.

1   The study of culture is primarily concerned with how meanings are generated and circulated in modern societies (Fiske, 1987), and especially how these meanings are put together by people so that they *interpret* (make sense of, or represent) social change in particular ways. Quite clearly, the myriad social groups that go to make up society will have different meaning systems (or cultures). These 'maps of meaning', to use a term first coined by Stuart Hall (1980), may be relatively discrete, or they may overlap substantially.

Two things need to be noted about this definition of culture as a set of 'maps of meaning'. First, meanings, and the interpretations of social change derived from them, are not conjured up out of thin air. They are handed down, learned, or otherwise picked up from concrete social institutions; mum and dad, school, the newspapers, television, and so on. But, secondly, the whole process by which this happens is very complex. Interpretations of change can come from all manner of sources. They can be made up in day-to-day conversations at home or at work, they can be gleaned from reading books, and they can be taken from magazines and the television. In addition, there are interpretations of change which most people in a society share, and other interpretations which are specific to particular social groups. And there are also interpretations of change that people in one place subscribe to which people in another place think are ridiculous or threatening. (For example, think of a white, middle-class, male stockbroker and his family living comfortably in a large house in Esher. Their interpretations of social change in the UK are likely to be quite different from those of a Bengali family eking out a living in Spitalfields and living in constant fear of racist attacks.)

In other words, we should expect to find in a country like the UK a multiplicity of 'cultures'. Maps of meaning will vary according to basic social grouping, for example class, gender, age, ethnicity and religion; they will vary by place; they will include various youth 'subcultures' (Hebdige, 1979); and they will take in the cultures of 'outsider' groups, like Gypsies (Sibley, 1981). People belonging to each of these groups use their own maps to 'read' the same events, objects and people in quite different ways.

2   The existence of such a multiplicity of cultures leads to a second feature of the modern study of culture, which is that the process of interpretation of change is *not* a neutral process. It involves producing and circulating meanings which favour one interpretation over others. Consciously or unconsciously, all kinds of social group want their interpretations of what is going on accepted as the norm, not for disinterested reasons, but to help them get what they want or keep what they have got. So, culture is an inherently *political* process in which different social groups vie to impose their interpretations of change on subordinate social groups, while, in turn, these subordinate groups contest the process, in various ways and to varying degrees, by trying to make interpretations that will serve their interests instead.

It is important to recognize that not all social groups have equal access to the institutions, like education or the media, that allow certain interpretations to become commonsense. Some social groups have the power (especially, but not only, through money) to dominate these institutions, and so have a correspondingly better chance of imposing their interpretations of the world on other social groups. Over time, these social groups may be able to impose a **hegemony**. That is, through the various institutions they dominate, they can produce and accumulate meanings which are favourable to their interests and which other groups accept as the 'natural' order of things. These more powerful social groups are able to mobilize *consent* from other social groups for their privileges:

> ascendancy of one group of [people] over another achieved at the point of a gun, or by the threat of unemployment, is not hegemony. Ascendancy which is embedded in religious doctrine and practice, mass media content, wage structures, the design of housing, welfare/taxation policies and so forth, is. (Connell, 1987, p. 184)

One of the best examples of hegemony in operation is the production and circulation of meanings which buttress men's ascendancy over women. Whilst women's subordination may have faded to some extent, various institutions still generate interpretations of masculinity and femininity – through strategies such as praising stereotypes and marginalizing groups that do not conform to these stereotypes – that reproduce current social relations between men and women. Hegemonic masculinity involves the production of meanings which emphasize the dominant role of 'men'. From teachers at school, from mates in the workplace, even from the media with its gallery of male fantasy figures like Humphrey Bogart, John Wayne or Sylvester Stallone, come all kinds of messages about the dominant roles men must take on if they want to be 'men'. Similar institutions also produce a hegemonic version of femininity, emphasizing a willing compliance. The dominant interpretation of women stresses women's *differences* from men:

> We put girls in frilly dresses, boys in running shorts and so on. But there is something odd about this. If the difference is natural why does it need to be marked so heavily? For the sex-typing of clothes and adornments really is obsessive. At some moments it reaches quite fantastic levels. No one is likely to doubt the femaleness of a nursing mother. Yet the front-opening dresses and dressing-gowns marketed for nursing mothers (in shops like the ... Mothercare chain) are an absolute mass of 'feminine' frills, tucks, bows, lace, ribbons and such like. When you think about the mess created by a nursing baby it is clear there is nothing functional about this. In fact (such) social practices are not reflecting natural differences with these marks of gender. They are weaving a structure of symbol and interpretation around them, and often vastly exaggerating or distorting them. (Connell, 1987, pp. 86–7)

3   All this said, culture is not a simple matter of one social group imposing its ideas on others. People do not uncritically and deferentially accept dominant groups' meanings. If that were the case, presumably there would be no strikes, riots or demonstrations. There would be no subcultures proclaiming their difference from the norm, whether rastas or punks or scientologists (Cohen, 1972; Hall and Jefferson, 1976; Hebdige, 1979). There would be no dissent.

Instead of the crude stamping of one group's interpretations of the world on to other groups, more subtle processes are at work. Meanings can be produced by dominant social groups but their circulation is always *negotiated*. Four related points need to be made here. First, when a meaning or interpretation is produced by members of a dominant group, it will not be taken on with equal enthusiasm by every social group (Hall, 1980). The meaning will probably be taken on in full by other members of the dominant group. But people who do not belong to the dominant group may take on only a part of the meaning, or they may interpret it according to their own local circumstances, or they may contest it, or they may reject it outright (see Chapter 7). The range of possibilities in this process of negotiation is enormous. For example, research shows that television may, or may not, influence how men and women think of men and women according to a bewildering variety of different circumstances (Morley, 1986). The picture is even more complicated because dominant groups may try to package meanings and interpretations in different ways to appeal to different groups, as often happens with television and newspapers.

Secondly, it is important to note that dominant meanings and interpretations are not always directed at other social groups. They may be used primarily to reinforce a dominant group's sense of cohesion, and have little or no meaning for other social groups. For example, certain kinds of clothes may produce appropriate feelings of identification for one social group, and mean nothing to other groups.

Thirdly, people may *seem* to accept dominant meanings, at least for the official consumption of researchers, whereas they are actually quite cynical about them amongst the people they know. One often-cited case is the example of wartime propaganda: the people at which it is directed regard it with cynicism, often as a bit of a joke.

Fourthly, social groups can both reject dominant meanings and build their own culture, yet still end up in a subordinate position. For example, Willis (1977) showed in research, in a Midlands town, how certain working-class school boys built a culture of rejection of middle-class ways and values, especially through an exaggerated idea of masculinity. But this culture ensured they would always be stuck in lowly jobs. In a sense, they colluded in their own subordination.

4   So, how can we end up with roughly similar interpretations of change at all? As we have seen, the interpretations that people put on social change can vary by subculture, by place, and so on. But, given that certain interpretations are common to many social groups in all manner of places in the UK, how have these dominant interpretations come to be fixed in people's minds?

The answer is connected with the rise of the state and the media in the UK (Corrigan and Sayer, 1985). The nineteenth century saw the growth of state apparatus (especially education) and of the mass media, like the daily newspapers. Together these institutions worked to produce and distribute similar meanings and interpretations to dissimilar groups and places. They made large-scale social engineering of the imagination possible. In the process they started to bind the people together as a 'nation'. Nowadays, the state and the media work in three ways to fix common national ways of seeing.

To start with, education and the media provide a common structure for the experiences of many people. For example, the ceaseless flow of headlines in the newspaper and programmes on the television provides a common history upon which people can hang their lives all across the country (Hall, 1977). Seen in this way, education and the media contribute to what Raymond Williams (1977, p. 131) has called a 'structure of feeling' to which each generation subscribes, the 'particular quality of social experience and relationship, historically distinct from other particular qualities, which gives the sense of a generation or a period' (see Chapter 7).

Secondly, education and the media are adept at providing slightly different versions of the meaning of social change to different social groups, suitably tailored to their tastes and outlooks. For example, national newspaper readership in Britain is very clearly stratified by class and age, but the underlying messages each of the newspapers retails have, if anything, become more and more similar as the ownership of newspapers has been centralized. In 1987, only 27 per cent of British daily newspaper readers saw a pro-Labour Party newspaper (Butler, 1988).

Finally, education and the media have been vital in creating **imagined communities** which provide a sense of belonging to a nation. These communities are 'imagined because the members of even the smallest nation will never know most of their fellow-members, meet them, or even hear them, yet in the minds of each lives the image of their communion' (Anderson, 1983, p. 15). The media and education do this both by providing social groups with images of the lives, meanings, values and practices of *other* social groups, and by relaying to social groups images of their *own* lives.

1.2.1   Consumer culture

This brief summary of culture inevitably leaves some questions unanswered. In particular, there is the problem of how interpretations of social change themselves change. Meanings and images change all the time. For example, the images of impressionist painting were greeted with general shock and outrage when they were first let loose upon the world. Now they tend to be seen as fodder for greeting cards, calendars and the lids of chocolate boxes. Thus, we can never assume that an interpretation will retain its original meaning over time. Worse than this, there is some evidence to suggest that interpretations are changing more rapidly than was the case in the past, especially because of the invention of advertising.

Advertising has been a method of selling goods almost since goods began (see the entertaining account of eighteenth century advertising in McKendrick, Brewer and Plumb, 1982). But it was not until the 1920s that it became the leading edge of an emergent 'consumer culture' which, in many ways, has become popular culture. This consumer culture consists of a set of market segments made up of people who, it is assumed, share particular tastes and values because of their similar social group characteristics (class, age, gender, race, place of residence, and so on). These market segments are an object of constant audience research (by media firms), and market research (by the producers of goods and services), with a view to matching products with social groups that have the appropriate tastes and values. This process of tying products and consumers together is co-ordinated by advertising agencies who add the cultural gloss of meaning (and so value) to products, by investing them with words and images that identify them with, and so appeal to, particular market segments. They provide 'commodity aesthetics' (Haug, 1986, 1987).

Since the 1960s the task of advertising agencies has been eased by the invention of the 'lifestyle ad', which makes a virtue of market segments by making each product into a badge or *sign* of group membership: 'the product has become a token, a representation of a clan or group that we recognise by its activities and its members' shared enjoyment of the product' (Jhally, 1987, p. 202). In these types of advertisements, the product is situated within a particular setting, which either includes people from the appropriate market segment doing appropriate things, or infers their existence. For example, in the advertisement in Figure 1.1, a car is associated with an appropriate social setting. This kind of advertisement relies on the fact that certain people will identify with the lifestyle portrayed, and buy the product

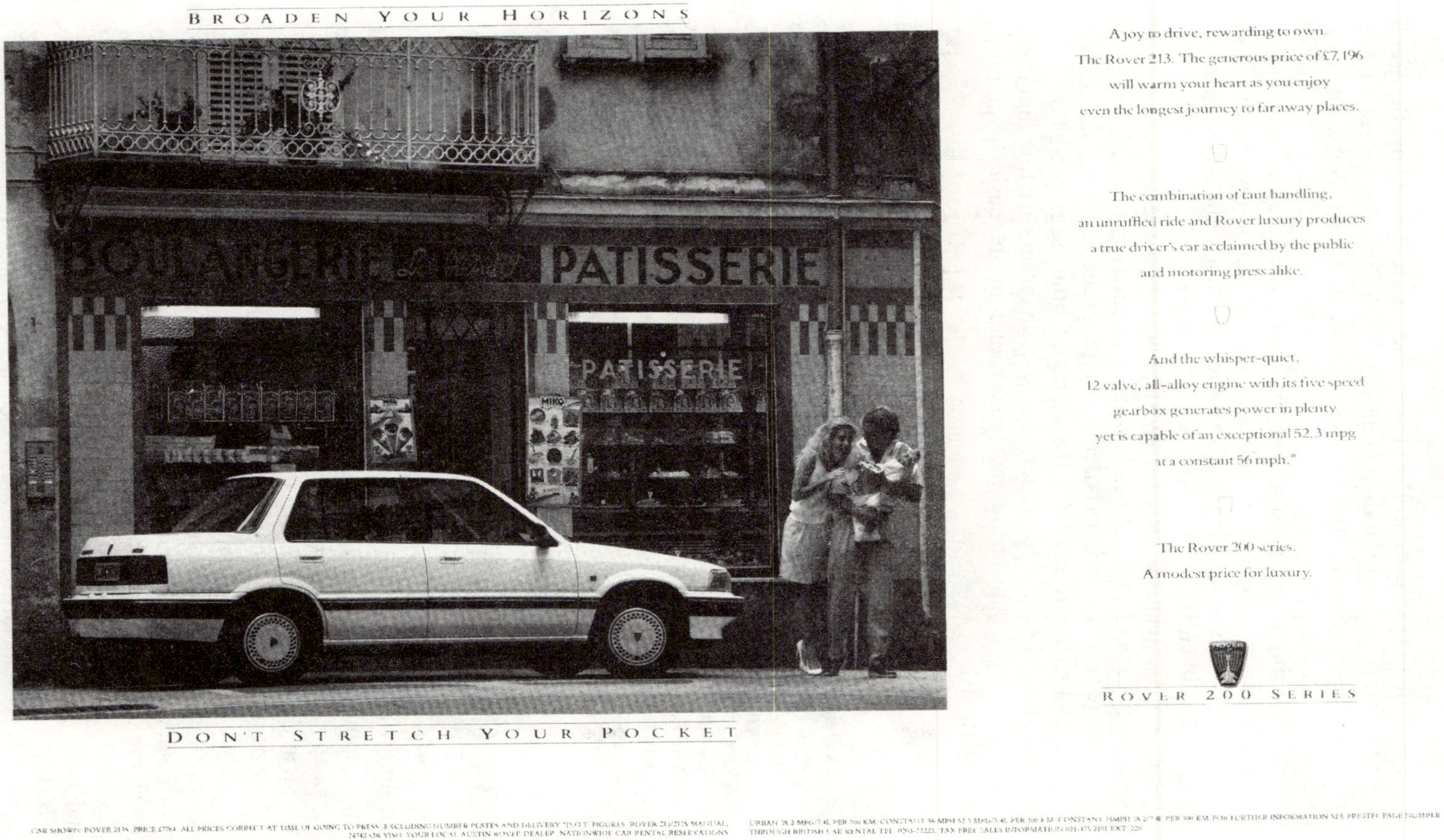

Figure 1.1 *Rover advertisement*

as proof of that identification. People become, or are defined by, the goods they buy, and never more so than in the case of clothes where certain labels have become associated with lifestyles – Levis, Benetton, Next, Barbour, Burberry, etc. Some lifestyle advertisements have become very abstract indeed, requiring that a person have the appropriate educational/cultural background in order to understand them. (It is worth noting that there is a controversy in the advertising industry over whether some advertisements are now too difficult!)

Thus, popular culture increasingly depends upon the consumption of appropriate signs of taste. It has become a minutely graduated empire of tastes, where each set of tastes is deemed appropriate to a particular market segment and carefully excludes the tastes of other segments. For some commentators, this new consumer culture is a vibrant, exciting thing. For others it is more sinister; a merry-go-round of increasingly pointless accumulations:

> The conscious, chosen meaning in most people's lives comes much more from what they consume than what they produce. Clothes, interiors, furniture, records, knick-knacks, all the things that we buy involve decisions and the exercise of our own judgement, choice, 'taste'. Obviously we don't choose what is available for us to choose between in the first place. Consuming seems to offer a certain scope for creativity, rather like a toy where all the parts are pre-chosen but the combinations are multiple. Consumerism is often repre-sented as a supremely individualistic act – yet it is also very social: shopping is a socially endorsed event, a form of social cement. It makes you feel normal. Most people find it cheers them up – even window shopping. The extent to which shop-lifting is done where there is no material need (most items stolen are incredibly trivial) reveals the extent to which people's wants and needs are *translated* into the form of consumption. (Williamson, 1986, p. 230)

1.3   Cultural change in the UK

The UK *is* culturally diverse. Within its boundaries are many cultures and subcultures formed out of the divisions, like class, ethnicity, gender and consumption, which are addressed in the following chapters. To complicate the picture further, these cultures and subcultures are all locally differen-tiated, as Savage makes clear in Chapter 7.

How is it possible to gain a purchase on the changes taking place in this diversity of cultures and subcultures? Williams' (1977) work gives us one means of entry into understanding how British maps of meaning are cur-rently being redrawn. Williams was particularly concerned with the extent to which the cultures of particular social groups wax and wane. Therefore he classified cultures into those that are 'dominant', those that are 'emergent' and those that are 'residual'. Dominant cultures are those which have achieved hegemony. Emergent cultures are still in the process of being formed. Residual cultures are ones which are being marginalized.

The thesis of this section is that, during the last 20 years of social change in the UK, one particularly important shift has been the emergence of a 'service class', an occupational group made up of managers and professionals (see Chapter 3). It was not until the 1960s that the service class was fully formed (Lash and Urry, 1987). Since then it has had considerable influence in the UK, and especially cultural influence. In Williams' terms, what can be seen is a service-class culture that is emerging and on the way to dominance, but not yet hegemonic at the national scale. Meanwhile, the traditional kind of working-class culture has become more marginal, partly because some of its members have taken on service-class interpretations of the world.

The rapid growth of the service class in the 1970s and '80s has, in turn, led to the spread of service-class culture, helped along by this class's favourable degree of access to education and the media (in which many of its members work). The values of the service class are firmly rooted in consumer culture. It gains much of its collective identity from consumption, from the value its members place on products as signs of the taste and dignity of their users. Since 1979, the service class has also increasingly absorbed and disseminated the ideas of competitive individualism inherent in the spread of an 'enterprise culture'. This is not a great surprise; consumption culture and competitive individualism are closely linked:

> Lifestyle advertising is about differentiating oneself from the Joneses, not, as in previous decades, keeping up with them. Put that simply, it sounds as if the marketers had just discovered individualism as a way of selling commodities. Of course, the special, unique *you* has been the staple diet of so many campaigns over the last 30 years. What we can say is that the 80s have seen a hyping of the process, an explosion of individualities – of the number of yous on offer. (Mort, 1988, p. 50)

Further, the private sector fraction of the service class is now in the ascendant, and more likely to accept the enterprise culture as a valid interpretation of social change in Britain.

Meanwhile, the working class is declining in numbers, and its culture is declining in influence from a high point in the 1950s and '60s (Laing, 1986). There are many reasons for this decline. One is the decreasing power of the workplace as a means of promoting collective identity; for example, on average, plants now employ fewer people. Another reason is the declining power of certain kinds of place as a basis for cultural solidarity. Single industry towns are dying out. (The Miners' Strike of 1984 was particularly symbolic of the decline of this kind of place.) Increasingly the working class is to be found living in New Towns and housing estates (Clarke, 1984; Marshall *et al.*, 1988). One more reason is that working-class leisure patterns have changed (see *Urry,** 1988, for an account of these changes in action).

---

* An author's name in italics indicates that this article has been reprinted in the Reader associated with this book (McDowell, L., Sarre, P. and Hamnett, C., 1989).

Finally, consumer culture is eating away at the fabric of working-class solidarity, promoting an individualism, which is further bolstered by government policies to privatize collective consumption, such as the sale of council houses (Chapter 6). Increasingly, working-class people are gaining their identity by being consumers.

It is important to note here that none of the above is meant to imply that working-class culture is dying out. Rather, we are arguing that it has taken on a new, more consumption-orientated, and probably a more privatized, form and it has less influence than before on the national cultural stage.

Clearly, an account of recent changes in British culture which concentrates on the increase in the dominance of one class culture, and the marginalization of another, is highly simplified in many ways. It ignores cultural differentiation based upon gender or race (and the richness of ethnic culture is an important element of British cultural life now). It ignores the culture of other classes, for example the upper class. And it ignores the multiplicity of youth subcultures – punks, skinheads, teddy boys and the like (Hebdige, 1979; Willis, 1978), which, although they are class differentiated and have an ambiguous relationship to consumer culture, still provide a site of resistance to the dominant culture.

But the rise in the influence of service-class culture and the decline in the influence of working-class culture is still significant, not least because the maps of meaning created by these emergent and residual cultures can also be mapped spatially; they have a geography. Increasingly, the south of England is the preserve of service-class culture and its consumption ethos. In many parts of the south service-class culture is dominant, perhaps even hegemonic, and many members of the southern working class also subscribe to its interpretation of the world. In the rest of the UK, however, the dominance of service-class culture is still contested, and it is arguably dominant only in pockets. Outside the south of England, working-class culture's hold remains strong, although it is a different working-class culture from 20 years ago. This vibrance is underlined by studies such as those of Jenkins (1982, 1983) on working-class boys and girls growing up in a Protestant housing estate on the outskirts of Belfast in the 1980s. There, in the face of very considerable difficulties, (Boal and Douglas, 1982), a distinctive working-class subculture has been fashioned. It has a dark side in its restricted ambitions, its sectarianism and its sexism, but it also shows a degree of independence and pugnacity.

Activity 1.1

What other cultural changes can you think of which have been significant in the last 20 years? Which social groups have been most involved with these changes? Do these changes have a geography?

1.4   Making a culture: the case of the British service class

In this section, we will consider service-class culture in more detail, and in particular the class's attempt to make a culture and then claim that it is the dominant *national* culture. Part of this attempt has involved tapping into some important traditions of a specifically English cultural life. There are two main reasons for this. The first is to help represent this recently formed class to itself. The meanings and interpretations provided by these traditions can strengthen a class's social cohesion in all kinds of ways. Secondly, such traditions can help to give a newly founded class legitimacy in the eyes of the rest of the population. They represent the new class as a 'natural' holder of privilege and power (Dodd, 1986).

1.4.1   Tradition

Modern traditions have usually been quite carefully *invented* for quite particular purposes (Hobsbawm and Ranger, 1983). Thus, Hobsbawm (1983, p. 1) defines modern tradition as a 'set of practices . . . which seek to inculcate certain values and norms of behaviour by repetition'. Normally, it will 'attempt to establish continuity with a suitable historic past' (ibid.). So, a tradition is a ritualized and symbolic set of meanings and images, the main purpose of which is to help establish or retain social cohesion by appealing to a past. There are other functions served by tradition as well. One is to legitimize the institutions which are connected with a tradition. In the British case, the monarchy is a good example (Cannadine, 1983; Hayden, 1987; Nairn, 1988). Another function is to foster the sense of the superiority of dominant social groups, both in order to bolster the sense of superiority of the dominant groups themselves, and in order to make other non-dominant social groups more likely to bow to them.

Since the nineteenth century, these traditions have been closely associated with

> that comparatively recent historical innovation, the 'nation', with its associated phenomena: nationalism, the nation-state, national symbols, histories and the rest. All these rest on exercises in social engineering which are often deliberate and always innovative . . . [for] . . . whatever the historic or other continuities embedded in the modern concept of ['England'] and the ['English'] – and which nobody would seek to deny – these very concepts themselves must include a constructed or 'invented' component. And just because so much of what subjectively makes up the modern nation consists of such constructions and is associated with appropriate and, in general, fairly recent symbols or suitably tailored discoveries (such as national history), the national phenomena cannot be adequately investigated without careful attention to the invention of traditions. (Hobsbawm, 1983, pp. 13–14)

In periods of rapid economic and social restructuring, such as that experienced in the 1980s, it is important for a dominant social group like the service class to provide interpretations of the national community that stress continuity and consensus, in the face of discontinuity and conflict. Ideas about the national culture can act as a kind of security blanket. The 1960s and early 1970s had seen post-war ideas about the UK come dangerously close to breaking down in the face of mounting economic and social conflicts, as well as overwhelming evidence that Britain was no longer a declining imperial power, but just another medium-sized European state. The late 1970s and '80s were a period in which attempts were therefore made to build a new sense of national community, which could cope with all the economic, social and political changes taking place, by interpreting them in a way that was favourable to the service class.

We will now consider, in more detail, two of the major modern English cultural traditions which the service class has tapped into and reworked, both in order to recognize itself and in order to gain recognition from other classes. These two traditions – which I will call, rather clumsily, 'countryside' and 'heritage' – are encapsulated in the advertisement for a service-class housing development (Figure 1.2). Notice, first, the rural appeals made in the text, the picture of the house (surrounded by trees), the name of the development, and the Laing Homes corporate logo, with its flowers. Next, note the appeals to the historic character of the area, made in the text, in the garb of the woman, in the typography, and in the carefully inserted date. The advertisement intertwines the countryside and the heritage traditions. In the next section, I will briefly consider the history of these two traditions, why they have been so enthusiastically embraced, or created, by the service class, and the variability of their meanings.

Figure 1.2   Housing advertisement

Activity 1.2

Search out examples of lifestyle advertisements in newspapers, magazines and on the television. How many of these advertisements use countryside or heritage themes? How do they use them? At which sections of the population are the advertisements aimed?

1.4.2 The countryside tradition

A key tradition in English culture has been that of the countryside and nature, in a suitably tamed and romanticized form. The roots of this tradition do go back a long time. It is an interpretation of the countryside which was invented, as Keith Thomas has shown, in early modern times. In 1600, much of what we now think of as a distinctively English rural ethos of good husbandry and preservation, leading to pleasing rural vistas, would have appeared as a quite alien philosophy to the inhabitants of England of that time:

> Man's task, in the words of Genesis, was to 'replenish the earth and subdue it'; to level the woods, till the soil, drive off the predators, kill the vermin, plough up the bracken, drain the fens. Agriculture stood to land as cooking to raw meat. It converted nature into culture . . . (Thomas, 1983, pp. 14–15)

By 1800, however, this unsentimental, utilitarian attitude to the countryside had been replaced by something much more romantic, although not without calculation. The new interpretation was probably strongest amongst the English aristocracy who had the wherewithal to indulge it:

> For centuries the English aristocracy had been country-based, because a heavily capitalised agriculture was the formation of their wealth. Farming and estate management were the central interests of the gentry. They pursued country sports; they took an obsessive interest in dogs and horses; they were knowledgeable about natural history; and they self-consciously designed a rural landscape which would provide for both profit and recreation. (ibid., p. 13)

But even in 1800 the interpretation of the countryside as a place in which to follow rural pursuits set against an increasingly idealized and often carefully manicured background – even 'wild' areas were carefully staged – was not restricted to the aristocracy. It was becoming more and more general in society:

> Already in the late eighteenth century [the feeling for the countryside] had begun to produce the characteristic home-sickness of English travellers abroad. As the factories multiplied, the nostalgia of the town dweller was reflected in his little bit of garden, his pets, his holidays in Scotland or the Lake District, his taste for wild flowers and bird-watching, and his dream of a

weekend cottage in the country. Today it can be seen in the enduring popularity of those self-consciously 'rural' writers who, from Izaak Walton in the
seventeenth century to James Herriot in the twentieth, have sustained the
myth of a country Arcadia. Whether or not the preoccupation with nature and
rural life is in reality peculiarly English, it is certainly something which the
English townsman has for a long time liked to think of as such; and much of the
country's literature has displayed a profoundly anti-urban bias. (ibid., p. 14)

As Howkins (1986) points out, the tradition of the countryside (and a
corresponding anti-urbanism) has certainly survived to the present, if anything becoming stronger over time (see Glass, 1968). It is now an especially
potent brew of rural images. But the images tend to be of a quite specific
kind, anchored in some imagined village community of the past. Often, it
seems that this rural community is peopled by bluff and manly squires and
elegant ladies taking the air in the grounds of their country houses, and by
jolly, rustic swains and giggly, rosy-cheeked milkmaids cavorting in the
fields. The community is set in a rolling landscape, which is full to the hori-
zon with stands of oak and elm, yellow corn fields, luxuriant green hedgerows, scurrying wildlife and drifts of wild flowers. In other words, what we
have is a bucolic vision of an ordered, comforting, peaceful and, above all,
deferential past. The countryside has rather rarely been quite like this! As
often, it has consisted of poor farm labourers with only sacking for a coat; of
farm labourers' wives with hands blistered from stone picking on frosty
mornings; of farmers as rapacious as any mill owner, swearing death to all
poachers and plotting to remove common rights; and of desperate riots.

Nowadays the countryside is even less like this 'ye olde Englande' village
vision of days of yore. As the cities have expanded, much of the countryside
around them has become a vast tract of manicured suburban space which
acts, for those who live within driving distance of it, as parkland, as a crucial
source of economic value for those with houses with rural views (no wonder
fights to keep rural land from being built on are amongst some of the most
determined in Britain), and, increasingly incidentally, as a place for production. Where the land is used for production, it has often become, what the
poet Wordsworth called, a 'vegetable manufactory', devoted to mass production of cereals, or root crops, or conifers, on larger and larger farms. The
land is owned by a mixture of landed aristocracy, other private landowners,
and owner-occupier farmers (Newby, 1982; Shoard, 1987). Surely,

> by 1970, no one ... could persist in seeing the [village] as the small, self-
> contained microcosm of England. It wasn't small, it wasn't self-contained –
> and by 1982 its rosy-cheeked postmistress would be running the Video Club
> from the Post Office and doing a nice trade in P-snuff movies and lacy erotica at
> £1.00 a night with Sundays free. (Raban, 1986, p. 176)

We are living through a time when the tradition of countryside images and
meanings has reached a crescendo of feeling (see Gentleman, 1982). The
increase in rural conservation societies is one indication of this (Table 1.1),

Table 1.1   Membership of various countryside and heritage organizations, 1971 and 1987

Group	1971	1987	Percentage increase 1971–1987
National Trust	278 000	1 404 181	505
National Trust for Scotland	37 000	150 000	405
Royal Society for the Protection of Birds	98 000	529 000[1]	539
Civic Trust	214 000	300 000 (est.)	140
Royal Society for Nature Conservation	64 000	180 000	281
English Heritage (founded 1984)		112 000	
World Wildlife Fund	12 000	110 000	916
Royal Horticultural Society		100 000 (est.)	
SAVE Britain's Heritage (founded 1975)		100 000	
Ramblers' Association	22 000	55 000	250
Council for the Preservation of Rural England		30 000	
Friends of the Earth	1 000	28 500	2 850

[1] Includes 102 000 young members
Source: CSO, *Social Trends*, 1987, p. 173; *Landscape*, 1987, pp. 36–7

as is the growth of folklife museums. A further indication is the increase in the readership of countryside-related magazines (Table 1.2). The very successful, new magazine *Country Living* (Consumer Magazine of 1987) makes no bones about its appeal. It is subtitled 'When your Heart is in The Country'.

1.4.3   The heritage tradition

Intersecting with, and supporting, the countryside tradition is another tradition, which I have called 'heritage'. This term has been recently applied to a new phenomenon: the way that the government, the media, retailers, and other institutions are generating more and more images of the past which are gradually intruding more and more into the present. At the centre

Table 1.2   Circulation figures for some old and new traditionalist magazines

Magazine	Date of founding	Circulation in 1987
The old traditionalists		
Country Life	1897	48 491
The Field	1853	
The Lady	1885	67 740
The new traditionalists		
Country Homes and Interiors	1986	88 130
Country Living	1985	114 808
Country Times	1988	
Landscape	1987	
Traditional Homes	1984	
Traditional Kitchens	1985	
Traditional Bathrooms and Bedrooms	1986	
Traditional Interior Decoration	1986	30 000
Homes and Gardens	1919 (revamped 1984)	198 000
House and Garden	1947 (revamped 1984)	133 000
The World of Interiors	1981	61 975

Source: *Willings Press Guide*, 1987

of this heritage tradition is the potent set of symbols provided by a monarchy suitably adapted to the times:

> Ceremonial which was badly performed has now become so well stage-managed that the British have been able to persuade themselves (despite overwhelming historical evidence to the contrary) that they are good at ritual because they always have been. And, however much literacy and education have increased, the liking which the British public has for royal pageant and display has grown rather than lessened. Old ceremonies have been adapted and new rituals invented, the combined effect of which has been, paradoxically, to give an impression of stability in periods of domestic change, and of continuity and comfort in times of international tension and decline. (Cannadine, 1983, p. 160)

The invention of heritage goes much further than just the many doings of the Royal Family, important though these are as constant, living reminders of a (mainly) invented national past. The heritage tradition takes in other 'traditional' institutions, which provide a whole national history and geography that people can fix on as quintessentially English. Such institutions include: the fresh-faced choirs of the public schools (founded in their modern form only in the late nineteenth century); punting on the rivers at Oxford and Cambridge; willow on leather at the major county cricket grounds; and the events of the 'season', like the Henley regatta, or Wimbledon, now revived under corporate sponsorship (Smith, G. 1987). These are lighthouse places and events, which can somehow appeal, even to people who have no intimate knowledge of them, as part of what it is to be English. The invention goes even further, into an obsession with 'traditional' interiors and exteriors of houses, shops and the like.

But nowhere has the growth of a national heritage tradition become more apparent than in the conservation of the built environment. Formal conservation of the built environment has had a comparatively short history – the National Trust was set up 1895 – and it is only recently that the desire to conserve has become something approaching a national mania. Central government now spends over £100 million per annum on conserving the built environment, much of it through agencies like English Heritage in England, Cadw in Wales, the Scottish Office in Scotland, and the Department of the Environment in Northern Ireland. Whole centres of some towns like Bath are conservation areas which cannot be altered except within strict guidelines.

Conservation mania is apparent in more than just government activities. There is the booming country house market, for example. Demand for these houses and what they represent is so great that new country houses are still being built (Robinson, 1984). There is also a booming market in towns and cities throughout the UK for any house which is 'historic' (Queen Anne, Georgian and Regency houses command a particularly high premium, but Victorian will do, if that is what can be afforded). Such houses provide their buyers with the opportunity to buy into history. There is the whole network of historic houses and stately homes around the UK. 4.2 million people visited National Trust houses in 1986 (Miller and Tranter, 1988) and, as *Hewison* (1987) makes clear, country houses provide an immense reservoir of meaning.

Finally, there is the museum. The 1980s and '90s may well be seen as the heyday of the museum in Britain: there are now at least 2160 and they are opening at the rate of one a fortnight. Of 1750 museums which replied to a 1987 questionnaire, half had been started since 1971 (*Hewison*, 1987). This new museum economy includes the many heritage centres now open around the UK. These are complete re-creations of the past, like the Ironbridge Gorge museum near Telford, the Wigan Pier Heritage Centre, the Beamish Open Air Museum, just south of Newcastle upon Tyne, the Jorvik Viking Museum in York, the Pilgrims Way Museum in Canterbury, or the Oxford Story Complex in Oxford (Lumley, 1988). To some observers we seem to be fast becoming a country which is creating its past in the present, or its present in the past, depending on the way you see it!

> Nowhere outside Africa, I thought, were the tribespeople so willing to dress up in 'traditional' costume and caper for the entertainment of their visitors. . . . By June and July it would be hard to stop at an English village without running into tabarded medieval knights in armour preparing for a joust, cars full of Cavaliers about to refight some old battle in the Civil War, or prancing morrismen in bells. The thing had become a national industry. Year by year,

England was being made more picturesquely merrie. These bucolic theatricals were a very new fad. Even the morris dancers, whose claim to stretch back through the mists of time was strongest, were new. Their dances and costumes had been researched and renewed by Cecil Sharp, the folklorist, in the 1890s. (Raban, 1986, pp. 194–5)

Activity 1.3

List examples of heritage sites in your locality? Who is employed in them? To whom are they meant to appeal?

1.4.4   The reasons for tradition

Why have the countryside and heritage traditions, interlinked as they are, reached such an ascendancy in English culture? There are three main reasons, each one connected to the others. First, the countryside and heritage traditions provide images which can produce cultural cohesion in a time of rapid economic and social change. These images are frequently appealed to by politicians and pundits as exemplifying the English way of life: solid and virtuous in the face of change. But there is more to it than this, or these traditions could not be so deep-rooted and appealing. The countryside also provides many members of the English population with a green haven in times of change, an imagined community of the past to fall back into when the real community of the present seems to be falling apart. The idea of happier, more innocent and very definitely rural times past becomes a kind of hiding place from the trials of the world (Williams, 1975).

Secondly, the countryside and heritage traditions have met and blended with consumer culture. Countryside and heritage *sell* products, and in turn these products strengthen the hold of these traditions.

One of the greatest plaudits for a product nowadays is that it is 'natural', that it comes from, or is inspired by, the countryside. The examples are almost endless. There is a flood of books on the country, many selling very well indeed. *The Country Diary of an Edwardian Lady* sold 2.6 million copies and spawned £75 million worth of related merchandise, including 'Country Lady' cosmetics (*Hewison*, 1987). Clothes that display the rural ethos are popular too: real or imitation green, waxed Barbour jackets, real or mock green Hunter wellingtons, brogues, tweeds, the lot. Marks and Spencer has started a 'Country Style' range of clothing.

Many home interiors are also getting a traditional country look. *Country Living*'s Design Editor has said of the 'modern' kitchen: 'I simply tell my readers what they want to see – and it's quite simple – everthing is going country. Kitchens are becoming retrospective in their designs and there is this whole bit with the environment. People are using natural finishes in their kitchen which they generally find more comforting' (Smith, 1988, p. 18).

Association with the past can also increase a product's consumer attraction. Consider the advertisement in Figure 1.3. Here a foreign import is given added dignity and selling power by associating it with a country house backdrop. The motor bike seems to grow in stature as it connects with a bucolic English past. (Figure 1.4 shows a similar appeal being made to consumers.)

Nowhere can the blending of tradition and consumer culture be better observed than in the 'historic' towns of England – Bath, Canterbury, Chester, Salisbury, Winchester, York and the like. All these towns are thriving as they tap into the deep vein of meaning associated with the heritage tradition, both to sell themselves and to sell goods. They are both a stock of historic built environment and consumer 'spectacles'. In effect, whole towns have become vast, theme shopping malls/entertainment complexes, whose evocative historical backdrops give the act of shopping, and the kinds of shops found in these places, an added veneer of respectability (Shields, 1988). The power of these backdrops is increasingly enhanced by all manner of new heritage developments – a museum here, a heritage centre there. The director of the Conran Foundation's new design museum, appropriately located in 'that temple of conservation-led redevelopment, London Docklands' (Samuel, 1988b, p. 23), gives the whole game a rationale:

> In a sense, the old nineteenth century museum was somewhat like a shop, you know, a place where you go and look at values and ideas, and I think shopping is becoming one of the great cultural experiences of the late twentieth century . . . The two things are merging. So you have museums becoming more commercial, shops becoming more intelligent and cultural. (quoted in *Hewison*, 1987, p. 139)

The blending of the countryside and heritage traditions and consumer culture has been further accelerated by one other factor, and that is the UK's increasing dependence upon tourism. The UK's countryside and its stock of historic places and buildings are now a vital national money earner. For example, in 1987, 15.6 million foreign tourists spent more than £6 billion in the UK. Only the United States, Italy, Spain and France made more money from foreign tourism. Tourists – British as well as foreign – have to have something to look at, and what they want to see in Britain is increasingly an idealized version of countryside and heritage, as *Urry* (1988) makes clear. The relationship is circular: more tourists, more countryside and heritage, more tourists, and so on . . .

Thirdly, and linked to each of the previous reasons, the increase in the hold of the countryside and heritage traditions on England's culture can be linked to the growth of the service class in at least three ways. To begin with, the service class seems to be the social group that has taken the countryside and heritage traditions most to heart. It uses the traditions as ways of defining itself – similar tastes, similar market segments, similar people – and

Figure 1.3   BMW advertisement

Figure 1.4 Yorkshire Television advertisement

as a way of excluding others. At the heart of the countryside and heritage traditions (or so it is believed), lie knowledge and values that are non-communicable to the outsiders from other classes (*Wright*, 1985). A useful by-product of adopting these traditions, for a newly formed class like the service class, is that they provide a short-cut to legitimacy. Its members dignify themselves with the trappings of the countryside and the past and so gain kudos in the present.

Following on from the last point, the essential service-class character of places replete with manicured countryside and/or heritage is strengthened as more and more members of the service class move into them. For example, census and other figures show that, especially around London, it is the service class which is leading the urban–rural push. Many studies (e.g. Hamnett, 1984b) have shown that at least one of the motives behind many of these moves is a desire to convert rural imaginings into a reality. Much of southern England has become a refuge for the service class with houses and villages carefully marketed by housing developers to appeal to its members. As one estate agent put it:

> 'Now we are selling dreams; in the old days we were selling houses. We tell people about the village the views and the lifestyle before we talk about the style of house itself'. The sales brochure of one development ... opens with pictures of the rolling Sussex countryside, ivy-clad village houses and even deer. Only later are there pictures of the houses.... This sales pitch is now common. (McGhie, 1988)

Of course, the service class is not just intent on colonizing the countryside. Its members are also intent on gentrifying inner city areas that have the right historic associations, as *Wright* (1985) demonstrates.

If members of the service class cannot live in the countryside, then they are more likely to visit it, drawn like bees to a honeypot. Figure 1.5 shows this tendency. Note the heavy use of the countryside made by those in AB categories. Similarly, members of the service class are more likely to visit country houses and museums than are members of other classes (Lumley, 1988).

Finally, as Pond shows in the next chapter, since 1979 in particular, wealth has been flowing into the coffers of the service class (and especially its upper reaches) so that, more and more, the class is able to indulge its rural-historical tastes. Perhaps the best gauge of this process is the growth of the country house market (Figure 1.6).

The country house is a potent symbol of economic and social success, what Williams (1973, p. 299) called 'the abstraction of success, power, and money ... founded elsewhere'. It also allows the instant gratification of the service-class longing for a rural lifestyle complete with a matching constellation of appropriately 'rural' products, dogs, guns and Range Rovers; houses, Hunter wellingtons and Barbour jackets; tweedy skirts and silk scarves (see Figure 1.2). Here is one comment from a member of the service class:

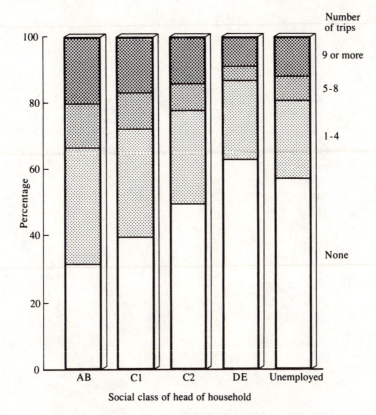

Figure 1.5   Recreational trips to the countryside: by social class of head of household, 1986, England and Wales

Source: Countryside Commission, 1987

> My husband and I first saw our house in Dorset advertised eight years ago in *Country Life*. We thought we couldn't afford it, but fell in love with the picture and drove over one sunny morning in June. We walked through the hall, across the dining room, and out of the French windows and on to the terrace past the most wonderful papery white poppies. We sat on the stone seat at the edge of the wood and said 'we'll have it' . . . In the summer I walk straight out onto the terrace, have a glass of wine, look over our bit of England, and I'd rather be there than anywhere else in the world. (Potter, 1987, pp. 46 and 50)

But, as *Hewison* (1987) points out, it is important to remember that these bits of England have their dark side too. Especially in the more spectacular of these houses,

> the values of the rural capitalist order are now being presented as the height of civilization. Now it is true that country houses and furniture have not ceased to be valuable in the sense that some of them are beautifully made. But . . . in the crudest way these houses were primarily sites of exploitation and robbery and fraud. If anything, the fact that some of them were well-built and are pleasant to look at makes that worse! (Williams, 1979, p. 312)

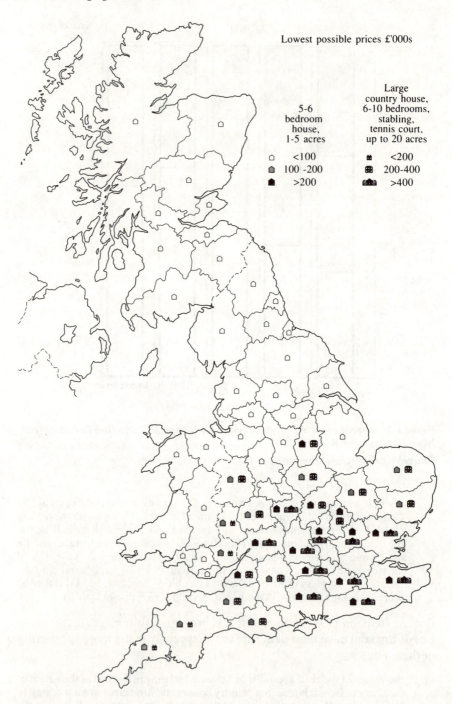

Figure 1.6   Country house prices, 1987

1.4.5 Contesting tradition

The maps of meaning laid over England by service-class culture are orientated according to suitably reconstructed countryside and heritage traditions. The meanings flowing from these traditions can be malign or beneficial. For example, the countryside tradition is not only about dignifying personal aggrandisment. It also links into, informs and is informed by the growing concern for the natural environment – the draining of wetlands, the grubbing up of hedgerows, the disappearance of wildlife, and many other issues. Similarly, the heritage tradition is not just about dignifying consumption. It can also inform us about the past and so allow us to hold a mirror up to the present. Conservation can be important.

The point is that each tradition is *contested*. The politics of culture consist of the work done by particular social groups, through the various cultural institutions, to produce interpretations, ways of seeing issues, that are favourable to them. Thus the countryside tradition *can* easily become a paean to private property (*my* little bit of England). Similarly, the heritage tradition *can* have a dubious aspect. Its recovery of the past is too often selective, sometimes spurious, and nearly always idealized. In the words of one commentator, the conserved landscape of historic buildings and museums can become 'a crash course in the bourgeois myths of history' (Lumley, 1988, p. 8).

Activity 1.4

Is there a museum or heritage site near you? Does it attempt to provide a balanced view of history, or is it a view of history biased towards one social group? How often do women appear in the exhibition, and in what roles?

Raphael Samuel's criticism of Christine Edzard's film adaptation of Dickens' novel, *Little Dorrit*, applies equally to the heritage tradition:

> Little Dorrit reflects . . . the 'heritage' industry. In the manner of a contemporary theme park, it invites us to take a Victorian Day Out, in the words of an admiring critic, 'to luxuriate in the recreation of a past world'. As a spectacle, it resembles nothing so much as a succession of Athena block prints. . . . It sets out neither to shock nor disturb, but to please, purging the novel of evil, and doing nothing to offend the canons of good taste. It is a Little Dorrit of our time, one in which (Victorian) London is not a prison house but a playground, and poverty – provided it is safely period – is picturesque. (Samuel, 1988a, p. 23)

Again, for some commentators, the heritage tradition can direct attention away from the problems of the present. Take the case of Beamish Open Air Museum, near Newcastle upon Tyne:

> The paradox of Beamish is not that it is false, the exhibits are as genuine as they could possibly be, but that it is more real than the reality it seeks to recall. The town street evokes an indistinct period of between two wars, at just that distance in time when memory softens and sweetens. But there is no need for personal nostalgia. Here the displays do it for you. The effect is so complete that it is the late twentieth century visitors, not the buildings, that seem out of place.... Yet while this charming world was being created, the life of the North East was being destroyed. Many of the thousands of items that the museum's first director was gathering and storing in the decade before the site was formed came to him because of redevelopment and dispersal as the old [working-class] communities were breaking up. (*Hewison*, 1987, p. 95)

Then, worst of all perhaps, there is the worry of some commentators that the heritage tradition reduces people to passive consumers; for Wright, England has entered 'an age of dead statues'. It has become

> a museum of superior culture and those citizens who are not lucky enough to be 'curators' of the 'collection' shouldn't worry that they have been left out of the action, for they are still subjects of the new archaism. Their position is to look, to pay taxes, to visit, to care, to pay at the door (even when entering cathedrals these days), to 'appreciate' and to be educated into an appropriate reverence in the process. (*Wright*, 1985, p. 71)

Activity 1.5

Do any of the trends described and analysed in *The Economy in Question* (Allen and Massey, 1988) have a bearing on the cultural changes described in this chapter? For example, what connections might there be between flexible specialization and lifestyle advertising? What connections might there be between the rise of certain kinds of service industry and the countryside and heritage traditions? What connections might be found between service-class culture and the north–south divide?

1.5   Excluded cultures?

The interlocking of the traditions of countryside and heritage, landscape and history by, and for, the service class provides a formal set of ways of imagining England as a nation, often called 'Deep England'. These ways of imagining England then affect the way that social change is interpreted. They provide a dominant interpretation, appealing above all to the service class, but ranging over considerable parts of the lower-middle class and working class as well. Their peculiar power can be seen with particular clarity in times of national crisis, for example, the Falklands War. Raban describes how the Falklands were a blank slate, hardly heard of by the

British population before the war, on which various government and media institutions could write cultural significance:

> Their blankness was their point: you could make them mean nothing or everything. [During the course of the war] the Falkland Islands accumulated a huge bundle of significations. They meant Tradition, Honour, Loyalty, Community, Principle – they meant the whole web and texture of being British. (Raban, 1986, p.13)

For Hewison, growing very cynical, the Falklands War

> proved to be the encapsulating heritage event: a battle for a distinctly 'British' and utterly remote piece of moorland, long neglected by the industrial corporations that owned it, against a group of fascist foreigners out of a Bulldog Drummond story. The campaign was short, though not without risks which recalled earlier foreign expeditions, from Henry V to the BEF in 1940. The final outcome appeared to be an extended version of the Royal Tournament, though with the added drama of actual loss of life. The effect of the Falklands expedition was to strengthen Britain's inward conservatism. 'We' had won. (*Hewison*, 1987, p. 142)

It is, however, important to recognize that the 'national' traditions of countryside and heritage, so beloved of the service class, are not truly national (despite the casual equation of 'Britain' with 'England'). They touch certain parts of the country more than others; they have a geography. Their strength is felt most deeply in the south of England, and less deeply in other parts of the country (see Hamnett 1984b). As they lap across the borders of Wales, Scotland or Northern Ireland, they meet other national traditions, often just as real, sometimes just as powerful (and just as carefully invented). Thus, the Plaid Cymru MP, Dafydd Elis Thomas, passionately insists that the spread of English national traditions into Wales must be stopped, for the good of both England and Wales.

> The creation of elected governments in Scotland and Wales would prove beneficial to the people of *England*. It would force them to realise that they are living, and always have lived, in a multi-national, multi-cultural, multi-lingual state – just like the rest of the world. Cultural diversity is not, after all, some new phenomenon invented in the 1950s and 1960s when (to quote a particularly obnoxious contribution from the Department of Education and Science) 'our society became multi-cultural'. The English . . . do not find it easy to think about their Englishness. But if nations are . . . 'imagined communities', then England needs to be re-imagined. And if thinking of England only conjures up thoughts of undulating green landscapes, peopled by women in Laura Ashley dresses (designed and manufactured in *Wales*), then the England that is imagined is an invented, mythical past. (Thomas, 1987, p. 17)

Further, the national traditions of Deep England do not find much room for certain social groups, who do not meet the exacting cultural citizenship tests that are required (Centre for Contemporary Cultural Studies, 1982). The Afro-Caribbean and Asian communities are a particular case in point. The British 'national' traditions sometimes seem to peter out in the black areas of the inner cities (see Chapter 4). Of course, black citizens are not all alike.

They come from many different cultural backgrounds. Some may accept the national traditions more or less willingly, but others dissent; 'there ain't no black in the Union Jack'. Why?

There are two main reasons. The first is that many members of the Afro-Caribbean and Asian communities are excluded from these traditions by a racism that in some ways is a part of the traditions. Black people are not seen as part of the imagined community conjured up by the traditions of country-side and heritage. They can never be 'true Englishmen', and the fear is that they will 'swamp' the culture; a 'tidal wave' of black immigrants will 'flood' the country with alien values and meanings (Smith, S.J. 1987). Hysterical media reporting on immigration is a barometer (and a creator) of this fear, made more poignant by the fact that it is a fantasy, since the various Nationality Acts of the last few years have made large-scale immigration by blacks into Britain impossible. (Meanwhile white South Africans have become a major immigrant group each year to the accompaniment of a deafening press silence.)

Chesshyre notes a few of the press subtleties with regard to black immigration:

> 'They're still flooding in' – London *Standard*; '3000 Asians flood Britain' – The *Sun*; 'Immigrants Paralyse Heathrow' – *Daily Mail*; 'Asians Start Housing Crisis' – *Daily Mail*. The *Star* commented 'Britain finally began to drop the portcullis and raise the drawbridge against the alien hordes'. The *Sun*, under the banner headline 'The Liars' reported 'the 1,001 lies used by immigrants to cheat their way into Britain'. One pop paper wrote: 'Remember too that every male immigrant to this country represents either an addition to the dole queues, or a job lost to a native Briton, or both. We can afford neither. . . . Some of their customs – child brides, arranged marriages, marriage to first cousins – are repugnant to western minds. Many of them refuse to conform to our way of life, our laws and our customs. (Chesshyre, 1987, p. 291)

The Falklands War brought into sharp relief the links between racism and the traditions that make up the English imagined community. Many politicians and commentators stressed that the Falkland Islands were a special case, because upon their soil lived a little piece of the national community. According to Peregrine Worsthorne, writing at the time of the war: ' Most Britons today identify more easily with those of the same stock 8000 miles away . . . than they do with West Indian or Asian immigrants living next door' (quoted in *Gilroy*, 1987, pp. 51–2). And so to the heart of the matter: 'If the Falkland Islanders were British citizens with black or brown skins, spoke with strange accents or worshipped different Gods, it is doubtful whether the Royal Navy and Marines would today be fighting for their liberation' (ibid.).

It is, then, something of an irony to realize that there were black British soldiers fighting in the Falklands. Sapper Pradeep Gandhi from Brent was killed in action. (It is also something of a consolation to know that for the black soldiers in the Falklands, under pressure of battle, 'the whole racist thing went out of the window. No one called me a nigger. Not once!' (Sweeney, 1988).

The second reason why blacks are so little represented in the national tradition is that the various black communities have their own cultures and subcultures, which are both excluded and excluding. These may be partly defined by the struggle against racism, but they are also very definitely their own diverse cultures and subcultures, with their own traditions, often recently invented and vibrant. To become part of any dominant imagined community would be to lose that identity.

Consider the Conservative Party election poster prominent in the 1983 campaign (Figure 1.7). For some commentators, this poster was a sober and responsible call to young blacks to enter the mainstream of the national

Figure 1.7   *Conservative election poster, 1983*

culture. For other commentators, it was an invitation for them to sell out their own culture:

> The slightly too large suit worn by the young man, with its unfashionable cut and connotations of job interview . . . conveys what is being asked of the black readers as the price of admission. . . . Blacks are being invited to forsake all that marks them out as culturally distinct before real Britishness can be guaranteed. National culture is present in the young man's clothing. Isolated and shorn of the mugger's key icons – a tea cosy hat and the dreadlocks of Rasta – he is redeemed by his suit, the signifier of British civilisation. The image of black youth as a problem is thus contained. . . . The wolf is transformed by his sheep's clothing. (*Gilroy*, 1987, p. 59)

Whichever interpretation is correct, it certainly seems to be the case that, for many commentators, being a citizen of Britain is not just a matter of a passport. It also requires subscribing to cultural traditions like those examined in this chapter.

2 The changing distribution of income, wealth and poverty

Chris Pond

Contents

2.1   Introduction

The distribution of economic rewards between different groups in the population, and different parts of the country, is an important determinant of the nation's economic and social structure. Economic and social inequalities are inextricably intertwined, and the distribution of income and wealth, the extent of poverty and privilege, have their effects on living standards, life chances and opportunities. Individuals' health and well-being are influenced by their position in the labour market, income and access to economic resources. Thus, class differences in health have persisted, despite an overall improvement in national standards. Moreover, inequalities in wealth have political implications, providing the wealthiest individuals with access to economic, social and sometimes political power. For this reason, inequalities can become self-perpetuating, having an influence on the institutions that reinforce the class structure.

In this chapter, we will examine the distribution of income and wealth in the mid-1980s, and consider how it has changed in the post-war period. We need to ask whether the degree of inequality that exists today is the product of a process of continuous change, or whether there was a radical transformation during the 1980s: Did the advent of the Thatcher governments after 1979 represent the end of the post-war 'welfare consensus', and usher in a period of increased economic inequality and social polarization?

The first two sections of the chapter consider some of the statistics concerning economic inequality. This material allows you to work through the evidence on the distribution of incomes, earned and unearned, and look at both the way it has changed since the Second World War, and the regional divisions in economic rewards. In attempting to analyse what has happened to inequality, we need to examine the different factors that result in inequality, and those that mitigate its effects. In a market economy such as Britain's, underlying economic factors are perhaps the most important determinant of the distribution of resources. In section 2.3 we look at the role of the labour market in shaping the distribution of employment incomes, which, in turn, contribute to overall economic inequality. Market forces are, of course, themselves influenced by social and institutional factors, including the class structure. Their effects can also be enhanced or mitigated through state actions, principally through the mechanisms of the tax system and public spending. These aspects of the role of the state in shaping the distribution of economic rewards are the subject of section 2.5.

Section 2.6 is concerned with the outcomes of this process of interaction between the state and the market. Here, we look at the extent of poverty and at inequalities in the ownership of wealth, the two extremes of the distribution. In addition to documenting the extent and nature of poverty as it existed in the mid-1980s, we consider whether changes in the distribution of economic resources have served to create a permanent underclass of the poor. And we ask whether there also persists something which might be described as an 'upper class' amongst the rich, maintaining itself through a process of inheritance, and wielding considerable economic and social power.

2.2   The changing pattern of inequality

Economic inequality is traditionally measured in terms of the distribution of income and wealth. The distinction between these two concepts is somewhat artificial, imposed by the way in which the statistics are collected by official agencies. Both income and wealth are measures of an individual's or family's command over economic resources, the former representing a *flow* of resources over time, the latter being the *stock* of resources held at any one point in time. The two concepts are closely interrelated: holdings of wealth generate an income, for their owners, in the form of interest, dividends or capital gains; and, if income is sufficient to allow for savings, these will accumulate into wealth-holdings.

A more enlightening measure of economic inequality would be a combination of wealth and income, but we are denied this by the nature of the statistics to hand. The Royal Commission on the Distribution of Income and Wealth had planned to devise such a measure, but met its demise at the hands of the 1979 Conservative government before it was able to achieve this. In the UK, as in most countries, the data on economic inequality are available only as a by-product of some administrative process. Figures on the distribution of wealth and income must be sifted from the tax returns submitted to the Inland Revenue, or derived from the Family Expenditure Survey, the main purpose of which is to construct the monthly Retail Price Index. No separate survey evidence, designed to discover the true magnitude and nature of economic inequality, is available. This is perhaps an indication of the low priority accorded to such questions by governments; there is scant purpose in devoting resources to the examination of something about which one intends to do very little.

The information available suffers as a result. Tax returns may be an adequate measure of the distribution of income or wealth which taxpayers see fit to disclose. Income which the Inland Revenue does not know about (much of which circulates within the 'black' or 'shadow' economy), or which it does not very much care about (such as fringe benefits and a large proportion of capital gains), will not reveal itself through tax returns. The adjustments which statisticians make to guess at the magnitude and distribution of this 'missing' income are not wholly satisfactory. (For a fuller discussion, see Atkinson, 1983; Playford and Pond, 1983.)

For these reasons, the statistics available on the **distribution of income** and wealth tend to understate the true degree of inequality. We should bear this in mind when assessing what the figures tell us. Nevertheless, we can at least begin to put together a picture of economic inequality by examining the data presented by Stark (1988).

2.2.1   The distribution of income

There has been a long-running debate among economists concerning the 'constancy' or 'stability' of the share of wages in national income. In recent years, the proportion of household income accounted for by wages and salaries has been far from constant, falling from 69 per cent of the total in the mid-1970s to less than 60 per cent ten years later (see Figure 2.1). About half of this decline in the share of money wages was accounted for by the rise in transfer payments, mainly social security benefits. In part, this reflected demographic changes, such as the continued growth in the number of pensioners (whose numbers increased by about one million to 9.6 million during the decade) and single parent families dependent on social security. More importantly, it is testimony to the effects of increasing unemployment. The numbers (excluding pensioners) claiming supplementary benefit increased from 1.2 million to nearly 3.2 million between 1979 and 1987 alone. When pensioners are included, the numbers receiving supplementary benefits increased from just under 4 million to nearly 8.5 million. The share of self-employment incomes traces the change in the numbers of self-employed, dipping in the 1970s and rising sharply during the 1980s. The decade following the mid-1970s also witnessed the revitalization of *rentier* incomes, from dividends, interest payments and rents: property incomes increased from 6 per cent to 8 per cent of the national income, while pensions and benefits from life assurance increased from 5 per cent to 7 per cent. This was largely a reflection of the effects of the recession, pushing more occupational pensioners into early retirement, and of the shift from social to private welfare encouraged by Conservative governments after 1979 (Central Statistical Office, *Social Trends*, 1988).

Figure 2.1 also illustrates changes in the burden and incidence of taxation over the period, which will be useful later for analysing what has happened to the distribution of incomes – and why. Taxes on income (which included the taxation of investment incomes as well as earnings) were a lower proportion of household income in the mid-1980s than ten years earlier. However, this was partially offset by a rise in employee social security contributions, so that direct taxes took virtually the same proportion of household income in 1985 (19 per cent) as they had in 1975 (20.1 per cent). Taxes on expenditure, such as excise duties and VAT, increased sharply,

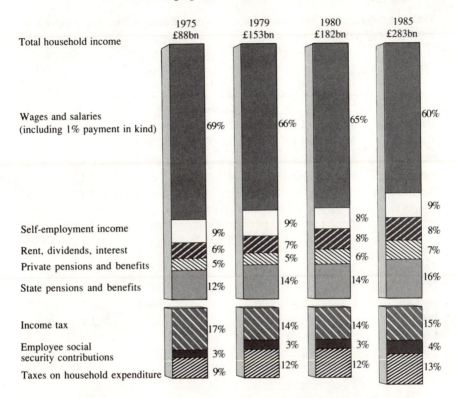

Figure 2.1   The make-up of household income, 1975–85, the United Kingdom
Source: Stark, 1988

taking, by the mid-1980s, almost as large a slice of household income as direct taxes on income.

The distribution of family incomes (taking together earnings, property incomes and social security benefits) is based on Inland Revenue data, supplemented by information from the Family Expenditure Survey. The results are shown in Table 2.1.

The distribution of incomes narrowed sharply in the post-war years. Over the thirty years ending in 1979, the share of income going to the richest one per cent more than halved, from 11 per cent to little more than 5 per cent. However, examination of the data shows that the main beneficiaries of the declining fortunes of the very rich were the not-quite-so-rich rather than the poor. While the share of the top ten per cent fell from a third of all personal incomes to a quarter, the remainder of the top half of income units *increased* their share from 43 to 50 per cent. The bottom half of the income distribution actually saw their share of income *fall* from 27 per cent to 23 per cent over the period.

Table 2.1   Percentage shares of income, before and after income tax, received by given quantile groups

	1949	1959	1970/1	1976/7 (old basis)	1976/7 (new basis)	1978/9	1984/5
			Before income tax				
Top 1%	11.2	8.4	6.6	5.4	5.5	5.3	6.4
Top 10%	33.2	29.4	27.5	25.8	26.2	26.1	29.5
Next 40%	43.1	47.5	49.0	49.7	49.7	50.4	48.3
Bottom 50%	27.3	23.0	23.5	24.5	24.1	23.5	22.2
Bottom 10%			2.5	2.5	2.5	2.4	2.3
Gini: %	41	40	39	37	37	37	41
			After income tax				
Top 1%	6.4	5.3	4.5	3.5	3.9	3.9	4.9
Top 10%	27.1	25.2	23.9	22.4	23.2	23.4	26.5
Next 40%	46.4	49.7	49.9	50.0	49.9	50.4	48.6
Bottom 50%	26.5	25.0	26.1	27.6	26.9	26.2	24.9
Bottom 10%				3.1	3.0	2.9	2.7
Gini: %	36	36	36	32	33	34	36

Source: CSO, *Economic Trends*

2.2.2   Inequality in the 1980s

What has happened during the 1980s? The share of the top ten per cent of income recipients increased before tax from 26 per cent of the total to 29.5 per cent between 1978/9 and 1984/5 alone. Meanwhile, the share of the poorer half of income units fell, from 23.5 per cent to just over 22 per cent. Thus, the distribution of incomes in the mid-1980s displayed a considerable degree of inequality. The richest one per cent of income recipients enjoyed a larger share of the nation's income (6.4 per cent before tax) than the poorest 20 per cent between them (5.8 per cent), and nearly three times as much as that going to the poorest tenth. The top ten per cent had a larger share of the total income (29.5 per cent) than the lower half of the population (22.2 per cent). Indeed, sixty per cent of the population barely matched the income between them enjoyed by the richest ten per cent.

The Gini coefficient is an overall measure of the degree of inequality.[1] The value of the Gini coefficient can vary between 0 (indicating a situation of complete equality) and 100 (indicating a situation in which all the income is enjoyed by one individual). Summary measures of inequality such as this have been criticized, especially by Atkinson (1980), for failing to take account of the value judgements built into any assessment of inequality. However, such measures do give some indication of what has been happening to the distribution of income over time. Using the Gini coefficient, we find that the degree of inequality in the pre-tax distribution of incomes declined steadily until 1976/7. By 1978/79, the Gini coefficient had started to rise again, indicating an increase in inequality. By the mid-1980s the distribution of incomes was as unequal as it had been in 1949, both before and after tax. (See pages 76 and 77 below.)

Activity 2.1

The data here provided cover the period up to the mid-1980s. Using the most recent article on 'The Distribution of Income in the United Kingdom' in CSO *Economic Trends*, published each year by HMSO, check what has happened since.

2.2.3   The regional divide

The growth of inequality during the 1980s is also reflected in sharper divisions between the regions of the UK. As the *Financial Times* reported, reviewing data from the Central Statistical Office:

> ... on virtually any measure of economic performance, the so-called north–south divide has widened during the 1980s. People in the south have produced more, earned more, spent more and been offered more job opportunities than their counterparts in northern England and in Scotland, Wales and Northern Ireland. (*Financial Times*, 18 February, 1988)

The CSO data reveal that spending per head in the South East increased from a level 13 per cent above the average in 1979 to 20 per cent above the average in 1986. In the north, spending per head fell from 94 per cent of the national average in 1979 to only 89 per cent in 1986.

The shift in resources towards the south was partly due to the decline of older manufacturing industries in the 'depressed' regions, and the growth of new service and high-tech employment concentrated in the south. This was reflected in the distribution of job opportunities. According to the Department of Employment's 1987 *Labour Force Survey*, nearly half the 1.4 million jobs created between 1983 and 1987 were in the South East, with many of the rest appearing in East Anglia and the South West. Meanwhile, Wales and Scotland saw virtually no new jobs during this period, and employment in the North West actually fell. These trends reflected themselves in changes in the distribution of earnings (see section 2.3.5), and also in the relative levels of household incomes. In 1986, households in the North had an income £40 per week below the national average and £80 per week lower than the average for the South East (Department of Employment, *Family Expenditure Survey*, 1987).

Although there is a clear divide between regions in terms of income and wealth, it is important to recognize that a similar, perhaps greater, division can exist *within* regions. Even in the prosperous South East and Greater London, poverty increased during the 1980s. A study carried out by Professor Peter Townsend found evidence of 'rapid social polarisation taking place in London as standards of living amongst the poor and rich diverge more rapidly in the capital than in the UK as a whole' (Townsend, 1987). This study pointed out that the government's own figures showed that 1.8 million Londoners lived in poverty, or on its margins (having an income no more than 40 per cent above the supplementary benefit subsistence level). It found sharp differences in levels of deprivation amongst the inhabitants of the poorer boroughs, such as Hackney and Tower Hamlets, compared with the more affluent areas such as Bromley. Townsend also calculated, using data from the Family Expenditure Survey, that between 1981 and 1985 the disposable income of the poorest fifth of households in London fell by 14 per cent, while that of the richest fifth increased by 7 per cent.

2.2.4   The failure of redistribution

The data show that income inequalities were very little different in the 1980s from those which existed before the establishment of the welfare state forty years earlier. This is despite the existence of a nominally progressive tax system, a social security system designed to increase the relative incomes of the poorest, and social services – including education and the NHS – intended to narrow the gap in opportunities and experience between different social classes. Moreover, the evidence suggests that the most recent period has seen a reversal of the modest narrowing in incomes which continued for most of the post-war period.

Recent changes in the degree of inequality were described by the Central Statistical Office (CSO) in the 1988 issue of *Social Trends*:

> Between 1976 and 1985 the distribution of household original income in the United Kingdom became steadily more unequal, with the share of the bottom 40 per cent falling from 10.2 per cent to 6.3 per cent, compared with a rise in the share of the top 20 per cent from 44.4 per cent to 49.2 per cent. (CSO, *Social Trends*, 1988)

The figures, which are derived from the annual Family Expenditure Survey, show that by 1985 the share of original income going to the poorest tenth of households had fallen to almost one third of its 1976 level (from 0.8 per cent to 0.3 per cent). Hence the underlying trends, powered mainly by the effects of the recession and unemployment, together with demographic changes such as an increase in the number of pensioners and single parent families, were towards an increase in inequality.

What role did the state play in influencing income distribution? The CSO data also show a decline in the share of income going to the poorest households after taxes and public spending have been taken into account, balanced by an increase in the share going to the richest households. So, what has prevented the redistribution of income?

There seem to be two sets of factors that help to determine the extent and nature of inequality. The first is the underlying influence of market forces and economic factors, although as Dorothy Wedderburn has argued, these are themselves influenced by class and institutional factors (Wedderburn, 1980). The second is the importance of state action to reduce (or increase) inequality through the use of the tax system and public spending, especially on social security and the social services. While both sets of forces, the state and the market, interact with each other and with class and institutions, it is important to try to separate them in order to analyse the forces that generate and perpetuate inequality. In the next section, we will focus mainly on the market distribution of incomes, the main component of which remains earnings from employment. As we will see, the evidence points to an increasing disparity in the distribution of earnings, partly because of changes in the structure of the economy and the labour market but also, most recently, because of government policy. In section 2.5 we will consider the role of the tax and social security systems, the main state mechanisms for influencing inequality.

2.3   Earnings inequalities

Although wages and salaries have declined as a proportion of household income in recent years, they remain an important determinant of living standards. Stark shows that, amongst households with the highest incomes, earnings are the most important source of income, and amongst the poorest households, social security benefits are the main source (Stark, 1988, Chart J). Changes in the labour market can therefore have a powerful influence on economic inequality.

2.3.1   The pattern of earnings

Stark's analysis documents the pattern of earnings, showing the influence of industrial and occupational factors, as well as the importance of age and sex differences. It does not, though, illustrate the difference in pay rates (for each hour worked) between part-timers and full-timers, which Hurstfield (1987) shows to be considerable. Nor does it provide information on racial differences in earnings, which are also important (Low Pay Unit, 1988).

These aspects of **earnings inequality** will be important when we come to look behind the changes in the distribution of economic resources later in this chapter. For the moment, consider what has happened to the overall distribution of earnings. Table 2.2 represents a distillation of the many different aspects of pay inequalities. The lowest decile represents the earnings below which ten per cent of workers fall. If you prefer, think of the lowest decile figures as the average (median) earnings of the poorest fifth of workers. The lower quartile is the point on the earnings distribution below which one quarter of workers fall (or perhaps the median earnings of those in the lower half of the distribution).

Table 2.2 Dispersion of earnings of full-time men in manual jobs, 1886–1987

	Lowest decile as % of median	Median (£)	Highest decile as % of median
1886	68.6	1.21	143.1
1906	66.5	1.47	156.8
1938	67.7	3.40	139.9
1960	70.6	14.17	145.2
1970	67.3	25.60	147.5
1976	70.2	62.10	144.9
1979	68.3	88.20	148.5
1982	68.3	125.20	152.6
1986	65.4	163.40	154.8
1987	64.4	173.90	155.9

Note: Figures for later years have been adjusted by the Low Pay Unit to take account of statistical changes in the New Earnings Survey.

Source: HMSO, 1971; updated by DE, *New Earnings Surveys*, 1970–87

The most comprehensive source of data on the distribution of earnings is the Department of Employment's *New Earnings Survey*. This reveals a widening of the spread of full-time adult male earnings since the 1960s. In 1960, the poorest fifth of male manual workers had average (median) earnings equivalent to 70.6 per cent of the overall average (median), while the best-paid fifth earned 45.2 per cent more than the average. By 1987, the relative earnings of the poorest fifth had declined to 64.6 per cent of the average, while the best paid fifth earned 56 per cent more than the average.

The dispersion of earnings amongst adult women working full time appears also to have widened, but to a less dramatic extent. However, we should bear in mind the changes taking place in the structure of the workforce. The number of women working part time has increased sharply, while the number of full-time jobs for men has fallen during the period in question.

2.3.2   Long-term stability and decline

Changes in earnings distribution since the mid-1970s have been dramatic. However, a longer-term analysis is possible, using earlier Board of Trade, Ministry of Labour and Department of Employment data on the distribution of earnings for adult men in manual jobs (there are no equivalent figures for women). The figures begin in 1886, and suggest a remarkable stability in the distribution of earnings for this group throughout most of the following century. The lowest decile earned between 68 and 70 per cent of the median in 1886, 1960, 1971, 1976 and 1979. Since the early 1980s, however, the distribution of earnings has widened sharply, so that, as we have noted, the lowest decile had dropped to little more than 64 per cent of the median by 1987.

It should be remembered that adult male manual workers now represent a much smaller proportion of the workforce than they did in the late nineteenth century, or even in the early 1970s. The significance of the recent decline in the relative position of the poorest amongst this group should not be overstated. However, the 1980s saw a sharp increase in divisions between the high and low paid. Between 1979 and 1987 alone, earnings for the best paid fifth of male workers generally increased by 42 per cent more than those of the lowest paid fifth, partly as a result of the rapid increase in City salaries in the mid-1980s. The same period witnessed a widening of divisions between different groups in the labour market: young and adult, part-time and full-time, black and white, men and women, low paid and high paid (Low Pay Unit, 1988).

2.3.3   The fragmentation of the workforce

In 1979, 16- and 17-year olds earned 42 per cent of adult earnings, on average; by 1987 they earned only 39 per cent of the adult average, and this proportion was expected to decline further as a result of legislation in 1988, which abolished their entitlement to social security payments, leaving them no option but to accept a training place or low-wage employment. Similarly, 18–20-year olds saw their earnings decline from just over three-fifths of the adult average to only 54 per cent. This group, too, might be expected to experience a further decline in its relative pay, given the abolition in 1986 of wages council minimum wage rates for people aged under 21.

Activity 2.2

Check the latest edition of the Department of Employment *New Earnings Survey* to see whether these changes are reflected in the up-to-date figures.

Despite the introduction of equal pay legislation in the mid-1970s, pay differences between men and women persisted, with a slight widening of the gap towards the end of the 1980s. Adult women working full time earned roughly the same proportion of the adult hourly male wage in 1987 as in 1979 (73.6 per cent as against 73 per cent). However, more than two-fifths (43.8 per cent) of women worked part-time in 1987, and the overwhelming majority of these were low paid. Four-fifths of all women working part time earned less than the Council of Europe's decency threshold for wages, set at £3.50 an hour for the UK in 1987. On average, women working part time earned 57.5 per cent of the male full-time hourly wage in 1987, compared with 59.3 per cent in 1979.

2.3.4   Wage inequalities and race

A major gap in the official earnings statistics is the absence of any data on the earnings of different ethnic groups, making it impossible to assess changes in the pattern of earnings inequality between black and white. However, the Policy Studies Institute (PSI) has carried out sporadic national surveys which throw some light on this aspect of earnings inequality. The latest data available relate to 1982, and since that time earnings disparities have generally increased sharply. This is likely to have had a disproportionate effect on those from disadvantaged ethnic groups. However, even in 1982, the average earnings of Asian and West Indian men were 15 per cent lower than those of white men. An earlier PSI survey, in 1974, had detected a differential of only 10 per cent. Indian and African Asian men earned more than West Indians, while Pakistanis and Bangladeshis earned less. The researchers were careful to point out that the apparent widening of the gap between the earnings of different ethnic groups between 1974 and 1982 may in part be attributed to the higher non-response rate among black people within the sample compared with whites in 1982. However, the study concludes that 'there has been no overall improvement in the situation' (Brown, 1985).

2.3.5   The regional earnings divide

The final aspect of earnings inequalities which must be considered is the regional dimension. The Department of Employment data indicate a wide disparity in earnings both between and within regions. The decline in manufacturing employment, its replacement with generally lower-paid service employment, and the overall growth in unemployment, have all had a differential impact on earnings between regions. During the 1980s, the smallest increases in earnings were experienced by workers in the North, while London and the South East fared rather better than the average. By 1987, average earnings in Greater London were £60 a week – more than

£3000 a year – higher than the average outside the South East. This reflected itself in a much higher incidence of low wages, as well as unemployment, in the 'depressed regions'. Overall, about one third (32.2 per cent) of full-time adult workers earned less than the Council of Europe's decency threshold; this was set at the equivalent of 68 per cent of the available earnings of all men and women together, and gave a UK figure of £135 per week (£3.50 per hour) in 1987. In the South East the proportion falling below the threshold was under one in four (23.1 per cent), but in Scotland 37 per cent of adult full-timers earned low wages, as did 36 per cent of those working in Wales, Yorkshire and Humberside, the South West and East Anglia (Low Pay Unit, 1988).

This differential between regions concealed a marked disparity in earnings within regions. In 1987, not only did London have higher average earnings than other parts of the country; it also had a more pronounced inequality of earnings than elsewhere, with the best paid fifth of men in white-collar jobs earning 6.5 times as much as the poorest fifth of women in manual jobs. In Yorkshire and Humberside, by contrast, the highest paid group earned only 4.8 times as much as the poorest. In order to understand this intraregional inequality, we have to take into account employment within regions, and the differences in pay between urban areas generally and poorer inner city or rural areas.

Summary of sections 2.2 and 2.3

● For three decades after the war, the distribution of incomes became more equal. But the 1980s witnessed a reversal of this generally egalitarian trend. By the mid-1980s, incomes were as unequally divided, both before and after tax, as they had been in 1949. The divisions reflected themselves, not only between rich and poor, but between and within the regions of the UK.

● Earnings from employment are the main source of income for most households, and so changes in the distribution of earnings can have a marked effect on inequality generally. The figures presented above suggest that the distribution of male earnings has remained almost stable since the late nineteeth century, with a tendency towards a widening in the 1980s.

2.4   Labour market segmentation

Given the importance of earnings in determining the overall distribution of incomes, we need to explain how this increased inequality has come about. There appear to be two sets of factors at work: longer term changes in the structure of the economy and the labour market and, especially during the 1980s, the effects of central government policy. These two sets of factors are closely interrelated, but it is helpful to consider each of them separately. In my view, the underlying changes in the structure of the labour market are more important, and I will deal only briefly with the effects of short-term policy change. When examining both types of influence it is perhaps helpful to consider the development of economic theory on labour markets.

2.4.1   Orthodox theory: the competitive labour market

Orthodox (neo-classical) theory of wages and employment takes as its starting point the assumption that the labour market operates through the process of competition to maximize employment and output. The mechanism for matching the demand for labour with its supply is the wage system. Assuming that market forces are allowed to operate freely, workers will be paid a wage equivalent to their contribution to value added (the marginal revenue product of labour). Those whose productivity, for whatever reason, is less than the average will be paid less, or will be unemployed. Higher wages, by contrast, are assumed to represent the rewards for greater productivity. Hence, 'the distribution of marginal product is identical with the distribution of earned income. If an individual's income is too low, his (*sic*) productivity is too low. His income can be increased only if his productivity can be raised' (Thurow, 1969, p. 26).

Orthodox theory emphasizes the importance of labour supply factors – the quality of labour measured in terms of effort, training, skills and qualifications – in determining rewards. It also implies that any intervention, whether by the state or by trade unions, to 'artificially' increase the earnings of workers will inevitably result in lower levels of employment, since the wage will then exceed the marginal revenue product of labour. Strict adherence to the neo-classical theory would attribute the generally low wages of women and ethnic minorities to the low productivity of these groups. For instance, the Institute of Directors argued recently, 'a statutory minimum wage discourages employers from taking on blacks, who for a number of socio-economic reasons have a lower marginal productivity than whites' (Institute of Directors, 1984).

Assuming that the distribution of innate abilities is constant, the theory would suggest that the only way of improving the incomes of the poor is to increase their productivity through training and education. Orthodox theory forms the basis of much conservative thinking about the economy and society. Its conclusion – 'if you are paid a lot it must be because you are worth a lot' – represents a comforting explanation for inequality. Yet it is open to challenge on both conceptual and empirical grounds.

Activity 2.3

Spend a few moments considering how you would challenge orthodox wages and employment theory. What problems with it can you identify?

The concept of 'marginal productivity' on which the orthodox theory rests is largely tautological. The marginal product of labour defies measurement, and so economists have tended to use wage levels as its proxy. Lester Thurow has pointed out the difficulty:

> There is practically no direct information on whether or not labour is paid its marginal product. Economists take it as an article of faith or else claim that it is the best null hypothesis, and economic theory is based on the assumption that labour is indeed paid its marginal product. Without this assumption, much of [orthodox] economic analysis falls apart. (Thurow, 1970, p. 20)

Empirically, the notion that wages are related to an individual's stock of 'human capital' (innate abilities, skills and qualifications) lacks credibility. A study of General Household Survey data carried out for the Royal Commission on the Distribution of Income and Wealth in the late 1970s could find little association between educational attainment and earnings. It found that there was 'an enormous spread of earnings', even amongst those with the same education and qualifications, and that 'if all educational disparities were eliminated the remaining inequality would still be over 93 per cent of what it is now' (Layard *et al.*, 1978). The marginal productivity theory is no better at explaining the rewards of the rich than those of the poor. Evidence submitted to the Royal Commission suggested that top executive salaries had little association with measures of company economic success. As one member of the Commission reported:

> If economic determinants were all important, we would expect to find some correlation between the level of salary of top managers and the profitability of their company, its rate of growth or its size, so these might be factors expected to help determine what the senior executive is worth in market terms. But the correlation is, in fact, very weak. (Wedderburn, 1980)

2.4.2   Labour market duality and segmentation

Few would be prepared to accept the logical conclusion of orthodox theory, that the consistently lower wages of blacks, women, and those living in the more depressed regions of the north, are the result of lower productivity. In an attempt to adapt the orthodox theory to take account of such persistent inequalities, labour economists (mainly in the United States during the 1960s) developed the theory of the **dual labour market**, divided between a primary sector and a secondary sector. The inhabitants of the primary sector of the labour market generally enjoyed higher rewards, more job security and better fringe benefits than those in the secondary sector, whose employment tended to be poorly paid, casualized and insecure.

Early versions of this theory drew a distinction between an 'internal market', guided by institutional rules, and an 'external market', in which the rules of competition continued to apply. The internal labour market had developed, it was argued, because of the increasingly job-specific nature of skills. Employees needed to invest in the training of new recruits, whose general skills would be inappropriate to the job in question. The employees concerned were rewarded with good pay and employment conditions, together with prospects for advancement within the organization, to discourage staff turnover and the loss of valuable skills. Entry to this internal labour market was allowed only at the bottom of the hierarchy, or at specified 'points of entry' higher up the job scale for suitably qualified candidates. For those in the internal labour market, external labour market conditions had little effect on earnings or job security; these conditions were felt most strongly by those in the external market.

These theories did not deny the validity of the competitive labour market model used in orthodox economics, and they rested heavily on the concept of 'human capital', which was common also to the 'marginal productivity' approach. Instead, they sought to adapt the simple competitive model to take account of the administrative rules that often operated in big business and the public sector. Their emphasis, like that of orthodox theory, remained on the characteristics of the labour supply.

During the 1970s new theories developed to challenge this emphasis, focusing instead on the characteristics of labour demand. These also argued that the labour market had come to be divided into primary and secondary sectors, but their explanations for the division were different and more radical. Both employers and worker organizations had an incentive in creating and maintaining those divisions. Firms, subject to fluctuations in the demand for their products needed to find a means of adjusting their costs to such fluctuations, while at the same time retaining their investment in the training of their more skilled or higher status staff. They therefore needed to ensure that sections of the workforce were sufficiently 'disposable' to allow the adjustment of labour costs to economic fluctuations.

This flexibility could be achieved by the employment of part-timers and homeworkers, casual and temporary workers, and groups whose vulnerability to unemployment and non-union status, rendered them acceptable as part of a labour reserve. Young people, black workers and some groups of women workers fulfilled these criteria. Privatization and the contracting out of public services helped in this isolation of certain groups, some of whom as full-time, permanent employees and members of trade unions were part of the primary or core labour force. Rubery (1978) argued that worker organizations had an interest in colluding in this process, ensuring, for their core membership, a greater measure of security of employment, and a differential in wages above those of groups in the secondary sector.

2.4.3   The peripheral workforce

Leadbeater (1987) documents the evidence available to support the analysis of labour market change outlined above. He argues that economic change has created a persistent pool of long-term unemployed, and a **peripheral workforce** of part-timers, temporary workers, and the self-employed. Meanwhile, many (although, as we have seen, not all) of those in full-time employment have enjoyed growing prosperity. Leadbeater cites data which show that, 'the peripheral workforce expanded by 16 per cent between 1981 and 1985 to 8.1 million workers, while the permanent workforce of full-time employees declined by 6 per cent. While some of this growth is a continuation of trends established in the 1970s, it seems to mark a permanent change in the structure of employment'. This **labour market segmentation** has gender and racial dimensions, as well as a geographical aspect. The majority of those who find themselves within the secondary sector of the labour market are women or black people, even though white men are still heavily represented amongst Leadbeater's 'outer core' of the long-term unemployed.

Economic factors have undoubtedly played an important part in helping to create such divisions. Employer and union strategies designed to increase flexibility of labour costs and security of employment, each contributing to the creation of the divisions in different ways, are both responses to economic uncertainty. Moreover, the decline in manufacturing industry since the mid-1970s, and the growth of service employment has tended to have an effect on the balance between core and periphery employment. Most jobs in manufacturing were held by men on a full-time and permanent basis; most of those in the service sector are held by women, often on a part-time or casual basis, and with poorer rewards and less security. Virtually all the new jobs created in the United Kingdom since the peak of unemployment in 1983 have been part-time, and most of them have been low paid (Hurstfield, 1987). Most of them, too, have been created outside the older industrial areas. These developments have been reflected in the growing disparity of earnings noted above, with the greatest divisions between men and women, full-timers and part-timers, black people and whites. As *Leadbeater* (1987) warns, however, and as our data above confirm, inequalities in pay between full-time male workers have also increased, largely as a result of the depressive effect on the wages of certain groups resulting from the competitive presence of the long-term unemployed and the peripheral workforce.

Activity 2.4

Summarize the main differences between orthodox, neo-classical labour market theory and the theories of labour market duality and labour market segmentation.

2.4.4   Labour market policies under Thatcherism

These changes in the structure of the labour market, determined principally by underlying economic developments, were encouraged during the 1980s by central government policy. Pursuing a generally orthodox approach to the labour market, the post-1979 Conservative governments developed a policy of 'deregulation' designed to encourage flexibility in employment. This took the form of reducing the scope of employment rights and minimum wages, especially for young people, part-timers and those working in small firms. The Thatcher administrations actively encouraged the growth of self-employment, and its policies of contracting out public services further extended the development of the unregulated secondary labour market. Wage subsidy schemes were used to persuade the unemployed to accept low wage employment (and employers to provide it), while a tightening of social security regulations was used to coerce the less willing to accept, or remain in, low wage jobs.

The decline in union membership, already an inevitable consequence of the changes in the level and structure of employment, was further encouraged by explicit government policy. Between 1979 and 1987 the number of union members fell by 2.5 million, to a level almost 20 per cent below the peak of 13.2 million established at the end of the 1970s (Government Certification Officer, 1988). In the Government's view, such measures were justified in helping to overcome labour market 'rigidities' which prevented wages adjusting downwards to take account of unemployment.

Summary of section 2.4

•   Explanations for the inequality of earnings – including pay differences between the sexes, races and age groups – differ according to alternative theories of the labour market. Orthodox theory attributes differences in pay to differences in skills, ability and the productivity of the workers concerned. More radical 'dual labour market' and 'segmentation' theories explain differences in pay in terms of the structure of labour markets rather than the abilities of individuals.

•   The extent of state intervention that is considered appropriate will be determined by which of these approaches is favoured. Orthodox theories suggest that the state should intervene as little as possible; those who believe in labour market segmentation advocate more state intervention to correct the inequalities generated by the labour market.

2.5 The role of the welfare state

Labour market changes help to explain much of the pattern of wider inequality which we examined in the first two sections of this chapter. But employment incomes are not the only determinant of market inequalities; capital and property markets are also important (see section 2.7). The effect of underlying economic factors such as this can be powerful in helping to shape the distribution of economic resources, and can operate in a self-reinforcing fashion. Market-generated inequalities can perpetuate and magnify themselves through their effects on institutions. The state can break into this cycle, or it can reinforce it, through the tax system and public spending, and mainly through social security which is the largest single public expenditure programme. Here we consider the effect of state intervention in this way during the decades following the Second World War and more recently.

2.5.1 Taxation and the redistribution of incomes

Taxation has had little effect on the overall **distribution of incomes**, contrary to what we might expect from an apparently progressive tax system. Thus, while we would expect the income tax system to reduce the degree of inequality, by taking larger proportions of the incomes of higher income groups, the data examined in section 2.2.2 suggest that the effect is marginal: in 1984/85 the share of total incomes going to the richest one per cent fell from 6.4 per cent before tax to 4.9 per cent after tax – a reduction in their overall share of less than a quarter. The top ten per cent saw their share of income reduced by even less, about a tenth. Tax also had little impact at the lower end of the distribution, increasing the shares of income going to the poorest tenth from 2.3 per cent to only 2.7 per cent – an increase in their share of income of little more than one sixth.

An examination of the effects of the tax system over time is also revealing. Comparing the distribution of incomes before and after tax, as in Table 2.1 above, we find that the share of the richest groups fell by less after tax than before tax. This is reflected in the Gini coefficients which have reflected a sharp increase in inequality in after-tax distribution since the mid-1970s. Indeed, using this measure of inequality, the distribution of income after tax was more unequal in 1984/5 than it had been in 1949.

2.5.2 Changes in the structure of taxation

The reason for this rather limited impact of taxation can be traced to changes in the structure of income tax since the war, combined with changes in the overall pattern of taxation. Over a period of forty years after the war, income tax was extended to sections of the workforce that were previously exempt. Thus, in the mid-1950s a stereotypical family of four would not pay any income tax if its earned income was less than the average wage, and even when it started to pay, it would pay at a rate of only 7p in the pound. By the mid-1960s, this type of family paid tax on incomes in excess of three-quarters of the average wage, and by the mid-1970s on less than half the average wage. Moreover, the rate at which tax became payable on entry to the tax system was now closer to 30p in the pound. The effect of these changes was to spread the burden of income tax towards those on lower levels of income, reducing the overall redistributive impact of the system. Meanwhile, taxes on capital and on corporate and unearned incomes diminished in import-ance, increasing further the burden on wage-earners.

2.5.3   The political economy of taxation

These trends in taxation were not merely a matter of accountancy. It can be argued that for much of the post-war period, taxation was used by the state as a mechanism for mitigating the effect of economic change, and perhaps declining profitability, on the corporate sector, and concentrating the burden of economic change on wage-earners. During the late 1960s and '70s, there was clear evidence of the development of a 'wage-tax spiral' in which governments were using wage taxation as a means of controlling the growth of net money wages, while wage-earners were seeking to compensate for the rising tax burden by demanding still higher increases in gross money wages (see Day and Pond, 1982). In this context, some have argued that taxation, and the welfare state generally, acted as a focus for competition between classes (Gough, 1979).

These developments entered a new phase with the election of the Thatcher governments of the 1980s. Tax changes now became explicitly a mechanism for redistributing incomes and wealth. Capital taxes on rentier incomes were virtually abolished, although taxation of the corporate sector was allowed to increase, perhaps reflecting government preference for finance rather than industrial capital. Wage taxation also increased, within the context of a sharp redistribution of the tax burden from the rich towards the poor. In 1988, the once progressive system of income tax was converted into a virtually single rate structure, with 95 per cent of taxpayers subject to the same basic rate of tax. Combined with the somewhat regressive effects of indirect taxes (such as VAT and excise duties), the tax system was deprived of most of its redistributive features.

2.5.4   Social security changes

Changes in social security also served to reinforce, rather than to challenge, the underlying growth in inequality. Beveridge's post-war reforms in social security were based on two important premises: first, that full employment would be maintained; secondly, that anyone engaged in full-time employ-ment would have sufficient income without the need to turn to the state for help, except with part of the costs of child-rearing. Beveridge's scheme was based on the principle of national insurance, with a residual of national assistance (later supplementary benefit, and later still income support) remaining as a means-tested 'safety net' for those few unable to accumulate sufficient contributions to insure themselves against periods of interruption of earnings.

The changes in the economy and the labour market described above rendered the social security system ineffective in its principle objectives. The growth in long-term unemployment meant that the proportion of the labour force able to insure itself against want was always less than had been envisaged, while the growth of a peripheral workforce has meant that many of those in employment are also unable to build up sufficient contribution records. As early as the late 1960s, it became clear that full-time employment would not act as a guarantee against hardship, bringing with it the necessity to extend social security to the working poor who had been excluded from Beveridge's original plan. This extension, in the form of rent and rate rebates (later to become Housing Benefit) and Family Income Supplement (later Family Credit) was offered on a means-tested basis which tended to increase stigma for the recipients, and extend the effect of the poverty trap to a large section of the workforce.

2.5.5   Social security in the 1980s

Once again, these developments entered a new phase during the 1980s with substantial reforms in the **social security system**. The combination of growing unemployment, an increasing low wage sector and demographic changes was creating what was perceived as a 'fiscal crisis' for the state. The response of the Thatcher governments was to restrict both the level of benefits and the groups entitled to them. Housing benefit, the cost of which had escalated because of the growth of low incomes and because of cuts in the rate support grant to local authorities, was subject to deep cuts. National insurance unemployment benefit was virtually scrapped, through a combination of changes in the rules for eligibility and abolition of the child additions and the earnings-related element. The real growth of pensions and child benefit was restricted, and cash payments to help claimants meet the cost of essential items, such as a cooker or pram, were converted into a system of discretionary loans. Increased means-testing was applied in the payment of benefits, and the growth of private provision was encouraged, where necessary by tax concessions.

There is an important regional dimension to this pattern of change. Inevitably, less prosperous parts of the country have a higher proportion of households dependent on social security benefits: benefits accounted for 20 per cent of the average weekly income in the North, 17 per cent in the North West, 15 per cent in the West Midlands and less than 10 per cent in the South East of England. The highest proportion of children receiving free school meals (before they were abolished in 1988) was in Northern Ireland (28 per cent), the North (25.4 per cent) and the North West (24.5 per cent). These same regions had the highest dependence on supplementary benefit. As we have noted, special payments for recipients of supplementary benefit were also abolished in 1988. Meanwhile, tax benefits such as mortgage interest relief were of greatest benefit to households in the more prosperous regions: only 1.3 per cent of mortgage tax relief revenue found its way to Northern Ireland, and only 6.8 per cent to Scotland. The North West of England received 9.4 per cent of the tax subsidy, while the South East received 41 per cent (Low Pay Unit, 1987). In these respects, social security and tax changes have effectively become a negative form of regional policy (CSO, *Regional Trends*, 1986).

The changes since the late 1970s, and especially during the 1980s meant that the role of the social security system in reducing inequality was severely curtailed. While the private and 'fiscal' welfare states, made up respectively of occupational provision of pensions and other benefits, and of an increasingly generous system of tax reliefs, continued to grow, the system of social welfare diminished in importance. Combined with the developments in earnings inequality described above, unmitigated by the tax system, the effect was an increase in the scale of poverty.

2.5.6   An end to the 'welfare consensus?'

During much of the post-war period a consensus seemed to have emerged about the role of the welfare state, based on Beveridge's conception of society's responsibility to destroy the 'five giant evils' of Want, Disease, Ignorance, Squalor and Idleness (Beveridge, 1943, p. 42). Despite differences in emphasis between governments of different persuasions (some placing greater weight on the welfare state as a mechanism for redistribution, others seeing it largely as a safety net) there was general agreement by both Labour and Conservatives that the welfare state had an important role.

This consensus came under increasing pressure during the 1970s: the escalating costs of public expenditure could no longer be financed by economic growth and required an increasing burden of taxation, much of it falling on wage-earners at relatively low levels of income. It has been argued (for instance, Day and Pond, 1982) that this helped to undermine the support for welfare spending amongst the working class who needed it most. By the late 1970s an assault had begun on the so-called 'nanny-state' from the New Right. As Margaret Thatcher asserted in 1977 ' . . . a vital new debate is beginning, or perhaps an old debate is being renewed, about the proper role of government, the welfare state and the attitudes on which it rests' (Thatcher, 1977).

Redistribution was no longer considered a legitimate activity for governments to pursue, or indeed to concern themselves about. And, since inequality was no longer a matter of policy, the collection of information about its dimensions became an unnecessary drain on public funds. As noted at the start of this chapter, the Royal Commission on the Distribution of Income and Wealth, established by the Labour government in 1975 was soon dismantled after the 1979 election. Likewise, the publication of annual figures on the numbers in poverty was considered an extravagence, and was first extended to once every two or three years before being abandoned altogether in 1988. Although the public presentation of government policy in the Thatcher years was that the role of the state was to intervene as little as possible in redistribution, in fact taxation, social security and labour market policy all resulted in a substantial redistribution of income and wealth, albeit in a direction previously considered unacceptable.

The failure of the post-war welfare state to redistribute economic resources was therefore followed, during the 1980s, by a government determined to shift resources from the state to the private sector, to encourage the growth of private rather than social welfare, and to use the tax system as a mechanism for encouraging incentives rather than redistribution.

2.5.7　The failure of redistribution

One of the themes running throughout this chapter is that of the role of the state versus economic forces in determining the degree of inequality. For much of the post-war period, as we have described above, the consensus in British politics saw the proper role of the welfare state to be that of assisting the redistribution of income and wealth, mainly through fiscal measures (the tax and social security systems), but also through labour market policy and the provision of services. Yet the effect of this long period of 'progressive' state intervention on the distribution of economic resources was less than dramatic. Even before the election of the first Thatcher government in 1979, extreme inequalities in wealth, income and life chances persisted.

LeGrand (1982) has argued that the principal failing of the post-war welfare state to narrow inequalities significantly appears to rest with '**the strategy of equality**'. This strategy was based on a reluctance to interfere directly in the processes that generate inequalities, or to intervene in the operation of market forces, but instead to adjust 'after the event' to remove the worst excesses of inequality that might otherwise result. He argues that, by failing to challenge the *causes* of inequality, the strategy allowed the inequalities to reassert themselves through the institutions of the welfare state. Hence, as LeGrand has demonstrated, a health service intended to provide equal provision to all classes has become a mechanism for allocating NHS resources unequally between socio-economic groups; the education system, designed to provide equality of opportunity, has in effect served to reinforce class divisions in the distribution of educational resources. Similarly, the tax system has done little to narrow inequalities in income or wealth, while social security has become a system of last resort, providing no more than a basic subsistence income that traps many families into poverty rather than lifting them free of its effects.

Summary of section 2.5

- During most of the post-war period, governments pursued a policy of 'redistribution', using progressive taxation and social spending to narrow economic inequalities. The policy failed to affect the distribution of economic rewards significantly, because it did not challenge the underlying *causes* of inequality, generated mainly through the labour market. The 1980s saw a reversal of policy, with changes in taxation and social security tending to reinforce the trend towards greater inequality.

2.6   Poverty and wealth

Having examined the overall distribution of economic rewards, and considered the factors that have helped to generate or alleviate the inequalities, it is time to consider outcomes. At one extreme of the spectrum of economic inequality are the poor; at the other extreme are the wealthy.

The concept of **poverty** refuses to fit the statisticians' distinction between income and wealth. Certainly, poverty is normally associated with an inadequate income; but the poor also tend to lack property and assets from which an income might be derived (Townsend, 1979).

2.6.1   Who are the poor?

A lively debate continues within the academic community as to how **the poor** are to be identified (see, for example, *Journal of Social Policy*, 1987). The poor themselves have no such difficulty. Stark (1988) neatly sidesteps this debate by listing the number of persons in families with 'low incomes'. Once again, the figures are derived from the annual Family Expenditure Survey (FES), although the DHSS analysis of the FES is far from regular. The latest estimates at the time of writing relate to 1985.

On the 'narrow measure' of poverty – which Stark defines as any individual or family either dependent on supplementary benefit or having an income which is at, or below, the level they would receive if dependent on supplementary benefit – 16.6 per cent of the population was in poverty in 1983, rising to 17.3 per cent in 1985. This compares with 11.5 per cent in 1979. Translated into numbers of the population, this represents an increase from 6 million to 9.4 million people – an increase of more than half. These are the latest available statistics of the numbers in poverty: in 1988 the Government decided to discontinue the series, making it difficult to make an assessment of the effects of the major changes in the social security system implemented that year as measured by the numbers in poverty (see Low Pay Unit/CPAG, 1988).

On the 'broad measure' of poverty – everyone having an income which is less than 40 per cent above the supplementary benefit level – 28.5 per cent were in poverty in 1985, compared with 22 per cent in 1979. The numbers of individuals within this broad category increased from 11.6 million to 15.4 million, a 33 per cent increase over the period.

2.6.2   The composition of the poor

In addition to an examination of overall numbers, we need also to consider what has happened to the composition of the poor. As we have noted, Beveridge assumed both that full employment would be maintained, and that those in employment would have an income above the poverty line (Piachaud, 1987). Neither assumption now holds valid. Unemployment and low earnings are now major causes of poverty. Whereas for most of the post-war period pensioners were the most visible group amongst the poor, this situation had changed by the 1980s. In 1985, the number of people below pension age living in poverty or on its margins (having an income less than 40 per cent above supplementary benefit level) stood at 11.3 million – three-quarters of the total. Of these, the largest single group were those where the head of household received a full-time wage. Only one third of the army of poor, defined on this broad definition, were pensioners (Low Pay Unit/CPAG, 1988).

Demographic changes have been important in determining the pattern of change in recent years. People are living longer, adding to the numbers of pensioners. There has been an increasing tendency, until recently, for people to set up their own households, rather than to share a household with parents or children. Because this means less income sharing, the inadequacy of incomes has become more apparent. There has been an increase in the number of single parent families, most of whom find themselves amongst the poor.

While these demographic changes have been important in influencing the extent and pattern of poverty, the evidence suggests that economic factors are more powerful still. The very sharp rise in poverty between 1979 and 1985 cannot be explained solely by demographic changes, which take decades rather than years to show their effects.

2.6.3   The distribution of wealth

Despite the substantial changes that have taken place this century in the economy and society, is there still an upper class in the UK? The received wisdom is that the power and influence of the upper class has been usurped by a managerial meritocracy, asserting control without ownership. Certainly, the older aristocratic families have been forced to make room for a newer breed of millionaire. In 1988, *Money Magazine* was able to report that, of the 200 richest men and women in Britain, each having wealth in excess of £250 million, only one in three had inherited their wealth. Certainly, too, much wealth has become institutionalized – in the financial institutions and the corporate sector – the control of which is divorced from its ownership. Yet the statistics on the distribution of wealth suggest that the ownership of property remains heavily concentrated in a very few hands, and that inheritance plays a central role in perpetuating that inequality.

The concept of an upper class implies not simply the existence of a top tier of society, measured in terms of status or wealth, but also a group whose ownership of wealth allows them to exert power and influence. If such a class still exists, who are their members? The statistics on the distribution of wealth are seriously deficient, being a by-product of the process of tax collection. Indeed, by the late 1980s, figures on the distribution of wealth were considered of too little importance to publish in the annual volume of *Social Trends*, but the figures are available in Inland Revenue statistics (see Stark, 1988, Chart R). Despite their very considerable drawbacks, they do give us some insight into the upper echelons of the class structure as it existed in the mid-1980s.

2.6.4   The changing distribution of wealth

The figures show that, in 1985, the top one per cent of the adult population owned more than a fifth of net personal wealth – three times as much as the poorer half of the population. To put this in a clearer perspective, we might reflect that one per cent of the adult population represents just 400 000 people. The top five per cent (about two million people) own almost 40 per cent of the total personal wealth, and the top ten per cent own more than half.

Activity 2.5

How does the degree of inequality in the distribution of wealth compare with the distribution of incomes or earnings?

Table 2.3 shows that the distribution of personal wealth was little different in the 1980s to that which existed 60 years before. At first glance, it appears that the decline in the share of the 'super rich' – the top one per cent – has been dramatic. Their share of personal wealth declined to one third its previous level by 1985. However, over a sixty year period, this rate of change is less than spectacular, the share of the top one per cent declining by an average of 0.7 per cent a year.

Moreover, this trend has not been even throughout the period. As Atkinson and Harrison (1978) point out, there was a once and for all shift in

Table 2.3 The distribution of wealth, 1923 to 1984: share of total wealth (%)

	1923	1938	1960	1971	1976	1980	1985
Top 1%	60.9	55.0	33.9	31	24	20	20
Next 4%	21.1	21.9	25.5	21	21	19	20
Next 5%	7.1	8.1	12.1	13	15	13	14
Top 10%	89.1	85.0	71.5	65	60	52	54
Next 10%	5.1	6.2	11.6	16.6			
Next 15%				21	24	23	22
Top 50%				97	95	94	93

Source: 1923 to 1960 figures are for England and Wales, after Atkinson and Harrison (1978). Figures for other years are for the adult population of the UK, from CSO, *Social Trends*, 1988

wealth holdings in 1959/60, after which the rate of change in the share of the richest one per cent slowed to a decline of 0.4 per cent a year. At this rate of change, the top one per cent can expect to own one eighth of the nation's wealth into the next millenium. In the early 1970s there was a further significant decline in the share owned by the wealthiest, primarily as a result of collapsing stock market prices. Since then, the rate of change in the share of the wealthiest has been slower still, although it will have been subjected to a further sharp decline in the October 1987 stock market collapse.

2.6.5 Wealth and class

The statistics do seem to give credence to the notion of a self-perpetuating upper class amongst the rich. A second glance at Table 2.3 reveals that the declining fortunes of the wealthiest were contained within fairly narrow limits. While the top one per cent saw their share diminish, the rest of the top five per cent retained almost as big a share of personal wealth in 1985 as they did in 1923 (20 per cent compared with 21 per cent 60 years earlier). The rest of the top ten per cent own twice as much wealth now as they did sixty years ago. This would seem to suggest that what we have witnessed over this period is not so much the redistribution of wealth, as the reordering of the affairs of the richest families. Largely as a means of avoiding estate duty, the wealthy have been encouraged to disperse their wealth amongst members of their families, most members of which remained within the top ten per cent of wealth holders.

There is a remarkable symmetry about wealth inequalities in the 1980s: while ten per cent of the population own more than half the nation's wealth, half the population own less than ten per cent. The Inland Revenue statistics show that those in the top half of the wealth owning adult population each enjoyed net personal wealth in 1986 of approximately £45 000 – that is after all debts such as mortgages have been taken into account. Those in the bottom half of the wealth owning population each own just £3500 net. The richest one per cent each owned wealth averaging £1–2 million – 143 times the average wealth holding amongst the poorer half of the population.

The data suggest that the richest groups have retained a significant share of personal wealth over a long period, and that there has been little change in the overall distribution since 1960. Two sets of characteristics might help to identify whether the rich represent a class or simply a collection of fortunate individuals (in the true meaning of the word). The first is whether the group is self-selecting; the second is whether this group exerts real power and influence. To consider the first aspect, we need to look at the process whereby wealth is transmitted – at the importance of inheritance in sustaining wealth inequalities. To decide to what extent wealth and power are associated with each other, we need to examine, not just the overall *amounts* of wealth owned by different groups, but also the *types* of property that they own. In particular, it is of interest to assess the impact of the growth of so-called 'popular wealth' – houses, pensions schemes and other forms of savings including, most recently, company shares. Margaret Thatcher's expressed objective is to create a Britain in which 'every man is a capitalist' (Thatcher, 1977). (Note the gender specification: of the 200 richest people in 1987, only 12 were women, and one of them was the Queen!) An examination of the make-up of the portfolios of different groups of wealth holders will help us assess how successful her governments were in this objective.

2.6.6   Wealth and inheritance

How do the rich acquire their wealth? One mechanism would be the accumulation of property through savings. As *The Times* once put it:

> in the most egalitarian of societies one would not expect the new born babe and the man on the point of retirement to have identical savings . . . and there must therefore be a concentration of wealth in a minority of hands in any society one can conceive of. Where inheritance is not allowed, only the old can be rich. (*The Times*, September 1968, quoted in Atkinson, 1972)

There is clearly a strong association between wealth and incomes. High incomes allow the recipients to accumulate savings and investments, which in turn yield income in the form of profits, dividends, capital gains and interest payments. Those dozen top executives with annual earnings in excess of £500 000 are undoubtedly amongst the top group measured in terms of wealth holdings, unless they enjoy an extremely extravagant life-style. However, savings can explain only a small part of the inequality in wealth. As the Royal Commission on the Distribution of Income and Wealth found, 'the distribution of wealth within age groups was generally similar to that of the population as a whole' (Royal Commission on the Distribution of Income and Wealth, 1979, p. 96). This would suggest that the association between wealth holdings and lifetime savings was relatively weak. The Commission also calculated that, at best, accumulated savings might account for no more than a third of the share of wealth enjoyed by the richest one per cent of the population, and for between half and two thirds of the wealth held by the rest of the top five per cent. While **inheritance** and entrepreneurial fortunes accounted overall for 40 per cent of all personal wealth, these sources accounted for three-quarters of the wealth of the top one per cent, and for over half of that owned by the richest five per cent (ibid., p. 98).

A closer examination of the process of wealth transmission through inheritance has been undertaken by Harbury and Hitchins (1980) who traced the pattern of inheritance between generations. They found that the top 0.1 per cent of wealth holders left, after their deaths, the equivalent (at 1980 prices) of £500 000. Of these, about half the men and three-quarters of the women had fathers who had left the equivalent of £250 000, an amount which at a compound interest rate of only 7 per cent would double in value in a decade, reaching the sum left by the heirs themselves. Three-fifths of the rich men and three-quarters of the rich women had fathers who had left the equivalent of £125 000, which compound interest and the process of time would have converted into £500 000 in just twenty years. The heirs needed to do nothing other than maintain the value of the wealth they had inherited to ensure their own position amongst the wealthy. Indeed, it appears that many had actually dissipated the wealth which they had inherited by the time of their own deaths. The researchers reported that 'without question, the firmest conclusion to emerge from this study is that inheritance is the major determinant of wealth inequality'.

2.6.7   Wealth and power

What is the association between personal wealth and power in the last quarter of the twentieth century? Does the disparity in wealth holdings have any significance in a society principally ruled by democratic institutions, especially given the growth of owner-occupation and share ownership amongst the broad mass of the population? As noted in Chapter 6 below, home ownership has spread rapidly since the 1950s, encouraged by Conservative governments' policy of 'the right to buy' for council tenants: between 1979 and 1987 the proportion of households who were owner-occupiers increased from 56 to 64 per cent. This is reflected in the importance of owner-occupied housing in overall wealth holdings: in 1970 'homes' represented 27 per cent of all personal wealth (net of mortgage debts), rising to 37 per cent by 1984 (Stark, 1988, Chart V). This reflected not only the extension of home ownership, but also the increase in the real value of property.

However, the effect of the 'right to buy' policy should not be overstated in terms of its effect on wealth holdings: between 1981 and 1986 the proportion of personal wealth made up of dwellings remained static. In part, this was because much of the value of the newly purchased housing was owned, not by the previous tenants, but by the financial lending institutions. The great privatization programmes of nationalized utilities also extended share ownership. A survey carried out for the Treasury and the Stock Exchange in 1987 found that nearly 20 per cent of the adult population owned shares, although three-quarters of these owned shares in the Trustee Savings Bank or in privatized companies, and half of these own no other shares at all. The survey found that shareholdings in privatized companies and TSB were not confined to the highest socio-economic groups. While one third of shareholders were classified as social class AB (managerial administrative and professional), and a further quarter as CI (supervisory or clerical, junior managerial, administrative or professional), nearly 40 per cent were from the three lowest social classes, including pensioners and manual workers. However, the survey does not record what proportion of total shares was held by each of these social classes (CSO, *Social Trends*, 1988). Moreover, the evidence is that these assets quickly found themselves back amongst the portfolios of the financial institutions rather than remaining in the hands of individuals (Neuburger, 1987). Chapter 6 considers the impact of these changes on class positions and ideology. Here we are concerned with the effect on wealth inequalities and the distribution of power. Table 2.4 shows the composition of wealth holdings in terms of the different types of assets that make up the nation's personal wealth. It is important to distinguish between different forms of wealth in making an assessment of their importance in determining economic and political power, as well as assessing the effect of property ownership on lifestyles and ideology.

Popular wealth, in the form of owner-occupied housing, pensions and insurance policies, confers on its owners greater security and control over their lives. The ownership of land or company shares and partnerships, by contrast, means not only an enhanced standard of living, but also control over the lives of others. Halsey has identified a distinction between 'property for power by which I mean property which carries control over the lives of other people, and property for use – possessions that free a man from other people's control. . . . A tiny minority has monopolised wealth, and an even tinier minority has monopolised property for power' (Halsey, 1978).

The growth of popular wealth has indeed extended to a larger section of society a greater degree of security and enhanced living standards, although it is a matter of contention whether this has been sufficient to provide the sort of independence suggested by Halsey; even share ownership and owner-occupation are unlikely to remove the need to work to earn a living. At a 10 per cent rate of return, an individual would need a share portfolio worth in excess of £200 000 to yield an income equivalent to the average in 1988. That represents a large number of shares in British Gas and British Telecom. Popular wealth may provide increased living standards, but it is unlikely to set its owner free, let alone confer control over the lives of others.

Table 2.4 The asset distribution of wealth, 1982

	Proportion of each type of asset owned by:			
	Top 1%	Top 2%	Top 5%	Top 10%
		Owning at least:		
	190 000	120 000	75 000	50 000
UK government and municipal securities	20	32.3	45.5	57.7
Overseas and foreign securities	65.4	84.0	90.0	96.0
Unlisted UK company securities	63.8	72.4	80.0	83.5
Listed UK company securities	45.6	64.0	78.3	88.4
Cash and bank accounts	8.0	14.8	23.2	35.6
Loans, mortgages etc.	37.6	47.2	56.2	67.7
Superannuation benefits	0.2	0.9	3.5	10.5
Insurance policies	5.6	11.7	22.3	37.0
Household goods	12.8	19.8	27.5	38.8
Trade assets and partnership shares	34.0	53.1	40.4	82.0
UK residential buildings	5.3	11.0	18.7	31.0
Other UK buildings	18.0	32.0	43.1	55.2
UK land	69.9	80.0	88.0	92.1

Note: Figures relate only to identifiable personal wealth; they are based on Inland Revenue estimates.
Source: Inland Revenue, 1986, author's calculations based on Table 4.11

A similar distinction has been suggested by Hird:

> Capital . . . is different from other forms of wealth: shares in an industrial company, for example, will typically grow in value over time, produce a regular dividend, confer legal ownership over part of the company's material assets, and are moreover, easily marketable when necessary. Other forms of wealth are quite different: consumer goods generally depreciate and have a low second hand value; the value of houses may in the main appreciate, but they are often difficult to sell and the owner generally needs to buy another as a replacement; pensions provide an entitlement to future income only as long as the pensioner lives, are not transferable, and often depreciate in value: and cash, although it confers immediate economic power through its purchasing power, generally depreciates. It is changes in the ownership and control of the means of production that need to be treated as the central criterion in assessing the distribution of wealth, for changes in other forms of wealth are intimately related to these. (Hird, 1979)

The important distinction for Hird is the difference between wealth in the sphere of consumption and that in the sphere of production (a distinction discussed in greater detail in Chapter 6, where the views he expresses about the importance of home ownership are also subjected to scrutiny). Hird argues that only the latter confers real power and influence.

2.6.8   The growth of popular wealth

Table 2.4 shows that, despite the extension of popular wealth, the ownership of power-conferring assets remains concentrated in the hands of a very few. Just one per cent of the population owns nearly two-thirds of the private land in Britain, while five per cent own almost 90 per cent and Stark (1988, Chart W) shows that ownership of land is becoming increasingly concentrated amongst the rich. While the richest one per cent own only 5 per cent of residential buildings, their portfolios include one sixth of all other privately owned buildings. The richest one per cent also own two thirds of unlisted company securities and foreign securities, almost half the listed company securities, and a third of the trade assets and shares in partnerships. The great privatizations are unlikely to have changed this pattern dramatically. The rich are not particularly interested in the ownership of assets which confer comfort and security but not very much power. Thus, the top one per cent own only 5 per cent of the value of privately owned residential buildings, only 8 per cent of cash and bank deposits, only 6 per cent of insurance policies, and only 0.2 per cent of superannuation benefits.

We should be careful here in assuming that assets which we may define as components of 'popular wealth' confer no power, no matter what form their ownership takes. The ownership of housing property, for instance, has always provided large landlords with a substantial degree of influence. It is when the purpose of ownership moves from that of profit to that of use that the nature of the assets themselves changes, and the link between ownership and control is broken. In the case of many forms of popular wealth, power and control have been separated from ownership, through the financial institutions. Building society deposits, for example, represent a massive accumulation of wealth, which might be expected to confer considerable influence on their owners, whose money ultimately determines who has the opportunity to become owner-occupiers, and whether they are allowed to keep the houses they have bought. However, this power has been transferred from the depositors to a tiny handful of people in control of the institutions. Indeed, it can be argued that the concentration of power deriving from institutional wealth is even greater than that from personal wealth.

The great share flotations in privatized industries provide another recent example. Here the power vested in such wealth has been transferred from the managers of the previously nationalized firms, not to the millions of individual shareholders, but to the City institutions.

Summary of section 2.6

●   The poor and the rich represent the extremes of inequality. Poverty increased sharply after the late 1970s, partly as a result of the effects of the recession, and partly due to policy changes especially relating to social security and minimum wage laws.

●   Alongside this increase in the numbers counted amongst the poor (rising to one in six by the mid-1980s) there was also a change in the composition of the poor. Whereas poverty during most of the post-war period was associated with pensioners, the poor were increasingly of working age, and therefore also responsible for children.

●   The rich appear to have held their share of income over a long period of time, and during the 1980s were able to improve their position still further. Most of the richest tenth of wealth holders increased their share of wealth between 1923 and 1985. The very richest one per cent saw their share of wealth diminish, although they still held a fifth of the nation's wealth even by the mid-1980s. The evidence seems to suggest that the upper class of the rich still wield considerable economic and social power.

2.7   Conclusion

We have now considered in some detail the nature and extent of economic inequality in the UK, and the way it has changed over time. This lays the foundations for considering other aspects of the structure and restructuring of society, many of which are shaped by the underlying distribution of economic resources. The evidence suggests that, for much of the period after the Second World War, market forces and state intervention had countervailing effects. The underlying pressures of market forces and demography, tending towards greater inequality, were mitigated somewhat, albeit without dramatic effect, by state taxation and expenditure. The period after 1979 appears to have marked a significant shift in the direction of greater inequality, and one which may prove to be long term in its effects. The explanation for this is, perhaps, that public policy was turned into the wind of economic change. During the 1980s, the state no longer sought to mitigate the effects of market forces in generating inequality. Indeed, government intervention (or non-intervention) tended to reinforce the underlying inegalitarian trends. However, the effects should not be overstated. Not all of the economic developments tended in the direction of greater inequality. The stock market 'collapse' of 1987 is likely to have had a significant impact on the asset portfolios of the rich, registering in the statistics as a decline in their share of personal wealth.

Nevertheless, by the end of the 1980s Britain was undoubtedly a more polarized society than that of either the 1940s or the 1970s. This social and economic polarization registered as an increase in poverty and a decline in the incomes of the poor, alongside an enhancement of the wealth enjoyed by the rich. It was a society marked by increased homelessness alongside a flourishing property market, by sharply increased problems of debt amidst a credit boom, and by increasing divisions in the living standards of different groups and of different parts of the country.

Inevitably, many of these inequalities came to be reflected in the structure of society and its institutions. While the prosperity generated towards the end of the 1980s extended to relatively large sections of the population, the trends in inequality tended still to reinforce the divisions between the extremes. We have argued that one result was the creation of a permanent underclass of the poor. A second result was the enhancement of the wealth of a much smaller group amongst the rich who, while finding their numbers swelled by those with market and tax generated fortunes, nevertheless managed to retain and reinforce their status as an upper class continuing to wield significant economic, social and political power.

Note

[1] The Gini coefficient is a measure of the distributional concentration of something among a given population. The range of the coefficient is from 1 – total concentration – to 0 – total equality of distribution. Its construction can be best demonstrated visually.

Figure 2.2 is a graph with the axes scaled from 0 to 100 per cent. The horizontal axis represents the cumulative percentage distribution of the population and the vertical axis the cumulative percentage distribution of wealth. If the top 10 per cent of the population own 10 per cent of the wealth, this would be represented by point A; if 20 per cent of the population own 20 per cent of the wealth, this would be represented by point B; and so on, up to point D where 100 per cent of the population own 100 per cent of the wealth. Connecting these points produces a straight, 45° line – X – which shows a situation of complete equality.

If we now consider a situation in which the top 10 per cent of the population own 50 per cent of the wealth, the top 20 per cent own 70 per cent, the top 30 per cent own 80 per cent, and the top 50 per cent own 90 per cent of the wealth, the resultant graph would be Y. The difference between lines Y and X (at 45°) represents the degree of inequality. This can be measured precisely. If the shaded area between line Y and line X is measured and divided by the area of the triangle bounded by the horizontal and vertical axes and the 45° line, the resultant figure is the Gini coefficient.

It can be seen that, if one person owns 100 per cent of the wealth, the resultant figure would be nearly 1 – total inequality. The greater the deviation of line Y from the 45° line X and the greater the size of the shaded area, the greater the degree of inequality and the larger the value of the Gini coefficient.

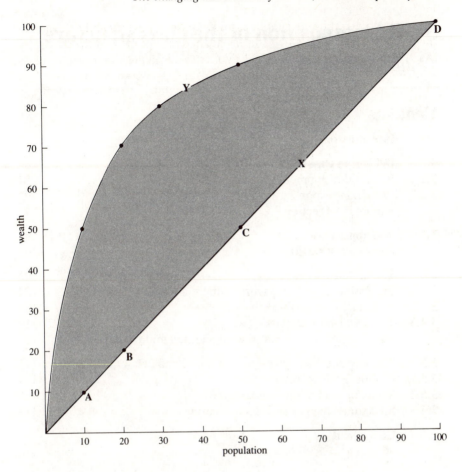

Figure 2.2

3 Recomposition of the class structure

Philip Sarre

Contents

3.1 Introduction

This chapter seeks to clarify how the British class structure has changed in recent years and whether this can be regarded as a restructuring.

At the simplest level, the chapters by Thrift and Pond have both indicated a substantial change which seems to be present both in cultural forms and economic strength. There appears to be a decline in the numbers and condition of the working class, and a growth in the numbers and significance of the upper-middle class – or, as Thrift terms it, the service class. This is in itself a substantial change, but it leaves many questions unanswered: is the rise of the upper-middle class accompanied by, or at the expense of, the upper class; what of the lower-middle class; and is the decline in the working class general, or is it concentrated in particular parts, e.g. among skilled craft workers or unskilled labourers?

In an ideal world, someone setting out to answer a straightforward question of change in the **class structure** would hope to find both clear and agreed definitions of the class structure at one or more points in time, and empirical data on the appropriate variables, systematically collected over the period in question for the population in question. In the real world, neither of these conditions is met. On the one hand, the social science literature on class shows the persistence of heated debates about the basis of **class** and the nature of the class structure of contemporary societies, with little sign of agreement within or between Marxist and Weberian camps. On the other hand, there is a massive amount of data collected by the Office of Population, Censuses and Surveys (OPCS), dating back most of the century, that focuses on variables which are, at best, loosely related to those emphasized by the theorists. A full answer to the question at hand will require detailed consideration of the theoretical debates and the available evidence, but a partial answer can be begun by a look at census data.

Table 3.1, which is taken from Beacham (1984), shows the change in social class between 1971 and 1981 for a 10 per cent sample of persons in employment in Britain, presenting men and women separately. It uses the standard OPCS classification of occupations into six classes and shows: substantial growth in the proportion of employees in professional and intermediate occupations; little change in the proportion in skilled non-manual jobs; and substantial decline in all manual categories, except women in unskilled jobs. As such, it confirms the erosion in numbers of the working class and the growth of the middle class – a shift more starkly portrayed by *Halsey*, who points out the reduction in the percentage of employees in manual jobs from 70 per cent in 1951 to 52 per cent in 1981 (1987, Table A5). However, Table 3.1 also leaves some questions unanswered: it deals with those in employment, and we know that unemployment had grown dramatically during the period. It also refers to the fact that the 1971 figures have had to be reclassified in the light of the new 1980 classification of occupations, which explicitly raises the issue of the basis of classification.

Table 3.1 Persons in employment – social class by sex, 1971 and 1981: Great Britain

Social class (occupations)	1981 (thousands)		Men (percentages)		Women (percentages)	
	Men	Women	1971*	1981	1971*	1981
All in employment	1376	915	100	100	100	100
I Professional	83	10	4.6	6.0	0.6	1.1
II Intermediate	320	194	18.7	23.2	16.1	21.2
III(N) Skilled (non-manual)	164	367	12.6	11.9	38.4	40.1
III(M) Skilled (manual)	483	75	37.0	35.1	10.3	8.2
IV Partly skilled	220	194	17.2	16.0	26.0	21.2
V Unskilled	72	65	7.5	5.2	7.1	7.1
Armed forces/unclassified	34	11	2.4	2.5	1.5	1.2

* The proportions for 1971 are based on the 1 per cent recoding exercise which were classified in the *Classification of Occupations* (OPCS, 1980)

Source: Beacham, 1984

These issues are addressed in Goldblatt (1983), who attempts both to document the effects of changing classifications of occupations used for the 1971 and 1981 censuses, and to separate out the effects of industrial change and the changing balance of occupations in surviving firms – though his analysis has the weakness of dealing only with men in England and Wales. His tables show that the net effects of the revised classification are appreciable, especially for social class I, and that the gross effects involve up to a third of class members moving in or out of their class classification between 1971 and 1981. This raises serious questions of principle about the validity of the classification, and raises serious practical difficulties in making intercensal comparisons over the span of several decades. His analysis shows that the 1981 labour force was nearly a tenth smaller than that of 1971, and the effects of this were much more serious in the manual categories. Surviving activities had seen a dramatic loss of unskilled workers, and serious losses of semi-skilled and skilled non-manual workers. On the other hand there was rapid growth in the higher classes (see Table 3.2).

The problem of reconstructing intercensal change in occupational classes over the post-war period has been tackled by *Heath and McDonald* (1987) and their conclusion is summarized in Table 3.3. This confirms that the fastest growth has been for professionals and technicians, followed by

Table 3.2   Change between 1971 and 1981 censuses in the number of employed men in each social class – components of change: England and Wales

| Type of change | Social class | | | | | | All employed men % |
	I %	II %	IIIN %	IIIM %	IV %	V %	
Conversion from 1970 to 1980 classification*	−11.8	+ 4.0	+5.2	− 2.9	+ 0.9	+ 2.1	0
Industrial effect†	− 1.4	− 0.9	−3.3	−15.1	−14.8	−18.6	−9.5
Occupational effect†	+17.8	+10.0	−6.4	+ 0.4	− 5.4	−29.0	0
Net change in size**	+ 2.6	+13.5	−5.0	−17.1	−19.5	−46.0	−9.5

*   Changes are expressed as percentages of the 1970-based class in 1971.
†   Changes are expressed as percentages of the 1971 size of the class (after converting to the 1980 classification)
** Net changes are expressed as percentages obtained by converting from 1970 to 1980 Classification and then applying the effects of structural changes

Source: Goldblatt, 1983; estimated from data produced by the Institute of Employment Research, University of Warwick

Table 3.3   Distribution of the economically active population by occupational category: Great Britain 1951–81

	1951	1961	1971	1981
Employers and own account	6.7	6.4	6.5	6.4
Managers and administrators	5.4	5.3	8.0	10.1
Professionals and technicians	6.6	9.0	11.1	14.7
Clerical and sales	16.3	18.6	19.5	19.3
Supervisors and foremen	2.6	2.9	3.9	4.2
Skilled manual	23.8	24.1	20.2	16.0
Semiskilled manual	26.6	25.1	19.3	19.0
Unskilled manual	11.9	8.5	11.6	10.4
Total	99.9	99.9	100.1	100.1
N (thousands)	22.514	23.639	25.021	25.406

Source: Heath and McDonald, 1987

managers and administrators, and the greatest reduction has been in manual classes, especially the skilled manual class. Again, this table raises further problems: although ultimately based on census data, it adopts a different, eightfold, classification of occupations, which differs from that of OPCS, and from other classifications used by other authors in the same area. This once more raises the question of the proper basis for the definition of classes.

The data discussed thus far have dealt with aggregate numbers of employees in different categories, but have not addressed the question of mobility between classes. This issue has been considered by Goldthorpe and Payne (1986), who analysed intergenerational mobility in a special survey in 1972, and reanalysed data from the 1983 General Election Study. Their results show that intergenerational mobility is long established:

> From at least the interwar years through to the time of the 1972 study, men of all class origins had become progressively more likely to move into professional, administrative and managerial positions – or into what we have termed the 'service class' of modern British society: at the same time they had become less likely to be found in the manual wage earning positions of the working class. (Goldthorpe and Payne, 1986, p. 1)

The changes between 1972 and 1983, summarized in Table 3.4, confirm this trend – except insofar as unemployment had been the destination of several million former workers. Again the empirical trend is confirmed, for men at least, but the basis of classification is further called into question by Goldthorpe and Payne's use of seven categories, defined differently from those of the other authors quoted. The sheer longevity of the trend to upward mobility also raises the question of what is meant by structural change.

The information and commentary above imply a number of possible lines for arguing particular change as being structural. First, as was the case for

Table 3.4 Distribution of respondents and their fathers, 1972 and 1983, according to new class scheme (percentages)

		Father 1972	Father 1983	Respondent 1972	Respondent 1983
I	Higher ⎰ Professional, administrative	7.0	9.7	11.7	16.0
II	Lower ⎱ and managerial	7.5	8.2	14.7	17.6
III	Routine non-manual	4.4	5.1	6.7	6.7
IV	Small proprietors and self-employed	13.7	14.0	9.0	11.6
V	Lower technical and supervisory	10.3	10.5	9.7	8.4
VI	Skilled workers	26.6	25.0	21.1	19.6
VII	Semi and unskilled	30.5	27.5	27.1	20.1
I–II	Service class	14.5	17.9	26.4	33.6
III–V	Intermediate class	28.5	29.6	25.4	26.6
VI–VII	Working class	57	52.5	48.2	39.8

Source: Goldthorpe and Payne, 1986

the change from a manufacturing economy to a service economy, a long-running gradual change might pass a threshold or tipping point where the whole balance of the structure changes; such an event probably occurred during the 1980s as non-manual employees became a majority for the first time. Secondly, the appearance or disappearance of a class would be a major structural change; for example many class theorists have focused upon the appearance of a 'new middle class' early this century. Given the confusion over categorizations of class, this kind of change demands theoretical clarification. Thirdly, a major change in the role of a particular class would arguably be a structural change; we have already seen great claims for the emergence of a new 'service class', and we will also consider claims that the 'de-skilling' of clerical work has effectively made most of what were previously regarded as lower-middle class occupations into working-class jobs. Fourthly, if mass unemployment were to become a long-term feature of British society, it would emphasize a serious problem for class theory: how to define the class position of people who are playing no part in the economy. This could be a major structural change.

All these possibilities combine to emphasize that an attempt to describe the recomposition of the class structure is on extremely slippery ground without a critical look at what is meant by the concepts of class and class structure.

To try to clarify these basic concepts, the next section looks at some recent debates in social science about the basis and significance of class. To keep this manageable, we have decided to be selective and to hold back consideration of race and gender, both of which interact with class as major social divisions, to later chapters. Sections 3.3 to 3.5 consider changes in upper-, middle- and lower-class groups over recent years. Section 3.6 sums up the debates about the recent restructuring of class, and relates the conclusion to other social divisions, and to political divisions and struggles which are discussed in detail in *Politics in Transition* (Cochrane and Anderson, 1989).[1]

3.2   Debates in class theory

In spite of a century of intense debate, social scientists still disagree about the basis of class divisions, and about the importance of class as against other social divisions. So strong are the bases of disagreement, that many accounts of class theory present Marxist and Weberian class theories as necessarily incompatible. Because the task of this unit is to illuminate the actual changes in the British class structure, we will adopt a different approach, selecting recent attempts to grapple with contemporary class structures which take partly distinctive, but partly overlapping, positions. It will be argued that Marxism has a particular strength in clarifying the different **class positions** in different kinds of economy, while Weberian interpretations have more to offer in clarifying the social processes which lead to **class formation** in practice.

As you study this chapter, you will have to evaluate these theoretical positions both as conceptual arguments and as they relate to the available evidence. As you read this section, concentrate on identifying the aims and assumptions of the different positions, their scope and limitations, and consider whether they are incompatible or complementary. You will find that there are debates and disagreements *within* broadly Marxist and Weberian approaches as well as *between* them. The two major issues within the theoretical positions are: which criteria are taken as central in classifying and relating social classes, and the nature of the class structure so defined. You will find that different criteria produce different views of the class structure. The broad views sketched in this section provide a framework for looking at particular debates about parts of classes or boundaries between classes, and at further evidence for change in sections 3.3 to 3.5. Finally, in section 3.6, you will have to consider whether the debates and evidence indicate a recomposition of the class structure.

3.2.1   Recent developments in Marxist class theory

Post-war debates in Marxist class theory have revolved around two major empirical developments which appear to contradict radically earlier expectations that capitalist society would see a polarization between **bourgeoisie** and **proletarians**. In fact, as *The Economy in Question* (Allen and Massey, 1988, Chapter 3) showed, and section 3.1, above, confirmed, the twentieth century has seen an enormous increase in the numbers of people in man-

---

[1] Marshall *et al.* (1988) give a detailed analysis of contemporary changes in the British class structure.

agerial, professional and service jobs. Not only has the traditional **petty bourgeoisie** of self-employed small businesses persisted, but it has been joined by a new middle class of corporate and state employees enjoying comparatively high salaries which allow a high living standard and acquisition of substantial assets in housing, pensions, life insurance or shares. Other members of the traditional middle classes, for example clerical employees, have seen their living standards eroded to the point where their incomes are now less than those of better paid manual workers. The result of these two developments – the growth in the middle classes and the high living standards of some workers – has been an intensive effort to reformulate Marxist class theory in a way which preserves its basic strengths but makes sense of the new groups.

In tackling these new problems, contemporary Marxists have come to accept that some aspects of traditional Marxist class theory need rethinking. In the process of rethinking, many authors have returned to read Marx to check whether their, or other people's, new proposals were consistent with his views. Thus, much has been done to clarify the essentials of his mature views and to contrast them with the simplistic stereotypical views, which were often based on early or manifesto accounts. Rattansi (1985) summarizes these stereotype views as follows:

- The basis of class differentiation is ownership of the means of production.

- Capitalist class systems would polarize into two classes – the owners and those obliged to sell their labour power.

- The working class as economically defined (class in itself) would become more self conscious and politically active (class for itself).

- Economic divisions determine political and ideological change.

- The development of the productive forces would inevitably lead societies towards socialism and communism.

- The future would see a dissolution of scarcity, class and the state.

Rattansi goes on to argue that, in spite of attempts at defence by some Marxists, many of these propositions have been subjected to damaging criticism. However, he returns to the later, post 1848, works of Marx to argue that the mature Marx had changed his position on all these issues.

Among these changes, the most crucial for this discussion is the first, concerning the basis of class differentiation. In his later work, Marx came to distinguish *ownership* and *control*, and to emphasize that there had to be **exploitation** of the lower class by the upper class. He saw production relations (i.e. production of goods) as the basis of class, with exchange as secondary, though essential. Production relations have two components: *exploitation* through capitalists' appropriation of the fruits of surplus labour; and *domination* through capitalists' increasing control of the processes of production. In this view of exploitation, the concepts of surplus labour and surplus value are central: they rest on the assumption that part of workers' labour is necessary to produce the equivalent value of the goods and services required to reproduce the labour force (i.e. food, housing, clothing, etc.), and that another part produces the extra or surplus value which is appropriated by capital as profit. Exploitation has the crucial property of being relational: the upper class gains from the labour of the lower and is therefore dependent upon it as well as dominant over it.

Changes in the other five stereotype views were prompted both by Marx's observations of political struggles and by his theoretical development. In particular, he recognized the growth of middle-class positions, like managers, administrators and sales personnel, as well as the growth of unproductive workers like domestic servants, as a result of increases in the productive capacity of industry. He also recognized the fragmentation of the proletariat by skill, gender, nationality and geographic area. This linked up with a growing realization that economic factors did not determine political and ideological responses, and that state power did not inevitably favour the upper class. As a result, he stressed more the uncertain and contested nature of class formation and politics, and moved away from any idea of historical inevitability. This shift included the loss of any necessary link between classes as defined by analysis of exploitation relations, and classes as perceived in society or as expresssed through political struggles. Rattansi concluded that the more sophisticated views of the later Marx legitimated a range of theoretical developments which had been thought to contradict Marx's views as presented in the simple stereotype.

One of these developments was that of E.O. Wright (1978). Drawing on earlier restatements by Carchedi (1977), Poulantzas (1975) and others, he argued that class remained central and relational, but sought to explain the middle classes by recognizing multiple dimensions of **domination**. Ownership of property was shown to confer control over investment, over physical capital like machinery and over labour, but, in modern economies, legal ownership tends to be separated both from investment and production decisions and from direct control of the labour process. Thus, it is now common for ownership of companies to be spread across a range of individual and institutional shareholders, while top management may have effective control over the use of assets, delegating control of the physical production process to junior managers and control of workers to supervisors. As a result, Wright concluded that many people are in class positions which are *objectively contradictory*: managers may control without ownership; the petty bourgeoisie may own without employing labour; some craft employees may own their own tools and have a great deal of control over their labour process, but remain employees (Figure 3.1). These contradictions are reinforced by Wright's view of the petty bourgeoisie as being outside the capitalist mode of production, though actually present in existing capitalist societies. This is a point which was clarified, but complicated, by the work of Roemer and Wright's later reaction to it.

Perhaps the most fundamental reconstruction of the foundations of Marxist class theory is that by Roemer (1982). He felt that by emphasizing aspects

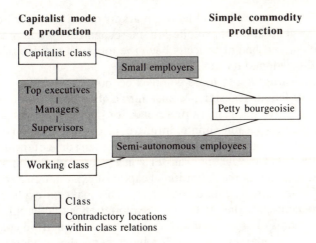

Figure 3.1   Basic class map of capitalist society
Source: E.O. Wright, 1985

of control Wright had mistakenly separated domination from exploitation, and so he set out to restore exploitation as the basis of class differentiation. Roemer argued that it was necessary to generalize Marx's notion of exploitation to make it applicable to socialist societies as well as feudal and capitalist ones. He claimed that his use of a historical materialist approach, showing the basis of class formation in different 'modes of production', makes his approach Marxist in method, though he ultimately reformulates some central Marxist concepts. His method is analytic and abstract and concerned with the economy and not with society or politics, so he concedes that further work is needed to apply his general principles to particular historic cases.

Roemer analysed a number of hypothetical economies to clarify Marx's concept of exploitation and how it could operate in different circumstances. He argued that in essence it involved a transfer of surplus labour, i.e. labour over and above the labour necessary to provide the worker's subsistence, so that the exploiters would gain and the exploited would lose. This was most obvious in feudalism, where serfs were obliged to work on their lord's land for part of the time. Roemer shows that in an economy with private ownership of the means of production plus a commodity market, this form of exploitation can occur without a labour market, if there is a credit market in which poorer producers hire credit from richer ones. Given the same distribution of productive property, a credit market produces an identical division of classes to that produced by a labour market. *This caused Roemer to reject the centrality of control of the labour process and appropriation of surplus value as the theoretical basis of capitalist exploitation.* Instead, he claims that this is produced by inequality in productive assets giving greater or less power in apparently free markets. In effect, this is closer to the early Marxian emphasis on ownership of the means of production rather than the later move to appropriation through the labour process. However, although

Roemer insists that credit and labour markets are in principle equivalent routes to the generation of exploitation, he recognizes that, in practice, the use of hired labour had historically been the foremost method of capitalist appropriation when Marx was at work.

Turning his attention to more complex economies, Roemer argues that any notion of labour transfer becomes intractable when labour is hetero-geneous in terms of skills and/or preference for free time as against income. Indeed, his models became counter intuitive, involving people whose labour was exploited, but were nevertheless better off than some of the exploiters. He concluded that the labour transfer concept of exploitation should be abandoned in favour of the definition of capitalist exploitation as possession of an excessive share of productive assets. This makes it explicit that the value judgement embodied in defining exploitation is that people ought to have equal shares of assets so that they can bargain equally in commodity, credit and labour markets. As a value judgement, this is open to dispute from other positions, but it has the merit of clarity.

Having put exploitation at the centre of his argument and recognized that definitions of exploitation are value-laden, the next stage of Roemer's argument was to identify different forms of exploitation as characteristic of different kinds of society. In feudal society, exploitation took the form of direct appropriation of labour in return for military protection. In the capitalist mode of production, ownership of saleable assets was defined as the characteristic form of exploitation. He also went on to consider state socialist societies and argued that, even though feudal and capitalist exploi-tation had been eliminated, two forms of exploitation persisted: *socialist exploitation* was based on the uneven distribution of skills and credentials, while *status exploitation* resulted from unequal access to official positions, for example on the basis of party membership. Roemer concentrated on identifying the characteristic forms of exploitation in pure modes of produc-tion, but stated that in particular real societies there is a mixture, and that present day capitalist societies combine at least capitalist, socialist and status exploitation. He focuses on underlying principles and does little to explore how his ideas relate to particular class structures beyond presenting a five class division in subsistence economies.

Roemer's discussion of exploitation under different modes of production has now been accepted by Wright (1985) and used to revise his previous analysis of contradictory class locations. As a prelude, he reformulated Roemer's notions of socialist and status exploitation. Wright argues that the notion of status exploitation is inconsistent with materialism, and that what is at issue is the occupation of *organizational positions which carry powers to direct investment and/or the labour process*, and that in state socialist socie-ties these are typically state positions (though in capitalist societies they could be held by managers in private or state corporations). Wright sees this strand of exploitation as subordinate under capitalism, dominant under state socialism, and absent from true socialism, where experts would be the last remaining exploiting class (but practising a socially necessary form of exploitation, since the experts would make the workers better off than they would be if left to their own devices). He points out that it is the use of *credentials* to limit access to influential positions rather than gradations of productive skills in themselves which are the chief socialist means of exploitation.

On the basis of this argument, Wright presents a summary table of modes of production (Table 3.5), and emphasizes that, unlike the early Marx, he sees no inevitable progression towards communism, but an indeterminate struggle between exploiters and exploited. He points out that in past transitions – from feudalism to capitalism, and from capitalism to state socialism – it has not been the previous exploited class but previous contradictory class which has become dominant in the new societies: the bourgeoisie were instrumental in curbing royal and aristocratic power in the French, and to a lesser degree in the English Revolutions; the Russian and Chinese Revolutions soon centralized power upon state functionaries who had absolute control over production and labour.

Table 3.5   Assets, exploitation and classes

Type of class structure	Principal asset that is unequally distributed	Mechanism of exploitation	Classes	Principal contradictory location
Feudalism	Labour power	Coercive extraction of surplus labour	Lords and serfs	Bourgeoisie
Capitalism	Means of production	Market exchanges of labour power and commodities	Capitalists and workers	Managers/ bureaucrats
Statism	Organization	Planned appropriation and distribution of surplus based on hierarchy	Managers/ bureaucrats and non-management	Intelligentsia/ experts
Socialism	Skills	Negotiated redistribution of surplus from workers to experts	Experts and workers	

Source: Wright, E.O., 1985

Wright goes on to consider the implications of this view of modes of production for contemporary capitalist societies. Here, like Roemer, he sees ownership of alienable productive assets as the dominant form of exploitation. However, state socialist and socialist forms of exploitation also exist, in the form of preferential access to organizational positions and exploitation of credentials to restrict entry to lucrative professions. He lays these out as a matrix of differentiation, assuming three levels of assets, skills and organizational positions (as in Figure 3.2), and goes on to present empirical data about the distributions of income, class attitudes and unearned income in the USA and Sweden, claiming to show that his definitions of middle and working class fit the data better than those of Poulantzas or the conventional manual/non-manual divide. He states that, in particular societies, the process of **class formation** operates to transform the matrix of differentiations into a small number of classes, but, apart from comments on the data analyses for the USA and Sweden, he does little to indicate how this happens. As a result, his book is sharply criticized by Carchedi (1986) for substituting distribution for production, using an individualistic methodology, and resorting to statistical rather than dialectical logic – in short, for abandoning a Marxist viewpoint.

While there are problems with the statistical exercise, an alternative view is that Wright and Roemer have provided a logical Marxist case for the existence of multiple strands of exploitation in contemporary capitalist societies. Because both see the transformation of these multiple strands into a particular class structure as open, rather than determined, neither has explicitly mapped out how this is likely to happen. However, the general nature of their structure of exploitation is clear in outline. The major reference axis must, by definition, be that of the capitalist sector. The logic of Roemer's argument is that, on the basis of ownership of assets and sale of

Assets in the means of production

	Owners of means of production	Non-owners (wage labourers)			
Owns sufficient capital to hire workers and not work	1 Bourgeoisie	4 Expert managers	7 Semi-credentialled managers	10 Uncredentialled managers	+
Owns sufficient capital to hire workers but must work	2 Small employers	5 Expert supervisors	8 Semi-credentialled supervisors	11 Uncredentialled supervisors	> 0
Owns sufficient capital to work for self but not to hire workers	3 Petty bourgeoisie	6 Expert non-managers	9 Semi-credentialled workers	12 Proletarians	−
	+	> 0		−	

Organization assets

Skill/credential assets

Figure 3.2   Typology of class locations in capitalist society

heterogeneous labour, there are five classes. Pure capitalists (1) and property-less workers (5) are clear extremes, and well-known from traditional Marxism, as is the (perhaps hypothetical) traditional petty bourgeois who, subject to owning an average per capita share of assets, provides a mid point (3) in the exploitation scale, separating an upper-middle class (2) with sufficient assets and control to be on balance exploiters, from a lower-middle class (4), with some assets and autonomy but on balance exploited (Figure 3.3). The petty bourgeois class might best be seen as *alongside* the two newer middle classes, as in Wright's (1978) diagram of contradictory class locations (Figure 3.1).

The state sector provides a secondary axis of differentiation on the basis of organizational assets or liabilities. This axis would range from government ministers and senior civil servants, who are on a level with the top of the new middle class (and may partially overlap the bourgeois class), down through a hierarchy of employees to poor manual workers, who are parallel to private-sector workers (Figure 3.3). The two hierarchies may be held together by recruitment of top decision-makers and senior managers from bourgeois families and/or élite educational institutions, and by the existence of credentialed groups (e.g. managers) who may move between state and corporate sectors. Professions, like teachers, who fall mainly into the state sector, tend to lag behind those, like engineers or architects, who have extensive private-sector roles in terms of income or status. The state sector also helps to make sense of the substantial group in society who are not exploited in the traditional Marxist sense of labour transfer, but who are materially worse off than workers – the unemployed and welfare recipients. The state provides an element of supervision and control in allocating benefits which makes much more tangible their abstract exploitation in Roemer's sense of possession of less than the per capita share of assets.

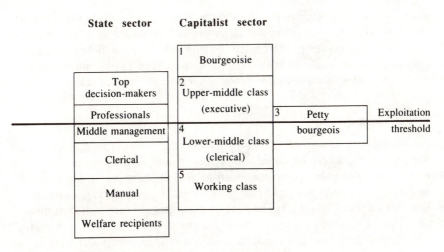

Figure 3.3   Relations between class positions in capitalist society

This schematic structure of class positions may apply to any capitalist society. The balance between sectors, access to privileged positions and formation of alliances or conflicts will vary between societies in response to differences in history, culture and class struggle. However, Roemer and Wright say little about class formation in practice. This is a process which has been of central interest to Weberian theorists.

3.2.2   Weberian responses

Just as Max Weber's sociology was in large part a response to Marx, so later developments in Weberian class theory have been an explicit or implicit dialogue with developments in Marxism. And, just as Marx scattered his references to class across many of his works, so Weber failed to provide a single co-ordinated statement of his views. As a result, Weber, too, is subject to oversimplification and selective interpretation. A stereotype has grown up that Weber's view of class was contingent and empirical, relying on outcomes of market position and on subjective views of **status**. The positive side of this stereotype is that it led professed Weberians to take a much closer interest in class attitudes and collective action as they occur in practice. The negative side is that Weberians have often neglected to consider the objective relationships which differentiate class positions, and have sometimes taken a completely empiricist view of class.

At the heart of Weber's thinking about class, and subsequent interpretations of it, was the notion that social divisions involve an interplay between three factors: *class*, *status* and *party*. The following account will try to clarify the implications of this idea in three stages: first, by looking at Weber's original intentions, second, by looking at neo-Weberian positions which emphasize the interactions between factors, and consequently face the problem of indeterminancy; and third, by considering attempts to argue the primacy of one or other of the three factors. Since Marxists have dealt with attempts to single out economic class, we will consider attempts to place status or party power at the centre. In summing up, it will be argued that emphasis on interactions between factors need not imply, analytically or practically, weak views of each factor or empiricist views of class.

Weber's original view

The clearest summary of Weber's views on class occurs in *Economy and Society* (1948), where he defines the concepts and roles of class, status and party. Far from being completely antithetical to Marx, he states 'property and lack of property are basic categories of class', though he goes on to say that, within these broad categories, class situations are further differentiated by different market positions. His treatment of status is more challenging, not because he takes status groups to be communities with certain styles of life, but because he argues that 'the road from this purely conventional situation to legal privilege, positive or negative, is easily travelled'. In other words, membership of a status group (e.g. Jews, women, blacks, or Free-masons) may, in some circumstances, be legally defined as entitling people to, or prohibiting them from, certain benefits.

One way this can be brought about is through the action of political parties, which Weber sees as being orientated towards the acquisition of social power for its own sake, or to influence a community towards a certain goal. Real life events suggest that such goals may include intervention in the rights of ownership and/or the operation of markets, including the labour market. Weber clearly anticipated this kind of possibility in his statement that 'classes and status groups influence one another and they influence the legal order and are in turn influenced by it'. Indeed, to read this passage on class, status and party is to see that Weber gave 'the legal order' a key role in determining class differences, and party political struggles a key role in influencing the legal order. Rather than shifting attention from economic class to subjective status, he seems to suggest that economic class might be an *outcome* of the legal order rather than the prime cause of social divisions.

Interaction between factors

While the assumption of multiple interacting factors has led many neo-Weberians to a conceptually weak empiricism, some authors have tried to develop Weberian thinking to help solve some of the central issues of class structures in contemporary societies.

Lockwood (1958) used a tripartite framework to analyse the class position of clerical workers, drawing the concepts of *market situation* and *status situation* from Weber, but adding the concept of *work situation* to take account of some aspects of Marxist concern with the social relations of production. Lockwood's analysis was quite successful in explaining the identification of most clerks with the middle class, in spite of their similarity in income terms with manual workers, and it became quite influential in 1960s British sociology, both in relation to empirical studies and further theoretical development. We return to it below in section 3.4.3.

A further step on this road was taken by Giddens (1973), who was particularly concerned to make sense of the different white-collar groups, e.g. professional, managerial and technical versus clerical and sales. He emphasized *market capacity* as crucial and as tending to create three classes based on ownership, qualifications and labour power. However, differences in market capacity were only the foundation, and classes were forged on this basis in a process of *structuration*. This was a complex process in which a range of situations could affect outcomes in terms of class affiliation and action. These ranged from the division of labour and authority relations in the workplace, through distributive groupings – for example, the neighbour-hood and perhaps housing tenure – to longer term expectations of social mobility. In effect, this turned Lockwood's framework into a general expla-natory framework for the processes of class formation.

Status-centred accounts

Most neo-Weberian writers have tended to emphasize status, but many have chosen to present it as a matter of prestige or lifestyle, and as more relevant to consciousness than to analytical differentiation. In spite of this tendency, we will consider some attempts, more or less successful, to construct a strong role for status in social differentiation.

Perhaps the sharpest avowedly Weberian challenge to Marxist class theory came from Frank Parkin (1979), who seems to differ from the Marxists in three fundamental assumptions. First, he challenges the notion that class divisions have been *historically* more important than other kinds of division in society, instead asserting that divisions based on status, and including race, culture and gender, are at least as significant. Secondly, he challenges the notion that there can be an objective analysis of class positions, and contends that all class theories are, in practice, no more than 'morally laden conceptual models'. Thirdly, he asserts that it is more important to deal with classes as they appear in collective action than to construct formal structural models of the effects of production relations.

Parkin sees a state of 'mutual antagonism and permanent tension' between classes, which presupposes a systematic underlying conflict of interest. The major concept which he develops to deal with these antagonisms between and within classes, and other groups, is the concept of 'social closure'. Privileged groups use strategies of 'exclusionary closure' to limit access to resources and opportunities, while less privileged groups use strategies of 'usurpation' to maximize their own strength and increase their access. Some groups may practice 'dual closure' – usurpation to break into higher positions and exclusion to resist encroachment from below. Parkin argues that these processes are more general than the capitalist mode of production:

> Credentialism flourishes as well in command economies as in market systems; the exclusionary rights attaching to productive property are a prominent feature of capitalist, socialist, feudal, slave and caste societies and their associated modes of production; collective social closure on the basis of sex and ethnicity shows a similar indifference to the type and quality of the material substructure. (Parkin, 1979, p. 113)

The problem with this argument is that it both affirms what it wishes to deny – namely, that there are different modes of production, in which resources and opportunities are somehow differently allocated – and fails to demonstrate what it asserts: the *occurrence* of credentialism or property rights in different kinds of society does not demonstrate that they are *indifferent* to the mode of production. They may be of different relative importance and operate on different criteria and through different social processes. The concept of closure seems to deal with how status groups struggle for advantage, but not to account for the existence of the groups, except as historically pre-existing.

Murphy (1986) argues that Parkin is wrong to try to shift neo-Weberian class theory entirely into the area of conscious collective action. He argues that Weber recognized that economic class situation was predominant in modern societies, but had formulated the concept of status in a way which would have met Parkin's need to explain racial and gender divisions while maintaining a grasp on an underlying structure of class positions.

> In fact, in his sociology of domination Weber made little use of his global conception of class but instead used primarily the components or sub types of class. These sub types, such as property classes, are based on particular structural relationships of domination and exclusion, such as the domination by the class that possesses property over the class that does not. . . . Power relations of domination and subordination, mutual antagonism and incompatibility of interests between social classes are hence much more complex than those between the entities along the component dimensions which make up social classes, but they exist all the same. (Murphy, 1986, pp. 252–3)

Barbalet (1986) extends the argument for a more powerful conception of status. He argues that if status is interpreted as an evaluation of prestige and is expressed only through lifestyle, then the concept is of limited use. However, there is another way of interpreting status which is much more central:

> In addition to inequalities based on given material conditions are those *based on socially accepted and enforceable norms*. The economic *rights* of unions and professional bodies, for example, are instances of status as privileged access to entitlements through socially constructed norms. (Barbalet, 1986, p. 562)

He traces this position back to T.H. Marshall, who defined status as 'a position to which is attached a bundle of rights and duties, privileges and obligations, legal capacities or incapacities, which are publicly recognized and which can be defined and enforced by public authority and in many cases by courts of law' (1953, p. 176). This strong concept of status as linked to enforceable norms is reminiscent of the way Weber related class, status and power to 'the legal order'.

Marshall's concept of status is a part of his main argument that the expansion of citizenship rights has been a significant challenge to capitalism as the main determinant of British society. He argued that struggles for, and achievement of, **citizenship** had established three sets of rights which had dramatically changed the position of people in the UK. These rights were: *civil* – formal equality in legal terms; *political* – the extension of voting rights and rights to organize pressure groups, including trade unions; and *social* – especially the establishment of a comprehensive system of social welfare after 1945. Taken together, these rights have modified the expectations and entitlements of all groups, and so changed the nature of the class system. Whether citizenship has really dislodged capitalism, or merely produced reforms which have humanized and legitimized capitalism, is another major debate which cannot be tackled here.

Power-centred accounts

The recognition of citizenship as the most influential statement of status, and of political rights as part of the concept of citizenship, seems to confirm the existence of some circularity between class, status and politics. There seem to be two broad interpretations in the literature: one, consistent with Weber, is that class, status and political party are all forms of access to power; the second, particularly common in the USA, is a reformulation whereby class, status and power are seen as three dimensions of differentiation that particularly interest economists, sociologists and political scientists. Rather than pursue such debates, this sub-section will look at an attempt to place power at the centre of class theory in place of economic definitions of class.

This case was most strongly made by Dahrendorf (1959) in what he called a 'positive critique' of Marx, but was a trenchant critique of the coherence of Marxist thought and its relevance to what Dahrendorf called 'post-capitalist' society. Dahrendorf focused on the separation of ownership from control, and argued that this demonstrated that it was not legal ownership which conferred advantage but the ability to control people and events. Accordingly, he substituted a Weberian concept, *authority*, as the central issue in class division, asserting that society was divided into two classes, the dominant and those in subjection. As industrial societies are characterized by complex hierarchies, both capitalist and labouring groups are heterogeneous in terms of their authority, but bureaucrats are ultimately linked to the capitalist class through the chain of command. This line of argument opens up questions about the position of industrial managers and public sector bureaucrats which are considered further in section 3.4.1 below.

While Dahrendorf has built a class system around the concept of authority, and Weber emphasized the role of political parties as a way of changing the legal order, the role of power at an international scale is also relevant to the evolution of class structures in the twentieth century.

An interesting recent insight comes from a paper by Mann (1987), who argues that, during the course of this century, capitalism has co-existed in different countries with five different citizenship systems from fascism to liberal democracy. The emergence of liberal democracy, with its wide spread of citizenship rights, is, in Mann's view, not a result of internal social struggles or of a special complementarity with capitalism but of Anglo-American victories in the war. The victories led both to extensions of civil rights in the UK to produce 'a land fit for heroes', and to the imposition of democratic forms on countries like Germany and Japan. Perhaps an interim conclusion to this debate is that status certainly exerts appreciable effects on the distribution of power and material rewards, that it may have had substantial effects in the UK, and might have the potential to shift the balance from a basically capitalist society to a genuinely socialist one. However, the balance between capitalism and citizenship is dependent on political and ideological struggle and, as *Politics in Transition* (Cochrane and Anderson, 1989) will show, the trajectory in the 1980s has been to reduce citizenship rights and expand the role of market capitalism. As Wright (1985) observed, there is no automatic progression from feudalism to socialism but a fluctuating balance between forms of social organization.

Summary of section 3.2

Looking back over this section, we can compare and contrast neo-Marxist and neo-Weberian views as regards:

- the nature of the differentiation between class positions;
- the main dimensions of differentiation at work in the UK, and
- the relationship between class positions and political struggle.

It should now be clear that:

- Neo-Weberians range from those who are content to take 'life chances', often as measured by occupation or income, as a convenient indicator of class to those who are trying to analyse the multiple underlying components of differentiation and to show that they involve oppression or domination of lower classes by higher ones. Neo-Marxists, on the other hand, after a period of emphasis on control, increasingly put *exploitation* at the centre of their theories, as did the mature Marx. In so doing, they generate the need for a theory of justice to define what is or is not exploitation. This is an area of profound philosophical disagreement.

- Wright contends that capitalist societies include capitalist (ownership), statist (organizational) and socialist (skill based) forms of exploitation, though the economic form is pre-eminent. Weberians also accept that property ownership is central to exploitation, though skills, status and political influence may exert significant effects on entitlements. Both schools of thought recognize complex strands of differentiation. While traditional Marxists emphasize that the use of capital for surplus appropriation makes their view of property different from that of Weber, Roemer's revised view of assets and markets seems to bring him very close to Weber on property classes.

- Neo-Marxists still seem to be fundamentally preoccupied with the analysis of class positions, often tacitly accepting that the economic determines the social 'in the last instance' – except when political struggle succeeds in transforming the mode of production. Neo-Weberians, however, seem to argue for a reciprocal relationship, with prior status influencing access to property, credentials and political power and hence to class, with economic class position influencing positions taken in political struggles (though emphatically not determining those positions), and with political struggles leading to legal changes in the rights of property and labour, and hence shifting the balance between economic classes. Paradoxically, the Weberian standpoint seems to be more dialectical than the stereotypical Marxist position, though Wright's position opens up similar questions of multiple causation.

Of course, there remain major differences between Marxists and Weberians, and these are not just differences in language. First, they differ in epistemological terms, with Marxists more concerned to theorize the underlying structures and Weberians more concerned to come to grips with observable social processes. Even if they were to agree on the description of a mode of production, they would disagree on its epistemological basis, Marxists being confident that it dealt with a necessary and concrete reality, and Weberians probably regarding it as a heuristic 'ideal type'. Secondly, the schools tend to disagree on the moral imperative attached to their concepts. Even the most academic Marxist would regard a theory of exploitation in different modes of production as implying a need to strip away the layers of exploitation and progress towards an ideal communist society. Weberians, on the other hand, tend to be more concerned with what is, to have a more restricted view of what is possible, and to be inclined towards a pluralistic view of politics. A thoroughgoing, rather than schematic, resolution of the differences between Marxist and Weberian class theories would have to resolve at least the epistemological differences, and should preferably have a clearer view of the relationship between the scholarly activity of explaining class differentiation and the use of such explanations in social struggles. (The distinctions between Marxist and Weberian class theories are explored further in Wright (1985, pp. 106–9).)

Activity 3.1

Does Parkin's assertion that class theories are 'morally laden conceptual models' apply to the theories of Roemer and Wright? If so, why? How successfully does Parkin's approach overcome this problem? Can other Weberian concepts overcome the incorporation of moral commitment into the analysis of class? Can they avoid using value judgements in defining classes?

For the purposes of the present chapter, which are to obtain a view of recent changes in the British class structure, neither a fundamental reconciliation between Marxist and Weberian methods nor a final solution to the ethical basis of class recognition is needed. Our next step is to use the overall sketch of the class system, and the process of class formation which has emerged here, as an agenda to look in more detail at changes in certain parts of the class system. All the major authors would concur that to look at data on occupational change is to focus on surface appearances. To understand and explain change in the class structure involves analysis of ownership, relation to job markets, social organization of production, political struggles and state intervention, especially as they relate to changes in legal entitlements.

Within this complex of influences, a number of empirical themes stand out from the theoretical literature and provide an agenda for the following sections:

1 The trend towards the separation of ownership and control suggests the development of new roles and relationships between owners and managers.

2 The persistence of the old petty bourgeoisie, and the growth of a **new petty bourgeoisie** of managers and experts, raises questions about the integrity of the middle class.

3 If selling one's labour and working in a routinized organization, being subject to constant supervision and receiving low pay is typical of a working-class position, are today's clerical employees really working class? Has the commonsense division into 'white collar' and 'blue collar' diverted our attention away from a significant change in class position?

4 If selling one's labour and being exploited by an employer is diagnostic of being working class, how do we regard the long-term unemployed who depend on welfare payments and who therefore obtain an income without working?

3.3 The upper class

Earlier parts of this book have already alluded to two developments affecting the upper class which imply different directions of change. In Chapter 2, Pond showed that taxation has reduced the peaks of income and wealth, which could imply a narrowing of the gap between the upper and middle classes, a move which is consistent with Thrift's discussion, in Chapter 1, of the adoption of previously upper-class lifestyles by the growing middle classes. On the other hand, theoretical Marxists stress the growing separation of ownership from control, which could bring about a separation between a **rentier** upper class (owning and receiving income from extensive portfolios of investments, but not engaging in direct control of production) and a managerial upper-middle class (controlling investments and production, but lacking substantial ownership). Before looking at evidence of recent changes, it is important to establish the nature of the British upper class.

The commonsense image of the British upper class is that it consists of the aristocracy, and that its economic power and social status depends ultimately on the possession of agricultural land. However, even lay people probably have some awareness that this has been far from the whole truth for a century or more, and that the contemporary upper class has been recruited from the industrial and commercial bourgeoisie as well as the aristocracy. If this is the case, it raises a crucial question about the process of class formation: how are groups which initially differ profoundly in terms of economic base and social status welded into a single class? To answer this question requires a look back over the history of the last century, but the main concern of this chapter is with *recent* change, and here a different question becomes crucial. Have economic change and state intervention through taxation diminished the significance of the upper class in wealth and control of production? In answering this second question, I shall try to show that some of the cultural features of the upper class that developed in response to the industrial revolution are still important in establishing indirect forms of class control.

A revealing study of the English upper class is by Wiener (1981). He set out to explain British economic decline, apparent since the late 1960s but developing over the last century, in relation to the culture of the élite. He argues that, although the aristocracy became financially involved with industry and commerce in the eighteenth century, the industrial revolution was achieved by new bourgeois entrepreneurs. The root of the 'British disease', in his view, was the nineteenth century *accommodation* of the aristocracy to industrialization, and the *assimilation* of successful entrepreneurs into the upper class: 'Through these mechanisms of social absorption, the zeal for work, inventiveness, material production and money-making gave way within the capitalist class to the more aristocratic interests of cultivated style, the pursuits of leisure and political service' (p. 13). Foremost among the mechanisms of absorption were the public schools, where the aim of producing gentlemen of good character was pursued through the study of classics and games playing, and where science, technology and commerce were excluded until the twentieth century. Similar patterns of recruitment and education were entrenched at the ancient universities. When members of the upper class had to work to maintain themselves, they turned to the civil service (at home or in the colonies), the professions or finance, but seldom to manufacturing industry.

Wiener argues that this 'gentlemanly' culture penetrated lower levels of society, including the working classes, via socialist writers like Ruskin and William Morris. Their dislike of big cities, industrialized production and hierarchical organization helped feed yearnings for a mythical rural past. This frame of mind was much more firmly entrenched in the rural areas and the soft south; in the urban and industrial north capitalist values were more evident. Many would recognize this as a picture of Britain's past, but Wiener shows that British political and economic life was still dominated by paternalism and amateurism until at least 1979: 'English history in the eighties may turn less on traditional political struggles than on a cultural contest between the two faces of the middle class' (ibid., p. 166).

Wiener's analysis of the culture and class formation of the upper class suggests, though he doesn't explicitly consider the possibility, that it would incline towards being a *rentier* upper class, content to draw on income from industrial ownership and to leave management to employees. This connects with recent arguments in class theory that capitalism is undergoing a **managerial revolution**, where effective control of the economy is moving from the capitalist class to professional managers. This process is thought to be most advanced in the very large corporations which increasingly dominate British economic life, because fragmentation of share ownership leaves the nominal owners powerless to direct the full-time expert managers. Moreover, ownership of shares by insurance companies and pension funds diffuses ownership rights widely, but leaves investment decisions in the hands of small numbers of professionals. These arguments have been empirically investigated in a series of studies by John Scott and his associates.

Scott (1979) confirms that power over corporate affairs is passing from the hands of individuals to impersonal organizations, though many family controlled companies are still in evidence. Banks in particular have 'spheres of influence' which co-ordinate numbers of companies. In spite of this, however, he concludes that:

> a propertied class still exists and that it derives its advantages from ownership of company shares and participation in strategic control. . . . There has been a managerial reorganization of the propertied class. Wealthy families hold shares in a large number of companies and they form a pool from which corporate managers are recruited. . . . Class domination takes a 'structural' form, because the transmission of social positions is less and less a matter of personal inheritance and more a matter relating to the structure of the class as a whole. (p. 175)

Scott's later work includes detailed network analysis of interlocking directorships in major British companies, and shows that multiple directors form an inner circle which differs from those who sit on only one top board. Whereas in 1904 the inner circle was mainly composed of entrepreneurial capitalists, by 1930 the core was provided by city institutions and, by 1976, finance capital had built out from the London core to forge an extensive national network.

> This whole sphere of interpersonal connections was the basis for cohesion and informality among directors at the level of social integration. People meet as kinsmen, friends, co-directors, and as colleagues of kin and friends, and each relation reinforces the others to produce multiple and multi-stranded, personal relations. If combined with the looser partial networks of common club memberships and common school or college attendance, a mapping of the structure of the establishment is produced. (Scott and Griff, 1984, p. 181)

Activity 3.2

Reread chapter 2, section 2.6, paying particular attention to:

● the degree of redistribution of wealth from the top one per cent;

● the importance of inheritance as a source of wealth; and

● the concentration of wealth holdings which produce economic power (i.e. securities in private firms and land ownership).

Does this data support or challenge Scott's argument?

Summary of section 3.3

The data concerning the upper class seem to be partly contradictory. On the one hand, during the last 50 years, the top one per cent's share of total wealth has declined and the next four per cent's share has been stable, but the position of the next 15 per cent has sharply improved. On the other hand, the top one per cent still own a majority of productive wealth, while the rest of the top ten per cent have more of their wealth as homes, domestic property, life insurance and so on. The role of inheritance remains crucial in determining wealth, but there are appreciable numbers of highly paid executives who are moving into the ranks of the wealthy. Overall, there does seem to have been a narrowing of the gap between upper and upper-middle class, but without a dramatic erosion of the position of the top one per cent.

As regards their position in the corporate structure, the evidence is also equivocal: the growing size and complexity of business organization has much reduced the role of the small family firm, but it has also increased the significance of financial institutions. The connections between finance and the upper class have been strong since the eighteenth century and remain significant, though bitterly disputed (Ingham, 1984; Barratt-Brown, 1988). Far from becoming a *rentier* class, the upper class seem to be more involved in investment decisions and industrial management than was the case in the Edwardian era. Much of the change is perhaps best conceived as an improvement in the income and influence of the upper-middle class rather than a worsening of the position of the upper class. Whether the cultural institutions of the upper class can assimilate rapidly growing numbers of newly rich people in the future as they have in the past remains an open question. The reduction in upper-class domination of the Conservative party during the Thatcher years seems to suggest a diminution in upper-class power.

3.4   The middle classes

The middle class, or classes, have long been the main problem of class theorists, both because of their intermediate position between the bourgeoisie and the proletariat and because of their heterogeneity. Even the old petty bourgeoisie was varied, including as it did the professions (e.g. medicine, the law and the church), the small shopkeepers and the bureaucrats of the civil service.

Throughout the twentieth century, the number of people employed in middle-class occupations has grown, both absolutely and as a proportion of the labour force, in the UK and other advanced countries. To make matters more complicated, this growth has involved new kinds of middle-class occupation, for example, technical specialists and state employees like social workers. In both state and corporate sectors, larger organizations have seen the emergence of more differentiated hierarchies of power and responsibility. Whereas a Victorian business may have been run from a counting house staffed by the entrepreneur, a bookkeeper and a few clerks, a modern corporation has a chain of command running from the board of directors through the chief executive, department heads and down through differentiated hierarchies to supervisors on the shop-floor – or perhaps on a variety of shop-floors in different regions or countries. As a further complication, people with the same qualifications, for example, as solicitors, might be found in independent small partnerships and as employees of the state or private companies. The growing size and complexity of the middle classes pose two important theoretical questions: first, how can they be separated from the upper class and the working class, and secondly, how should internal differentiation be treated – as unimportant, as divisions into class fractions, or as divisions into separate classes?

In general, these were not problems which were easily addressed by traditional Marxists because of the influence of the notion that Marx had defined only two classes in capitalist societies, and that the intervening classes would gradually polarize either into the bourgeoisie or, more likely, into the proletariat. A typical traditional Marxist response would be to conclude that even senior managers were employees, and hence workers, and that their failure to recognize the fact was a result of 'false consciousness'. Carter (1985) has argued that more constructive Marxist responses to the middle classes were pioneered in Weimar Germany, as a result of the rapid growth of technical and office employment in Germany's late and rapid industrialization.

In Britain Marxist responses had to wait until the 1970s. Even then, these responses were not consistent or particularly convincing, as Parkin (1979) has rather acidly pointed out. He contrasts *maximalist* definitions of the working class – separating only extreme and unproductive roles like landlord, *rentier* and property speculators as bourgeois, while all roles which could continue in a 'rationally ordered society', including managers, were classed as productive and hence workers. *Minimalist* definitions, especially that of Poulantzas, eliminate from the proletarian class all unproductive (non-industrial) workers, all supervisors and all technically qualified personnel, and leave a tiny rump class, perhaps only 15 per cent of the labour force. Between maximalist and minimalist definitions fell some intermediate ones, for example, locating the primary division in the class system between the managerial class and 'administrative labour'. However, the work of Wright and Roemer, as reviewed in section 3.2, does seem to restore the possibility of a dichotomy between exploiters and exploited, as well as recognizing a variety of positions where ownership, control, expertise and the need to sell labour varies.

Many other authors have argued that the middle classes are more amenable to treatment from a Weberian, rather than a Marxist, stance, emphasizing in particular his concern with varying life chances brought about by different market positions, and the relationship to his ideas of bureaucracy.

Barbalet (1986), after discussing the way different dimensions of domination could feed into a complex class structure (as summarized in section

3.2.2), went on to argue that the new middle class was clearly working class in view of its lack of productive property, but equally clearly separated from the manual working class by status considerations. Unlike earlier suggestions that the middle class was to be separated from the working class by lifestyle and prestige, Barbalet applies the idea of status as enforceable norms to argue that the new middle class has established conventional and legal expectations about remuneration, negotiating rights and security of employment which sets its members apart from the working class. (He also notes that securely employed members of the primary working class enjoy similar status advantages over those in the secondary labour market. His solution to the problem of the new middle class is therefore linked to propositions about the working class which we will consider in section 3.5.) While Barbalet's solution seems a simple one, it leaves open the question of why the new middle class has been able to secure such a beneficial position, which might involve command over skills or organizational assets, and whether there are further status divisions within the class. Finally, it offers little to explain how, or whether, the new middle class establishes common cause with the old, property-owning petty bourgeoisie and small employers.

Recent decades have seen three persistent debates about changes in the middle classes. First, and overlapping with ideas about a managerial revolution discussed in the previous section, is the debate about the position and role of the professional and managerial classes, and the proposition that there is a distinctive *service class*. Secondly, there is a more restricted, but still significant, debate about the persistence of the old petty bourgeoisie, and thirdly, there is a long running discussion of the proletarianization of clerical occupations. I will look briefly at the main issues in these debates in their own terms and in order to develop the proposition that a strong definition of status, plus the ideas of Roemer and Wright on modes of production, provide the optimum platform for assessing current changes in British society.

3.4.1   Professionals and managers: is there a service class?

Many aspects of the debate about professionals and managers have been briefly anticipated in sections 3.2 and 3.3 above. In general terms, we are dealing with groups which do not own amounts of property comparable to the bourgeoisie, though they may well own domestic property and industrial shares. However, they exercise a good deal of day-to-day control in industry or in bureaucracies, they tend to enjoy quite secure employment, and may find it possible to move jobs advantageously. Many possess formal credentials for employment in specified occupations. In Marxist terms, they are a mixture of, or a contradiction between capital and labour. In Weberian terms, they are privileged employees, their privilege being based on status qualifications and scarce skills.

Rather than rehearse previous arguments in more detail, I will focus on the proposition that the twentieth century has seen the emergence of a new class – the service class. This proposition has gained wide acceptance recently (to the degree that the term is used as if it were self-evident), and has the advantage of bringing together some elements of Marxist and Weberian concerns, as well as drawing attention to culture. However, it seems to me that the proposition involves unresolved difficulties, which have interesting implications, but throw major doubt on the notion of a single service class.

The term **service class** was put forward by the Austro-Marxist Karl Renner in 1953 (see Renner, 1978), and is therefore at least an indirect continuation of earlier debates about the new middle classes in Weimar Germany. Renner proposed that capitalists were agents of circulation and were handing these functions over to paid assistants or substitutes, who performed these services for salaries, fees or commissions. Typically, there would be an employment relationship based on trust and with a good deal of security. However, although Renner defined the service class as performing services for capital, he took as his model the *public service* which had first paid salaries. The fundamental output of the public service was seen as *law and order*, but Renner also extended his analysis to social services (distributing welfare), and economic services performed by managers. He noted that, at first, the public services had had the character of castes, separated from society at large by particular qualifications and functions, and integrated from top to bottom – 'from Generalissimo to private soldier and from Cardinal to village priest' – by caste pride and loyalty and a clear hierarchy of authority and promotion. Chillingly, he reminds us that, in pre-war Germany, these castes had tended to support Nazism in the hope of maintaining privilege. After the war, Renner saw a greater separation of the service castes from the bourgeoisie and closer affiliation to workers as these castes took on the character of classes. Even the most mildly sceptical reader of Renner would see his arguments about the public service as more indicative of a vertical division between private and public sectors, empowered by the state's legal and coercive machinery, rather than a horizontal division, allying public, social and economic services. However, it is the latter view which has reached the present.

A possible reason for this is that one of the main importers of the idea of a service class into the English language was Dahrendorf (1969), who tended to assimilate it to his own project of replacing property as the main concern of class theory with a focus on power. He therefore separated more powerful members of the 'new middle class', such as the bank manager or senior civil servant, from less powerful, such as the shop assistant, waiter and postman, calling the former at first bureaucrats and later a service class. Dahrendorf argues that since bureaucracies exist to exert the power of the rulers upon the ruled, the service class should be seen as an appendix of the ruling groups. 'The main expectation attached to service class positions is the administration of laws, whether public or private, formal or sanctioned'

(Dahrendorf, 1969, p. 145). However, he goes on to discuss the routine functioning and conservative attitudes of this class in a way which seems much more appropriate to civil servants than to business executives. Finally, he concludes that the service class is not a class at all, but a subordinate fragment of the ruling class.

More recent discussions of the concept of a service class seem to continue to accept the contradictions between services for capital and state bureaucracies, without explicit discussion of how the two aspects are to be brought together. Abercrombie and Urry (1983), for example, start with Dahrendorf's notion that the service class performs services *for* capital *in* bureaucracies. Later they note that most members of the service class are found in bureaucracies where the scope of their authority and the expectations placed upon them are quite clear. Only for technical specialists is there significant self-determination, though many expert positions are regulated by the professions. The functions performed by the service class are said to be control, reproduction and conceptualization. Later still, Abercrombie and Urry argue that, as a class, the service class has distinctive causal powers, though they are not necessarily manifested. These powers are to restructure capitalism to maximize the separation between conceptualization and execution, hence de-skilling the labour force and maximizing the educational and research requirements of the service class itself.

Only very late in their argument do they note the existence of distinct fractions of the middle class: the traditional petty bourgeoisie, the state sector and the private sector. Indeed, they go on to criticize other authors for neglecting the separation between 'entrepreneurial business' and the 'professional and governing class' in analysing the functions of the middle class in nineteenth century England. Yet in thinking through the definition, functions and causal powers of the service class, they too neglect to consider the distinctions between state employees – who tend to be more highly qualified, but are often in the most bureaucratic work situations – and managers in private companies – who tend to have fewer formal qualifications, and whose reputations often depend on successful innovation rather than routine reproduction or cultural elaboration. Their emphasis on the role of social struggles in class formation opens up the possibility of alliances between state and private sector groups to form a distinctive service class, but Abercrombie and Urry do not attempt to provide such an argument.

Activity 3.3

The discussion of the service class has counterposed vertical divisions – between state and capitalist sectors – and horizontal divisions – between powerful and powerless white-collar positions. Which view seems more consistent with political changes in the UK since 1945?

Post-war experience in the UK has seen a growth in the size and influence of the state (based on taxation, nationalization and increased welfare provision) and, in the 1980s, an explicit attempt to 'roll back the state' through public expenditure cuts and privatization. These changes are explicitly seen by their protagonists as involving competing principles of social organization vying for supremacy. Within this wider struggle, different middle-class groups have taken different positions, illustrated by the fact that, in the 1987 election, the votes of people with degrees were divided almost equally between Conservative, Labour and Alliance parties, while those of managers without degrees were more than 75 per cent Conservative. The current ideological supremacy of private sector organization is indicated by the harsh treatment meted out to white-collar professions in state employment, such as teachers and social workers, and the wide gulf between their material expectations and political affiliations and those of corporate sector middle-class groups. The irony, of course, is that this shift in the balance between state and corporate sectors is being pursued through a combination of state power and petty bourgeois ideology. The debate over the service class cannot be resolved fully without going on to look at the related questions of the petty bourgeoisie itself and the proletarianizing of former middle-class groups. At present, it is best left as 'not proven'.

3.4.2   The petty bourgeoisie

The distinctive feature of the traditional petty bourgeoisie is that it simultaneously owns a share of the means of production *and* uses its own labour. In the ideal case, where the share of the means of production is about the societal mean and where no labour is employed, this class is neither exploiting nor exploited, either in terms of ownership, or in terms of control or appropriation of surplus value. For traditional Marxists, this contradicts their basic belief in a polarized class conflict between bourgeoisie and proletariat, and I have already mentioned two reactions: first to predict that the petty bourgeoisie would disappear over time as polarization reduced its members to proletarian status, or, second, to regard them as a relic of a previous mode of production, usually described as petty-commodity production. Wright (1978) used the latter device to identify the petty bourgeoisie as a 'contradictory class location' and to identify a range of intermediate positions, small employers being intermediate between petty and high bourgeois, and self-employed artisans being intermediate between petty bourgeoisie and proletariat.

The petty bourgeoisie has not attracted discussion by as many academics as the major classes, but there has been a scattering of empirical studies over the last two decades, and interest in this class has grown recently. *The Economy in Question* (Allen and Massey, 1988) established that the UK economy has been increasingly dominated by large organizations. There was also a long-term decline of self-employment to only 7.9 per cent of men and 4.2 per cent of women in the labour force in 1966. Since then, however, there has been a slight recovery. The proportion of small firms varies greatly in different areas of the economy, but personal ownership is most significant in agriculture, construction, retailing and decorating, as shown in Table 3.6. The variety of sectors where self-employment plays a part also points toward the fact that self-employment can range from very significant asset owner-ship (e.g. among farmers) to possession of tools alone (e.g. in decorating or construction).

Scase and Goffee (1982) have documented the range of positions which exist within what they term the entrepreneurial middle class, and what Wright identifies as contradictory positions between the bourgeoisie and the petty bourgeoisie. They draw a distinction between established and marginal positions: the established often inherit assets and expertise and may employ labour, while the marginal rarely do so and are often upwardly mobile from manual occupations. They then divide each group into two further categories. The marginal are made up of the *self-employed*, most of whom are tradesmen and effectively depend on selling their labour, and the *small employers*, who work alongside their employees and face substantial administrative complexities for only a few workers. The established include the *owner-controllers*, who concentrate on management, and *owner-direc-tors*, who can rely on a management structure and are therefore effectively small capitalists. Scase and Goffee assert that technical and managerial qualifications are most frequently found among the established groups. They found that, although the motives for self-employment included econ-omic ones, there was considerable emphasis on establishing independence and autonomy at work. Hence, psychological and ideological factors were quite important.

Scase and Goffee did note that, although much of their work was done in the building industry, they deliberately omitted workers who were in fact 'labour only subcontractors'. This practice, commonly known as 'the lump', is a reminder that 'freedom and autonomy' may, for many self-employed people, be the result of the employer's wish to escape the responsibilities of an employer – for example, sick and holiday pay, insurance and so on. As was shown in Allen and Massey (1988), the move to flexible employment strategies has often meant a move away from direct employment towards subcontracting, sometimes of the same people. These kinds of employer strategies are undoubtedly a significant factor in the recent growth of self-employment. The past record of small clothing manufacturers, whether self-employed outworkers or small sweat shops, is that recession can bring pressure through market prices, which is every bit as severe as the exploi-tation of labour by the most ruthless employers.

In spite of these growing pressures on at least the marginally self-employed, the small business sector has become more significant for theory and policy. Curran and Burrows (1986) have reviewed some of the theoreti-cal issues and conclude that the survival and growth of the petty bourgeoisie is based on the fact that it is functional for capital. This is so both materially,

Table 3.6 Distribution of male self-employed by occupation, 1971

Occupation	Employees in employment (thousands)	Self-employed (thousands)	Number in employment (thousands)	Self-employed as a % of number in employment (%)
All economically active	13 560	1 471	15 031	9.8
Farmers, foresters, fishermen	378	246	623	39.4
Miners and quarrymen	233	-	234	0.2
Gas, coke and chemical makers	122	-	122	0.2
Glass and ceramic makers	60	1	61	1.8
Furnace, forge, foundry, rolling mill workers	148	3	152	2.1
Electrical and electronic workers	488	27	515	5.2
Engineering and allied workers	2 307	98	2 405	4.1
Woodworkers	335	63	398	15.8
Leather workers	49	7	55	12.2
Textile workers	134	2	135	1.4
Clothing workers	63	13	75	16.6
Food, drink and tobacco workers	217	34	250	13.4
Paper and printing workers	208	6	214	2.9
Makers of other products	187	11	198	5.4
Construction workers	364	154	517	29.7
Painters and decorators	198	62	260	23.9
Drivers of stationary engines, cranes, etc.	288	3	291	1.0
Labourers	942	22	964	2.3
Transport and communications	1 141	68	1 209	5.6
Warehousemen, storekeepers, etc.	477	-	478	0.2
Clerical workers	1 035	7	1 043	0.7
Sales workers	833	313	1 147	27.3
Service, sports, recreation	717	148	865	17.1
Administrators, managers	830	-	830	-
Professional, technical workers	1 472	180	1 651	10.9
Armed forces	240	-	240	-
Inadequately described	95	4	100	4.3

The total number in employment (column 3) is rounded to the nearest thousand
Source: *Royal Commission on the Distribution of Income and Wealth, Report No. 8*, 1979, Table 2.13

because it can be a useful source of flexibility and customer sensitivity, and ideologically, because it represents the core of *laissez-faire* capitalism. However, they argue that there is no necessary ideological identity with monopoly capital, and that the petty bourgeoisie have at times taken a radical stance. The current use of petty bourgeois ideals to advantage corporate capital against nationalized industry and services is but one example of the possible ideological alliances which could be forged between the petty bourgeoisie and other classes or class fractions.

3.4.3   The lower-middle class

The most persistent debate in relation to what I have provisionally termed the lower-middle class is whether routinized white-collar, and especially clerical, employees are to be regarded as middle class (as they are in commonsense usage), or whether the nature of their employment should be regarded as proletarian. Within this debate, the majority of Marxist writers tend to argue that clerical workers have been **proletarianized** during the course of this century, while many pluralist writers have been more concerned to argue, as we shall see in the next section, that manual workers have become more middle class.

The context for this debate has already been sketched in above. Clerical occupations have grown rapidly since the late nineteenth century, reaching over 10 per cent of the labour force by 1951 and nearly 20 per cent by 1981. Where clerks existed in small numbers in each firm a century ago, they now work for much larger organizations, and at the lower end of much more elaborate hierarchies. As a consequence, they tend to carry out much more tightly defined tasks and to be distant from areas of real power. Finally, the substantial differential in pay between clerks and skilled manual workers in the nineteenth century has been narrowed to the point where there is no difference between averages, and some clerks are paid substantially less than some skilled workers. In spite of this, it appears that clerks perceive themselves as different in class from manual workers, and their political behaviour has tended to be different, even where white-collar unions have grown. How has this discrepancy between 'objective' indicators and 'subjective' affiliation been interpreted?

The most influential study of this question was by Lockwood (1958). As described in section 3.2, he took a fundamentally Weberian position by focusing on market and status situations, but added 'work situation' to take account of neo-Marxist concerns with degrees of control at the workplace. As regards *market situation*, all clerks share with manual workers the need to sell their labour, but they have typically enjoyed much more secure employment and pension rights. Lockwood shows that there has been a wide gap between the relatively high pay of groups like bank clerks and the low pay of railway clerks, so that only for a minority has significantly higher pay set them off from workers. Historically, clerks had some expectations of social mobility, into management and even into partnership, but in more recent times the growing stress on formal qualifications for higher positions has reduced this kind of mobility. The *work situation* of most clerks has also changed: in the Victorian 'counting house', clerks worked with the proprietor and could influence policy and day-to-day decisions, and even in the 1960s mass production industries' clerks would usually work with management and be separated from manual workers. In today's larger offices, direct contact with authority has lessened, but there is no concomitant increase in contact with workers. In considering *status situation*, Lockwood uses the term in its weak sense to indicate prestige, and, beyond noting the significance of the manual/non-manual divide in European society and noting that many clerks come from middle-class backgrounds, he makes no serious attempt to argue that status is of comparable importance to class. His conclusion in relation to status is effectively the conclusion to the book, but is ambiguous: 'In the case of clerks we have tried to show how their original claim to middle-class status has been slowly undermined during the rise of the modern office. . . . And yet we are forced to recognize that not being middle class is not identical with being working class' (p. 133).

Lockwood's solution to the problem of this 'non-middle and non-working' class dominated the debate until Braverman (1974) renewed the case for the de-skilling of the clerical labour process and revived the argument for ascribing clerks to the working class, as summarized in *Crompton and Jones* (1982). This line of argument has been strengthened, but qualified, by Crompton and Jones' (1984) empirical study of clerks in three large offices. They found that most clerks were performing routine tasks which did not require particular skills. However, they stress the enormous variety of clerical work, including the different atmospheres in state and private offices, and the continued possibility of substantial promotion for those – almost all *men*, though only about 30 per cent of clerks are men – who perform well, improve their qualifications and accept geographical mobility. For the majority of clerks, who are in positions with little scope for promotion or autonomy and whose status and pay are low, they unhesitatingly conclude that they are dealing with a 'white-collar proletariat'. Crompton and Jones' discussion of the gender differences between clerks helps to explain the apparent discrepancy between aggregate studies of social class and social mobility, which show increasing numbers in the higher social classes, and studies of the labour process, which emphasize de-skilling of manual and clerical jobs: it now appears that upward mobility relates to men and clerical de-skilling to women. The massive concentration of women into clerical and sales occupations is reflected in the difference in the proportions of men and women in the skilled (non-manual) category in Table 3.1. The interactions of class and gender are explored further in Chapter 5.

Two main issues seem unresolved in these discussions. First, if the 'real' basis of class in selling relatively unskilled labour is hardly different between today's clerks and manual workers, how is it that residual status differences can so effectively conceal the fact from these occupational groups?

Secondly, is Lockwood's neglect of the difference between the state sector and the corporate sector justified? As regards the first point, Barbalet (see section 3.2.2 above) would surely argue that, if status is interpreted as 'enforceable rights' attached to particular categories of worker rather than as prestige, the benefits to clerks, in terms of security of employment, pension, pleasant working conditions and such like, are significant and material, even though they evolved as norms under previous conditions. Their significance would be clarified by studies which enquired whether employers have reacted to the weakened position of clerks by withdrawing these benefits.

A particularly instructive employer in this respect is the state. While the public servant may have been the original model of the service class, Lockwood's data does show that clerks in local government, the civil service and British Rail are far more unionized than those in the private sector. This was confirmed by the high level of unionization in Crompton and Jones' state sector sample office. Restraints on public spending have led to slow pay increases and even redundancies for state employed clerks. Some groups, especially Inland Revenue and DHSS clerks, have been involved in long-term disputes over the pressure of work. Hence, the position of clerks *vis-à-vis* the state as a very large scale employer does seem to be less favourable than that of private sector clerks. A countervailing factor is that where clerks are involved in allocating state benefits, such as welfare payments or council housing, their effective power over their clients may well prevent them from too close a class alliance. In effect, these arguments do seem to confirm rather than weaken Lockwood's conclusion: in objective terms clerks are separate both from other parts of the middle class and from manual workers. In terms of self-perception and political behaviour, they have, in the past, tended to align with the middle class, but this need not persist, especially if the future sees the emergence of a relatively privileged 'core' working class, as discussed below.

Finally, technological change may have unpredictable effects on clerks. If the main reason for failing to keep ahead of manual workers in levels of pay has been the rapid growth in mechanization and automation of industrial production, with growth in productivity per worker, the current rapid automation of office work could have two kinds of effect on clerical work. First, it could reduce the number of clerks required, and hence subject others to unemployment. Secondly, this would increase the productivity of those remaining, and perhaps their expertise, and hence justify higher pay. The overall result could therefore be either subjection to poorer conditions or a move back towards the service class. Computerization of office work is such a recent and rapid phenomenon that no clear answers are currently available on its implications for the position of clerical workers in the class structure.

Summary of section 3.4: the fragmented middle classes

The discussion of the main components of the contemporary British middle classes and the thumbnail sketches of the major theoretical debates does seem to confirm the existence of real divisions, both vertically and horizontally. The vertical divisions are, centrally, the capitalist sector (which is by definition the dominant one in a capitalist society and is being made even more dominant by Thatcherism), and the two subsidiary modes of production, the state sector and the sector of small capital.

The horizontal divisions are somewhat more elusive, but they can usefully be related to the gradations of small capital: from owner-controllers and directors at the top, through the classic petty bourgeois (with assets but without employees) and down to the self-employed artisan. The expert managers and controllers of both private and public sectors can look forward to using high incomes to become substantial owners of domestic property, life assurance, unit trusts and direct investments in shares and securities. The lower ranks of private and public bureaucracies have their favourable conditions of service to set them off from manual workers, but only improved qualifications and successful job performance give them any hope of progression from lower-middle to upper-middle class. The issue of upward mobility is highly relevant to the working class also and will be discussed in the next section. The issue of how the fragments of the middle classes become forged into politically conscious class movements is taken up in Carter (1985), but as both upper and lower sections of the middle class are subject to rapid change, no clear or stable picture has yet emerged.

3.5   The working class: erosion from above and below?

The empirical evidence discussed in section 3.1 has already identified one major change in the position of the working class – its decline as a proportion of the labour force as the number of middle-class positions has grown. While this change seems undramatic, it does steadily reduce the possibility that the working-class vote could elect a radical left-wing government which could significantly transform British politics and society. However, this numerical erosion is slower than some other changes which may be taking place as the rapid changes in the economy over the last twenty years alter the material position of different parts of the working class.

This section will consider two debates about the changing class position of parts of the working class, each of which is partially consistent with the arguments over the proletarianization of the lower-middle class. First, the so called **'embourgeoisement thesis'** takes a reciprocal view, namely, that affluence among workers has moved them into effectively middle-class positions. Although this was a major debate twenty years ago, it both sets the scene for and has relevance to contemporary debates about the effects of mass unemployment and the use of part time and temporary labour in separating a lower class, or underclass, from the working class. This debate about downward mobility relates to changes in the labour process, as does the proletarianization debate. The concluding sub-section will both sum up changes in the position of parts of the working class and raise questions about their consequences for politics, and especially for the Labour Party.

3.5.1   Embourgeoisement and after

One of the best known and most influential studies of the British class structure was carried out in the 1960s and published as 'The affluent worker in the class structure' (Goldthorpe *et al.*, 1969). The question addressed by this study was whether affluent workers had or had not adopted 'bourgeois' – or, more realistically, 'middle-class' – lifestyles, values and aspirations. The authors' review traced the origins of the debate back to the realization, even in Marx's lifetime, that neither the polarization of the class structure nor the anticipated commitment of the proletariat to revolutionary class struggle had come about as expected. The concept of *embourgeoisement* was introduced by Engels with a double meaning: in terms of objective class position, the British working class effectively benefited from the exploitation of the colonial masses to enjoy an enhanced income; in subjective terms, they seemed to accept, and aspire to conform to, the prevailing values of the bourgeoisie and were consequently deferential in social and political behaviour.

As the twentieth century progressed, and particularly in the 1950s and 1960s, many commentators in Britain and other advanced societies began to note the improving economic position of the working class and their surprising ineffectiveness in turning numerical superiority into class domination of politics. Goldthorpe *et al.* (1969, p. 5) saw this as producing an implicit alternative theory to Marxism: a progressive *integration* of the working class into the institutional structure of capitalist societies and a consequent blunting of its revolutionary potential. By about 1960, and related to the 'end of ideology' thesis of Daniel Bell, some authors went beyond this integrationist argument to put forward an alternative historicist theory, which included a new view of 'embourgeoisement'.

According to authors like Kerr *et al.* (1962) the whole thrust of social and technical change was acting to break down the structure of class societies, and particularly to merge the working class into a broad 'middle mass'. Three sets of factors were combining to produce this effect. *Economic growth* had brought working-class incomes and ownership of consumer goods to unprecedented levels. *Technical change* was seen to have transformed the labour process so that many workers were technicians supporting automated or continuous process production. *Geographically*, the redevelopment of run-down urban areas was scattering working-class people into suburban estates and new towns where individualized lifestyles replaced the communal solidarism of traditional working-class areas. It was widely believed by social scientists and politicians in the late 1950s that these changes were making many manual workers effectively middle class in their lifestyles, including their voting – a view apparently endorsed by the three successive Conservative victories at general elections.

This theoretical viewpoint was challenged by Marxists, not so much denying the tendency towards affluence, but questioning its nature and consequences. For example, Marcuse (1964) argued that the pursuit of consumer goods was engendered by advertising for the benefit of capitalism, and tended to produce workers alienated in consumption as well as in production. Goldthorpe *et al.* (1969) point out that, in identifying the role of the mass media, together with government and employer propaganda in tranquillizing the workers, these neo-Marxist responses seemed to concede the 'embourgeoisement' argument at the material level, but try to counter it at the ideological level – a position rather discordant with traditional Marxist principles.

Their own theoretical critique of the embourgeoisement thesis dealt with both the material and the ideological levels. First, they note that the proponents of embourgeoisement are not clear whether the assimilation of workers to the middle classes is at the level of income similarities, the adoption of middle-class values by manual workers, or the acceptance of affluent workers as social equals by the middle class. Secondly, they point out that the reduction of differentials in income and consumption do nothing to eliminate differences at the level of production and that even affluent workers are still exploited. Thirdly, they argue that observed changes in the social life of manual workers might just as easily be an adaptation of working-class lifestyles to new environments as a shift to middle-class patterns.

Given their expectation that the thesis would prove vulnerable, Goldthorpe *et al.* chose to test it in a situation which was as favourable as possible. They carried out a survey in Luton, where workers were not only affluent, but fairly newly arrived in a town without a long history of industrial working-class settlement, social organization or politics. Their interviews were carried out in the early 1960s, in the era of Harold Macmillan and 'you've never had it so good'.

The results bore out their theoretical scepticism at every level. First, at work, they found that improved pay and conditions had done nothing to change the class situation of people who were still paid labourers without control of the labour process. Indeed, they found no general tendency towards better working conditions, and a *contradiction* between achievement of high incomes and improvements in conditions. Higher pay, which was a major goal, meant overtime, shift work and even the acceptance of dirty or dangerous conditions. Secondly, they found that changed styles of life did not involve adoption of middle-class habits or contact with middle-class people (except for respondents with previous middle-class connections), but were an adaption of working-class traditions to a new environment. Neither at work nor at home did higher incomes lead to striving after middle-class status. Finally, there was no trend away from trade union membership or Labour voting – though there were indications that these institutions were perceived instrumentally, as likely to produce immediate individual benefits, rather than in terms of class solidarity.

Goldthorpe *et al.* concluded that the embourgeoisement thesis was incorrect and proposed a different interpretation. In their view, what was happening was a *convergence* between upper-working class and lower-middle class, in which they were growing more alike but remaining separate. Affluence was seen as having far-reaching consequences in producing a more individualized, instrumental and consumerist lifestyle among workers, but not as transforming their class position. The only possible exception to this was the respondents' high aspirations for their children, which would have led to a move to middle-class occupations. The other side of this 'convergence thesis' was the reduced incomes, increasing hierarchical domination and greater unionization of lower-middle-class people, which was making them more like the working class, as discussed in section 3.4. On the basis of their findings, they concluded that convergence need not imply a decline in Labour votes, and that much depended on the effectiveness of political leadership in mobilizing potential, but not guaranteed, Labour supporters.

3.5.2   Segmentation of the labour force

The affluent worker study was published just at the peak of the post-war period of full employment. Since then, as *The Economy in Question* showed, the British economy has passed into a period of crisis in which there have been dramatic changes in the structure of the economy. For our purposes here, the central changes have been the decline in the number of manufacturing jobs and the restructuring of the labour process towards 'flexible specialization'. The result, as discussed by Pond in Chapter 2 and *Leadbeater* (1987), has been a segmentation of industrial workers into at least three groups. First, the *core* workers, who continue to enjoy permanent jobs, and may indeed have improved their working conditions and income. Second, the *peripheral* workers, a diverse group of temporary, part-time, agency and nominally self-employed people, who provide employers with the flexibility to expand and contract their labour force. Third, the *long-term unemployed*, who pose the problem of the class position of poor people who are not employed.

The graph in Figure 3.4 shows that real earnings have risen rapidly since 1982, and that earnings in manufacturing industry started rising earlier (1981) than in other sectors, and exceeded them from 1984 onward. In spite of a 9 per cent fall in manufacturing output and a 25 per cent fall in manufacturing employment between 1979 and 1986, the post tax earnings of

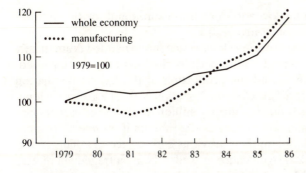

Figure 3.4 *Post-tax real earnings, 1979–86, United Kingdom*

those who remained in employment rose by 20 per cent. A part of this change can be accounted for by the higher incidence of job-loss among manual workers, and consequently a higher proportion of white-collar employees in the later years. However, even manual workers have, on average, obtained pay rises above the rate of inflation, although many lower paid workers have not kept up. The pressures toward embourgeoisement have remained for core manual workers, and have been intensified by the campaigns to sell council housing and privatize nationalized monopolies and foster wider share ownership. They have been complemented by the closure of many large plants, where unionization and Labour voting were more entrenched than in small plants. The effects of these changes will be sketched in section 3.5.3 below, and considered in more detail in Chapter 6, and *Politics in Transition* (Cochrane and Anderson, 1989).

The nature of the emerging 'flexible firm' and dual labour force has been sketched by Atkinson and Gregory (1986). They emphasize both the need for 'functional flexibility' among core workers, who may have to perform different roles as trading conditions change, and the increasing role of peripheral workers in providing numerical flexibility. The peripheral workers fall into two groups, those directly employed by the firm and those employed by subcontractors. For direct employees, the role of part-time working has grown, especially in services like retailing (where part-timers form a majority of the labour force in many areas), as has that of temporary contracts (from 20 per cent to 35 per cent of job centre placements since 1979). As later chapters will show, a high proportion of part-time and temporary work is done by women and members of ethnic minorities.

The second category of peripheral workers is that of subcontractors, agencies and those who are nominally self-employed, and therefore deprived of benefits like sick and holiday pay. Many of these people, whose continuity of employment depends entirely on the maintenance of the subcontract, were previous employees of the main company who were encouraged or obliged to leave direct employment and then compete with other subcontractors for the contract to do the work. By its very nature, the size and fortunes of the peripheral workforce are hard to establish and subject to rapid change, but it is a growing group, and one whose interests are both fragmented and partially contradictory to those of core workers. It has consequences both for low and insecure incomes and for the political affiliations of the people concerned.

The third segment of the working class, which has expanded dramatically since 1979, is the unemployed, and especially the long-term unemployed. This has dramatically increased the proportion of the British population dependent on state benefits (see Chapter 2, section 2.6). The growth in long-term unemployment has brought a further million former wage earners into dependency on supplementary benefit as the time limit on unemployment benefit removes any relation to their previous earned incomes. This shift is of considerable theoretical significance as well as being a tragedy in human terms. To traditional Marxists, supplementary benefit claimants are no longer being exploited because they generate no surplus value which can be appropriated by capital. Yet, in commonsense terms they are surely worse off than those in manual work. Friend and Metcalf (1981) and Harrison (1983) have vividly recorded the problems of claimants, especially in run-down inner city areas, and they demonstrate that administrative pressures play a significant role in creating stress, as well as low income and social heterogeneity. Although material deprivation is arguably less than in the 1930s, the absence of stable solidaristic communities seems to worsen the problems, and to separate the experience of the new poor from that of the traditional working class. There seem to be strong practical arguments for regarding them as separate class groups.

The contrasts between the new poor and the traditional working class have led some observers to designate them as an **underclass** (Dahrendorf, 1987). At its most extreme, the concept of an underclass blames the poor for their own position, through ideas like 'the cycle of deprivation', which implies that situational and/or genetic disadvantage makes some poor children unemployable – an affliction they pass on to their children. A related argument is that of the 'culture of poverty', which is also thought to disincline its adherents from employment. Such arguments have been challenged by MacNicol (1987), who shows that the concept of an underclass has long historical roots, but that the size and composition of the poor changes over time, as the demand for labour changes, and that the research findings are inconsistent with simplistic genetic or cyclical notions of inferiority. Low pay, old age, disability and single parent status are sufficient causes for the current incidence of poverty without resorting to blaming the victims.

Indeed, a wider look at history suggests that the notion of a single working class may be a misreading of the experience of the past. Thus, Neale (1972) separates the eighteenth century working class into an upper and lower fraction. Much of British sociology, even during full employment in the 1950s and '60s, separated working-class people into respectable (usually in secure jobs) and rough (often in insecure and discontinuous employment). American usage has for decades discriminated between working class and lower class (i.e. those who don't work, at least on a consistent basis). Yet the distinction was then based on relation to the labour market, implying a dualism between core and marginal workers, the latter either being undesirable employees or those temporarily in 'the reserve army of labour' because of short-term unemployment. The new feature of the post-war period, and especially that since 1974, is that the bottom fraction of what was the working class has been shifted into the orbit of the state. By taking responsibility for their subsistence, the state and its agents have taken control of their lifestyle. Many studies of the allocation of state benefits show the effect of stereotypes reminiscent of the nineteenth century division between the deserving and undeserving poor.

Perhaps the crucial factor in whether the current division between those in work and those dependent on the state becomes a real class division is whether it persists. Here the debate links back to that on post-industrial society. It may be that high technology and the resulting automation of manual jobs in industry, and increasingly in services, will increase unemployment in the future. The issue then will surely become political rather than economic: can society at large endure the long-term existence of a large group of second-class citizens, or will there be a move towards genuine redistribution?

Activity 3.4

● Identify the three headings used by Goldthorpe *et al.* to state and then refute the 'embourgeoisement' thesis.

● Use these three headings to summarize the recent changes associated with the segmentation of the labour force.

In carrying out this activity, and particularly when dealing with the third heading, it will be helpful to relate your summary to the discussion in *The Economy in Question* (Allen and Massey, 1988) concerning employment change in different parts of the UK.

3.5.3   Structural changes and Labour voting

Both Marxist and Weberian theories of class concur in the view that the economy, and especially the division of property and labour, is an underlying cause of the differentiation of class positions. They also agree that politics can potentially play a decisive role in redefining the rights of property, labour and citizenship. For Marx in particular, the political objective of promoting a cohesive and revolutionary working class was the practical objective of theoretical understanding. Weberians have long argued, and neo-Marxists have more recently accepted, that the process of class formation is a problematic one in which shifting economic position and varying political strategies and effectiveness lead to fluctuating affiliations and advantages. The British working class was forged principally through

the Trades Union movement and the Labour Party, but the recent restructuring of the economy and the class structure have led to a new situation in
which manual workers are no longer in a majority. While much of the debate
revolves around political conviction and the desirable response to the
present situation, there is a more analytical component which focuses on the
degree to which structural changes account for changes in the Labour vote.

A key contribution to this debate has been that of Hobsbawm. Under the
title 'The forward march of Labour halted?' (1978), he argued that support
for Labour had been in decline since 1951, and that a central feature of the
decline had been the reduction of the proportion of manual workers from
three-quarters of the labour force in 1870 to a bare majority in 1976.
However, although some commentators linked this simplistically to a
decline in Labour voting, Hobsbawm refused to accept simple economic
determinism and looked in more detail both at the early development of
Labour politics as well as its post-war decline. In particular, he noted that
trade union organization was strongest among skilled workers, the so called
'labour aristocracy', and that it often excluded or worked against the
interests of the unskilled and the poor. Moreover, the skilled workers were
the very group which Engels had shown to be buttressed by British manufacturing supremacy, and hence prone to respectable and moderate views.
Changes in British industry and the loss of Empire have subsequently
radicalized skilled workers to a degree, but growing sectionalism between
segments of the working class has prevented the numerical superiority of
manual workers from producing a concomitant superiority of the Labour
vote. In later papers (1983, 1987), Hobsbawm concedes that the years since
1979 have seen a dramatic collapse of Labour voting, not as a result of the
decimation of the manual labour force, but as a result of losing majority
support even *within* the working class. He concludes that the chief cause of
this is a failure at the political level to define and present policies which will
mobilize potential Labour support, and he argues that the tide can be turned
by new approaches to policy.

A recent analysis has sought to clarify the effects of the changing structure
of the labour force in terms of occupational class, trade union membership
and housing tenure. *Heath and McDonald* (1987) argue that changing class
structure accounts for only 5 per cent of voters leaving Labour between 1964
and 1986, while the Labour vote fluctuated from 48 per cent in 1966 to 28 per
cent in 1983. They conclude that explanations for voting change should
primarily be sought at the political level, though they also point to internal
divisions within the salariat (between union and non-union), and within the
working class (between integrated and marginal). These kinds of intra-class
divisions in voting behaviour seem to imply that the incipient divisions
discussed from a theoretical viewpoint in this chapter have already begun to
exert a discernible effect. However, the multiplication of class positions
seems unlikely to make it easier to anticipate changes in voting, since it
leaves more room for political activity to reconstruct coalitions between
sections of society.

3.6   Conclusion

Activity 3.5

Look back to the four possible forms of 'restructuring' of class relations outlined in section 3.1. For each: consider the theoretical arguments and the evidence outlined in this chapter and try to reach your own view about whether there has been a structural change. In doing so, be explicit about what you consider to be the relevant criteria for class recognition, and in separating a gradual change from a restructuring.

My conclusion to this exploration of changes in the British class structure is that, on the basis of possession of property, credentials and organizational positions, there are considerably more class positions than are recognized either by the majority of theorists or by everyday commonsense usage. There seems to be a good case for recognizing five horizontal divisions and three vertical ones. Horizontally, commonsense usage seems to have some support from Roemer's analyses in recognizing an upper class (based mainly on ownership), an upper-middle class (with a large measure of control and some ownership), a lower-middle class (in routine white-collar work, with moderate pay but benefits in conditions), and a working class (based on sale of labour power). I would also add a lower class based on occasional work plus welfare benefits; this would seem to be a structural change in the post-war period. Vertically, the central axis is the corporate sector, with the private sector adding a range of mainly petty bourgeois positions alongside the middle classes, and the state sector constituting a hierarchical structure analogous to that of the corporate sector (though with its largest numbers in the clerical areas and with overtones of social control from many state employees to welfare claimants). Such a wholesale proliferation of class positions, plus the narrowing of the differences between classes, seems almost to amount to a decomposition of the class structure, rather than a recomposition.

Such a complex set of class positions may seem startling to most readers, accustomed to thinking of the British class system as tripartite and the dominant political division between working-class Labour and middle- and upper-class Conservative. From an international perspective, it may look less surprising, given the wide range of party systems in other advanced societies. For example, Vanlaer (1984), in attempting to map political groupings in 18 countries of Europe, notes that these societies contain mixtures of four fundamental cleavages: church–state, centre–periphery, capital–labour and rural–urban. The emergence of political parties, and hence of politically active alliances of party positions, differs sharply from country to country, with the UK being an exceptional case of capital–labour bipartisan division, and with several countries having major Christian democratic or agrarian parties. *Politics in Transition* (Cochrane and Anderson, 1989) provides a fuller exploration of the way political divisions and disputes have changed in the UK, but the implication for the present argument is that, unless we are to conclude that economic class is unimportant as a basis for politics, it seems arguable that economic class creates a variety of class positions which then interact with contingent factors in generating a system of self-conscious political parties.

An approximate indication of the proportions of the UK labour force in some of these positions is given by Rose and Marshall's (1986) attempt to fit British socio-economic groups into Wright's (1985) matrix of divisions between property, organizational and skill assets, as reproduced in Figure 3.5. The relatively small proportions in all the cells except 9 and 12 emphasize that there is a wide range of possibilities for alliances and antagonisms between groups. Wright's own surveys in the USA and Sweden confirmed this by showing different patterns of similarity and differences between cells for different variables (such as income and attitudes) and between countries. Moreover, his formulation does not recognize the state/capitalist division, so even these multiple cells may be heterogeneous. The more complex the structure of class positions, the more difficult, and yet the more important, the process of class formation, which has the potential to reduce them to small numbers of self-conscious class groupings.

Assets in the means of production

Owners of means of production		Non-owners (wage labourers)					
1 Bourgeoisie 2.0%	4 Expert managers 5.2%	7 Semi-credentialled managers 8.7%	10 Uncredentialled managers 2.9%	+
2 Small employers 4.5%	5 Expert supervisors 1.6%	8 Semi-credentialled supervisors 4.3%	11 Uncredentialled supervisors 3.5%	> 0
3 Petty bourgeoisie 6.0%	6 Expert non-managers 2.1%	9 Semi-credentialled workers 22.4%	12 Proletarians 36.9%	−
	+	> 0	−	

Organization assets

Skill/credential assets

Figure 3.5   Distribution of the UK labour force into new Wright classes according to socio-economic group

The process of class formation which intervenes between economic differentiation and the formation of active self-conscious classes and other groupings is often characterized as an open-ended and somewhat nebulous process. However, one strand of it seems both more approachable in practice and more significant in principle. This stems from Barbalet's (1986) discussion of status as involving *enforceable* norms, and leads on to the use of state power to intervene in material rewards, through tax and welfare systems, and to alter groups' ability to negotiate or compete successfully – for example, in defining employment rights, union powers and responsibilities, or monopolies legislation. The tendency of the British state has been to consolidate the position of owners, but with some appreciable gains by other segments of the population. Some of these gains may have been attributable to other strengths (e.g. possession of credentials), but, at the extreme, welfare payments depend not on economic power but on some notion of the rights and duties of citizenship. It is perhaps significant that the two periods this century when there has been greatest emphasis on redistribution have been after the two world wars, when the benefits of national solidarity were apparent. Beyond that, the existence of state socialist societies is a reminder that state power has the potential to radically revise the meaning of economic power. The political processes by which enforceable norms are created and modified then begins to look like the *central* question in class formation. The tendency of the liberal democratic state to allow capital to remain pre-eminent in terms of economic and political power becomes a more important problem than the operation of capital *per se*.

In this regard, Roemer's definition of capitalist exploitation offers a much sharper view of the contemporary class structure than do the multi-class structures discussed above. Using figures given in Chapter 2, section 2.6, one can see that the national average holding of wealth, Roemer's 'alienable assets', was about £24 250 per adult in 1986. Thus the top one per cent of wealth owners have twenty times their per capita share, the top ten per cent five times their per capita share. The next 15 per cent have one and a half times their per capita share, while the next 25 per cent have only three-quarters of their share. In Roemer's terms only the top quarter of wealth owners are exploiters while three quarters of the adult population are exploited. In those terms, a proportion of the professional and managerial groups, and all intermediate and manual groups, remain exploited. If one accepted that complete equality is not a reasonable criterion, and that some variation from the average is reasonable to reward hard work and/or special ability, perhaps only the top five or ten per cent would be seen as exploiters. This is a figure not far different from the number of owners, so in these terms Marx's division of people into the two classes of owners and non-owners is not removed from actual experience, as it is in terms of the functions, consumption and lifestyles of different kinds of worker.

Finally, it is important to acknowledge that the view of class presented here is necessarily incomplete. There are a number of other social cleavages which have not been fully discussed. Three of these are taken up in succeeding chapters: *race* and *gender* are two of the significant status groups recognized by Parkin, and *consumption cleavages* are the result of state intervention increasing or decreasing opportunities for consumption. As further social divisions, cross-cutting those based on economic class, these cleavages further fragment society and multiply the options for divisions and alliances.

4   Race and the class structure

Philip Sarre

Contents

4.1 Introduction

One of the most obvious changes in British society since the Second World War has been the growth of identifiable minorities in the population. From the 1950s, the minorities which attracted most comment, both in the mass media and the academic literature, were those coming from the West Indies and the Indian subcontinent, who were initially referred to as 'coloured immigrants', officially defined as of 'New Commonwealth ethnic origin', and more recently recognized as black British. The range of terms used to describe these groups is partly a result of their variety, and partly a result of change over time (from a period of immigration in the 1950s and '60s to the emergence of relatively settled minorities in the 1970s and '80s), but particularly because of the intense political and academic debates about the nature of the changes which were taking place. In these debates, questions of newness, national origin and culture were very much in play, but the empirical emphasis on non-white groups provides prima facie evidence that race was a major factor.

These debates ranged from straightforward empirical questions (who were these immigrants, how many were there, what were they doing in the UK?), through rather more difficult questions of intention (why had they come, would they stay?), to even more difficult theoretical questions (how did these migrants from the Third World fit into the British social structure, how they might change it?), and to deep moral questions (had they a right to be here, should be regarded as fully equal?).

Within this context, this chapter concentrates on one major issue: *how have these minorities fitted into and/or changed the British class structure*? The previous chapter has shown that to answer this requires evaluation of (a) the position of the racial minorities in relation to the ownership and control of the means of production, including sale of labour power, and (b) the effects of status categories, in this case of racial categories and of citizenship. In seeking an answer to these questions, this chapter will draw on empirical materials about origins, intentions and activities and also touch upon moral issues, but it will concentrate on relations to the economy, the state and the majority society. This is to recognize that the discussion of the relationship between race and class cannot be confined to analysis of abstract categories: the relationship is a particular and concrete example of the process of class formation taking place over time, which involves the assimilation of pre-capitalist differences, for example race, caste and religion, into an advanced society. It involves group values and perceptions forged under imperialism, as well as those generated in particular places, especially the inner cities, at particular times. To simplify these complexities, the following analysis divides the subject into two periods: the first (section 4.3) covers the period of immigration, from about 1950 to 1970, and the second (section 4.4) covers the position of the minorities during the period of recession, starting in the early 1970s and continuing until the present. Before these substantive analyses, section 4.2 will outline a range of theoretical views of the relationship between race and class in the UK. This should help to orientate your reading of the descriptive sections, which will, in turn, provide evidence against which the theoretical views can be assessed.

4.2   Race and class: theoretical debates

4.2.1   Introduction

The debates about the importance of race and class as influences on the experience and action of the minorities are complex, because they potentially involve all the disagreements about class (as introduced in Chapter 3), plus disagreements about the concept of race, and about the relative importance of, and interactions between, the two. This chapter will rely on Chapter 3 to help identify positions and arguments about class, and focus on the discussions of the interactions between race and class. In doing so, it will avoid being drawn into debates about race per se, and adopt the following position on the nature of racial differences.

The term '**race**' is an extremely problematic one and has been applied in the past to many groups, which no one would describe as races today. Banton (1987) has recently reviewed the vast literature relating to the concept of race and shown conclusively that there is no valid connection between the scientific use of the term and societal definitions. This is confirmed in Rose and Lewontin (1983). In science, a race is characterized by genetic homogeneity, whereas social definitions of race are usually unsystematic and centre on a few characteristics, notably skin colour, regardless of the great variation in other characteristics. As a result, racial groups may be very varied in biological characteristics and lack clear boundaries. The West Indians are even more complex because they are varied in terms of proportions of African, European and sometimes American or Asian stock, and hence of skin colour. Britain also contains many children resulting from marriages and relationships between members of 'different' groups. In spite of this, commonsense usage and academic debates tend to treat minorities as if they can be unequivocally categorized in one group or other.

This rough and ready tendency is compounded by a tendency to assume a correlation between racial and cultural characteristics, often using territorial origins as a label. 'West Indians' and 'Asians' are often treated as if they were homogenous groups rather than categories which lump together people of different racial, cultural and national origins, some of whom are drawn from different sides of conflicts, like those between India, Pakistan and Bangladesh, Sikh and Hindu, or Trinidadians of African and Asian origin. For these varied groups and subgroups, the major unifying factor is their shared experience of suspicion, discrimination and hostility at the hands of the white British. This leads on to a further paradox – which I propose to participate in – namely, the designation of this highly varied collection of different people as *black*. In the rest of this chapter I shall at times use the term '*black*' to span people of African, Caribbean and south Asian ethnic origin. I do so while recognizing that it is a non-literal umbrella term for highly varied people, many of whom would not accept it as referring to themselves. However, it is not only a better term than alternatives, like non-white (negative) or coloured (has different usage elsewhere), it has the positive feature of accepting that the meaning of the term is defined in relation to the prevailing 'white' British culture, and it has overtones of a rallying cry to unite to secure better treatment. It is explicitly an ideological term as well as a (rough) description, but as such it may be a two-edged sword, used by insiders to promote solidarity, but by outsiders to impose separation and closure.

For this purpose a cultural definition of ethnicity is sufficient. There have, though, been attempts in the past to construct theories of 'scientific' **racism**, but these were primarily attempts to justify certain forms of social programme – for example, imperialism, genocide of the Jews and apartheid – and they do not stand up well to critical examination. There is also a tendency to extrapolate from ethnicity to other characteristics: British history over several centuries shows a repeated tendency to assert that immigrant groups (both white and black) are lazy, dirty, dishonest and, most unforgivable of all, prone to breed like rabbits. There have been attempts to provide scientific proof of some of these beliefs, for example by using IQ tests to assert that American blacks are on average less intelligent than whites. The problem for such tests is that cultural differences overlay racial ones, and that differences between groups tend to narrow as their culture and experience become more similar. In this chapter, I take the view that race is not a scientific concept, but a socially defined one. In other words, what matters is the way groups are separated in general usage. This tends to vary between places, so that, for example, in Germany and Switzerland racist language is used against white groups whereas in the UK it is now selectively applied to groups of black people.

To say that race is not a scientific concept is not to deny that race as socially defined has real effects. Centuries of imperialism have created a status distinction in which blacks are in general expected to be inferior to whites in abilities and entitlements. The independence of India was sufficiently recent for the notion of black equality to have hardly begun to penetrate British society before immigration brought appreciable numbers of blacks into Britain – usually to inferior areas, jobs and housing. The facts of racial disadvantage could then feed the stereotypes of inferiority in an ongoing vicious circle.

4.2.2   Views of race and class

When discussing the relationship between the complex concepts of race and class, there are three broad positions which can be argued: (1) that class is the major division with race having minor and secondary effects; (2) that race is the major division, with class being secondary; and (3) that the two factors are interrelated in a complex way, with both having significant effects. All three positions have been argued in interpreting the position of post-1950 black settlers in Britain. As you might expect from your reading of Chapter 3, there is a tendency for Marxist scholars to emphasize class and for Weberian scholars to give more primacy to race. However, this tendency is by no means absolute and there is considerable overlap of views. Some of the most interesting developments have been among neo-Marxists concerned with the roles of race, class and culture in political struggles. The easiest way into these debates is to look first at the positions which prioritize single factors, and then to consider the more complex interactions.

The argument for *class primacy* is inherent in traditional Marxism, with its emphasis on the economic determination of social relations and the fundamental antagonism between bourgeoisie and proletariat. In this view the objective position of black workers is as workers, and the only role accorded to race is in retarding the emergence of a self-conscious proletarian class-for-itself, because divisions between black and white workers prevent recognition of their objective identity of interest. This does leave room for racial divisions to affect the process of actual class formation, though not in defining objective class position. In fact, few scholars interested in immigration and race relations took up this position. Perhaps the closest approximation came in a more general study of the British class structure by Westergaard and Resler (1975), who argued that, 'preoccupied with the disabilities that attach to colour, liberal reformers and research workers have been busy rediscovering what in fact are common disabilities of class . . .' (p. 359). However, after reducing the question to one of class, they made it more complex by going on to argue that it was wrong to assume that all New Commonwealth immigrants were in unskilled manual work, and that 'professional, white-collar and skilled manual blacks tend to be left aside in the stereotypes of public debate and research alike'. In so doing, they posed a problem that many other theorists have chosen to ignore.

An elaboration of the class primacy position, derived originally from Engels, is to note that British workers were favoured in class position because they participated in the exploitation of workers in the colonies. The immigration of ex-colonial citizens into the UK, and into manual work with poor pay and/or conditions, could then be regarded as 'internal colonialism': the black immigrants were physically present in the UK, but in effect in the same subordinate position as they had been in the colonies. A reformulation of this argument came from Castles and Kosack (1973), who interpreted the massive influx of migrant workers into Western Europe as capitalism drawing on an international 'reserve army of labour'. The fact that most of these workers came from countries without former colonial connections, were on temporary contracts, and did not enjoy European citizenship rights led them to argue that they were objectively a lower division of the working class. They extended this argument to the UK and 'Commonwealth immigrants', but the fact that the latter were entitled to remain indefinitely, and to full citizenship rights, leaves a question over this interpretation.

A smaller-scale study of West Indian workers in London led Phizacklea and Miles (1980) to formulate a different interpretation. They accepted that their respondents were, in economic terms, working class, but argued that a range of differences between them and the native working class could best be clarified by using the notion of a class being divisible into *fractions*. In their terms, West Indians were a **racialized class fraction**, for whom the ideological category of race produced different treatment, attitudes and political behaviour. In later developments of this idea, *Miles* (1982, 1984) also recognized the existence of a racialized fraction of the petty bourgeoisie.

The effective overlap of neo-Marxist and neo-Weberian thought in the face of the complexities of the position of the minorities is shown by the conclusions of Rex and Tomlinson (1979) from a study of Asian and West Indian migrants to Handsworth, Birmingham. Using a Weberian analysis – which accepted that the minorities were working class in economic terms, but which argued that they were disadvantaged in status and power by their colour, and hence less favoured in areas of consumption, like housing – they concluded that the migrants were an underclass, torn between the British class structure and their Third World connections and aspirations. Using an argument and method quite similar to those of Phizacklea and Miles, Rex and Tomlinson reached the same conclusion as Castles and Kosack reached on the basis of economistic reasoning!

A more single-minded attempt to move away from class primacy and to construct a sharper Weberian interpretation, drawing on Marshall's concept of citizenship, was made by Rose (1969) who argued that a crucial determinant of the early period of New Commonwealth migration was, or ought to have been, their status as 'Citizens of the UK and Colonies'. This gave them full civil, political and social rights immediately on arrival, as well as free entry and exit, and so placed them in a quite different *de jure* position from that of alien guest workers in Europe. However, the results of the Survey of Race Relations, many of which appear later in the book, showed that the importance of the *de jure* status of citizenship was directly challenged by the *de facto* status of colour or race. This leads on to theoretical positions which stress that race and racism are the key factors in explaining minority settlement.

One theorist who was willing to focus on *de facto* processes rather than search for underlying structural explanations, and who therefore began his analysis with race and not class, was Parkin (1979). He returned to Weber to argue that the status attached to racial differences could potentially form a social cleavage independent from class, and that it could at times be more important as a basis for collective action. Indeed, he refers with approval to other authors who contend that race has been a more important division than class during much of history, though he does not commit himself to this view. According to Parkin, status groups engage in two forms of collective action to maximize their access to desirable positions, goods and services, namely, **closure** against lower groups, and **usurpation** into the privileged position of higher groups. The definition of, and the balance between, status groups then becomes an outcome of success and failure in political and ideological struggles.

Parkin's view of struggles between status groups does not dwell on the possibility that underlying class positions might determine the distribution of resources for struggle. However, it is clearly the case that the fate of a relatively small minority is likely to be determined principally by decisions taken within the majority, and that the collective actions of the minority are in large part reactions to the majority. This explains why the position of ethnic minorities within a society cannot be explained by focusing on the minority alone; the reaction of the whole society is important. Many crucial changes result from struggles within the majority about the proper treatment of the minorities. Parkin's theoretical position leaves open the possibility of a wide range of processes and causal effects, spanning all the influences suggested by the other theorists.

An attempt at an interactionist view has been undertaken over a decade by the staff of the Centre for Contemporary Cultural Studies at the University of Birmingham. In a pair of major books (Hall *et al.*, 1978; CCCS, 1982) and associated papers, they have developed a neo-Marxist approach which has moved away from production relations to cultural relations. Although the existence of class fractions is recognized, this analysis gives much more attention to relations between racial minorities and the state, especially in the form of the police, than relations to the economy. In these conflicts, the distinctive cultures of some of the minorities have been a basis of resistance, linking back to struggles against colonialism in their countries of origin.

A recent development of this line of argument has come from *Gilroy* (1987). He argues that there are very subtle interactions between race and class, so that race may be seen by black people as an alternative basis of political action to class, but in the process be a factor in class formation. He argues that the 1980s have seen the development of a new racism which emphasizes affiliation, or lack of affiliation, to a supposed British national culture and focuses hostility on culturally separate groups – whether Asians with distinctive dress and social organizations, or West Indians exhibiting the symbols of Rastafari – rather than the mere possession of a black skin. Another key argument is that, at a national level, left-wing politics have failed to represent racial minorities, and resistance to economic disadvantage and state repression is increasingly focused in particular urban communities, where black and white residents work together on issues of mutual concern and contribute to a shared culture. Gilroy's analysis makes the point that a thoroughgoing interactionist view involves renegotiating the practical meaning of terms like race, class, culture and racism in the course of social change.

Activity 4.1

In formulating the concept of a racialized class fraction, *Miles* (1982) treats class as given and race as ideological. In the light of the arguments presented above, assess the validity of Miles' view.

Summary of section 4.2

Before moving on to look at some of the events of the last forty years in the light of these theoretical debates, it will be useful to summarize the range of factors which may be involved, and to recognize that what is at issue is their relative strength and the degree to which they exert a fixed effect or are subject to revision as a result of other influences. In doing so, it will be helpful to refer to the conceptual diagram in Figure 4.1.

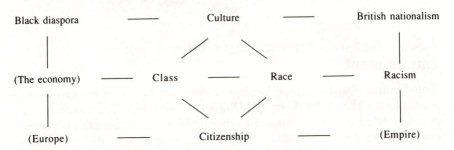

Figure 4.1   Race and class: a conceptual agenda

In thinking through the relationship between class and race, it is necessary to assess the strengths of influences in each direction between pairs of factors. Thus economic class may limit black groups' economic and political power, but the relationship may not be one way – black people may be chosen for some economic roles but excluded from others on the basis of race. Class affiliations as perceived and acted upon may be defined in racial terms as well as in terms of measures like asset ownership, organizational power, credentials and skills. Race is not itself an objective scientific designation but one which is culturally and ideologically defined; systematic or casual racism conditions the attribution of racial status. This status may be acted upon in relation to ethnic cultures and/or biological characteristics, and these cultures may be defined in an inner city community and/or in an international diaspora of Asian and Afro-Caribbean people. A part of the negotiation between the majority and the minorities concerns the recognition, or withholding, of full UK citizenship, an issue which has strong links back to the British Empire, and weaker, but still significant, links to current moves to redefine Britain as a part of Europe.

Having outlined a range of theoretical positions on the intersection between race and class, and identified a number of strands to be considered, it is time to look in more detail at some of the events of the last forty years. Inevitably, the following account is nothing like objective evidence; I have necessarily been selective and may have favoured particular interpretations, so you should scrutinize it carefully and also look for additional evidence. Part of the evidence is itself a matter of interpretation and debate: the effects of immigration control and the causes of the urban riots being examples. These particular debates may fit into particular overall positions or might be compatible with several. You will have to study sections 4.3 and 4.4 very actively. To encourage this, you might like to look ahead to the activities at the end of these two sections.

4.3   Immigrant labour and the class structure

4.3.1   Reasons for coming: citizenship and employment

British contacts with black people have a very long history – reaching back, according to Hiro (1973), to AD 200 when Septimius Severus, a north African, ruled Britain as Roman Emperor. Most of the contacts occurred overseas, notably in the slave trade of the sixteenth to the eighteenth centuries, and in the imperial system of the nineteenth and twentieth centuries. Yet, some blacks have long found their way to Britain, as evidenced by an attempt by Queen Elizabeth I to expel them. During the first half of the twentieth century there were black settlements in many British seaports and appreciable numbers of black students in colleges and universities. Large numbers of black people, from the Empire and the United States, came into, or passed through, the UK during the Second World War, but were sent home after 1945. The official expectation was of a return to the pre-war situation, but this expectation was quickly shattered abroad by the Indian push for independence, and at home by the arrival of ships full of West Indians looking for work in Britain.

In 1951, there were just over 1.5 million people of foreign birth resident in the UK, of whom 200 000 came from the New Commonwealth (including India, Pakistan, Africa and the West Indies). By 1971, there were 3 million overseas-born residents, of whom just under 1.15 million came from the New Commonwealth. These New Commonwealth (NC) immigrants had produced a further third of a million children born in the UK, to produce a total of just under 1.5 million UK residents of New Commonwealth Ethnic Origin. Clearly, during this period, there was substantial immigration from the New Commonwealth, though the figures also show continued growth in the Irish, EC and Old Commonwealth (i.e. Australia, Canada, New Zealand and South Africa) categories which together equalled the NC born population in 1971. Two principle questions arise from these figures: why was there so much movement into the UK and why were NC people so outstanding a feature?

The distinctive feature of the British economy from 1946 to the late 1950s was a chronic shortage of labour. The British government made strenuous efforts to alleviate this shortage in the immediate post-war period by admitting refugees from Eastern Europe, and then by actively seeking European Volunteer Workers. Yet, in spite of the rapid influx and the cultural contrasts between Poles, Latvians, Ukranians and their British hosts, there were few major problems. As early as 1969, Rose wrote:

> Between 1946 and 1950 this country experienced immigration on a scale not matched either previously or at the height of the entry from the Commonwealth ten years later. . . . Twenty years later, the very existence of this migration is almost forgotten and the term 'immigrant' automatically suggests colour – although now, as before, coloured faces are in a minority among newcomers. (Rose, 1969, p. 20)

Perhaps the crucial reason for the different response to European and New Commonwealth migration was the fact that the British view focused on 'colour and citizenship' and not upon **labour migration**.

The major events which focused attention on citizenship were the independence of India and Pakistan in 1947, and the consequent British Nationality Act of 1948. This Act, the first in a series of revisions of the legal basis of citizenship, was the most liberal. The status of 'British subject', previously shared by all citizens of the Empire, was divided into two categories. 'Citizens of the UK and Colonies' included both British born and bred and the populations of dependent territories. 'Citizens of newly independent Commonwealth countries' were recognized as such, but given freedom of entry to the UK, full civil rights on arrival, and the right to register as a citizen of the UK and Colonies after four years. In spite of this 'open door' arrangement, immigration from the New Commonwealth was slow until 1952 when the United States stopped migration from the West Indies. Then, as early arrivals sent back news of success, and a few British employers travelled to the West Indies to recruit, numbers of West Indian migrants grew rapidly to 30 000 in 1956.

The emphasis in the 1950s, even in sober social science texts, was on the sudden appearance of these 'dark strangers' with the assumption that they had come for their own reasons, and not because British industry needed them. In only a few years, conflicts over jobs, housing and places of entertainment, plus generations of imperial attitudes, were enough to unleash race riots in Notting Hill and Nottingham (in 1958), in which large groups of whites, including Teddy boys, attacked black people and their property. The result of these tensions was increasing pressure to control Commonwealth immigration, which led to the Commonwealth Immigration Act of 1962. This removed freedom of entry from Commonwealth and colonial citizens whose passport was not issued by the British government, and made entry conditional on application for an employment voucher. Thus, access to citizenship rights was removed from former colonial citizens except for those needed by the economy.

Growing British hostility also helped to stimulate immigrant political organization. Scattered groups joined together in 1958 to form the Indian Workers Association of Great Britain, and there were attempts to join with West Indian organizations, as in the Committee of Afro-Asian-Caribbean Organization, which lobbied against the 1962 Act. However, the heterogeneity of origins and differences over goals between moderates and radicals made these national organizations hard to hold together, though the local organizations continued, often sustaining a large membership and running recreational and welfare facilities. Much of the political activity of associations like the IWA has been in support of Labour candidates in local and Parliamentary elections, stimulated by hostile Conservative proposals and candidates like Peter Griffiths ('If you want a nigger for a neighbour, vote Labour') in Smethwick in 1963. The decision to use the title Indian *Workers* Association – which Hiro (1973, p. 140) states was quite deliberate – and to support Labour, does show an explicit link between migrant organizations and class in the early years.

The conventional view is that the 1962 Act saved the UK from a 'flood' of New Commonwealth immigrants. However, severe doubt is thrown on this in a detailed study of West Indian migration by Peach (1965, 1968). His argument separates into four stages. First, he showed that the rate of West Indian immigration in the 1950s was closely matched to the availability of vacant jobs in the UK. When vacancies fell in late 1956 and again in late 1958, arrivals fell well below 3 000 per quarter, while, when vacancies soared in late 1959, arrivals rose to a peak of over 15 000 before falling back. The second phase of the argument was that arrivals grew in 1960–1 although vacancies fell, precisely because it was apparent that the government was moving towards controls, in spite of pressure from employers and the Treasury to maintain free entry. Thirdly, Peach shows that, although New Commonwealth immigration fell in the year after controls were introduced, only 14 680 of the 44 750 vouchers issued were used – which he interprets as self-regulation. Thus under-use of vouchers persisted through the 1960s.

The final point in Peach's argument was that the Act changed the nature of migration from the movement of single workers, arguably with the intention of returning home, towards the movement of their dependants. In other words, the act changed what had been intended as short-term labour migration into permanently settled minority communities. However, the change was not unequivocal: Bohning (1972) later showed that, of those admitted for settlement, only about a third did settle in the sense that they stayed four years and took British nationality. Also, Peach's argument is not totally conclusive: others have pointed out that the period of self-regulation was short (though he later extended the analysis to 1974, and confirmed his case (Peach, 1978)), and that there were other important factors, notably the ending of Indian controls on emigration in 1960. The immediate result of this was to increase the rate of arrivals from 6000 in 1960 to over 20 000 in 1961.

The seriousness of the challenge posed to successive governments by black immigration and hostile white response is demonstrated by the frequency, and critics would say incoherence and dubious morality, of legislation. The 1962 Act was extended in 1968 to apply controls to people with UK-issued passports but without 'substantial personal connection' to the UK. This was apparently an attempt to deter entry by East African Asians, who were forced to choose Kenyan or Ugandan citizenship or leave. In practice it became necessary to admit substantial numbers of both groups, who would otherwise have become stateless in effect while holding UK passports.

One result of the Acts was to leave substantial confusion as to who should be regarded as UK nationals when the UK joined the EEC. It therefore became necessary to bring in the Immigration Act 1971 to try to clarify the matter. This Act adopted two principles: (1) British subjects having the right of abode, established by at least five years' residence in the UK, and (2) Citizens of the UK and Colonies by their own, or a parent's or grandparent's birth, registration or naturalization. This is usually interpreted by critics as using the principle of 'patriality' to restrict British nationality as far as possible to whites and keep out the very large numbers of British and Commonwealth blacks who had not already gained a foothold. However, the result was somewhat more complex, especially because of the special status of Gibraltar:

> Thus we have patrial British subjects with and without the right to free movement in the EEC and non patrial British subjects with and without that right. And we have coloured citizens of the UK and colonies who are legally settled in the UK without the right of movement and white citizens of the UK and colonies who have never settled in this country but possess this right. (Böhning, 1972, p. 154)

By 1971, the preferential treatment of former colonial citizens as against aliens had been substantially eroded, and EEC citizens were now replacing them as the preferred group. However, the complexities of post-colonial arrangements, plus the contradictions produced by using administrative formulae to achieve selective controls on black groups, had produced legislation which, as Böhning puts it 'completely baffled the Eurocrats' (p. 133), and was arguably both racist and contrary to the Treaty of Rome. The definition of British nationals used in joining the EEC was even more restrictive than the 1971 Act, as it excluded from freedom of movement in the European Community, not only Citizens of the UK and Colonies without right of abode in the UK, but also citizens of independent Common-wealth countries with right of abode.

The contradictions in the immigration and nationality legislation were exacerbated by their counterpoint with race relations legislation. The early migrants had met explicit racial discrimination (documented irrefutably and at great length by the Political and Economic Planning (PEP) survey, (Daniel, 1968)), which was abhorrent to the ideology of a multiracial Commonwealth and the liberal conscience of some British legislators. While it was widely accepted that control on black immigration was necessary 'to calm public anxiety', one of the rationalizations was that this would improve race relations for those already here. Accordingly, the Race Relations Act of 1965 was brought in to outlaw discrimination in public places, like restaurants, bars and dance halls, and the Act of 1968 extended the prohibi-tion to discrimination over housing and employment. However, whereas immigration controls were imposed with great, and often excessive zeal, race relations legislation aimed largely at conciliation, so few prosecutions occurred and *de facto* discrimination remained a common feature of British society requiring further legislation (see section 4.3).

A crucial influence in the late 1960s was Enoch Powell, whose speeches, notably the 'Rivers of blood' speech (20 April 1968) put into words the most lurid fears and prejudices of the British. Although Powell's speech was condemned by Labour and Conservative leaders, over 100 000 people wrote to him, 98 per cent in support of his views. There were hundreds of strikes and demonstrations, including London dockers who lobbied Parliament against the Race Relations Bill. Public pressure for further restrictions on immigration and against firm implementation of the Race Relations Act provoked politicians of all parties to take ever more hostile positions. The upsurge of white hostility led to a rapid reappraisal of their situation by many blacks, resulting in a new identification with the Black Power movement in the USA and the West Indies, and the development of a new solidarity with West African migrants in Britain. New militant black organizations were formed, for example, the Black People's Alliance – 'a militant front *for* Black Consciousness and *against* racialism'. The liberal dream of assimila-tion had been replaced by a new polarization between black and white, in which the best that could be hoped for was coexistence between separate communities, and the worst that could be feared was a growing climate of racism and violence.

Academic responses to the growth of black minorities in the UK evolved quite dramatically through the period. As already mentioned, it was common in the 1950s to dwell on the 'strangeness' of the new arrivals, and ascribe British avoidance or hostility to the fear that they would not know the unwritten rules of how to behave in the UK. More considered judge-ments, most notably the volume resulting from a five-year group project organized by the Institute of Race Relations, recognized that these groups were not strangers, but people with a well defined and inferior situation as colonial citizens, who had rather surprisingly turned up in the 'mother country'. However, in the course of an 815 page book with enormous amounts of detailed information and policy suggestions, focusing on the question of colour and citizenship, there is an odd silence about the fundamental question of *why* the minorities had come (Rose, 1969).

This issue was dramatically reorientated by the publication of a book taking a Marxist view of labour migration in the whole of Europe. Castles and Kosack (1973) revealed to the insular British that, while they had been experiencing New Commonwealth immigration, every other country in Europe had also experienced immigration from less developed countries. Furthermore, where countries had lacked former colonial citizens to provide labour, they had been obliged to recruit aliens, especially from southern and eastern Europe. From this point of view, the fact that many of our arrivals were colonial citizens was accidental, except in so far as it provided greater political rights once here. The crucial cause of migration into Europe was European capital's shortage of labour.

This type of migration has had a long history: France had one million foreign workers in 1886, and Germany contained large numbers of Poles before the First World War. The main sources of labour before the Second World War were Poland, Czechoslovakia and Italy, but France and Britain recruited many coloured colonial citizens in the First World War, an action repeated by Britain in the Second World War.

After 1945, Europe was expected to have a labour surplus, especially in West Germany which received over eight million refugees from East Germany. The opposite soon proved to be the case as economic expansion exceeded the local supplies of labour, and foreigners were sought to fill the least wanted jobs. The number and origin of workers in the EEC countries in 1973 is shown in Table 4.1. It is clear from this table that West Germany and France had considerably larger numbers of foreign workers than the UK. In fact, this table omits two of the countries most dependent on foreign workers: Switzerland, which had one million, comprising 16 per cent of the population and 27 per cent of the labour force, and Sweden with almost 700 000.

The experience of these large immigrant groups varied from country to country, but they had reduced civil and social rights, except where they were colonial citizens. Power (1972) characterized France and West Germany as two extreme cases. In France, *laissez-faire* had prevailed, with immigrants moving spontaneously, and bringing about one dependant per worker, so that there were about 3.5 million foreign nationals in all. The main sources were Algeria, Portugal, Spain and Italy. Many of the foreign workers lived in appalling conditions in shanty towns, cellars, attics and doss-houses, although the government was making increased efforts to cope. There was racial tension, though this was mainly directed at Algerians rather than black Africans or West Indians. By contrast, immigration in West Germany was controlled by inter-governmental agreements, and more migrants had a definite job to come to. Many lived in company hostels somewhat segregated from fellow workers. Dependants could only enter if the worker could

Table 4.1 Migrant workers employed in the communities, 1973

| Country of origin | Country of employment | | | | | | | | | Estimated total of migrant workers employed in the Communities by nationality during 1973 |
	Belgium yearly average 1972	Denmark 1.1.71	Germany at the end of January 1973	France 31.12.72	Ireland 1972	Italy yearly average 1971	Luxembourg yearly average 1972	The Netherlands 15.6.72	United Kingdom 1971 (approx.)	
Belgium	-	155	11 504	25 000	50	539	6 700	23 308	13 500	80 000
Denmark	200	-	3 954	1 000	50	248	-	180	2 000	7 500
Germany	4 500	4 080	-	25 000	210	7 190	3 800	12 000	20 000	78 000
France	15 000	526	54 669	-	210	4 145	6 200	1 700	20 000	102 000
Ireland	100	150	806	1 000	-	300	-	180	470 000	472 000
Italy	87 000	477	409 448	230 000	500	-	10 900	9 000	121 000	869 000
Luxembourg	1 400	1	2 209	2 000	7	32	-	60	500	6 200
The Netherlands	13 500	593	75 127	5 000	250	1 146	600	-	6 000	102 000
United Kingdom	5 000	2 515	19 839	10 000	-	4 500	100	3 800	-	46 000
EEC	126 700	8 497	577 556	299 000	1 277	18 100	28 300	50 228	652 000	1 762 700
Spain	30 000	934	179 157	270 000	-	2 006	1 700	12 981	30 000	526 000
Greece	7 000	3 453	268 408	5 000	-	768	-	1 126	50 000	332 000
Yugoslavia	1 200	4 520	465 611	50 000	-	4 103	400	8 388	4 000	538 000
Portugal	3 500	934	63 991	380 000	-	631	8 500	2 567	5 000	469 000
Turkey	12 000	5 730	528 414	18 000	-	317	-	21 588	3 000	589 000
Algeria	3 000	-	1 700	450 000	-	-	-	-	600	456 000
Morocco	16 500	1 645	15 261	120 000	-	-	-	12 843	2 000	168 000
Tunisia	2 100	-	11 124	60 000	-	-	-	-	200	74 000
Other non-Member countries	18 000	11 148	230 575	118 000	843	18 205	2 000	12 259	918 205	1 341 000
Total number of non-Member countries	93 300	28 364	1 769 244	1 471 000	843	26 030	12 600	71 752	1 013 005	4 493 000
TOTAL	220 000	36 861	2 346 800	1 770 000	2 120	44 130	40 900	121 980	1 665 005	6 255 700

Source: EEC Commission, 1973

prove they had accommodation, which was extremely hard to find. Earlier in the process, the West German government had expected to repatriate migrants during slumps, but during a recession in 1966–7 only 300 000 left and one million stayed. It now seemed that migrant labour was a permanent requirement of European economies.

Castles and Kosack's account of the causation of labour migration into Europe differed from earlier accounts in that it contained a built in statement of the position of the 'guest workers' in the class structure. Not only was it the case that migrant workers were being pulled in to fill job vacancies, but it was also argued that they would be left with the most unpleasant and unrewarding jobs, because the locals would take opportunities for upward mobility. In other words, the migrants were definitely part of the working class, and arguably formed a lower division of that class. This was particularly the case in countries that intended to reduce numbers of guest workers during slumps (e.g., West Germany): here the function of the migrants was explicitly to act as an 'industrial reserve army'. As regards Britain, Castles and Kosack's view ignored the substantial proportion of black immigrants in skilled or middle-class jobs (e.g., as doctors and nurses). It also ignored the possibility that concentration in unskilled jobs might itself result from discrimination, so that divisions in terms of race or status were the cause of inferior class position. It was certainly the case that many immigrants, especially in the earlier years, had had higher qualifications, skills and jobs at home than the jobs they were able to secure in the UK.

To clarify the class position of black immigrants in the first periods we are considering, the next sub-section will look at more detailed evidence of their employment position, consumption position (epsecially as shown by housing), and at influences on class formation through education and local area.

4.3.2   Area and jobs: a replacement population

The greater awareness of black immigration in the 1960s led to the appearance of a number of major studies which attempted to give a national perspective on the situation, drawing on the 1961 census and special surveys. Their conclusions tended to mirror at an empirical level the theoretical debate sketched above. The central explanation, first articulated by Peach (1966), of where the migrants lived and of the jobs that they were doing, was that they were acting as a **replacement population** – in other words, they were largely doing unskilled and unpleasant jobs which the native British were not available to do. This led them to concentrate in the areas where these jobs were available, notably in London (which has 11 per cent of the UK's total population and 40 per cent of the black population), the West Midlands (the only other conurbation with a higher proportion of the country's blacks – 15 per cent – than whites – 10 per cent), West Yorkshire and Lancashire, and to occupy poor, inner city housing, often initially in rooming houses. The pattern of settlement, as shown in Figure 4.2, confirmed that jobs were the central cause: relatively few immigrants went to areas where long-term

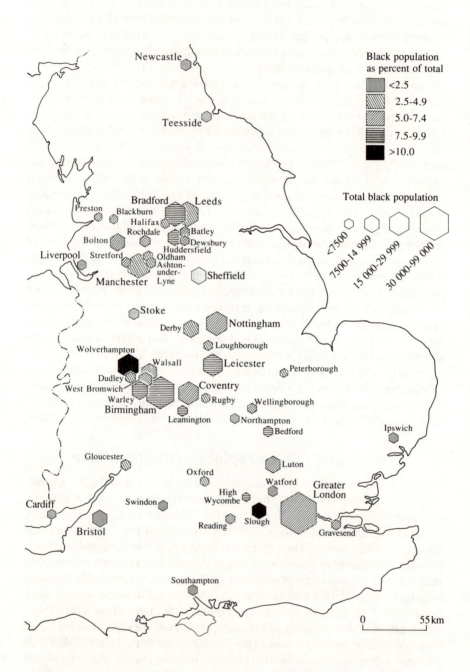

Figure 4.2   Population of New Commonwealth ethnic origin as a percentage of total urban population, 1971

Source: Jones, 1978, Figure 5

economic decline held back job growth even in the boom years of the 1950s and '60s; thus, Tyneside and Glasgow have smaller minority populations than the West Midlands, even today. Even fewer went to the most prosperous areas where job growth meant white-collar work for white Britons. The difference between minority and majority population is so great that three-quarters of the black population live in a set of census enumeration districts that contain only a tenth of the white population (Brown, 1985, p. 20).

Although work was the fundamental reason for the immigrant's presence, jobs did not dictate other aspects of their experience. From the pioneering PEP study (Daniel, 1968) onward, studies repeatedly found that immigrants' housing, schooling and consumer outcomes were poorer than their jobs or incomes would imply. Racial discrimination, which had previously been seen as an essentially individual, psychological aberration, increasingly began to be seen as built into the whole of British society. On the other hand, the migrants had their own reasons for coming, which often involved more than performing the role of unskilled labour, and they began to respond to their disadvantaged situation, both individually and in workplace, neighbourhood and religious groups. For many, 'underclass' or 'racialized fraction of the working class' was a far cry from what they intended.

Before moving on to consider developments in the UK from the mid-1970s to the late 1980s, it is worth looking again at the European context. Böhning (1972) pointed out that it was false to contrast Britain as a country of Commonwealth immigration for settlement too sharply with West Germany as a country of short-term labour migrants. On the one hand, he showed that only about a third of New Commonwealth migrants admitted to the UK actually stayed permanently (the same was true of the earlier European immigrants). But he also showed that even migrations which were intended as short-term by *both* migrants and host country actually developed a momentum of their own. First, they became, in his term, *self-feeding* as the availability of unskilled labour encouraged employers not to move to more capital intensive forms of production and even to reorganize the production process to adjust to less skilled workers. Secondly, they became more permanent as immigrant workers either despaired of earning enough to transform their lives at home, or as they began to aspire to the goods and lifestyle of their new home. In turn, longer stays would lead to family reunion, the birth of children who might have the new nationality, and would be at least partially socialized as Europeans. Again, the growing population would generate new business employment opportunities to serve the needs of migrants. Overall, even the guest workers turned out to generate settled minorities. This process was quite advanced through Europe by the early 1970s, when economic downturn led all European governments to place restrictions on further labour migration. Even before recession began in 1974, as Castles (1984) later showed, Europe was no longer dealing with labour migrants but with racial and ethnic minorities which were 'here for good'. The reserve army of labour had refused demobilization and dug in in their forward positions.

Activity 4.2

In the light of empirical evidence presented in section 4.3, review the range of theoretical positions sketched in section 4.2, and answer the following questions.

1   In view of the evidence, are there any theoretical positions which are clearly inadequate? Why?

2   In constructing an explanation of the place of the ethnic minorities in British society, what emphasis would you put on: (a) economic class; (b) citizenship; (c) 'race'; and (d) interactions between these aspects?

3   Do you think that there are any groups in British society for whom immigration from the black Commonwealth had the intended consequences?

4.4   Responses to recession

The Economy in Question (Allen and Massey, 1988) has established the changing fate of the British economy in the second half of the post-war period. The experience of full employment lasted until 1967, serious recession first appeared in 1974, and worsened dramatically in 1979, lasting, as far as manual workers are concerned, until the present. The move from a situation of labour shortages to one of mass unemployment was a dramatic reorientation of the context of the minorities. It was paralleled by a significant change in the nature of the black minorities themselves: in the early 1980s the proportion of the population of New Commonwealth ethnic origin who were born in the UK, and hence had full citizenship rights, passed 40 per cent. Since then, the proportion has continued to grow, emphasizing that we are increasingly dealing with a black British population rather than an immigrant one. Moreover, although black immigration was increasingly tightly controlled, total numbers of ethnic minority population continued to increase, to 2.1 million in 1982, and 2.4 million in 1985 – some 4.5 per cent of the total population of Great Britain (Shaw, 1988).

The new situation has seen further evolution of legislation dealing with the citizenship status of minority groups, and a continuation of the contradiction between law intended to prevent racial discrimination and a racially discriminatory immigration policy. The first half of this contradiction was expressed in the Race Relations Act, 1976. This both widened the scope of anti-discrimination legislation to prevent discrimination in anything except an ethnic association (e.g. the London Scottish), and extended the concept of discrimination to prohibit indirect discrimination – that is any policy or practice, such as council house residential qualifications, which effectively produces differential results between ethnic groups. Also, the new body charged with applying the act, The Commission for Racial Equality, was given power to subpoena evidence, and its judgements were given the force of law. Although falling well short of the United States' policy of 'affirmative action' (i.e. positive discrimination to offset past inequalities) the Act does represent a quite positive official rejection of racial discrimination. Unfortunately, it has been undermined by the retention, and later tightening, of the effectively discriminatory 1971 Immigration Act and its concept of patriality.

Provoked, perhaps, by the beginnings of recession and disapproval of government liberalism, the early 1970s saw the emergence of the extreme right-wing National Front party as the first serious right-wing political party since Mosley's inter-war British Union of Fascists. Particularly in poor, inner city areas, where blacks and whites were seen to be in competition for scarce resources of housing, employment, and such like, the National Front were able to mobilize whites to the point where in 1975–6 they were seen as posing a serious challenge, even in parliamentary elections. This heightened the pressure on the minorities and their defensive organizations. It also provoked two kinds of response. The obvious response was the formation of the Anti-Nazi League in 1977 and the associated work of Rock Against Racism; their high-profile campaigning seemed to help turn the propaganda tide against the National Front. But a more serious and long-lasting political change was at work, which effectively eliminated the National Front as an electoral force: the Conservative Party was moving to the right and adopting policies which proved even more successful than the National Front in attracting working-class votes. Any satisfaction at the loss of voting support for the National Front must be tempered by allegations that their activities moved to the promotion of racial harassment and violence in areas like the East End of London.

The contradictions of the 1971 Act and the change in the political climate, led to the 1981 British Nationality Act, the need for which had been recognized in the 1970s by the Labour administrations, but which was enacted as one of the earliest laws passed by the Thatcher government. The 1981 Act dismantled the category of 'Citizen of the UK and Colonies', separating British citizenship from citizenship of British dependent territories, but leaving a residual category of British Overseas Citizens, mainly living in Malaysia and Singapore, who were neither entitled to settle in the UK nor to pass on their citizenship to their children. Moreover, Commonwealth citizens, who previously only had to register as British citizens after five years' residence, now had to apply for naturalization in the same way as aliens and were subject to tests of language and good conduct. Whereas all children born in Britain had automatically qualified for British citizenship, the 1981 Act laid down that after 1983 citizenship would only be granted if the parents were *legally settled* in the UK. This status itself was eroded for 'non patrials', as the Act opened up the possibility of deportation for those who committed a crime. Finally, restrictions on bringing in dependants were further tightened, making additional difficulties for older children and parents, making some admissions subject to the ability to support them (in effect, withdrawing rights of access to the welfare state), and withdrawing the Labour government's 'concession' that wives with the right of abode in Britain could bring in husbands without that right, just as British husbands could bring in non-British wives. Critics have argued that this move made the Act sexist and well as racist.

The 1981 British Nationality Act therefore tightened and consolidated previous restrictions on non-white immigration and maintained the legitimation of the argument that race was the crucial problem. Since then, there has been a further hardening of attitudes to NC migration and, at the time of writing (1988) a new Immigration Bill has been introduced to make it even harder to bring in dependants, in spite of the fact that in 1986 the total number of arrivals from the Indian subcontinent was less than 3000. The official determination to reduce black immigration to zero shows that the situation is regarded as too serious to allow any compromise. However, after more than a quarter of a century of legislation on immigration and citizenship, the absurdities remain: it is now easier for a resident of French Guiana to settle in the UK, via France and the EEC freedom of movement policy, than for a resident of (the formerly British) Guyana.

4.4.1   The impact of recession

In considering responses to recession, a major question concerns the impact of unemployment upon different minority groups. Even in the 1960s, it was apparent that black workers tended to suffer more rapid growth of unemployment in recessions. It is also well known that the post-1974 and post-1979 recessions hit manual workers hardest, and that most black workers are manual workers. What, then, were the effects of unemployment on black groups?

This was one of the questions addressed by the 'Third survey of black and white Britain' by the Policy Studies Institute in 1982 (published as Brown, 1985). This survey had the benefit of allowing comparisons with the second (1974) PEP survey. It showed that there had been a selective impact of unemployment: in 1974, white and black groups had shared an unemployment rate of 4 per cent, but by 1982 men of West Indian origin suffered an unemployment rate of 25 per cent, men and women of Asian origin a rate of 20 per cent, and women of West Indian origin a rate of 16 per cent – all well above the white rates of 13 per cent for men and 10 per cent for women. Rates were higher for black youths and in inner city areas. The survey made it possible to analyse the factors underlying these very high rates.

The analyses show differences both on the basis of variations among the minorities and in relation to their situation in the UK. For example, among Asians, the unemployment rate for Muslim men is 27 per cent – twice that of Hindus and Sikhs, whose rate of unemployment is similar to that of white men. Similarly, Asians fluent in English have unemployment rates only a few per cent higher than whites while Asians not fluent in English have rates twice as high. As regards region of residence, the effects are not great; blacks have higher unemployment rates in all regions where they live in considerable numbers. In the inner parts of large cities, the gap between blacks and whites is narrower than elsewhere, while in the outer areas blacks are twice as likely as whites to be unemployed. A good deal of the difference between groups is due to job level: if white men had the same occupational structure as blacks, their unemployment rate would be 18 per cent, rather than the actual 13 per cent, but this is still appreciably less than the 25 per cent rate among West Indians. This suggests that while job structure and concentration in the inner cities explains part of the higher rate of black unemployment, there are appreciable differences which might well result from racial discrimination. Moreover, job structure and residential concentration are themselves influenced by discrimination, as shown in all three of the surveys of the situation of blacks in Britain (Daniel, 1968; Smith, 1977; Brown, 1985).

What, then, is the occupational structure of the black minorities? Table 4.2 gives the breakdown of occupations into five 'classes' for men. Overall, there is a much higher concentration of black men than white men in manual occupations: 83 per cent of West Indians, 73 per cent of Asians and 58 per cent of whites. Within that more blacks do semi-skilled and unskilled jobs. However, there is a large degree of variation between sub-groups of the black population: West Indians and Sikhs have few non-manual workers, but a large preponderance of skilled workers, while Bangladeshis have the highest proportion in semi-skilled and unskilled work. East African Asians and Hindus (partly overlapping categories) actually have more non-manual workers than the white sample, though within the manual groups they have fewer skilled workers.

Brown's analyses show that part of the difference between blacks and whites can be explained by the blacks' lower qualifications, but that, even when qualifications are matched, there remain substantial differences. Moreover, since the majority of manual workers, white as well as black, have no academic or vocational qualifications, lack of qualifications cannot explain the higher concentration in less-skilled manual jobs. When 1982 results were compared with 1974 results, there was little overall narrowing of the occupational gap between blacks and whites to set against the great growth in unemployment.

The job distribution of women (shown in Table 4.3) is markedly different from that of men. Black women are even more disadvantaged than black men, with much lower proportions in professional and managerial positions or in skilled manual work, though with much higher proportions in 'other non-manual' posts. However, because of the greater disadvantages of white women as compared to white men, the discrepancies between white and black women are much less than among men. Even so, there is still twice as high a proportion of black women in semi-skilled jobs as white women.

These survey results both clarify some impressions which began to emerge

Table 4.2 Job levels of men: all employees by ethnic group (percentages)

	White	West Indian	Asian	Indian	Pakistani	Bangladeshi	African Asian	Muslim	Hindu	Sikh
Professional, employer, management	19	5	13	11	10	10	22	11	20	4
Other non-manual	23	10	13	13	8	7	21	8	26	8
Skilled manual and foreman	42	48	33	34	39	13	31	33	20	48
Semi-skilled manual	13	26	34	36	35	57	22	39	28	33
Unskilled manual	3	9	6	5	8	12	3	8	3	6
Base: male employees										
(weighted)	1490	972	2167	847	611	177	495	998	571	452
(unweighted)	591	467	1041	401	298	96	227	507	258	213

Source: Brown, 1985

Table 4.3 Job levels of women: all employees by ethnic group (percentages)

	White	West Indian	Asian	Indian	African Asian	Muslim	Hindu	Sikh
Professional, employer, manager	7	1	6	5	7	(7)	8	3
Other non-manual	55	52	42	35	52	(36)	49	19
Skilled manual and foreman	5	4	6	8	3	(1)	4	10
Semi-skilled manual	21	36	44	50	36	(52)	37	66
Unskilled manual	11	7	2	1	3	(5)	2	2
Base: female employees								
(weighted)	1050	1020	760	431	237	102	322	229
(unweighted)	495	502	340	195	102	45	146	105

Source: Brown, 1985

earlier and pose new questions. They confirm that while there is appreciable aggregate disadvantage in occupational groups, the minorities are quite heterogeneous, and some groups are well established in non-manual occupations. The overlap in occupations is great enough to erode any idea that blacks can be ascribed *en bloc* to the working class, and certainly prohibits the notion that they are all in an underclass in occupational terms. Yet for many blacks, with their great predominance in less skilled manual occupations and their exposure to unemployment, there is a clear concentration in the lowest bands of the class system. Their prospects in an era of mass unemployment, reductions in welfare benefits and tightening immigration controls are not encouraging. At the other end of the occupational ladder, the Asian groups who are apparently overtaking the whites in membership of the top levels demand attention. Accordingly, the next two sections will focus on these two extremes of black experience, and in doing so, questions of culture emerge as central to forms of black response.

4.4.2   Blacks in the inner cities

Black people are so identified with the problems of the inner cities that some statistical indices designed to define problem areas have included concentrations of people born in the New Commonwealth as part of the definition of such areas, along with overcrowding, lack of amenities, unemployment, etc. We have already shown that this logic is false and that black people were concentrated into inner city housing and employment because it was the least attractive to the British, rather than being the cause of the problems. We have also shown that the degree of concentration is overstated and that many blacks, indeed a majority of Asians, live away from the inner areas of the big cities. Yet there is a kernel of truth in the association of the least favoured black people with the inner cities. West Indians are seven times as likely to live in inner London, Birmingham or Manchester as whites, and Asians four times as likely (Brown, 1985, p. 62).

Cross (1987) has argued that location within the inner cities is a more serious source of unemployment and barrier to future recovery than racism. He points out that the male unemployment rates in inner city areas of Birmingham, like Handsworth and Sparkbrook, are over 40 per cent – not because blacks live there, but because of deindustrialization which has caused similar unemployment rates for whites in those areas. In outer city areas, where overall rates of unemployment are much lower, blacks do better, though differentials in relation to whites are larger. Cross recommends both improvements in black education and training, pointing to the existence of highly successful schools in the West Indies, and moving talented black youngsters to areas of job growth, like Swindon and Crawley. He concedes that the inner cities have served as sources of cheap housing, as a political base and a bastion against racial attacks, but he does not regard their problems as soluble without decentralization. However, he admits that it would be impracticable to escape the inner cities altogether, so his 'solution' seems to be one which would increase polarization between deprived inner cities and affluent shires. It appears that he is writing off the inner cities to a spiral of decline, containment and police control.

Cross's view is correct in recognizing the macro-economic pressures on the inner cities, but it may well underestimate their political and cultural significance. After all, the inner city riots, which began in Bristol in 1981 and spread to most major cities as far north as Liverpool and Manchester, did focus the attention of the media on inner city and race problems in a way that rational argument had failed to do, and did place the inner cities on the political agenda of a government which had previously been utterly uninterested in urban problems. The effectiveness of the resulting policies was not great, and was aimed more at developing certain sites with potential for big business, notably the London Docklands, than at any overall improvement. However, non-governmental interests were also active, and the Archbishop of Canterbury's study *Faith in the City* (1985) and the Duke of Edinburgh's enquiry into housing problems joined the Scarman report (HMSO, 1981) on the Brixton disorders as statements of 'establishment concern', which helped legitimate the claims of black political groups to better treatment.

The 1987 election, which saw the inner cities confirmed as the last redoubt of the Labour Party in southern England, and which, for the first time, saw the long-established Labour ethnic vote translated into the election of black MPs, caused Mrs Thatcher to put the inner cities at the centre of policy formation for her third term. After a period in which liberal opinion mistakenly supposed that she meant to tackle urban problems by an injection of state funding, it has become clear that the chosen instruments of policy, including bills on housing, education and the introduction of the 'community charge', are actually calculated to break down existing local authority power. The overall results of this assault on the local authorities are unpredictable, and could well exacerbate inner urban problems, but for the ethnic minorities they could have some positive results. One can envisage that Muslims would be among the first groups to opt to take schools out of local authority control, and black council tenants could well be sufficiently disenchanted with their treatment to opt for self-management or transfer to a housing association. The opportunities for black institutions and leadership could well increase appreciably. Of course, these local gains will have serious costs, perhaps the most important being the erosion of the growing solidarity between blacks and whites on the basis of shared experiences of unemployment, poor housing and environment, and aggressive policing – the latter most vividly expressed when black and white youths fought shoulder to shoulder against the police from Brixton to Toxteth.

Gilroy (1987) has documented two kinds of attempt to combat racism. Official local government policies were tried in the 1980s, but seem to have been little better thought out than the 1970s 'Rock against racism' and the Anti-Nazi League. Noting the impact of rock music, Gilroy goes on to trace the way that black, and especially West Indian, culture has created connections between blacks in Britain, the West Indies, the United States, and even in South Africa, and it has done so in a way which is at least partially shared by white youth. The roots of modern pop in southern negro blues, the contributions made by black musicians to struggles in the US for civil rights and black power, and the equal representation of black and white performers on television pop shows must contribute to a destruction of the barriers between races, though they may also increase the gulf between generations. Gilroy even shows that pop culture has begun to reach young Asians in London, and hence to break down a cultural divide which was strong enough to survive centuries of British control in India.

A particularly important example of the role of culture in resistance to deprivation and racism has been the Notting Hill carnival. This grew from small beginnings in 1966 to reach an attendance of hundreds of thousands. Cohen (1982) argues that in the first few years it was multi-ethnic and under white leadership, and that only from about 1970 did it become predominantly West Indian. He shows that the costumes, music and dance rediscovered a link back to carnivals in Trinidad. Even the violent confrontations between the police and blacks at various carnivals since 1976 have precursors in Trinidad's colonial period. Yet he notes that the themes of the masquerades and dances remain in a love-hate relationship with British culture, just as the British press reactions fluctuate between pleasure at the vitality, excitement and multiracial harmony of most activities to condemnation of the violence which flares on occasion. To date, the carnival has resisted all attempts to repress or ban it, and it continues to provide an annual focus for expressions of black culture and solidarity.

The political alliances which exist in the inner cities are shifting and uneasy. They are opposed by the acute hostilities which still exist between some black and white areas, and by the racial harassment and attacks which are so frequent in areas like the East End. The effects of pop culture are pervasive but conditional. Nevertheless, underlying these features is the steady progress of the black minorities from the status of immigrant labourers to British citizens born and educated here. The change in status seems certain to produce an increasing assertiveness, expressed either through groups, like political parties or trades unions, or through individual struggles.

4.4.3 Asian enterprise

The high proportion of some Asian groups in non-manual occupations has already been mentioned. Closer examination shows that the most striking component of these statistics, and the most rapidly growing, is the number of Asians who are self-employed or small employers. For Indian men, the proportion of self-employed rose from 6 per cent in 1971 to 18 per cent in 1982, and for East African Asians the proportion was then 23 per cent. This compares with 14 per cent for white men – a figure matched even by Asian women. Subsequently, these figures have probably increased still further, judging by some local studies. Indeed, the phenomenon of Asian enterprise has become so visible that some commentators have even suggested that it might be a major contributor to the economic revival of the inner cities. Such a view is almost certainly overstated, but small-scale Asian enterprise is a development which demands some attention.

Some critics of the notion that Asian small business is a growth area have argued that many of the supposedly self-employed Asians are, in fact, home workers, and in effect suffer the disadvantages of employment without the advantages of sick and holiday pay and employer contributions to National Insurance. This certainly appears to be the case in many small Asian clothing workshops. However, Brown (1985, Table 105) states that two-thirds of self-employed Asians are in distribution and catering and only 10 per cent in manufacturing. Hence Asian shops and restaurants seem to be the central issue: why are there so many, and how successful are they?

Waldinger *et al.* (1985) have situated Asian small business in the UK in an international context, arguing that the last decade has seen an upturn of small business in Europe and North America, and that ethnic minority groups are particularly concerned with small business. They review two approaches to an explanation. On the one hand, many have argued that certain minorities are *culturally* predisposed to succeed in small business. Such predispositions may include religious beliefs which support hard work, self control and material success, but may also include solidarism in terms of kinship and/or area of origin which may provide access to expertise, information, credit and labour. A particular strand of the cultural argument is that certain groups, including the Chinese and Indians, have a long-established tendency to act as a 'middleman minority' in a range of overseas locations. In the case of Asians in Britain, those from East Africa come from such communities, which existed for generations under British colonialism and had their roots in pre-Imperial trading patterns. As well as a cultural predisposition, many were able to bring in substantial capital and start businesses on arrival.

The second line of argument connects better to the notion that Asians came to Britain primarily as migrant labour and only moved into self-employment as circumstances changed. This *ecological* approach stresses the limitations on business activity posed by the structure of the modern urban economy, noting the long-term decline of small business numbers and significance. Against this trend, ethnic segregation produces a demand for goods and services which was not met by existing British-run businesses, many of which were closing down or moving out. As those businesses became vacant, they tended to be taken over by Asians, though not to the same extent by West Indians. Aldrich *et al.* (1984) carried out a major study of this process in Bradford, Leicester and Ealing from 1978 through 1980, '82 and '84. They concluded that Asian retailing was economically marginal, relying on very long working hours to scrape a living in inherently unprofitable niches, and represented an aggregate waste of resources rather than a source of dynamic growth and upward mobility.

Waldinger *et al*, saw the cultural and ecological approaches as contributing to an *interactionist* approach which stressed the need for both cultural resources and ecological opportunities to allow successful economic growth of ethnic businesses. *Ward* (1985) has shown how different interactions have occurred in different British cities as a result of different local employment market conditions, and the different size and composition of minority populations, to produce a highly differentiated geography of ethnic economic and cultural activity. In cities such as Birmingham and Coventry, where factory jobs were both plentiful and highly paid before the late 1970s, he found a 'replacement labour population' with little business development. At the other extreme, Manchester and Newcastle had less favourable labour markets, and hence much smaller minority populations, but they were more educated and more business orientated. Their early and extensive growth in textile manufacturing, retailing and restaurants was characterized as a '**middleman minority**' pattern. Many towns had initially attracted replacement labour, but, with an earlier decline in job availability, had experienced a growth of Asian retailing catering for the ethnic market, in what Ward dubbed an 'ethnic niche' pattern – Bradford is one example. A few other towns had a mixed pattern of replacement labour, ethnic niche and middleman minority activities – Leicester being the classic example.

The interactionist view is particularly sensitive to change over time, especially in terms of the change of labour markets, from job availability in the 1960s to mass unemployment in the 1980s, and the situation will have evolved considerably since Ward's study. Simple observation suggests that there has been both considerable elaboration of some Asian shopping centres (such as Melton Road, Leicester, and Ealing Road, Wembley) to offer a wide range of products to a regional clientele, and a spread of Asian groceries and restaurants into predominantly white areas. At least some of these businesses give every appearance of prosperity, perhaps consistent with Brown's finding that 20 per cent of Asian businesses employed more than five people in addition to the owner.

Patel (1988) has argued that, although many Asian shops do resemble the negative stereotype identified by Aldrich *et al.* (1984) – particularly first businesses started in ethnic concentrations by former wage labourers and funded from savings, redundancy payments and informal loans – there are at least two ways out of this dead-end. The problem of increasing numbers of similar shops competing for a limited ethnic market can be overcome by moving out into white areas, though in so far as this move is restricted to corner shops, restaurants and newsagents it is only a modest step forward from inner area convenience goods. However, another option is to move into higher-order functions, such as retailing fashion clothes, where larger margins are possible, and this seems to have been the choice of experienced Asians who came to Britain from East Africa. Werbner (1980) has also pointed out that large numbers of Asian businesses require integrating activities, such as landlords, wholesalers and financiers, and that these less visible businesses may well provide substantial earnings and security.

What do these empirical changes imply for the position of black Britons of Asian origin in the class structure? I have already queried whether Asians could be regarded as straightforwardly in or, at the extreme, under the British working class, given their substantial presence in non-manual employment. The growth in numbers of Asian businesses is both an expression of a desire for upward mobility and an indication that there are problems with the 'normal' route to upward mobility via education and a better job. Many of the children of the immigrant generation of Asians have been successful in British schools and higher education, but Ballard and Holden (1975) have shown that they suffer from greater discrimination than do unqualified blacks seeking manual work. Although some have succeeded in getting professional jobs, many have been frustrated in the British job market. Small business then provides an avenue to independence and possible self-advancement both for qualified and unqualified Asians. In effect, they have sought to use the 'contradictory class locations', identified by Wright (1978, 1985) and reproduced in Chapter 3, Figure 3.1, as a ladder which could take them from the bottom to the top of the class system without having to face the institutional closure which operates against employees with a status handicap. For example, even an inner city grocery store may be a step up the class structure for a former wage labourer, and, if successful, it offers at least the prospect of joining a solid Asian petty bourgeoisie with significant ownership and autonomy. Beyond this, there are indications that some British born children of Asian origin are combining professional qualifications with shops and services, for example as pharmacists. Other successful businesses are becoming employers, thus climbing the ladder from petty bourgeois to small capitalist class positions. This strategy effectively depends on the assumption that racial closure will be less monolithic in a business world where cost cutting and profit maximizing are more important than the ethnic origins of the people who staff small businesses.

The indications are that most Asian small businesses are somewhere along the path from proletariat to petty bourgeoisie. Self-employment allows the owner to avoid exploitation by an employer and to enjoy some ownership of the means of production (of services if not of manufactured goods). However, until the capital value of the business reaches the 'national average' of productive assets per capita, the business remains exploited in Roemer's terms (see Chapter 3, section 3.2.1). It may well be exploited in practical ways by suppliers and, especially in manufacturing, by the larger firms who buy the output and can make or break small firms by granting or withholding a contract. Many of these small firms fail, but they seem to be replaced by new firms, sometimes with the same personnel. Even where Asian firms are successful in accumulating capital and growing to viability, they pose an interesting paradox for class theory, and indeed for British ideas of social justice. Most Asian small businesses rely on family labour, yet many of these groups retain an overt partriarchal form more extreme than is common in white British society. In effect, a self-employed man running a shop may be employing members of his own family on terms which would be seen as unacceptable in the formal labour market. As a result, the business may be able to accumulate capital and expand in a situation where a white-owned business would be seen as unprofitable. In the short term, the situation seems unjust to an outsider, but in the long term the family may achieve considerable affluence.

The use of family labour also poses a problem in assessing when a small business has moved into the second contradictory position: the transition between petty bourgeois and bourgeois. Here a key indication is becoming an employer, as well as using one's own labour. For Asian businesses, a more realistic indication is becoming a *formal* employer by offering a contract and a regular wage, though the tendency to do this is probably greater where whites are employed rather than other Asians. Patel (1988) has found appreciable numbers of Asian businesses employing white labour to deal with the public, and offering no obvious indications of Asian ownership. The target for Asian businessmen is to follow the earlier example of Jewish immigrants and build up mainstream businesses comparable to Marks and Spencer or Tesco. In some ways their task is harder, because they face a retail industry where ownership is much more concentrated than when a Sieff or a Cohen began to trade. A few Asian businesses are already very substantial, and they would typically relate to the diaspora of an Asian 'middleman minority' in many countries across the world. They may light the way for the small inner city businesses, just as the old Jewish community eased the way for the Ashkenazim Jews early in the century.

However, in discussing the class positions of Asians in Britain, it would be wrong to over-emphasize the number of substantial businesses. Such small numbers can disappear – as did the Asians who were at public schools, Oxbridge and even became Members of Parliament in the 1890s. For affluent Asians, with their strong economic motivation and weak links to British society, the option of a return to India or Pakistan, or more likely a move to the thriving Asian minority in Canada, is always open. For the majority, a slow move from manual into clerical, and from clerical into professional, is an alternative avenue of advance to the route via self-employment. Whether, and how fast, this can be achieved, depends both on the elimination of mass unemployment and the degree to which racial closure persists as a response of British society to these new citizens. Like other processes of social struggle, the outcome is unpredictable, particularly since the Asians have shown every sign of being an irresistible force while British racism has proved very close to an immovable object.

Activity 4.3

Consider the following questions as a means of reappraising the theoretical positions outlined in section 4.2:

1   Do the events of the late 1970s and '80s strengthen or weaken the proposition that blacks form an underclass?

2   Is culture always a result of economic or political forces, or are there instances where culture plays a more active part in determining economic or political change?

3   If ideology and politics can create 'racialized class fractions' of the middle classes as well as of the working class, how could one assess the relative importance of class and race as determinants of the social structure?

4.5   Conclusion: ethnic minorities and class formation

The post-war period of labour migration and the subsequent establishment of substantial ethnic minority communities in the UK have been important events, both empirically and conceptually. Empirically, the availability of migrant labour probably encouraged British firms to persist with labour-intensive production methods, and its limitation may well have encouraged the export of capital to overseas locations after 1962. The presence of ethnic and racial minorities also put to the test the British self-perception of tolerance and liberality; the results of the test confirmed a deep-rooted suspicion of foreigners and especially blacks. Conceptually, these minorities have been a problem in terms of race, citizenship and class. The inter-relationship of these categories is complex and shifting: as I write this paragraph, today's *Independent* reports that the government is suppressing results of a study which used DNA testing to prove that, of a sample of Bangladeshis denied entry to Britain on the grounds that they are not really the children of men settled here, nearly 90 per cent are genetically proved to be bona fide. The cross-cutting of the status categories and class can be treated at two levels – a static cross section of current class position and an ongoing process of class formation.

As regards current position, you can draw your own conclusions from the information presented here, but the evidence seems to indicate that the relationship of black groups to the overall class structure is somewhere between Miles' 'racialized class fraction' and Parkin's 'ethnic cleavage'. The class fraction view has to take account of the fact that black groups, particularly early arrivals from India and those of East African origin, are present in categories of employment and ownership which are at least petty bourgeois and arguably even higher. They may be seen as 'racialized fractions' of several classes, from welfare recipients, through marginal and core working class and into the middle classes. It may be that these fractions join into a kind of 'geological fault' slicing through the class strata and causing the blacks to drop in status in relation to whites. Miles' view that the divisions between class fractions are real and significant in ideological and political terms seems not all that far from Parkin's notion of a status cleavage cutting across class.

If status is viewed in Barbalet's terms as 'enforceable norms', it begins to make sense of the persistence of government efforts to withdraw citizenship rights from black Commonwealth citizens, and even black Britons, as against the rather modest efforts to enforce the Race Relations Acts, since the framing and enforcement of legislation is influenced by public opinion, and especially so when the laws deal with fundamental civil rights and widespread activities. The attitudes and stereotypes created over centuries of British Imperialism seem to have been more enduring than the economic and political institutions of the Empire, and they continue to exert major effects. Indeed, racial hostility feeds from disadvantage as much as it helps to perpetuate it, so that there is a vicious circle in which stereotypes of inferiority prompt discrimination and produce disadvantage which seems to confirm inferiority.

The cross-cutting and interaction of divisions based on class and on race creates a highly differentiated society, and these differentiations are multiplied by deep divisions within racial categories – on the basis of place of origin, religion and caste – and are related to the great variation between the areas of the UK. This heterogeneity creates major uncertainties for individuals and groups in terms of self-perception, group membership, the formation of alliances and political behaviour. Some have looked inward to family or group solidarity, and hence to an ethnic identity, others, especially West Indians, have tried to participate in British institutions, and occasionally have been accepted. At present, the situation is highly fragmented and could develop in a variety of directions, from a move to colour-blind class politics right across the spectrum to an immutable caste-like separation of black groups. Much may depend on directions taken by the first generation of British born blacks as they take over leadership of their groups from the immigrant generation.

Finally, it is worth noting a number of instances where immigration, race and culture have exerted a causal influence on British society at large, with far-reaching consequences. These go beyond the particular aims of this chapter, but are included here as an indication that social divisions can have significant effects on the economy and on politics.

The effects of the availability of cheap but inexperienced labour in the 1960s in encouraging the de-skilling of the labour process have already been mentioned. In turn, this form of cheap labour may have helped to inhibit two other possible responses to the labour shortage and to encourage a third. The coincidence of high profits and labour shortages could have allowed British manufacturers to expand production through higher capital investment – a strategy which might have produced both high pay and high profits and maintained international competitiveness. Conversely, the short-term expansion of the labour supply could have relied even more on that other 'reserve army' – British women. The use of Third World citizens in the UK helped to show that industries could rely on their labour and helped promote the export of productive capacity to Third World locations. The major role of Commonwealth immigrants was not inevitable, but an easy short-term option with long-term effects.

A second major effect which has already been mentioned is the 'blackening' of the inner cities. Problems of overcrowding, poor amenities and dereliction had been endemic in British cities since the early nineteenth century and had been exacerbated by two wars and the depression of the 1930s. In the 1950s and '60s, rising prosperity, improved mobility and rapid development of both private and public housing in outer city and suburban areas encouraged the depopulation of the inner cities. The influx of black immigrants with restricted resources was a major contradictory force, producing expansion in areas otherwise contracting. Through a process of guilt by association, many people came to regard blacks as the cause of run-down city areas. Even for the unprejudiced, the expectation grew that inner city problem areas would have large proportions of black people. Ben-Tovim and Gabriel (1982) argue that the Urban Programme of 1968 onward was 'devised as an attempt to defuse a potentially explosive situation'; i.e. that it would provide support to the areas where most black people were concentrated but without being seen by hard-liners as positive discrimination. However, the effect may well have reversed in the 1980s as the nature of inner city problems made it politically easier to redistribute rate support grant from the inner cities to the shire counties. This was reinforced by a further effect of the black minorities.

It has already been mentioned that the black minorities began to vote Labour in the 1960s. At the 1987 election, three-quarters did so, making them the most Labour-inclined sector of the electorate. Twenty years of support were at last sufficient to persuade Labour to field a few black candidates in safe seats. The reverse face of this is, as we have already noted, widespread racial prejudice, hostility and discrimination, not least among the working class. One result is certain, the Labour Party has been internally divided over how to involve black people, with many blacks demanding separate black sections, but the party as a whole preferring to assert its colour blindness and inviting blacks to participate in mainstream activities. Beyond the party, it is impossible to quantify the effects, but it seems likely that an appreciable number of former Labour voters have ceased to vote for a party seen to be relatively pro-black. Since the centre parties are at least as egalitarian as Labour in relation to race, the logical consequence would be to switch to voting Conservative – which is now more common for manual workers than at any time this century.

The last impact of the minorities on the economy which I will mention here is the impact on small-scale manufacturing. In some respects this is similar to the effect on retailing, but in the case of manufacturing there can be no argument that the minorities are merely 'taking in each other's washing'. Perhaps the most dramatic case is the Asian creation of a substantial textile industry in the West Midlands – an area which has never pre-viously been involved in textiles. While many of these enterprises are on a small scale, and subject their workers to very poor conditions and generate restricted profits, they do demonstrate a high degree of energy, initiative and enterprise and are in most respects an embodiment of the Victorian values so often recommended in the 1980s. At the least, they are an integral part of flexible specialization, at most they could be the seed beds of future industries, or even an emerging pattern of manufacturing like that of the 'Third Italy'.

These four examples show that, while 1960s commentators were right to claim that black groups were like a dye or an indicator used in science to make processes and structures more easily visible, they were wrong in suggesting that they did not promote or provoke new processes and structures.

5 Gender divisions

Linda McDowell

Contents

5.1 Introduction

Chapters 1 and 2 have shown, using different kinds of evidence, how the class structure of contemporary Britain has undergone a series of profound changes since the mid-1960s. Decades of relative prosperity and economic growth have been followed by a period of economic recession and greater social inequality in British society. Changes in the economy, which were the focus of *The Economy in Question* (Allen and Massey, 1988), have resulted in the decline of the traditional working class in the UK, the opening up of new divisions between a growing **underclass** of the poor in temporary or casual employment, and those who are unemployed or retired and dependent upon state welfare benefits. At the other end of the spectrum, the wealthy few have maintained their control over a large share of national income and resources. What we have not looked at in detail so far in our examination of the restructuring of social and economic relations in Britain is the impact on **gender relations**.

The changing sectoral division of the economy and the associated 'shift' effects on occupational and class structures have resulted in the feminization of the paid labour force. Not only have absolutely greater numbers of women been drawn into wage relations, but women's relative share of the labour force has increased significantly as jobs for men, in the manufacturing sector in particular, have disappeared. It may be that we are faced not with the end of the working class, but with its changing gender.

Studies of the impact of **economic restructuring** on gender divisions have moved from the descriptive level – showing how the growth of service sector employment has been based, in large part, on drawing women into the labour market – to critiques of conventional definitions of 'work' as waged labour. There is growing recognition of the need to broaden the scope of our understanding of 'economic activity' to include unpaid as well as paid employment. This recognition is based primarily on feminists' attempts to reconceptualize the links between **domestic labour** and waged labour. Such reconceptualizations have interesting parallels with some of the work in economic theory in the late 1980s; for example, analyses of the links between changes in the labour process and in the labour market that result in a growing periphery of workers in temporary and casual employment (see *The Economy in Question*, Allen and Massey, 1988, Chapter 5) are beginning to take gender divisions into account in their explanations.

Women's growing participation in waged labour also has profound consequences for gender divisions in the home and in the community, particularly in areas where high male unemployment is challenging conventional assumptions about men's roles as breadwinners and providers. A set of recent studies, primarily by sociologists, has begun to investigate the renegotiations of gender divisions within the home and the community which are related to the recession and to male unemployment.

Women's increased participation in waged labour has made gender divisions a central issue in debates about the impact of restructuring. However, there is further reason why gender has become a central issue since the mid-1970s. The coincidence of the social and economic changes in the UK (and also at an international level) with government commitment to reduce state expenditure on welfare has produced this centrality. British economic and social relations, since 1979 in particular, have been based on a fundamental contradiction between material changes that have challenged but also reinforced women's traditional roles as carers and providers in the home, in the community and as waged labourers. Women have been recruited as an essential part of the wage-labour force but, at the same time, as real cuts in welfare expenditure have reduced state provided services, individual women's labour has become even more essential in caring for children, the sick and the elderly, as well as servicing the day-to-day needs of other workers. These two trends – welfare cuts and increased participation in waged labour – have deepened the contradiction between what is often known as women's 'dual role'. Associated with this deepening contradiction has been a strengthening of an ideology of domesticity, that is, of women's role in the family, and a reinforcement through the tax and social security systems of the institution of heterosexual marriage. The aim of this chapter is to investigate the impact of these contradictions on social relations between men and women in contemporary Britain.

The investigation is divided into three parts. The aim of section 5.2 is to examine the impact of economic restructuring on the gender division of labour, primarily in the workplace but also in the home. We will look at a range of different approaches to the question of why increasing numbers of women have been drawn into the waged labour market; the extent to which this participation is challenging conventional assumptions about women's work; and the distribution of financial rewards between men and women, and between different types of households. We need to enquire whether women's waged labour is reducing or increasing income inequalities in Britain. Two incomes may be required to purchase the commodities of the middle-class lifestyle described in Chapter 1; on the other hand, women's increased earning capacity may mean the reduction of their economic (and emotional?) dependence on men. The growing number of single mothers, for example, may be related to changes in the economy as well as to changing attitudes towards marriage and divorce.

In the second part of the chapter (section 5.3) we will outline the consequences of the cuts in welfare spending for women's work in the family and in the community. Since 1979, government policies have exacerbated the contradictions in women's position by simultaneously asserting a belief in individual liberty alongside a moral and legislative reassertion of the sanctity of the nuclear family. The contradiction itself, between waged labour and responsibility for the activities of **social reproduction** (childcare, childrearing, informal nursing, loving and caring and most of the tasks that constitute housework), is not a new phenomenon. Indeed, the interconnections between women's domestic and waged labour are a central part of the different forms of explanation of why women remain segregated into particular parts of the occupational structure in the economy. Before the radical right administrations headed by Margaret Thatcher after 1979, governments had been equally wedded to the view that women's place is in the home. In the post-war consensus about the role of the welfare state, initiated by the Beveridge Report in 1943, married women's primary task was spelled out as ensuring the continuity of care for men and children provided by the traditional family. The welfare state and the structure of the tax system until the end of the 1980s reflected the assumption of women's economic dependence on men. Throughout the post-war period, Labour, as well as Conservative, administrations have reasserted the sanctity of marriage and motherhood, sometimes in the face of social changes that challenged this.

The difference since 1979 has been that the coincidence of an economy increasingly based on the exploitation of women in the labour market, where they are 'secondary' workers working for 'pin' money, with high male unemployment rates, and the continuing abolition of collectivist welfare provision by the state has provided the strongest challenge yet to traditional ideas about men and women's respective roles in society.

Finally, in section 5.4, we will evaluate evidence about how gender divisions are being renegotiated in the context of the material changes just outlined. In particular, we will focus on studies of young men and women who are growing up in a society that is based on values, assumptions and expectations about the role of waged work in people's lives which are different from those of the previous generation.

5.2   Women in waged work and the gender division of labour

5.2.1 Women in the labour market

One of the enduring features of British society is the dichotomous division between men and women. **Gender** is fundamental to the way in which life is organized: home and work, the public and the private, production and consumption are characteristic social divisions within a capitalist society that are associated with the distinction between men and women. In this section, I shall argue that the **gender division of labour** – that is, the allocation of work on the basis of sex, both within the home and in the workplace – is as important as are class divisions in Britain today. If we are to understand the ways in which waged work is currently being restructured, gender is an essential part of our analysis. Further, I aim to demonstrate that gender is not a category that can be added to, or superimposed on, explanations based on class divisions, but that it is an integral part of the analysis of structural change in contemporary Britain. Gender relations and class relations are interconnected; each shapes the other. Struggles in the workplace, forms of industrial restructuring, and current changes in the labour process are about the divisions and the maintenance of, or challenge to, the hierarchy of power between men and women, as well as changing class divisions.

In this chapter, I use the term 'gender' to refer to the *meaning* of being a man or a woman. It is important to distinguish this concept from the term 'sex', which refers to biological differences between men and women. The distinction between sex and gender is made to emphasize that gender is both a social construct and one that is subject to variation. Despite constant references to the 'natural', to the inevitability of distinctions between men and women ('women are naturally more loving'; 'it's inevitable that women care for children', and so on) the gender division of labour is neither inevitable nor immutable. The *content* of men's and women's work is subject to change; new types of division within the labour process and new forms of job are created, and these become 'gendered', that is, labelled as 'men's' or 'women's' work. What appears to be fixed, however, is the existence of a *distinction* between men's and women's work. Here, we are concerned to explore the reasons for this and the ways in which gender divisions are a crucial part of the restructuring of British society.

Women's participation in waged labour has been a feature of industrial Britain. In the hundred years between 1851 and 1951, women accounted for about a quarter of all waged workers, although the precise numbers are difficult to establish and there were considerable variations within and between different regions.

Activity 5.1

Figure 5.1 is based on statistics of women's participation in waged labour between 1901 and 1981.

1   In which regions were women the most noticeable part of the labour force?

2   Why do you think there were these wide regional variations at the beginning of the century?

3   Why has there been a decrease in the extent of regional variation in the post-war period?

4   Do you think these 'official' statistics accurately represent the extent of women's participation in waged labour?

In the early part of the twentieth century, women were a significant part of the labour force in the textile industry that dominated the economy of the North West, but also in a variety of trades and industries in the South East. It

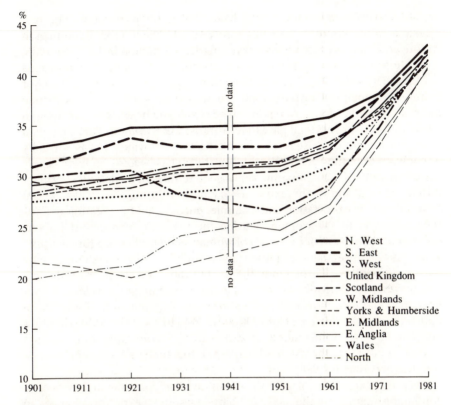

Figure 5.1 Female employees as a percentage of total employees by standard region, 1901–81

Source: Geography and Gender, *1984*

was in the heavy industrial areas such as the North and Wales, where hard manual labour for men imposed heavy demands on women's labour in the home, that female participation rates were lowest. In the post-war period, but particularly since 1961, these differentials have declined as women were recruited for service sector employment, and also in the 1950s and '60s into assembly line work in manufacturing industries. The fastest rates of expansion were in the regions where, traditionally, few women had worked for wages; these include heavy manufacturing areas and more rural regions, like the South West and East Anglia.

Statistics of women's participation in waged labour are, however, seldom completely reliable because many women are employed on a temporary or casual basis, or in areas of employment that are either not enumerated – prostitution is a classic example – or undernumerated – the numbers of domestic servants and governesses were often underestimated in the early years of this century, as nannies and mother's helps have been in recent years.

Since the Second World War, the extent, nature and pattern of regional variation in women's waged work have changed considerably. The first change is in the extent of women's involvement. The number of women in waged work has risen steadily from just under 7.5 million in 1951. By 1986, 9.4 million women worked for wages, accounting for 45 per cent of all waged workers. The second change is in the nature of their participation. A major feature of women's rising participation in waged work has been its part-time basis: 40 per cent of all women in waged employment worked part time in 1986, and 86 per cent of all part-time workers were women. Part-time paid work (as opposed to seasonal or contract employment) was virtually unknown before the Second World War, but it has become an increasingly evident feature of the labour market since that time. In the labour shortages during the war and in the expansionary period during the 1950s, central government, by exhortation and example, encouraged the creation of part-time employment for women. During the war, the Ministry of Labour published a booklet, 'Mobilization of woman-power: planning for part-time work' (1942), to persuade employers, who initially were reluctant to employ part-time workers. Throughout the 1950s, the state itself created large numbers of part-time jobs for women in teaching, nursing and clerical work in central and local government departments. The numbers of women in part-time employment rose from 700 000 in 1943 to 750 000 in 1951 (despite a post-war fall in the total number of women in the labour force) to 1.7 million in 1961. Since then, the rise has been rapid, to a total of 4.1 million women working part time in 1986.

Thus the expansion of part-time employment for women has been a continuing feature of the UK economy. Despite the radical changes in sectoral divisions in the economy that have occurred since the 1960s, and the overall fall in the number of men in waged labour, women's employment has continued to grow. The apparent paradox of the expansion of part-time employment for women in both periods of labour shortages *and* excesses, in periods of growth *and* recession, needs explanation. Part of the reason lies in women's apparent disposability, and in an argument that waged labour is less significant for women compared with men, because of the structure of family relationships and the assumption that women and children are, in the main, economically dependent on a male breadwinner. The expansion of part-time employment was specifically to facilitate the entry of *married* women into capitalist wage relations. In the post-war period there has been a shift in the marital status of women working for a wage compared with previous periods. Before the Second World War the majority of women waged workers were single. Part-time employment was seen as a way to resolve the contradiction for individual women between their responsibility for domestic labour and their entry into the labour market. As Winston Churchill remarked to the cabinet in 1941: 'Employers might well be encouraged ... to make further use of the services of married women in industry. This would often have to be on a part-time basis, and means must be found to ease the dual burden on women who are prepared to play a dual role' (quoted in Briar, 1987).

In the mid-1950s, part-time work was proposed as ideal for women but suitable only for men near to retirement age (Ministry of Labour, 1955/6, Cmnd 9629 para. 55). In the very different economic circumstances of the mid-1980s, part-time work for women seemed to be the one constant theme – 'flexible part-time work is particularly welcome to women' (Department of Employment, 1986, Cmnd 9794 p. 37). Part-time employment is thus seen as particularly appropriate for married women because it enables them to continue to shoulder their 'dual' role – caring for their families and adding to the family income, without radically disturbing the gender divisions of labour within the home.

Despite women's increased participation in waged labour, men's participation in domestic labour has hardly risen. Table 5.1 shows how household labour was divided between men and women in the mid-1980s. It is interesting to compare the actual distribution of work with the way in which the respondents think these tasks *should* be shared. Even in this situation, it seems that household work is often assumed to be a woman's responsibility. And the means to ease women's dual burdens, proposed by Churchill half a century ago, have yet to be found by the state. Indeed, as I shall argue in section 5.3, for many women these burdens have increased.

The increase in the number of women in the labour market in the last two decades has occurred in a different context from the rises in the previous two decades. What is sometimes called the 'feminization' of the labour force has been the result of *two* changes which have taken place since the early to mid-1970s, but have been particularly noticeable since 1979. These are: (1) the overall growth in the numbers of women employed, and (2) a large fall in the numbers of employed men. The latter has been of greatest significance in the 1980s in the overall rise in the proportion of waged workers who are women. Indeed, by 1986 the total of 9.4 million women in waged labour was still 0.1 million below its peak in 1979. But male employment fell over the same period (1979–86) from just over 13 million to 11.5 million, a decrease of 11 per cent.

The context of women's rising participation is the 'crisis' in the British economy which was the subject of *The Economy in Question* (Allen and Massey, 1988). Through capital relocation, labour intensification, rationalization and occupational shifts, employers shed male labour. The main factor associated with the loss of male employment and the rise in women's participation rates was the shift from manufacturing to service employment. Between 1979 and 1986, almost 30 per cent of manufacturing jobs were lost in Britain, the majority of them in the north of England. Although women in manufacturing also lost their jobs, most of the jobs lost were ones which had been carried out by men. The loss of these jobs and the continued growth of service sector employment meant that, by 1986, service sector jobs accounted for 67 per cent of total employment compared with 59 per cent in 1979. Over the same period, manufacturing jobs fell from 31 to 24 per cent.

Table 5.2 indicates the trends in aggregate employment numbers in Britain from 1979 to 1986, and Table 5.3 shows the broad sectoral gender

Table 5.1   Household division of labour: by marital status, 1984, Great Britain (percentages)

	Married people[1]						Never-married people[2]		
	Actual allocation of tasks			Tasks should be allocated to			Tasks should be allocated to		
	Mainly man	Mainly woman	Shared equally	Mainly man	Mainly woman	Shared equally	Mainly man	Mainly woman	Shared equally
Household tasks (percentage[3] allocation)									
Washing and ironing	1	88	9	-	77	21	-	68	30
Preparation of evening meal	5	77	16	1	61	35	1	49	49
Household cleaning	3	72	23	-	51	45	1	42	56
Household shopping	6	54	39	-	35	62	-	31	68
Evening dishes	18	37	41	12	21	64	13	15	71
Organization of household money and bills	32	38	28	23	15	58	19	16	63
Repairs of household equipment	83	6	8	79	2	17	74	-	24
Child-rearing (percentage[3] allocation)									
Looks after the children when they are sick	1	63	35	-	49	47	-	48	50
Teaches the children discipline	10	12	77	12	5	80	16	4	80

[1] 120 married respondents, except for the questions on actual allocation of child-rearing tasks which were answered by 479 respondents with children under 16

[2] 283 never-married respondents. The table excludes results of the formerly married (widowed, divorced, or separated) respondents

[3] Don't knows and non-response to the question mean that some categories do not sum to 100 per cent

Source: British Social Attitudes Survey, 1984, Social and Community Planning Research

Table 5.2   Employment trends in Great Britain 1971–1986 (millions)

	1971	1976	1979	1981	1983	1984	1985	1986
Total employees in employment	21.6	22.0	22.6	21.4	20.6	20.7	20.9	21.0
All men	13.4	13.1	13.2	12.3	11.7	11.6	11.7	11.6
All women	8.2	9.0	9.5	9.1	8.9	9.1	9.2	9.4
FT women workers	5.5	5.4	5.6	5.3	5.0	4.9	4.9	5.4
PT women workers	2.8	3.6	3.9	3.8	3.9	4.2	4.3	4.0
Total unemployed	0.7	1.2	1.2	2.3	2.9	2.9	3.1	3.2
Women as a % of all employees								
All women workers	38.0	40.9	42.0	42.5	43.2	44.0	44.0	44.8
FT women workers	25.0	24.5	24.8	24.8	24.3	23.7	23.4	25.7
PT women workers	13.0	16.4	17.3	17.8	18.9	20.3	20.6	19.0
Total working population*	24.6	25.5	24.8	26.1	25.9	26.4	26.8	27.3

* Includes self-employed and HM forces
Source: DE, *Labour Force Survey*, figures at June each year

Table 5.3   The gender division of labour in manufacturing and the service sector, 1986 (in millions)

	Male employees		Women employees		
	Full time	Part time	Full time	Part time	All
All industries	10.9	0.8	5.5	4.1	21.1
Manufacturing	3.6	0.05	1.6	0.3	5.2
Services	6.5	0.7	4.0	3.7	14.2

Source: DE, *Labour Force Survey*, 1986

division of labour. They illustrate that the service sector is the largest employer of both men and women but that, in 1986, women outnumbered men by 0.6m. Table 5.2 shows that the rise in total employment since 1983 has been in women's jobs rather than in jobs for men.

The aggregate rise in women's employment conceals continuing gender segregation in the labour market. An enduring feature of the labour market has been women's concentration into a narrow range of occupations. Figures 5.2 and 5.3 show the occupational distribution of men and women working in full- and part-time occupations in Britain. The concentration of women into a smaller number of the occupational classifications than men is clear for 1986. Men and women tend to be concentrated in different jobs. For example, in 1986, half of all employed men worked in jobs where the workforce was almost exclusively male (90 per cent), and half of all women

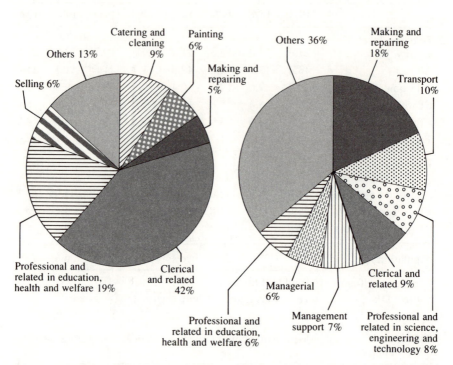

Figure 5.2   Distribution of full-time waged workers by occupational grouping, 1986, Great Britain
Source: DE, New Earnings Survey

where three-quarters of their co-workers were women. This is known as **horizontal segregation**. A range of jobs and occupations thus exists that is commonly regarded as 'women's' work. In 1986, of the women in full-time waged employment, 42 per cent were in clerical and related occupations, and a further 19 per cent were in professional and related occupations in education, health and welfare, many of them as primary school teachers, nurses and social workers. Part-time women workers were more likely to be concentrated in catering, cleaning, hairdressing and other personal service occupations.

Within those occupations where both women and men are employed, despite almost two decades of equal opportunity legislation that makes discrimination on the basis of sex illegal, women remain concentrated at the bottom of the hierarchies of pay and promotion opportunities. This is known as **vertical segregation**. The combined result of the two forms of segregation is that average pay rates for women remain significantly lower than for men. Despite the sectoral shift in the economy and the rising numbers of women in waged labour, since the early 1970s women's average full-time earnings

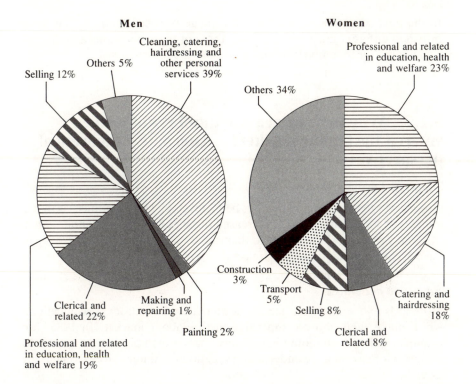

Figure 5.3 Distribution of part-time waged workers by occupational grouping, 1986, Great Britain

Source: DE, New Earnings Survey

per week have continued to fluctuate slightly at around two-thirds the level of male full-time weekly average earnings. And, as was pointed out in Chapter 2, women working on a part-time basis tend to be even more poorly paid in comparison with men.

This outline of the major changes in the extent and nature of women's waged labour raises a number of questions:

● Why have increasing numbers of women entered the labour market?

● Why have service sector employers apparently preferred women workers?

● Why and how, despite overall rises in the number of women workers, changes in types of work, the application of new forms of technology and wider social changes, has the gender division of labour in waged work remained?

● What are the consequences of women's increased involvement in waged work for social relations between men and women, not only at work but in the home and in the wider community?

In the next section, we shall look at a range of social theories that have provided different answers to the first three of these questions and then at some of the recent empirical evidence about the fourth.

5.2.2   Why have increasing numbers of women entered the labour market? – Alternative theoretical perspectives

Supply and demand theory

One answer to this question that has been developed by economists is that a number of social changes have increased the supply of female labour – that is, more women are able to make themselves available for work. Changes have occurred in the following areas:

Education and skills

More girls and women are gaining academic and vocational qualifications which make them more competitive in the labour market. In 1985, for example, girls gained more GCE O-level passes than boys in the same age groups. More women are undertaking vocational training. More women can drive.

Demography and form of the family

The birth rate has fallen from 811 per 1000 women in 1961 to 661 in 1986. Women born since 1945 are projected to have, on average, slightly under 2 children compared with almost 2.5 for women born between the wars. Women's age when the first child is born has increased and has decreased for the birth of the last child. So the time spent bearing and raising children has declined for most women. Although the incidence of marriage has not declined – in the mid-1980s less than 10 per cent of all women over 16 had never been married – the rate of divorce has increased, and more women spend more of their lives living alone, as single mothers, or in some other form of household, and hence they are more likely to need the greater economic independence achieved by entering the labour market.

Social changes

These range from the greater availability of a wide variety of goods and machinery that, in theory at least, reduce the drudgery of housework, cooking and washing, to wider changes in women's position and in social attitudes towards women's roles. These are evidenced by campaigns around 'women's issues' such as abortion and childcare, initiated by certain local authorities and by women's organizations, and by the changing representation of women in the media and in publishing.

Legislation

In 1975, the Equal Pay and Sex Discrimination Acts were passed in Britain outlawing certain types of discrimination against women. In theory, these acts should result in the gender of workers being immaterial to employers. Whether, in fact, this increases the supply of women workers is debatable. As we shall see later from our consideration of alternative theories, one of the attractive features of women as potential workers is their relative cheapness and exploitability as compared with men. Legislation to make discrimination illegal should reduce the gender differential.

The net result of these changes, according to simple supply and demand theory, is that greater numbers of women have been available for waged work since the end of the Second World War. This argument seems unexceptional, although we might want to ask more searching questions about the actual effects of technological innovations on housework, for example. The limited empirical evidence that is available indicates that the time expended on domestic tasks has actually fallen very little, and that the rather simplistic assumption made in these theories that the application of new technology to tasks reduces the labour time expended on them is incorrect.

Turning to the demand side of the equation, we find that this type of approach assumes that the demand for women's labour is a simple function of overall levels of demand within the economy as a whole. In times of economic prosperity and a strong demand for labour, women are drawn into the labour market; in periods of downturn, they are expelled. This assumption relies on a prior assumption about the nature of women's attachment to waged labour: that women's involvement in waged labour is a flexible or peripheral one. Behind this model is the implicit acceptance that women's primary role is in the family, and that their main source of financial support is another, invariably male, breadwinner. There is also the further assumption that employers are indifferent to the sex of their workers, which, as we shall see later, is incorrect. However, the major problem with this simple supply and demand model is that it conflicts with the empirical evidence that we have already examined. In Table 5.2 we saw that the rise in the numbers of women in the labour market in the post-war period seems to have been remarkably unaffected by both upturns and slumps in the economy, and has continued to rise throughout the entire post-war period, with the exception of the depths of the recession in the early 1980s when the number of women in *full-time* employment fell in absolute terms. The number of women employed on a part-time basis, however, continued to rise.

A number of neo-classical economists have developed the basic supply and demand model to include a more thorough investigation of how and why the potential supply of women workers is translated into actual workers. An interesting variant of these approaches is that known as the **human capital theory** and is represented by the work of Mincer (1962) and Becker (1965, 1975). In this approach, the assumptions left implicit in simple neo-classical models – about gender divisions in domestic work, childcare and the role of the nuclear family – are made explicit. It is argued that the conventional gender division of labour in most families, whereby women are the primary domestic workers and men the primary wage earners, is a perfectly rational one made on the basis of the amount of human capital invested in individuals of each gender, and the respective rates of return that result from their participation in waged labour. Thus, it is argued that, as men in general are better educated and have invested more time and/or money in acquiring professional and vocational qualifications, it makes more sense for them to enter the labour market as they receive proportionately greater financial rewards, commensurate with their qualifications. These arguments, as you will see, take the status quo for granted and they are unable to explain the structures of discrimination against women, such that women and men with identical qualifications receive differential rewards in the labour market. They are also not interested in *why* women are less well educated or trained in the first place.

In order to explain women's actual entry into waged labour, human capital theorists further assume that the correct unit of analysis is the household rather than the individual. The argument runs as follows. Each household has a finite amount of work, both waged and unwaged, that must be undertaken in order to ensure its basic functioning. Within the household, rational decisions are made on the basis of available information about how to apply the units of human capital available (labour power, in the terms of a different theoretical discourse) in order to achieve maximum returns for minimum effort. As we have already seen, the returns to male human capital are, in general, greater than to female human capital in the labour market, so it makes complete rational sense for each household to choose to apply its capital in a particular way – men to earning income in the labour market, women to performing unpaid work in the home. Further, if women do choose to enter the labour market, it makes economic sense, in the terms of this model, for them to work part time and/or close to home as the returns for each extra hour worked, or mile travelled, are lower than for men.

As we have seen, women are occupationally segregated into a small range of jobs with relatively low pay differentials between them. In explaining when women chose to participate in waged labour, the human capital model is more flexible than the simple supply and demand model, and to some extent it argues it both ways. The model suggests that women's participation is related in some way to the ups and downs in the economy. But the key issue, which is left to be determined empirically in particular cases, rather than established a priori by the conceptual structure of the model, is whether or not this participation is more likely in upturns or downturns in the economy. In periods of expansion, women enter the labour market because jobs are available, adding to total household earnings; this is known as the *income effect*. In periods of economic recession, when male earnings may decline either because of loss of overtime or rising levels of unemployment, women may be more likely to earn to supplement overall household earnings; this is known as the *substitution effect*.

The human capital models are initially appealing, not least because they appear to accord well with the reality of women's work, its part-time nature, the likelihood that women enter and re-enter the labour market during their lives rather than pursuing an uninterrupted lifetime career, that most women are responsible for childcare and housework and, partly (mainly?) to be able to continue to provide these domestic services, they tend to seek waged employment close to their homes.

But, we need to stop for a minute and think carefully about the propositions of these models. Do they actually explain the reasons for the gender division of labour or is their conceptual structure reliant on the current divisions? If girls and young women continue to gain the credentials that improve their 'human capital', how successfully will these models be able to explain either continuing gender divisions along current lines, and women's lower rates of return in the labour market, or alternatively a radical shift in the nature of gender divisions of labour in waged and unwaged work? It would require a reworking of the main assumption that women's earnings are secondary within a household headed by a man for these changes to be incorporated within human capital models.

We also need to interrogate these models' assumptions about the household as a rational decision-making unit with what we know about the nature of social relations within households and the structure of power between men and women. Studies of income distribution between household members, of the use and accountability of 'free' time, and of control over resources reveal that, in general, men are the dominant members of many households. In studies of women's decisions about entering waged labour, there is evidence that men's desires to assert or reassert their position of authority influence whether or not women take up waged employment. In addition, current social security regulations, which deduct part of a wife's earned income from an unemployed husband's benefit, act as a considerable economic disincentive for women in this situation to search for waged employment. I would therefore argue that while supply and demand and human capital models may be a reasonable representation or description of women's current position in the labour market, they fail to *explain* the basis of gender divisions and how these may change in the future.

Reserve army of labour theory

From a completely different theoretical perspective, the Marxist concept of a *reserve army of labour* has been utilized in two different ways to explain women's participation in waged labour. First, an argument has been conducted, primarily within explicitly feminist work, about the utility of the concept in explaining why *married* women increasingly have been drawn into capitalist wage relations. There are those who argue that it is a useful concept (e.g. Power, 1983; Beechey, 1978), and those who disagree (Anthias, 1980). Secondly, the concept has been used in discussions about what happens to women's employment relative to other groups in economic upturns and downturns (e.g. Breugel, 1979). Let us look at the conceptual basis of these arguments and the empirical evidence cited by adherents and opponents.

First, it is important to know that Marx's original formulation of the concept of an industrial reserve was sufficiently ambiguous to allow a number of different interpretations to co-exist. As Power has pointed out, at a basic level, 'every labourer is part of the industrial reserve army whenever she or he is unemployed or only partially employed' (1983, p. 74). Thus the reserve army consists of a surplus working population. The surplus may take one of three forms:

1   A floating category – this category is created when demand for labour falls in particular industrial sectors, resulting in redundancies and/or lower wages. These 'freed' workers are then available for new industrial developments. The 'floating' reserve is, it has also been argued, related in contemporary Britain to de-skilling, the process whereby unskilled labour is substituted for skilled workers as the nature of jobs in the economy changes.

2   The stagnant category – these are workers who are irregularly employed in industry or agriculture.

3   The latent category – these are workers expelled from agriculture as it is transformed, modernized and mechanized in capitalist modernization.

So how do women fit into one or other of these categories? Two major approaches can be distinguished, one dominated by US authors, the other by British. Authors in both the traditions have based their arguments upon concrete empirical investigations of the phenomenon of women being drawn into the paid workforce. As this phenomenon is taking place in similar ways in the USA and in Britain, it is difficult to find empirically based reasons for the theoretical disagreements between scholars adapting the concept to women's waged work in the two countries.

Beechey, the British feminist scholar who has been most influential in the use of the concept in Britain, has argued that women are part of the reserve army, but in a different sense from the ways in which Marx defined the term. Thus, she argues that Marxist theory must be extended in order to explain the radical shifts in the extent of women's participation in waged labour. While women may fit into any of the three categories Marx identified, Beechey also believes that, because of the particular characteristics of women as waged labourers, they constitute a further category in the reserve, which she left unnamed. Married women, because of their domestic responsibilities, offer special 'advantages' to capitalist employers. They are constituted as a uniquely flexible, disposable and low paid workforce because domestic work is seen as their primary responsibility. Women are thus distinct from other categories of workers in the reserve army. Beechey identifies a set of further reasons, that are specific to the particular historical period in Britain in which she is writing (the late 1970s/early 1980s) that also construct women as this uniquely disposable workforce. The reasons are based on their traditionally low levels of union membership, their ineligibility in many cases for redundancy payments, and the fact that many women are ineligible for state unemployment pay. As we shall see in the next section, cuts in welfare provision and changes in the social security system, as well as the continuing assumption in legislation relating to the tax and benefit systems that married women are and *should be* economically dependent on men, are an important element in explaining the deepening contradiction between women's waged and domestic labour.

The strength of Beechey's analysis lies in her insistence that, unless we specifically introduce the connection between women's waged labour and their domestic labour into a Marxist analysis, we can not understand why the restructuring of the labour force from the mid-twentieth century onwards resulted in women being drawn into it. However, it does seem that, rather like the neo-classical analysis outlined previously, Beechey takes women's domestic labour as given, although unlike the neo-classical economists, she does not see the current gender division of domestic labour as either based on rational choice or unproblematic. Indeed, the central essential element of any form of *feminist* theorizing is its commitment to challenging established gender divisions.

Feminist scholars in the United States have taken a different position on the utility of the concept of the industrial reserve army. It has been argued (by Power, 1983, Quick, 1977 and Vogel, 1983 among others) that women fit into Marx's concept of a latent reserve. They base their arguments on a particular point of view about what has happened, during the twentieth century, to the nature of those tasks that are defined as housework. Power, for example, has argued that housework has changed from being concerned with 'production' of goods used in the home to being concerned with maintenance or domestic reproduction tasks. Needs previously catered for in the home by the production of goods and services by individual women have been, throughout this century and indeed earlier, taken over by capitalist manufacturing organizations based on factory production, or provided by the state. As this happens, household and domestic labour is tied into capitalist production.

This is a long-term process. Huws (1985), for example, has argued that what she calls 'unsocialized labour', that is, work carried out in the home and community not for profit, has gradually been taken over by the manufacturing sector. The abolition of household production often reduces disposable family incomes as additional goods and services have to be purchased. It also reduces any last traces of women's economic independence. Power argues that, thus, by a combination of push and pull factors, women are drawn into waged labour. The push lies, in Power's eyes, in the reduction in the time required to do housework. Changes in its nature and the widespread availability of technologically sophisticated domestic appliances mean there is less (perhaps little?) for women to do in the home now. These arguments parallel those of Gershuny and Miles (1983; and see *The Economy in Question*, Allen and Massey, 1988) albeit in a different context.

Ursula Huws has written widely about new technology and its impact on the gender division of labour, in the home and in the workplace. Like Power, she has argued that the penetration of capitalist relations into domestic production has been an extremely significant, and long-term element in the restructuring of work and its division between waged and unwaged forms. Figure 5.4 shows two examples of this restructuring taken from Huws: food preparation and caring for the sick. In the boxes on the left, the nature of unsocialized labour, which includes community work by women as well as more strictly defined domestic labour within an individual home, is illustrated before the wholesale penetration of capitalist production. This work is then gradually transformed – the process is slow and uneven in time and space but the second and third columns illustrate two major changes. One change is a transformation of these tasks to service sector work, where services are available for purchase, although the technology and the work process may remain the same as when individuals provided the service in their own homes. The second major change, however, transforms these activities into manufacturing ones. Technological change results in what Huws calls the 'commoditization' of these activities. It is this set of changes that Power relies on in her analysis of why women became part of the latent reserve. She argues that the changes in housework parallel Marx's description of the transformation of agriculture under capitalism.

What is particularly interesting about Huws' diagram, in my opinion, is the final set of boxes on the right showing the changes that are occurring now, at the end of the twentieth century. Unlike Power, I think Huws would argue, not that there is little left for women to do in the home, but that the nature of the changes has merely altered the nature of women's tasks and women's exploitation. Using manufactured goods and services significantly reduces whatever elements of creativity and satisfaction there used to be in household production. What it does not *necessarily* do is reduce the time expended on housework. This question is open to empirical verification. In fact, there are few reliable surveys, based on representative samples, of the time spent on domestic labour. This partly reflects the marginalization of domestic work in academic studies of the labour process. However, what limited evidence there is (Oakley, 1974) suggests there have not been significant reductions in the time spent on domestic labour in the post-war period. The need to purchase domestic appliances may also be an important element pushing women in to the labour market now as Pahl (1983) has suggested, *and* it is happening at the very time that cuts in state services, such as care for the elderly and the young, are increasing the amount of domestic and community work for individual women involved in caring for dependants.

Where does this leave us in assessing the utility of the concept of the reserve army of labour? I would argue that the great value of the work of adherents of this approach is that it draws attention to the need to recognize, both theoretically and empirically, the changing nature of the links between waged labour and domestic labour. This marks a great advance on previous

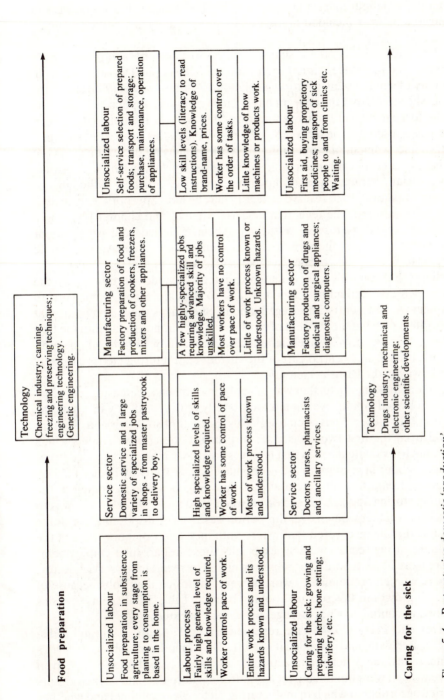

Figure 5.4   Restructuring domestic 'production'
Source: Huws, 1985, pp. 154–5

theories of labour market changes which either relied solely on changes in waged labour or included domestic labour as a universal and unchanging category.

However, critics of the variants of the reserve army of labour thesis have argued that the concept is not useful and has been applied too uncritically in studies of women's entry into waged labour. Anthias' work (1980) is important. She argues that the concept has been inaccurately applied as it 'can only refer to a determinate active labour force that is made unemployed and then used as a reserve'. The term should be restricted to this *category* of workers. Of course, women, or ethnic minority workers, may fill these categories but what the concept cannot explain, she suggests, is *why* workers with distinctive social characteristics occupy this category. Further, although she accepts that the 'latent reserve' category may be most appropriate to analyse women's position, she feels that because women (and children) have in a sense always been a reserve, as they have been excluded from waged labour for various reasons, the term loses any explanatory value. Anthias would prefer to restrict the concept to a particular usage in Marxist theory – she believes that domestic work cannot be treated as a mode of production in the same sense as agricultural labour – and to develop a new framework to explain women's entry into waged labour. She makes the telling point that one effect of using the concept of a reserve is to continue to fall into the trap of regarding women's waged labour as a marginal or peripheral phenomenon rather than a central part of the current restructuring tactics currently underway in the British economy.

Before looking at a further way of analysing women's increasing participation in waged labour, we should look briefly at the third way in which the concept of a reserve has been used. This third set of studies is at a different level from the first two. It is a set of primarily descriptive studies which attempt to evaluate the idea that reserves are drawn into, and expelled from, waged labour in relation to the economic cycle. A study by Breugel (1979) examined data for full-time and part-time waged work by women in the manufacturing and service sector between 1950 and 1978. Her aim was to discover whether women over this period were a more disposable workforce than men. She discovered that where both men and women worked in the manufacturing sector, women, especially those in part-time employment, were more likely to lose their jobs than men. However, in the service sector, where women predominate, women were not losing their jobs because of overall growth in this sector. Looking back to Table 5.2 it seems that this trend has continued since Breugel undertook her study.

Dex and Perry (1984) have repeated Breugel's study, using more disaggregated data, and extended it to 1981. They found, contrary to Breugel's conclusions, that when manufacturing was disaggregated into sectors, even here women were not unequivocally suffering more than men. Their results varied according to which manufacturing sector was examined and whether absolute or percentage, full- or part-time jobs were compared by sex. Part-time jobs underwent greater proportionate fluctuations than full-time in manufacturing, but the result was the same for men and for women. Thus, perhaps we should rephrase our questions about women's work. In this context, it is worth quoting how Dex (1985) concluded her own survey of different ways of looking at women's waged labour:

> Women are not a marginal workforce and should be viewed as permanently attached to the labour force. The sectoral distribution of women between occupations has been found to be an important factor in how they are affected by fluctuations in the business cycle. In services, women's employment has been found to be relatively unaffected in recent times by economic fluctuations. There is no evidence suggesting that women are a more disposable workforce than men. In fact the results suggest that 'disposability' is not a characteristic which applies to population groups as such: it may be better to discuss the vulnerability of certain industries. . . . The issues of whether women are a reserve army of labour or a disposable workforce buffeted by economic fluctuations have both been found to be asking the wrong questions about women's employment. The questions have been informed by too much male-centred theorizing. More specific gender-related questions need to be formulated about *women's and men's work* [my emphasis] as a further step towards the reconceptualization of the socio-economic changes that are occurring. (pp. 203–4)

Dex's book ends there but she raises a very important issue. In recent years, there have been moves towards this reconceptualization. Before we turn to these I would like to emphasize two points. First, the work which we have just considered, itself undertaken within the last decade (1978–88), has been enormously important in making questions about women's work a more central issue in academic analyses of socio-economic change than they have ever been before. It is difficult to give the impression in a single chapter of how exciting the last decade has been for all scholars interested in questions about gender and about feminism. Secondly, a framework which links women's position in the labour market and in the home to *men's* position in both these spheres, and which explains recent changes in both these areas, is far from being fully worked out at present. So, in this chapter, we are not only concerned with questions of socio-economic restructuring and changes in the social relations between men and women, but also questions about restructuring the social sciences. We are concerned with theoretical issues that are not themselves fully worked out but which are proving a challenge to conventional ways of explaining social change and the position of women and men in contemporary Britain.

5.2.3   Taking gender relations into account in studies of waged work

In this final part of section 5.2, I want to look at a number of studies that try to link men and women's position in the home into their analysis of women's entry into waged labour. They also attempt to integrate this consideration with an analysis of the horizontal and vertical segregation that results in women's subordinate position in waged labour. This set of studies is united by the combination of a theoretical position that places the structure of **power relations** between men and women at its centre with detailed empirical analyses of particular occupations. The studies are divided, however, by a theoretical disagreement about whether or not the integration of power relations into analyses requires the adoption of the concept of *patriarchy* as a separate and distinctive set of social relations, analytically distinct from capitalist social relations.

Before turning to a definition of the concept of patriarchy, I would like you to read Extract 1 from the introduction to a book called *Gender at Work* by Game and Pringle (1984). The authors' aim is to 'make sense of the social processes which generate changes in the sexual division of labour, and the ways in which it is reproduced'. In the extract they explain what they believe is the significance of power relations and gender identities in maintaining women's subordinate position.

Extract 1

Social processes and the sexual division of labour

The sexual division of labour is remarkably flexible given that it is supposed to be based on biology. Why then, if it *is* so flexible, does it continue to exist at all? The answer to this lies in the nature of the relations involved. Gender is not just about difference but about power: the domination of men and the subordination of women. This power relation is maintained by the creation of distinctions between male and female spheres – and it is the reproduction of these distinctions which accounts for the persistence of the so-called 'naturalness' of it all. It is because of this power relation that women are assumed to be much closer to nature than men. Whereas men are considered to have some agency in creating their social world, women are limited by biology – they bear children.

Here we try to make sense of the social processes which generate changes in the sexual division of labour, and the ways in which it is reproduced. Gender identity is crucial here. Masculinity and femininity are not just psychological states or attributes of sex roles that could be easily shaken off with, say, a change or 'reversal' in roles. They run much deeper than this. Our fundamental identity is as sexed beings, men or women. And in claiming that identities are constructed through social practices such as work, we are also suggesting that sexuality is a fundamental aspect of this. For example, men's sense of self is affronted if they do 'women's' work. They feel they have not only been reduced in status but almost physically degraded. (The Freudians would call this castration anxiety.) Men who do 'women's' work may be seen as weak, effeminate or even homosexual. Men's work has to be experienced as empowering. Thus men work on new *powerful* machines; technology and masculinity are very closely connected. (A mere typewriter is a different matter.) If women move into male areas of work they are made to feel awkward in a number of ways. They may be called castrating bitches, or excluded from a pub scene. Sometimes they are accused of 'sleeping their way to the top' or denied their sexuality altogether as asexual 'career women'. Frequently they are subjected to sexual harassment, which is a means of keeping them in their place and ensuring that they stay there.

Changes in the organization of work frequently provoke anxiety in men about the loss of power or the gaining of power by women to which they are not entitled. Power and sexuality are integral to work relations. As with all power relations, gender is constantly renegotiated and recreated. This process is particularly visible at points when work is being reorganized and new technologies introduced. By focusing on these it also becomes clear that masculinity and femininity are not fixed essences. There are different masculinities and femininities. Gender identities, like the power relations they embody, take a range of different forms.

In stressing the broader social relations of production we confront not only biological determinism but *technological* determinism as well. Technology does not fall ready made from the sky as an external 'cause'. It is a result of social processes. Yet the forms technology takes, and the pace with which they develop, are often assumed to be historically inevitable. Changes in the nature of work are thought to spring from some sort of technological imperative. This is analogous to the way in which gender is assumed to follow 'inevitably' from nature or biology.

Recent studies of the labour process have shown how new technologies are introduced to enhance management control over the work situation. Technology does not have an inherent dynamic of its own but is designed in the interests of particular social groups, and against the interests of others. These studies have focused on the class dimension of the social relations of technology, the struggle for control of the labour process between capital and labour. We take this further by considering the gender context of the implementation of technology. This makes the pattern of relations and the struggle over technology and control of the labour process a more complex matter. Not only are there conflicts between management and the workforce over machines, but there are also conflicts between men and women over machines; over who, for example, is to operate them. These two sets of relations mediate, overlap, and sometimes contradict each other. It is not simply that the latter conflict distracts attention from the former, as a functionalist analysis would have it.

Considering the gender context of technology raises questions about some of the central concepts in labour process analyses. In particular, we must reconsider very carefully the idea that work has been systematically deskilled under late capitalism. Whose work? Where does that leave those whose work has never been defined as skilled? Are jobs inherently skilled or are they only acknowledged as such as a result of struggle? What about new skills, including those associated with coping with pressure and monotony? Why have women never been in a position to assert that *they too* have skills? While deskilling is an important and useful concept it needs to be applied with somewhat more caution than it frequently is; it cannot be used as an all-embracing term that encapsulates processes related to technological change. While it clearly applies to old craft skills in some areas of manufacturing there are doubts about how far it is applicable to other areas of work in, for example, the tertiary sector. An analysis which focuses on deskilling is also likely to represent the interests of the most privileged sections of the workforce to the exclusion of others. Skilled tradesmen are frequently seen to be representative of the whole workforce but most men and women work in jobs that are already deskilled, defined as unskilled or, perhaps, more correctly, jobs that are not recognized as skilled.

If the deskilling hypothesis does not come to grips with the complexities of class, it is also gender blind. The definition of skill is gender biased. The process by which some jobs are defined as skilled and others as unskilled is complex, but by and large women's 'skills' are not recognized as such in the definitions of their jobs. Skilled work is men's work. To a considerable extent this is the result of trade union struggles to maintain the definition of jobs as skilled in order to preserve male wage rates.

These struggles have usually taken the form of attempting to maintain the definition of jobs as male; 'male' and 'skill' have been synonymous. There is a long history to this. Trade unions argue that *re*skilling rather than *de*skilling is occurring as a result of technological change, as a basis for wage increase claims. They do not find it at all helpful for academics to insist that deskilling has taken place, without taking any account of the particular difficulties faced in new jobs. While this still largely applies to a male workforce, for example, metal workers, there are some interesting new developments where unions cover industries such as retailing which have become predominantly female. In such cases trade unions are forced into defining the skills in women's jobs, having given up on the fight to maintain the area as male.

Another example of the relation between gender and skill – or at least of the way it is experienced – is the common assumption, held by unions, that the movement of women into a male area will not only lower wages but lead to deskilling. As we will show, the reverse is frequently the case – work is 'deskilled' and then women move in. But it cannot be assumed that this will necessarily happen. The relation between feminization and deskilling is much more complex than this. We take the view that general theories about technological change cannot be developed in the absence of concrete, specific studies.

Source: Game and Pringle, 1984, pp. 16–18

Game and Pringle set out the key issues which feminist analysts have concentrated on in studies of areas as varied as office-based secretarial work (*Webster*, 1986) working on the line in the car components industry (Cavendish, 1983), on the factory floor in a hosiery factory (*Westwood*, 1984), and in specific studies of new technology. Game and Pringle themselves, for example, undertook case studies of the factory production of white goods, retailing, the computer industry and nursing in Australia. Cynthia Cockburn in Britain has done similar work on gender, power relations and control of technology in the printing industry (1983; a book aptly entitled *Brothers*), in the clothing and distribution industries and in radiography in hospitals (Cockburn, 1986). In all these studies, women are seen as active agents, colluding in, and struggling against, male control of their labour power and **sexuality**. The innovative feature of this work is that it emphasizes that, as Game and Pringle suggested, **masculinity** and femininity are produced and reproduced in the workplace itself, as well as in the home, at school and through the media. Power relations between men and women must become an integral part of analyses of changes in the labour market.

Where Game and Pringle differ from many of the British feminists who are working on the detailed documentation of how power and gender identities are created, maintained and reproduced in the workplace is in their denial of the necessity of an analytical separation of **patriarchy** from **capitalism**. This issue, of a single system or of a **dual systems approach**, has generated a long debate within feminist theory and it is important to consider it here. Patriarchy has been defined as:

> a set of social relations between men, which have a material base, and which though hierarchical, establish or create interdependence and solidarity among men that enable them to dominate women. (Hartmann, 1981, p. 14–15)

Adherents of a separate systems approach argue that it is useful to separate patriarchy from capitalism because such a separation helps to explain the intractability of male domination, and the fact that it not only pre-dates capitalism, but that the system of sexual dominance does not seem to change at the same pace as **modes of production**.

On the other hand, Game and Pringle, among others, believe that such a separation results in an untenable trans-historical definition of the concept of patriarchy. They argue that the sexual division of labour takes specific forms in different modes of production. Within capitalism, they do not regard the particular form of this division as something pre-existing which has been 'taken over' to become a functional element of capitalist social relations, but rather as 'a defining feature of capitalism as central as wage labour or surplus value'. It is important to recognize that the particular set of power relations and sexual division of labour as experienced in capitalist societies is highly specific, but that it also varies over time and across space.

The adherents of the separate systems approach argue that distinguishing patriarchal relations as a separate system is essential to explain why the interests of men as waged labourers and capital have coincided in the past in excluding women from the waged labour force or from positions of power, when it might appear against the interests of capital to continue to employ higher paid male labour rather than replace it with cheaper women's labour. The adherents of the single system approach counter this by arguing that the particular division of labour within the home and workplace at any one time is a result of the negotiated contradiction between the short-term need to maximize profits and the long-term requirement to reproduce the labour force on a daily and generational basis which is achieved, in the main, through women's domestic labour.

Despite the theoretical disagreements between feminist scholars, detailed studies of particular labour processes that have been undertaken are re-markably similar in research design and in execution. Indeed Cockburn, who has taken what seems to be an intermediate position in the debate between the single system and dual systems proponents, has argued exactly this (see Extract 2).

Webster (1986), *Westwood* (1984) and Coyle (1982) have undertaken

Extract 2

Class and gender

The relationship between sex/gender systems and modes of production is still far from being fully understood. Modes of production (slavery, feudalism, capitalism, 'state socialism') seem to shift and change at a different pace from changes occurring within and between systems of sexual dominance. One way of looking at the world, therefore, is to see it as the interaction of two distinct systems. That way we can ask, what bearing one has on the other and where, and in what form, contradictions develop between them. This is a view I must admit to favouring. Another way, preferred by Ann Game and Rosemary Pringle, is to think of ourselves as living within a unitary system that is both capitalism and patriarchy, so tightly enmeshed is the power play of sex with that of class. *In practice, however, I think it matters little which over-arching theory we start with, provided that it is tested meticulously, by detailed analysis of material situations and historical processes.*

The project, then, is to show how masculine and feminine are produced in relation to each other through work. And the story unfolds like a grotesque dance, the unending dance of the sexual division of labour. Round the Maypole go men and women. One of the rules of the dance is that the two sexes will remain separate, though small deviations from the choreography may be tolerated. Men and women wear different costumes, men in pin-striped suits or white coats, women in trim skirts, pink overalls or nurses' aprons. Another rule is that men will normally have the initiative. The strands that are woven together, in and out, are new technology and old traditions, deskilling and hyperskilling, fragmentation and unification of tasks, the making and breaking of career ladders. The master of the dance is capital, the patriarch. And the web that is woven around the Maypole is the fabric of class and gender, in which women are firmly plaited into place.

Source: Cockburn *in* Game and Pringle, 1984, p. 10

detailed studies of the labour process within particular firms, often through direct participation as employees or through participant observation. Detailed records of the nature of the tasks undertaken by women, and of the structure of authority on the shop floor, or in the office, focusing in particular on how men exert power and authority over women, are the basis of each study. In a small number of studies, the researcher also became involved in the home and the social life of her co-workers or subjects of research. It is interesting that the higher level conceptual disagreement about the relationship between patriarchy and capitalism did not affect the execution or results of these analyses. All the authors, however, were working within a feminist perspective that emphasized the unity of women's home life and position in the workforce. Adherents of both approaches, moreover, stress the necessity of empirical research to document the nature and variety of gender relations in particular industries and particular parts of the country at any one time. They also emphasize the significance of looking at struggles and contradictions and the ways in which gender divisions are negotiated and renegotiated in the context of social change.

In the final section of this chapter, we will return to this question of renegotiation in the context of change and consider some of the lines of contemporary changes among young people. Before that, however, we will shift our focus a little, and consider a set of questions about how changes in the role and responsibility of the UK state, especially since 1979, have had an impact on women's non-waged labour. In particular, we will look at the role of the welfare state and its basis on women's unpaid caring work in the home and the community. Women are also significant employees in the welfare services, but it is the former aspect on which I shall concentrate.

Summary of section 5.2

1   Increasing numbers of women have become waged workers since the end of the Second World War in Britain.

2   Women have entered the labour market as low paid and poorly skilled workers.

3   Certain occupations are constructed as 'women's work'. The designation of a skill label and appropriate financial rewards to an occupation are as much to do with the gender of the worker as they are attributes of the job.

4   The factors that are considered to be important in explaining women's position in the labour market depend upon the theoretical perspective of the investigator:

•   Neo-classical economists and human capital theorists focus on supply and demand factors in the market, and household decisions about total income.

•   Reserve army of labour theorists focus on women's role in the family and cyclical variations in the economy.

•   Theorists who focus on gender relations between men and women look at questions about male power and control over women as well as the operation of the economy. In both single and dual systems approaches the importance of patriarchal relations is emphasized.

5.3   Women and welfare

The reasons for looking at changes in welfare provision and their relationships to gender relations is twofold. First, there has been a radical restructuring in the ideology and material basis of the provision of welfare services and social security in the UK since 1979. This restructuring has been based on an ideology that emphasizes *individual* liberty and *individual* moral responsibility, but in practice is based on the strengthening of *family* obligations. The second reason is that the shift in the extent of state-provided and funded welfare services has significantly affected the material resources and quality of life of many working-class people, but of women in particular. The result is that, at the same time as women are an increasingly central element of waged labour, their labour is also of growing significance in the area of social reproduction. For many women, this exacerbates the burdens of their 'dual' role.

This section is shorter than the preceding section on waged labour. This is partly because the changing distribution of income and wealth and the impact of social security changes in the 1980s have been discussed in Chapter 2; issues of housing, health, education are taken up in Chapter 6; and the changing role of the state is the major focus of *Politics in Transition* (Cochrane and Anderson, 1989). But it is also because the whole area is less theoretically developed than the area of waged work we have just considered, and despite changes in the nature of welfare services, women's place in this provision has *not* changed.

The contradiction created by women's participation in waged labour and their continued responsibility for the tasks of social reproduction is not a new feature nor solely a consequence or reflection of political changes since 1979. The institutions of the post-war welfare state were based on the assumption that a married woman's primary responsibilities were to her husband and children, and the structure of the tax and social security systems have continued to reflect the assumption of women's economic dependence on men. There is now a reasonably well-developed feminist critique of the post-war settlement and the institutional practices of the welfare state (see Land, 1983, 1986; or Wilson, 1977 for useful introductions to this critique). What I want to do here is illustrate how the successive policies of Conservative governments, with their commitment to dismantling the welfare state and abolishing collectivist provision, have raised in its starkest form yet the contradictions that are inherent in the current restructuring of the British economy and society. The economy, as we have seen here (and in *The Economy in Question* (Allen and Massey, 1988) if it is read carefully for the gender implications of the changes), is increasingly based on the exploitation of women in the labour market, where they are constructed as workers alternately labelled as marginal, peripheral, secondary or flexible. However, there is continued reliance on women's domestic and unwaged labour to maintain and reproduce the relations of social reproduction. This uneasy contradiction exists in the context of a society that seems to deny the necessity of renegotiating traditional gender divisions. The structures of inequality in the labour market and within the family appear to be remarkably resistant to change, as we shall see in detail in section 5.4.

5.3.1   The welfare state and women's roles

The institutions and legislation of the welfare state provide one of the clearest examples of the way in which women's domestic and caring responsibilities are constructed as their primary responsibility. Welfare legislation thus reinforces women's position in the labour market as part-time, often temporary (over their own life cycle at least) and low paid workers. Women's caring and servicing roles within the family, undertaken for love, have a parallel in their waged labour in the welfare state. Nursing, ancillary work in the health service (catering, cleaning and laundry work) and social work are all occupations dominated by women and relatively low paid. Attributes that are used to define femininity such as patience, dexterity, sympathy and tolerance for others' weakness are all used to construct these occupations as 'women's work' and to justify their low pay. The same attributes are used to explain gender divisions within the family. Since 1979, there has been a noticeable strengthening of rhetoric about 'the family' and a reassertion of 'Victorian values' to justify cuts in welfare spending, and an increased reliance on the voluntary labour of women to provide essential support services. The vision of the family that underpins Conservative social policy is reminiscent of a particular sector of nineteenth century society rather than a reflection of contemporary reality. It is a family based on strict sexual division of labour where the paterfamilias is the main economic provider, and the woman is primarily a homemaker and mother.

Consider for a moment: what proportion of households in Britain conform to the 'ideal' of an employed father, a mother at home and two dependent children? Senior managers in a selection of Britain's major firms were asked this question in early 1988. Their estimates ranged from 85 per cent to 20 per cent. They all overestimated the correct percentage of 8. Of course, statistics can be used selectively to give a particular picture. Look critically at the very narrow definition of an 'ideal' family – it must include two children, and only two, and both 16 years old or under. The tiny proportion of 8 per cent also represents a static snapshot at one point in time. The majority of the present population did in fact grow up in this type of family. But household patterns are changing. Figure 5.5 shows the distribution of households of different types and the proportion of people living in different types of households. The first chart shows that what is assumed to be the 'normal household' – a married couple with children – was only just over a quarter of all households in 1985, only a slightly larger proportion than the households consisting of a single person. But, of course, this means that statistically, as the second chart shows, almost one half of all individuals do live in traditional nuclear families of couples and children.

Despite the variation in family forms and relationships, throughout the 1980s there has been a strong emphasis not only on the family but on motherhood as an ideal and a full-time occupation. One of the earliest and frankest assertions of the ideology of the Conservative right was a statement in a televised debate in 1979 by Patrick Jenkin, then newly-appointed Secretary of State for the Social Services:

> Quite frankly, I don't think that mothers have the same right to work as fathers do. If the Good Lord had intended us to have equal rights to go out to work he wouldn't have created man and woman. These are biological facts.

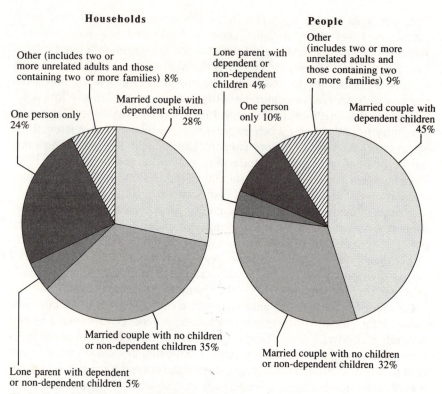

Households

Other (includes two or
more unrelated adults and those
containing two or more families) 8%

One person only
24%

Married couple with
dependent children
28%

Married couple with no children
or non-dependent children 35%

Lone parent with dependent
or non-dependent children 5%

People

Lone parent with
dependent or
non-dependent
children 4%

Other
(includes two or more
unrelated adults and
those containing two
or more families) 9%

One person
only 10%

Married couple with
dependent children
45%

Married couple with no children
or non-dependent children 32%

Figure 5.5   Households and people by type of household
Source: General Household Survey, *1986*

A rather more sophisticated view of motherhood than this crudely biological
determinist view can be traced in the acts of the governments since 1979.
Miriam David, in a survey of key issues in social welfare debates between
1979 and 1986 has argued thus:

> There is a core value of 'motherhood' in the conservative notion of the family.
> This notion underpins the various issues about the family which have domi-
> nated the political agenda. They range from the Gillick case on parental
> consent over contraceptive advice to girls under 16 years old, to the Warnock
> Committee's report on human fertilization and embryology and the conse-
> quent debates on reproductive technology and surrogate motherhood, and
> Enoch Powell's two Private Members Bills in parliament on the protection of
> (unborn) children. There has also been a debate about child care as well as the
> conditions of maternity and childbirth, namely over the taxation of workplace
> nurseries, and parental or family leave from employment to care for sick
> children and other families. In other words, there has been a sustained debate
> about *motherhood* [David's emphasis] in all its ramifications: from child
> bearing to child rearing. (1986, pp. 40–1)

Since her survey, other issues about motherhood have arisen, for example,
the defeated attempt in 1988 to alter the 1967 Abortion Act. It is clear that
the rights and responsibilities of 'motherhood' will remain a contested area.

5.3.2   The 'new right'

The 'new right' tends to argue that it is previous state interference in the family that has caused a range of so-called family problems, from teenage 'promiscuity', separation and divorce, to the growing numbers of single mothers. By invoking the Victorian family and reasserting women's primary caring role, it is assumed that these problems will eventually disappear. The ideological centrality of the nuclear family is thus constantly invoked to justify changes in the structure and coverage of welfare provision. In the theoretical writings and public statements of the proponents of reduced state expenditure, the role of the individual and the role of the state have been counterposed in terms of propositions about moral responsibility. In one of the few speeches she has made about welfare services, given in 1978, just before she became Prime Minister, Margaret Thatcher explained the new Conservative ideology as follows:

> We know the immense sacrifices which people will make for the care of their own near and dear – for elderly relatives, disabled children and so on, and the immense part which voluntary effort even outside the confines of the family has played in these fields. Once you give people the idea that all this can be done by the state ... then you will begin to deprive human beings of one of the essential ingredients of humanity – personal moral responsibility. (quoted in Croft, 1986)

Similar arguments – about how state provision saps the moral fibre of the nation – have been pronounced many times since 1978 in debates in Parliament and elsewhere about the welfare state. Indeed, in a major statement of her beliefs in a speech to the General Assembly of the Church of Scotland in May 1988, the Prime Minister reasserted her belief in individual responsibility and self reliance. The ways in which such principles enable the poor and deprived to challenge the structures of inequality in contemporary Britain were not dwelt upon. As a principle, it is difficult to deny the importance of personal responsibility; it is the ways in which this might be achieved that form the focus of debate. There is a similar argument about the role of '**community care**' in Britain today.

The role of women as volunteers in the community has been an important element in the debates about 'community care'. Reducing the institutionalization of the elderly, disabled people and mentally-ill people is one aim of this policy. Although it may or may not have advantages, it would seem to require the introduction of support services within 'the community' to enable the policy to be implemented. However, as Groves and Finch (1983) have shown in an assessment of the 'caring' services, community care relies on the unpaid domestic and voluntary labour of women, and it is an inexpensive solution to the care of the growing numbers of the dependent population. The projected rate of growth in the elderly population is such that by the year 2025, every ten economically active citizens will support nearly four pensioners and three children. This projection (see Figure 5.6) is reasonably accurate for the number of old people because the next century's elderly are already born; for births and for economic activity, the projection is less certain. What also seems certain is that women will feature in growing numbers among the elderly, the economically active and the carers.

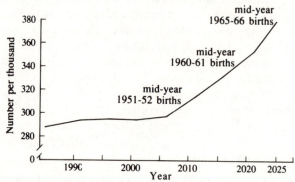

Figure 5.6   Projected population of pensionable age per thousand population of working age 1985–2025, Great Britain (mid-1985 projections)
Source: Office of Population, Censuses and Surveys

In the field of social security, some of the clearest evidence about recent assumptions about the centrality of women's familial roles, and their economic dependence within the household, is to be found in the Social Security Act 1986, implemented in April 1988. The net result of measures in this Act is to increase women's insecurity. In the Green Paper that preceded the Act, emphasis was placed on increasing 'self reliance' and 'personal independence', based on the assumed moral superiority of personal rather than collective responsibility. In fact, however, the act is based not on the presumption of *individual* responsibility but on *family* responsibility. Its provisions place greater reliance on means-tested benefits calculated on the aggregation of household or family resources. This is both incompatible with a rhetoric of personal responsibility and assumes an equitable division of resources between family members which, as studies have shown, is often not the case (Graham, 1984; Pahl, 1983).

Specific changes that will increase women's dependence, and the extent of inequality between men and women, include changes to pensions and maternity benefits, and to women's eligibility for unemployment benefit. The universal maternity grant was abolished in 1987 and replaced by a means-tested benefit available only to those claiming income support or family credit. At the same time, statutory maternity pay was introduced to be administered by employers, with a new qualification test that excludes large numbers of pregnant women. In addition, the 1986 White Paper, revealingly entitled 'Building businesses . . . not barriers', included a proposal to weaken the right of part-time workers to reinstatement after maternity leave. In other ways too women's dependency is deepened by the Social Security Act 1986. Alterations to the State Earnings Related Pension

Scheme will reduce its value for elderly widows. Similarly the introduction of the social fund and the abolition of special needs payments are based on a belief that women should be economically dependent on men, without regard to the actual financial circumstances of individual families. Women's eligibility for unemployment benefit has also been affected by the introduction of stringent conditions to establish a claimant's availability for work. These penalize, in particular, women with pre-school children who are required to demonstrate that they have already existing child-care arrangements before they are entitled to benefit. In a situation where there is minimum state provision for pre-school children and costly private alternatives, this measure, as David (1986) succinctly states, 'fails to grasp the reality of such women's lives' (p. 48). Women's right to child benefit payments has also been under attack in the last decade. Vigorous campaigns seem to have ensured that it is still paid directly to mothers, rather than through men's wage packets, but in 1987 the commitment to maintain its real value relative to inflation was abolished, and the planned April 1988 rise was reduced.

The operation of the social security system may also result in women withdrawing from paid labour when their partners become unemployed. This is an interesting proposition to consider because it contradicts one of the sets of assumed behaviour in the neo-classical approach outlined in section 5.2. There it was argued that women's entry to waged labour may be related to a 'substitution' effect as their partners' wages either fell or they became unemployed. However, evidence from surveys in Britain (Cooke, 1987) suggests that, when married men become unemployed, their spouses tend also to withdraw from waged labour. This appears to be a contradictory response, most obviously because it has been shown that in low income families with two earners, the second income is an important factor in raising total incomes above the poverty line. However, part of the reason for women's withdrawal is the way in which the additional earnings 'disregard' works for unemployed claimants. There are two disregards that concern the unemployed: the one for unemployment benefit (£2 a day in 1987) and the more stringent one (£4 per week) for supplementary benefit. The husband's unemployment benefit is paid to him as of right, and it is unaffected by any earnings of his wife; it is only the addition of the wife as a dependant that is reduced to take account of her earnings. Means-tested supplementary benefit, on the other hand, is assessed and paid on a *family* basis and is affected by any income of either spouse. After 12 months, entitlement to unemployment benefit is exhausted and it is replaced by supplementary benefit and so may increase the likelihood of women's withdrawal from waged labour.

Other factors have been found to be important, however, in explaining women's withdrawal. These include greater likelihood of poor health among unemployed men, and women's decisions to care for them, and attitudes and social conventions about the role of the breadwinner. There is evidence of 'strong endorsement' of the male breadwinner role by unemployed women and by women with unemployed male partners (Sinfield, 1981; Marsden, 1982; Campbell, 1984). Indeed, in a survey conducted across the member states of the EC (Commission of European Communities, 1984), 59 per cent of women surveyed agreed with the statement that 'in a period of high unemployment a man has a greater right to work than a woman.' However, as we have seen from the evidence of occupational segregation, men and women do not, in general, compete for the same jobs, and it is not likely that women's withdrawal will facilitate male re-entry to the labour market. On the other hand, where the men affected are near to retirement age, and the boundary between unemployment and retirement is blurred, the finding (Joshi, 1984) that wives of retired men withdraw from the workforce to share leisure time might also be part of the explanation. Whatever the particular mix of reasons, it is clear that the belief that women have less right to waged labour and to an earned income of their own has a tenacious hold on the general public and on public policy makers.

The taxation system is based on similar beliefs about women's economic position. The right for married women to be taxed individually on their earned and unearned incomes was finally introduced in 1988 (and implemented in 1990), but other changes in the taxation position of married couples introduced in the same year *increased* married women's dependence by increasing the tax advantages to well-paid men of non-working wives. As the Green Paper on 'The reform of personal taxation', published before the new legislation was introduced, made clear, the aim was 'to remove the present special incentive for two earner couples. Such positive discrimination is neither necessary nor economically desirable at a time of high unemployment, particularly among the young.' The message is clear: married women have less right to jobs than the young. In the event, the legislation introduced was a compromise which on the one hand introduced separate taxation for all individuals regardless of marital status, but on the other hand retained the married man's allowance which could be transferred from husband to wife if this improved the overall financial position of the family. *The Times* leader, commentating on the changes, congratulated the Chancellor for strengthening the position of marriage and the family which was regarded as 'a key institution essential for social stability'. The sanctity of wedlock was further strengthened by the rectification of the anomaly which allowed unrelated adults purchasing a single dwelling together to claim multiple tax relief on mortgage interest payments.

Such policies, together with the restructuring of the welfare state that is currently underway, are magnifying a central contradiction in Britain today – that between women's productive role in the economy and their reproductive role in the home and the community. The interconnection between the two is the way in which the tasks undertaken by women can continually be recreated and redefined as 'women's work' despite changes in the nature and content of these jobs. Once defined as 'women's work', these jobs and occupations are then expected to be undertaken 'for love' within the family, and for inadequate financial rewards in the labour market. This essential interconnection between men's and women's roles in the family and in the labour market, and the gender division of labour that has evolved in Britain means that women are a central element of growing significance in both the spheres of waged and unwaged labour. Yet in their position as waged labourers they are continually re-endowed with so-called 'marginal' characteristics. This central contradiction can only be resolved by a transformation of the relationship between waged and unwaged labour and a renegotiation of current gender divisions.

In the concluding section of this chapter, I thought it would be appropriate to examine what evidence there is about the nature of gender relations between young men and women whose social and economic experiences have been structured by growing up in a period of high unemployment, cuts in state spending and many years of a radical right government. It seems inevitable that the current contradiction will lead to a crisis, for individual women if not for the economy as a whole. In an interesting challenge to the usual practice of not including domestic labour as an integral part of the economy, and so not recognizing the contradiction, the London Industrial Strategy (GLC, 1985) not only investigated the contribution of domestic labour to the London economy but pointed to the forthcoming crisis, if state support for domestic and community work continued to be cut. Unfortunately, there is little evidence of changing policies.

Summary of section 5.3

1   As well as their growing participation in waged labour, women play an essential role in the social reproduction of the population through their unpaid labour in the home and the community.

2   The advent of a 'radical' right wing government in 1979 led to increased reliance on women's unpaid labour as state provision was reduced in many areas.

3   An ideological emphasis on self-reliance and individual moral responsibility actually meant the strengthening of *family* responsibilities and women's increased economic dependence on men.

4   The coincidence of economic and social changes has led to a deepening contradiction for individual women and the society as a whole between women's roles in waged and unwaged work.

5.4   Renegotiating gender relations

It is interesting that a great deal of the research evidence about youth culture, and particularly about young people's attitudes to employment, is based on studies of boys only. However, research on the attitudes and expectations of girls and young women, both middle and working class, has demonstrated the central importance of love and marriage in their current lives and in future expectations. For girls still at school, having a boyfriend gives them a certain status. Once out at work, previous studies have demonstrated that working-class young women exhibit a remarkably clear-eyed recognition of economic realities. Given their generally low wages compared with young men of their age, their spending power is low and greatly enhanced if they have a young man to take them out regularly (Leonard, 1981; *Westwood*, 1984). Such women seldom make a positive decision to marry; there is simply no alternative. Economic considerations and social expectations pull in the same direction. In addition, there is little or no affordable housing for young, single, working-class women. Consequently, they become locked into dependency on men. Social security and taxation policies, as we have seen, reinforce this dependency.

But what is the impact of the rapid rise of youth unemployment among young men and young women. Does unemployment and a levelling of income differentials reduce or reinforce gender divisions? In addition, given the continued expansion of service sector employment for women, albeit poorly paid, what is the impact on gender relations between couples where only the young woman has waged employment? To what extent are these couples challenging stereotypical gender divisions of labour?

In order to address these questions, I have looked at three general studies of youth unemployment which, although not focusing in detail on the issue of gender relations, do provide some pertinent evidence, and also at a study of young working-class women in employment who have unemployed boyfriends. The first three studies were originally presented at a conference in 1984 on 'Work, employment and unemployment', and later published in *The Experience of Unemployment* (Allen *et al.*, 1986). Each of the three authors deals with a specific location: Brah with the inner area of Leicester; Coles with four rural or small town locations in a shire county; and Allatt and Yeandle with a ward of a city in north-east England. They each use different methods: Brah concentrated on group discussions and in-depth interviews with unemployed Sikhs, Muslims and Hindus; Coles used survey methods to sample two cohorts of young people; and Allatt and Yeandle undertook interviews with young people looking for work and with their families. Despite these differences in location, methods and populations researched, which impair the comparability of results, each author made similar observations about gender divisions.

In all the studies, both the young men and the young women interviewed were keenly aware of the loss of independence entailed by being unemployed, and they regretted their inability to make their expected contribution to social relationships with the other sex. Young men were ashamed of not being able to pay for their companions when out with young women; young women were anxious about their future financial contribution within a permanent relationship. These feelings were particularly strong amongst Brah's sample of Asian young people – for example, the inability to provide for their widowed mothers, siblings and in a few cases wives, weighed heavily on Asian men in the sample. As Brah concluded, 'unemployment brings into sharp focus the centrality of the wage as an affirmation of masculinity' (p. 69). Asian women who were married regretted not being able to contribute financially to their household, and unmarried women to their own eventual marriage provision. Interestingly, the young Asian women in the sample spoke of, and apparently accepted, the 'double burden' of combining work outside the home with domestic duties. They knew too that they would earn less than men, and that there were domains of the labour market from which they were excluded. But they saw unemployment as eroding the steps that they had made towards greater independence.

Other studies of women's employment (Coyle, 1982; *Webster*, 1986; *Westwood*, 1984) have analysed women's cultures at the workplace, and reveal deep contradictions. Workplace relations are shot through with divisions of gender, race and ethnicity, and for ethnic minority women they often reaffirm racist, patriarchal practices in the wider society. However, entry to wage labour also widens social contacts, which are often very important for young Asian women, and the **workplace culture** is also a site for the development of resistance to gender and social stereotyping.

The three studies by Brah, Coles, and Allatt and Yeandle revealed little evidence of young people challenging conventional gender divisions. In order to further examine the possibility that changes in men's and women's economic prospects may affect gender relations, Beuret and Makings (1987) have undertaken a very interesting study of patterns of dating behaviour and courtship among a sample of unmarried working-class men and women in Leicester and the north of England. In order to test ideas that differential economic power between men and women affects the balance of power in personal relationships, the authors interviewed couples where the woman was in waged employment and the man was not. This reversed the more common situation, where men in general have a greater degree of economic power, and hence it is argued greater power in personal relationships with women. Some sociologists have suggested that the recession and male unemployment might 'herald a breakdown in patriarchal structures' (McKee and Bell, 1986) relating to married couples. The evidence we have discussed earlier (in section 5.4) does not lend support to this hypothesis, so it is important to look at couples in less established relationships to see what evidence there is about the impact of the recession on gender relations.

Beuret and Makings' sample consisted of twenty-five hairdressers aged between 16 and 27. They were all unmarried and, at the time they were interviewed, all had unemployed boyfriends. Despite this situation being an increasingly common one in the UK, this is the only study that I could find when writing this chapter which examines the behaviour and ideas of young women in these circumstances. Beuret and Makings found that the women in their sample of hairdressers were very aware of the effect of their boyfriends' unemployment on their relationship, but that they engaged in various strategies to try to ensure that their public 'courtship' appeared to conform to expected patterns of male and female behaviour. Here is a selection of responses which the young women made to questions about how they managed the unequal economic relationships when the couple went out:

'Yes, well of course Barry only gets his dole money plus a bit he makes on the side helping out at the Club, whereas since I changed salons I've been coming home of a Friday with £130 clear. My Mum won't take more than £10 so I'm sitting pretty. It makes going out with Barry a bit awkward. Up here (the North East) everyone expects the fellows to pay. When I'm out with me mates I drink Bacardi and coke but when I'm with Barry I have lager. He saw me drinking with the girls once and got upset when he saw the shorts, but I said it was Linda's birthday and we were having a treat.' (pp. 67–8)

'I like my man to look good on a Saturday but Mike is a bit touchy if I buy him anything pricey. So I pretend that one of the customers works for 'Next' and gets seconds cheap. I got him a smashing jumper last week, it cost me £39 but I told him it cost £5. He insisted on giving me the fiver too, poor sod. Men have no idea do they?' (p. 68)

'I let him pay for the everyday things like drinks when we do go out, but I pay for the larger items, especially holidays. We're going to the Canaries in May and I've already paid for both of us. It's all in, meals as well, so this won't leave him much to find for drinks and that when we go out.' (p. 68)

The authors comment as follows:

These and similar strategies for handling the financial aspects of the relationship were designed to preserve the appearance, both to the boyfriend and to other outsiders, of him being in financial control. To this extent they can be interpreted as attempts to maintain the man's traditional provider role. However, it is noticeable that the women felt themselves to be in charge of these situations. The various economic subterfuges were of their own devising; they frequently involved duping their boyfriends (the comment above; 'Men have no idea do they', was by no means atypical), and their purpose was often to make sure that the woman achieved her desired goal – a foreign holiday, a smartly dressed boyfriend, favourite drinks, or whatever – rather than deny herself these things as a consequence of his straitened circumstances. (p. 68)

The authors found that the women they sampled were prepared to initiate relationships with men, and that they were also clear-sighted about the disadvantages of early marriage or marriage at all in their current circumstances.

'If I ever do take the plunge, it will definitely be with Jo, but I can't see it for a bit until he gets himself a job. I wouldn't like to keep him on my wages.'

'I hear a lot from my customers. It seems that unless you find a man with a good job you're worse off getting married.' (p. 72)

Although this study is based on a limited sample, and the conclusions must be tentative, the authors suggest that their results show that 'the recession and male unemployment *are* [emphasis in original] having an impact on courtship, and in the situation described here – employed girlfriend, unemployed boyfriend – the effects seem to be weakening the dependency syndrome of women' (p. 72). However, as the authors also recognize 'numerous other variables such as class, level of education and training, occupational environment and region can act in different combinations to influence results' (p. 72).

Research remains to be undertaken to discover whether the tentative changes in gender relations outlined above will herald widespread future changes. Women's increased participation in waged labour is a geographically widespread phenomenon, and previous regional differences in participation rates have been reduced in recent decades. This is partly a consequence of the expansion of 'women's' jobs in the service sector, which geographically is more evenly distributed in relation to population than manufacturing employment, and also because regions that previously had the lowest proportion of women in their waged labour force, such as East Anglia and the South West, have expanded more quickly in recent years.

However, local differences between places remain important, and we are as yet only at the beginning of theorizing the implications for changing gender relations of the radical social and economic changes that have taken place in post-war Britain. The evidence presented here is only limited. We need to think carefully how to conceptualize the relationships between gender relations in the home and the community and in the labour market. We also need to devise criteria to assess the validity of evidence from studies based on different sources, undertaken at different spatial scales, and for different purposes. On the basis of the limited range of material presented here, it seems as if we could draw contradictory conclusions about the ways in which the restructuring of social and economic relations is affecting gender relations and women's subordination to men. Survey research, such as that of Beuret and Makings, may indicate that old patterns of dependencies are beginning to be challenged. National statistics on patterns of marriage, conception and childbirth may show this as well. But, the current restructuring of the welfare state and the labour market is deepening the contradiction for women of their 'dual' roles. Further, the creation of an economy increasingly based on jobs for 'women' that are constructed on a set of taken-for-granted assumptions – about women's economic dependence on men and their primary role in the family – *that are no longer true*, makes these contradictions increasingly unstable. 'Women's' jobs are *central* to individuals' household economies *and* to the economy as a whole as high rates of male unemployment appear to have become a permanent feature of the UK economy.

Placing this central contradiction – between an economy restructured along lines that reflect outmoded assumptions about women's attachment to waged labour (and, interestingly, this restructuring affects *all* workers, as the discussions in *The Economy in Question* (Allen and Massey, 1988) about core and peripheral labour markets and numerical flexibility revealed) and a welfare state restructured to rely increasingly on women's unwaged labour – at the forefront of analysis allows us, I would conclude, to reveal more clearly the nature of contemporary social changes.

Starting from the viewpoint of women allows us to start to give different and fuller answers to questions such as: Has the working class declined? Why do the trade unions and left-wing political parties currently seem incapable of addressing the key issues of the late 1980s? How is the economy being reorganized, and why is it impossible to understand these changes without considering the systems of production and social reproduction together? Social and economic changes in the UK are producing new contradictions which the state is struggling to overcome. It may be that the central contradiction embodied in the lives of the majority of women in the UK today can only be resolved by a transformation of the economy and a new relationship between the public and the private. As we move into the 1990s I believe that the necessity for a transformation in gender relations will become increasingly urgent. Time will test this prediction, but perhaps this chapter will need rewriting in the not too distant future.

6 Consumption and class in contemporary Britain

Chris Hamnett

Contents

6.1   Introduction

We have shown in previous chapters that the social structure of Britain is sharply differentiated in terms of class, race and gender. It is also highly unequal in terms of the distribution of income and wealth. These divisions are extremely important and they play a major part in determining people's social and economic opportunities. But the social structure of Britain is differentiated in a number of other ways which also play a major part in shaping the quality of people's lives and their 'life chances'. Differences in provision of, and access to, different forms of consumption, such as housing, education and health care, stand out as being of particular importance in this respect. Access to good housing, education and health care can play as crucial a role in influencing the quality of people's lives, as can access to good jobs and incomes. Housing conditions, educational attainment and health also play a major role in influencing people's occupational and income opportunities. It is, therefore, important to examine the major changes which have occurred in the provision of, and access to, these forms of consumption since the war.

Two major changes can be identified. First, the establishment of what is often termed 'the welfare state' at the end of the Second World War meant that a variety of welfare benefits and entitlements, such as national insurance, secondary and higher education and health care, became available to everyone on the basis of need rather than ability to pay. In addition, there have been major changes in housing consumption as private renting has been replaced by owner occupation and council renting as the dominant tenures. This has led to a widespread improvement in housing conditions, but also to a growing social division between those reliant on state housing and those able to afford private provision. It has been suggested that since the late 1970s, the public–private division in housing has been paralleled by the expansion of private education, health care and pension schemes, which are collectively leading to the emergence of a widening division in access to the **means of consumption** between those who have access to private provision and those who rely on state provision.

As well as changing people's life chances, these changes in the structure of consumption have raised several important theoretical questions regarding the relationship between consumption and class. It has long been recognized that the marked, and well-documented, differences in educational attainment, health, housing conditions and other key aspects of consumption, are strongly associated with occupational and income differences determined in the workplace (see Chapter 2). But, since the late 1970s, it has been argued by Peter Saunders (1978, 1984) that differences in consumption, particularly between those who have access to private means of consumption, and those who are reliant on state provision, constitute an *independent* dimension of social stratification, rather than just a reflection of social class.

This debate has parallels with the debate over the determinants of social class discussed in Chapter 3. Whereas Marxists see the relationship to the means of production as the chief determinant of class, Weberians argue that classes can arise in a variety of market situations, not just those between capital and wage labour. Similarly, some Weberians have argued that consumption locations are now as important as production locations in shaping social divisions in Britain. As *Saunders* (1984) suggests:

> Just as the main social division arising out of the organization of production in capitalist societies is that between those who own and control the means of production and those who do not, so the main division arising out of the process of consumption in such societies is that between those who satisfy their main consumption needs through personal ownership (e.g. through home ownership, personal means of transportation, private medical insurance and private schooling) and those who rely on collective provision through the state. (p. 208)

It has also been suggested that the growth of private forms of consumption and the decline of collective forms of provision and consumption have led to marked changes in the *culture of consumption* and in political orientations and alignments, because people who are less dependent on the state for provision of the means of consumption align themselves with those political parties which emphasize the importance of individual self-reliance and market modes of provision. Whereas social class determined through the workplace was thought to play a dominant role in the creation of political alignments, it is now argued by some commentators that consumption sector divisions are of equal, if not greater, importance.

These arguments have major implications for our understanding of the changing social structure of contemporary Britain and they will be examined in detail later in the chapter. First, however, section 6.2 summarizes and assesses some of the major changes which have occurred in the structure of housing, health and educational provision and consumption since the war. Particular attention is paid to the changes which have taken place in housing consumption. The reasons for this focus are twofold. First, it is difficult to deal adequately with all the changes in housing, health and education in the space of a single chapter. Secondly, it is argued by consumption theorists that housing tenure is the single most important consumption divide because of the potential afforded by home ownership for wealth accumulation. Although education and health play a major role in shaping life chances, they do not provide access to a source of income or wealth in the market. They therefore do not provide a basis for class formation in the strict Weberian sense.

Section 6.3 examines the empirical evidence on the relationship between class and consumption. Again, particular attention is paid to housing.

In section 6.4 we will consider the extent to which the differences in consumption may be seen to be class related and/or class determined, and the extent to which these consumption inequalities compound or ameliorate inequalities deriving from position in the paid labour market. It also outlines some of the major arguments that have been put forward regarding the extent to which consumption locations can be said to be an independent dimension of social stratification and social class. It will examine whether or not it is possible to distinguish classes based on consumption cleavages rather than relations of production, occupation, income and wealth.

Finally, section 6.5 looks at the debate regarding the culture and politics of privatized versus collective or socially provided consumption. Again, particular attention is paid to housing.

6.2   The changing structure of consumption in the UK

The post-war period has seen major changes in the structure and organiza-tion of housing, health care and education provision in the UK. Prior to 1945, direct state subsidized provision of social facilities was limited to council housing (introduced in 1919 by Lloyd George) and primary educa-tion; health care, secondary and higher education were still provided priva-tely on a fee-paying basis. But, with the commitment to full employment in 1944, the introduction of the 1944 Education Act, the National Health Service in 1947, and a national insurance scheme in 1948, the foundations of what has come to be known as the 'welfare state' were firmly established. As a result of these reforms, together with the rapid expansion of council housing in the 1950s and '60s, state provided forms of what have been termed '**collective consumption**' became available to the majority of the population for the first time.

This system of direct state provision, subsidized or paid for through taxation and national insurance, represented a sharp break with the pre-vious market forms of provision which were largely based on ability to pay. Henceforth, provision was to be available on a universal basis according to need or, in the case of entry to grammar schools and universities, on the basis of ability rather than ability to pay. The foundations of the welfare state were laid down by the 1945–51 Labour government but, despite right wing criticism, the three subsequent Conservative administrations (1951–64) accepted its popularity, and a broad consensus emerged regarding its continuing existence. In fact, the level of new house building under Macmil-lan in the mid-1950s has never been equalled. When Labour were re-elected in 1964 they set about strengthening aspects of the welfare state, legislating for comprehensive schools and increasing council house building.

But, from the early 1970s, the welfare state was subject to rapidly rising costs as inflation increased, Conservative support weakened and, at their Selsdon conference in 1971, the Conservatives adopted a much more market orientated political philosophy. The foreign exchange crisis of 1976, the request for assistance from the International Monetary Fund (IMF), and the limits on government expenditure set by the IMF as a condition for their help, led Labour to make cuts in government expenditure, particularly in council housing. The Conservatives made further sharp cuts in council house building during the early and mid-1980s.

Private forms of consumption also grew in importance during this period. Although the council sector had grown rapidly from 1.5 million households (12 per cent of the total) in 1945 to 6.5 million (31 per cent of the total) in 1979, owner occupation grew even more rapidly (from 25 to 56 per cent of households). This trend towards greater home ownership has been reinforced since 1979 with the introduction of the 'right to buy' policy for council tenants. Between 1979 and 1987 a million council houses were sold and by 1987 64 per cent of households owned their own home. There has also been rapid expansion in both private health schemes and private education during the 1980s. In 1987 5.7 million people (10 per cent of the population) were members of private health schemes and 8 per cent of children were educated privately. Also, with the rise of widespread private car ownership since the early 1960s (60 per cent of households owned one or more cars in 1986 against 21 per cent in 1961), there has been a rapid decline in both the provision of and usage of public transport.

As noted in the introduction to this chapter, these changes have led some commentators to argue that we are witnessing a major shift in the structure of social provision and the organization of consumption away from collective provision and towards privatized and individualized forms of provision. This, it is argued, is leading to a new division in British society between those who are dependent on state provision and those who can afford private provision. As *Saunders* (1984) puts it:

> We are moving towards a dominant mode of consumption in which the majority will satisfy their requirements through market purchases (subsidized where necessary by the state) while the minority remain directly dependent on the state. . . . If this is the case, then the division between the privatized majority and the marginalized minority (which is already evident in respect of housing) is likely to create an increasingly visible fault line in British society, *not along the lines of class* but along the basis of the private ownership in the means of consumption. (emphasis added)

This is an important argument on two accounts. First, because Saunders suggests that private provision will come to cater for the majority of the population as it already does in housing, and, secondly, because he views the public–private division as separate and distinct from that of class. The remainder of this section assesses the first argument. The second argument is taken up in sections 6.3 and 6.4 of the chapter.

6.2.1   Housing provision and consumption

To what extent is it correct that Britain is experiencing a general shift away from collective to individual forms of provision? In attempting to assess this it is first important to determine the extent to which collective forms of provision have been dominant in the post-war period. If we look at housing it is clear from Table 6.1 that the post-war period has witnessed a radical transformation in the structure of housing tenure in Britain. From 90 per cent of *households* renting privately in 1914, the proportion was reduced to 10 per cent in 1986, and the other two tenures have grown dramatically. Owner occupation first became the majority housing tenure in 1971, and today nearly two-thirds of households own their own home. It is also clear that the period of most rapid transformation has been the years since 1945. The number of owner-occupied *dwellings* in *Britain* almost doubled from 1945 to 1960, and doubled again from 1960 to 1986 (14 million). By contrast, council housing grew more rapidly between 1945 and 1960, during which time the number of dwellings more than tripled from 1.1 million to 3.6 million. The council sector reached its peak in 1979 with some 6.5 million dwellings. Since then, the size of the sector has fallen considerably as a result of the large cuts in council house building (now 25 000 per year compared with 200 000 a year in the mid-1950s and mid-1970s) and the introduction of a statutory tenant's 'right to buy' in the Housing Act, 1980. Between 1980 and 1987, one million council houses have been sold in Britain – almost 15 per cent of the stock.

Table 6.1   Housing tenure in Great Britain, 1914–1987

	Owner-occupied %	Public rented %	Private rented %
1914	10	0	90
1945	26	12	62
1951	29	18	53
1961	43	27	31
1971	50	31	19
1981	56	31	13
1986	63	27	10

Sources: Boddy, 1980, Figure 2.5; DoE, 1977; Census of Population, 1981; and Building Society Association estimates

The reasons for this differential growth are not hard to find. Both Labour and Conservative governments placed a major emphasis on the role of council housing in meeting the housing shortage in the period from 1945 to 1955 and, when Macmillan was minister of housing from 1953 to 1957, the Conservatives achieved a higher rate of council house building than at any other time before or since. Although the size and quality of dwellings were both cut at this time in order to maximize output, the council sector grew at an unprecedented rate. After 1957, however, when the immediate post-war crisis was thought to be over, the Conservatives cut back sharply the level of new council building in favour of a greater emphasis on the private sector (see Figure 6.1). They also switched to a greater emphasis on the role of high-rise industrial building systems. Although Labour have tended to build more council houses than the Conservatives, most government White Papers on housing since 1960 have accepted the central role of the private sector and owner occupation in housing provision.

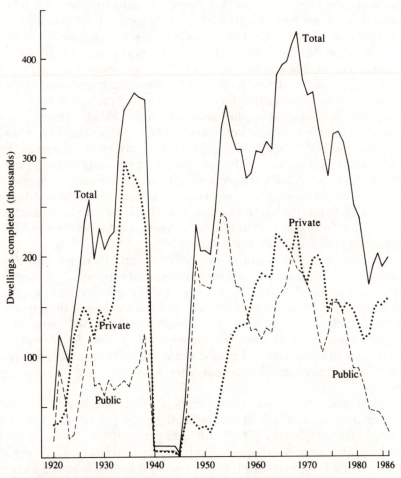

Note   Public housing includes New Towns, the Scottish Special Housing Association, the Northern Ireland Housing Executive, but excludes other housing associations. Private housing is principally built for owner occupation. Total output includes other housing tenures not included in the public or private housing categories

Figure 6.1   Public and private housing completions, 1919–86, United Kingdom

The geography of housing tenure

Because cities tend to grow outwards over time by a process of peripheral accretion, the radical changes in the structure of housing tenure have been reflected in equally radical changes in the *geography of housing tenure*. The old nineteenth century privately rented housing was concentrated in what are, today, the inner cities. The first wave of owner-occupied development between the wars led to the creation of a large new owner-occupied suburbia. This was particularly true of London and the South East, where, as today, the bulk of private house building was concentrated.

The reason, then as now, is simple. The South East escaped the full force of the recession and was the most affluent part of the country. In the midlands, the north and Scotland, council housing formed a much larger proportion of new building (Bowley, 1937; Marshall, 1968; Jennings, 1971; Dickens *et al.*, 1985). This pattern has been greatly reinforced in the post-war period, so that today the older inner city areas in England and Wales are surrounded by a large ring of suburban owner occupation interspersed with peripheral council estates. In Scotland, where the importance of owner occupation has historically been much less than in the rest of the country, much new development in cities such as Glasgow, Edinburgh and Dundee has taken the form of large peripheral council estates. These are found in England and Wales, in places like Kirkby in Liverpool or Chelmsley Wood in Birmingham, but much of the post-war council housing boom in England and Wales took the form of high density inner city redevelopment and, to a lesser extent, New and Expanded Towns. The years from the mid-1950s to the mid-1980s saw the transformation of many old inner city areas, such as St Annes and the Meadows in Nottingham, Ardwick in Manchester and almost the whole inner ring of Birmingham.

As a result of these changes in housing tenure, there has also been a dramatic improvement in housing conditions since the war. The amount of physically substandard housing has been rapidly reduced, and the proportion of households living in badly overcrowded conditions, or in dwellings without exclusive use of such basic facilities as inside WC, hot and cold running water, or a bath, are now relatively small. In 1947, for example, only 50 per cent of households in England and Wales had sole use of a fixed bath. By 1978 the figure had fallen to 4 per cent (Department of the Environment, 1977).

Apart from these *intra-urban* variations, there are large *interregional* variations. As Table 6.2 shows, in Scotland, 34 per cent of households owned their own homes in 1977, while 55 per cent rented publicly. In the Clydeside conurbation, the proportion of council tenants rose to 63 per cent. In the South East by contrast, 61 per cent of households owned their own homes and 25 per cent rented publicly. The Scottish figures were almost the inverse of the national ones. Table 6.3 shows the 1987 figures.

Table 6.2   The regional pattern of housing tenure in 1977

	Total number (thousands)	Percentage of total number		
		Owner-occupied	Public rented*	Private rented†
Northern	1 171	45.1	40.8	14.1
Yorkshire and Humberside	1 834	53.6	32.9	13.5
North West	2 416	57.8	30.5	11.7
East Midlands	1 413	55.8	29.5	14.7
West Midlands	1 864	54.8	34.2	11.0
East Anglia	701	56.2	27.1	16.7
Greater London	2 709	47.5	30.6	21.9
South East (excl. GL)	3 657	61.1	24.6	14.3
South West	1 626	62.1	22.3	15.6
England	17 391	55.5	29.6	14.9
Wales	1 042	58.8	29.0	12.2
Scotland	1 942	34.1	54.4	11.5
Great Britain	20 375	53.6	31.9	14.5
Northern Ireland		50	37	13

* Local authorities and new towns
† Includes housing associations and other tenures
Source: DoE, *Housing and Construction Statistics*, No. 25, 1978

Table 6.3   Tenure distribution by region, June 1987

	Percentage of all dwellings			
	Owner-occupied	Public sector rented	Private sector rented	Rented housing association
North	56.4	33.2	6.9	3.5
Yorkshire and Humberside	63.0	28.0	7.1	1.9
East Midlands	68.1	22.8	7.3	1.9
East Anglia	67.6	20.6	9.6	2.2
Greater London	56.4	28.1	10.6	4.9
South East (excl. GL)	71.7	18.7	7.8	1.8
South West	70.9	17.6	9.6	1.9
West Midlands	64.6	27.1	5.7	2.6
North West	66.2	25.1	5.8	2.8
Wales	67.9	22.6	7.9	1.7
Scotland	42.5	49.0	6.2	2.3
Great Britain	63.5	26.3	7.7	2.6
Northern Ireland (1984)	57	35	8	-

Source: Building Societies Association, Housing and construction statistics

Activity 6.1

Compare the 1977 figures with the 1987 figures and assess whether the pattern of regional differences increased or diminished.

It is clear from Tables 6.2 and 6.3 that owner occupation has increased in every region by about 10 percentage points (from 8.5 percentage points in Scotland to 12.3 points in the East Midlands). But despite the rapid growth of owner occupation in Scotland from a very low base, the gap between the regions with the highest proportion (the South East and the South West) and the region with the lowest percentage (Scotland) has widened slightly from 28 to 29.2 percentage points.

These differences have been intensified by the geographical distribution of council house sales under the right to buy legislation. Studies by Dunn, Forrest and Murie (1987) and Kleinman and Whitehead (1987) show that council house sales have been strongly concentrated in those regions where owner occupation is high, and in the suburban and rural areas where the more desirable houses are concentrated. There have been fewer sales in inner city areas where flats tend to form a much higher proportion of the stock and where tenants are often older and incomes are lower. It is clear from these figures that where people live plays a key role in determining the housing opportunities open to them. Conversely, because access to different tenures is unequally distributed, the geographical distribution of tenures also plays a key role in determining where people are able to live. This in turn influences access to health and educational facilities.

6.2.2   The rise and fall of collective consumption

It is clear from section 6.2.1 that there have been major shifts in the tenure structure of housing consumption since the war and that, although the council sector never exceeded more than 31 per cent of all households, it was of great importance in the 1940s, '50s and '60s. But, as a result of the massive cuts in new council building and subsidies since 1979, the introduction of the right to buy, and the changes introduced in the Housing Act 1988, collective provision in housing is now in total retreat. Murie suggests that in retrospect:

> It is reasonable to argue that since the last half of the nineteenth century a fundamental change has occurred in the way in which housing has been consumed. In the nineteenth century the most appropriate mechanism for financing housing production and consumption was private landlordism, but for various reasons this situation has changed. Individual private ownership (owner occupation) has emerged as the most appropriate mechanism in the twentieth century. But the period of transition and transfer ... involved particular strains and shortages which (through political action) have been offset by state intervention. The development of council housing ... redistri-

buted housing resources in the interests of the working class and has served the interests of capital and the 'social order' by minimising the effects of the restructuring of the private market. By the 1980s it is argued that the period of transition is over. The transitional role of council housing is therefore being abandoned and its permanent role is a more limited one. (1982, p. 35)

This threefold periodization of housing consumption in Britain has been given a more general expression by *Saunders* (1984). He suggests that it is possible to identify three distinct phases (not evolutionary stages) in the **mode of consumption** which he terms the *market*, *socialized*, and *privatized* modes. He argues that in the first phase, during most of the nineteenth century, consumption was organized primarily through the market, and that the role of the state was limited to regulation of the market in certain crucial areas, such as public health legislation. But, as a result of the social problems generated by the contradiction between low wages and the low standard of provision, the growth of working-class organization and pressures for social reform, he argues that:

> A second phase developed in the latter part of the nineteenth century in which direct state provision of key items of consumption – health, housing and education – whose cost was still prohibitive for most working people, came to supplement and eventually replace the subsistence provisions of the Poor Law Guardians and the handouts of private charities. In Britain, this new mode of consumption became firmly established before the first world war and reached its final maturity in the wake of the second. (p. 210)

Saunders argues that this new socialized mode of consumption largely overcame the contradiction between low wages and a decent standard of provision. He suggests, however, that this was achieved only at the expense of a second contradiction between the growing costs of the welfare provision and the availability of government revenues. In common with several other authors (O'Connor, 1973; Gough, 1979), he suggests that this second contradiction became increasingly manifest during the 1970s in the form of a **fiscal crisis** of the state. The response has been a marked shift in recent years towards a new third phase – the **privatization of consumption** or what *Harloe and Paris* (1984) term the '**de-collectivization of consumption**'. But, while both authors argue that the growing strain placed on government budgets by welfare spending has been a major factor in encouraging the shift to private forms of provision, they also both stress the longer-term increase in real incomes which has underpinned this shift. Saunders terms it 'the necessary condition of privatization'. He suggests that, since the 1950s, an increasingly large proportion of working families has been able to afford private provision, first in private transport in the 1950s, then from the 1960s onwards in housing and, most recently, in health care. Saunders concludes, like Murie, that:

> Collective consumption is proving to be not a permanent feature of advanced capitalism but a historically specific phenomenon and the period of collective provision may come to be seen in retrospect as a temporary 'holding operation' or period of transition between the decline of the old market mode and the emergence of a new mode of private sector provision which has today become

> both possible and attractive for an increasingly large proportion of the population. (1984, p. 211)

This is an important argument because it seems to completely contradict the argument put forward in the early 1970s by a number of Marxist theorists, notably Manuel Castells (1974), that the direct state provision of various forms of collective consumption is *functionally necessary* for the reproduction of labour power in modern capitalist societies. The basis of the argument was that the provision of adequate health, education and housing facilities for the mass of the population is necessary to ensure an efficient and productive labour force, continued economic growth and social order. But, as these facilities could not be profitably provided by private enterprise for those on lower incomes, it was necessary for the state to intervene and provide them collectively. Indeed, Saunders states that he is explicitly denying the claims of those who continue to argue that state provision in the sphere of consumption is necessary for the reproduction of labour power in modern capitalism:

> Such arguments ignore both the rise in real incomes of many middle- and working-class households which has made privatisation possible, and the widespread desire for personal control in the sphere of consumption which has made privatisation politically feasible. While it remains the case that private provision is still underpinned in some instances by the state (e.g. through mortgage interest subsidies, paybeds in National Health hospitals, tax benefits for private schools, and so on), and that the shift to a privatised mode of consumption does not therefore represent a return to the market mode of the nineteenth century, it is also clearly the case that universal *direct* provision by the state is in no sense functionally necessary in advanced capitalist societies and is now in a process of decline. (1984, p. 211, emphasis added)

It should be clear from the brief outline of Saunders' threefold periodization that it is not simply an attempt to describe the historical development of forms of consumption. It is a theoretical interpretation which explicitly challenges the notion that direct state-provided collective consumption is functionally necessary on a long-term basis. Like Harloe and Paris's interpretation, it rests on the argument that rising real incomes and the emergent fiscal crisis of the state in financing welfare provision have played a major role in bringing about the transition from the second to the third phase of consumption. Where Saunders differs from Harloe and Paris is in the stress he also accords to the role of individual choice and preference in underpinning the growth of private consumption.

6.2.3   Debate

Saunders' threefold periodization of the organization of consumption and the causal factors he emphasizes raise a number of important questions. The first concerns the extent to which socialized forms of consumption can ever have been said to be dominant. The second concerns the extent to which there has been an 'established and enduring' shift from collective to private consumption as Saunders suggests. The third is whether state intervention in the provision of the means of consumption and social reproduction necessarily have to take a direct, collective form. The fourth concerns the extent to which private forms of provision are directly or indirectly subsidized by the state in Britain, and the role of the state in fostering a shift to private provision.

Taking each of these arguments in turn, it can be argued that the post-war state intervention in education and health represented a distinct shift towards the dominance of collective provision. For thirty years after the war, private education and health consumption was limited to a small minority of the population. The position is more complex where housing is concerned. From 1945 to 1957 council housing made up two-thirds of new house building, and from 1965 to 1971 it totalled about half of new building (Merrett, 1979; Ball, 1983). But, while council housing clearly dominated new building in these periods, it has never comprised more than 31 per cent of the *total* national housing stock. Private provision – whether private renting or owner occupation – has always numerically dominated the existing housing market, although social provision was very important in the post-war period up until 1979.

The case for a marked shift to private provision in housing since the late 1970s is more problematic. Not only have one million council houses (15 per cent of the total stock) been sold between 1979 and 1987, but the level of council house building has also fallen dramatically, from over 200 000 dwellings a year in the mid-1950s (under Macmillan) and the late 1960s (under Wilson) to 33 000 in 1986 and 25 000 in 1987. This is the lowest peacetime level since the late 1930s. As a result, the number of council houses in Britain fell from 6.5 million in 1980 (31 per cent of the total stock) to 5.8 million in 1987 (26 per cent of the stock). The growth of council housing has been stopped dead in its tracks and thrown into sharp reverse.

The evidence for such a shift is less clear cut in education and health. Although private education and health care have both expanded rapidly since 1979 (for the latter, see Figure 6.2) – the number of private sector beds increased 50 per cent between 1979 and 1986 to a total of 10 025 in 198 private hospitals – the numbers and the proportions are still relatively small compared with the state sector. In 1987, approximately 10 per cent of the population had private health care and 8 per cent of children were educated privately. Also, private provision is still very unevenly distributed across different socio-economic groups. Saunders argues that this is no different from the early spread of owner occupation and private car ownership, but Harloe believes that:

> The chances of private health care replacing, either wholly or in large part, the state-provided service are remote. It is well established that private health specializes in limited aspects of medical care, mainly those which involve relatively short-term hospitalization for outpatient attendance. Long-term care is simply too costly to make its provision an attractive commercial

proposition. . . . In short, limitations on the levels of private incomes among more than a very tiny proportion of the population are a serious constraint on the expansion of private health care to provide more than a very partial replacement for the range of care provided by the NHS. (1984, p. 230)

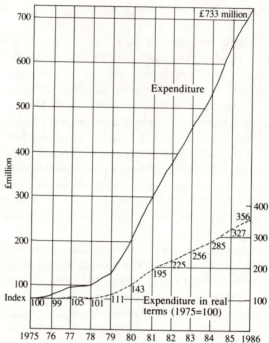

Figure 6.2   The growth of private health care, 1975–86, United Kingdom
Source: Laing, 1988

This argument was supported by a study of the potential role of private health insurance carried out by the Institute of Health Service Management (1988) which suggested that the private sector share of health care was unlikely to exceed 20 per cent, even with radical changes to the NHS. It concluded that: 'It is unlikely that the private health insurance industry will ever cease to rely on the NHS as the major provider of health care'.

Saunders argues, however, that the further privatization extends, and the worse state provision becomes as a result, the greater the pressure for people to join the exodus to private provision. In Saunders' view, private provision has a built-in momentum once it begins to erode state provision and the flight into private provision begins. Few people with any choice want to be left in socially and financially marginalized forms of provision. This process can be encouraged by government under-funding of state provision and the introduction of subsidies or tax relief for private provision. It is important to note in this context that the 1981 Finance Act allowed companies to offset against tax the cost of private health insurance for their employees. And, despite the growing public pressure in late 1987 and 1988 for increased government spending on the NHS, the government stated in February 1988 that it would not use its growing revenue surplus to further increase the NHS budget.

Until the 1980s, it could be argued that private health insurance and the older hospital pay-bed scheme were of limited importance. While they allowed individuals to get priority treatment or queue jump for certain non-priority operations, the standard of care provided in the National Health Service was such that people dependent on public health care were not significantly disadvantaged. But, with the under-funding of the NHS since the early 1980s, staff shortages, bed shortages, ward closures, rising waiting lists and cash limits on treatment, it can now be argued that members of private health schemes possess a significant advantage over those dependent on the NHS for certain non-acute forms of care. If, as seems likely, this is reflected in a flight into private medical schemes by those able to pay (possibly assisted by government tax relief on private insurance premiums as hinted by John Moore, the Secretary of State for Health in early 1988), the NHS-private sector divide may assume a new, and much more disturbing importance. We may be moving towards 'Two Nations' in health care, where private choice and public delays are the order of the day.

These developments have an important bearing on the argument that the cost of private provision is beyond the reach of most of the population. While this is probably correct in the absence of subsidies, there is no necessity for state subsidized consumption to be directed towards state provided forms of consumption. There is a very strong argument that the growth of owner occupation has been dependent on the growth of tax relief on mortgage interest and other forms of subsidy, and that it has been fostered by the Conservatives as part of their policy of creating a privatized, property-owning society. Ball has suggested that:

> Owner occupation is now the majority tenure for the 'economically active' sectors of the working class (on virtually any definition of that class). If the 'middle class' is included, with its contradictory social location, most groups which have a major power to push up wages at the expense of profits are substantially affected by the cost of owner occupation. In terms of the social groups receiving state housing subsidies the shift of housing subsidies away from council housing towards owner occupation consequently has been a shift away from a housing tenure where households increasingly are economically marginalised (either through not being 'economically active' or being one of the weaker ones of those that are) towards the tenure of those with greater economic power to undermine the profitability of capital. (1982, p. 63)

He goes on to argue that, while the state may find it politically desirable, or expedient, to subsidize housing consumption, it is not necessary for the state to subsidize direct state provision. The state may intervene to subsidize any form of house tenure, directly or indirectly. If this occurred in housing, there is no reason why it cannot occur in other areas of social consumption. As Harloe (1984) has argued, 'Privatization is dependent to a major degree on the extension rather than the reduction of public subsidies'.

What of the argument that the fiscal crisis of the state from the mid-1970s onwards has compelled governments to cut back on expensive social welfare programmes? There is no doubt that the post-war period has been characterized by the rapid growth of government social expenditure in Britain and most other Western capitalist countries. Table 6.4 shows that the percentage of gross national product (GNP) devoted to social services in Britain grew from 10.9 per cent in 1937 to 17.6 per cent in 1961, and 28.8 per cent in 1975. But is it correct to argue that the cuts in government social expenditure in the late 1970s under Labour, and subsequently under the Conservatives, are a direct response to the fiscal crisis of the state as *Harloe and Paris* (1984) suggest? It is possible to make two major criticisms of this view.

Table 6.4   The growth of social expenditure in the UK

| | Percentage of GNP at factor cost | | | | | | | |
	1910	1921	1931	1937	1951	1961	1971	1975
All social services	4.2	10.1	12.7	10.9	16.1	17.6	23.8	28.8
Social security		4.7	6.7	5.2	5.3	6.7	8.9	9.5
Welfare		1.1	1.8	1.8	4.5	0.3	0.7	1.1
Health						4.1	5.1	6.0
Education		2.2	2.8	2.6	3.2	4.2	6.5	7.6
Housing		2.1	1.3	1.4	3.1	2.3	2.6	4.6
Infrastructure	0.7	0.6	1.0	1.0	3.6	4.8	6.3	6.8
Industry	1.8	4.5	3.2	2.8	6.9	4.9	6.5	8.3
Justice and law	0.6	0.8	0.8	0.7	0.6	0.8	1.3	1.5
Military	3.5	5.6	2.8	5.0	10.8	7.6	6.6	6.2
Debt interest and other	1.9	7.7	8.2	5.2	6.9	6.3	5.9	6.3
Total state expenditure	12.7	29.4	28.8	25.7	44.9	42.1	50.3	57.9
Total state revenue	11.0	24.4	25.0	23.8	42.7	38.5	48.6	46.6
Borrowing requirement	1.7	5.0	3.8	1.9	2.2	3.6	1.7	11.3

For more precise definitions of each term see Table 2 of I. Gough, 'State expenditure in advanced capitalism', *New Left Review* 92 (1975) p. 60
Sources: Gough, 1979, p. 77; based on Peacock and Wiseman, 1966 and CSO, *Social Trends*

The first criticism is that, while major cuts have been made in certain areas, such as new council building, these have obscured the fact that the total volume of government social expenditure has not been cut overall. Instead, it is argued by *Forrest and Murie* (1987a) and Robinson (1986) that the 1980s have seen a *reorientation* of state social expenditures away from subsidies for collective forms of provision and towards private forms of provision, and away from universal towards means-tested benefits. It is significant that, while council housing subsidies have been severely cut since 1979, mortgage interest tax relief for owner occupiers has been preserved and increased – in 1986/7 it cost the Inland Revenue some £5 billion in tax foregone. While this is not counted as public expenditure, it represents a considerable cost.

The second criticism is that expenditure cuts cannot simply be interpreted as proof of a direct economic response to the fiscal crisis of the state. They may reflect other, more directly political or ideological considerations, such as the desire to foster privatization. Thus, it has been argued (Hamnett, 1987; *Forrest and Murie*, 1987a) that the cuts in council housing expenditure since 1979 owe more to the Conservative's desire to reduce the size of the council sector, expand owner occupation and create a mass property-owning society than they do to any pressures to reduce the level of housing expenditure. This argument has particular power where it can be shown that cuts have involved political choices, or where resources have been spent in other areas. Thus, it can be argued that the decision of the Chancellor of the Exchequer to cut tax rates at a cost of £2 billion in the 1988 Budget, but not to provide the additional £2 billion required by the NHS, reflects a political choice rather than a fiscal crisis.

Peter Saunders stressed the desire for greater personal autonomy and control as a key factor in the growth of privatization. While it is true that there is a high level of consumer dissatisfaction with the shortages, waiting lists and bureaucracy of state provision, it is important not to fall into the trap of arguing that the switch to private provision has occurred simply as a result of consumer preferences. While there has been a rapid expansion of private health schemes and private schools, it can be argued that central government has played an active part in reducing the attraction and raising the cost of publicly provided services by increasing rents, introducing user charges and raising them to 'market' levels. While this has taken place under several governments, the cut back of public services, the promotion of owner occupation and different forms of private provision has been most actively promoted by the Conservative governments since 1979. In public transport, government subsidies for bus services have been cut back, bus routes deregulated, and fares raised to 'market' levels during 1986 and 1987. In education, the Conservatives announced prior to the 1987 election that they intended to promote inner city community colleges, and to permit individual schools to opt out of local authority control, and in early 1988 they announced the break-up of the Inner London Education Authority (ILEA). At the time of writing in early 1988, the Conservatives announced that they are to conduct a major review of the way in which the NHS is funded. All the indications are that this will lead to the growth of private health insurance and health care. Also, the government Housing Act 1988 set out plans to allow council tenants to opt out of local council control and to revitalize the private rented sector. And, as Saunders has argued, it is important to recognize that part of the demand for private provision reflects not a straightforward preference for private provision but a desire to escape from a declining and under-funded state sector.

Activity 6.2

How far is it true to say that the UK has experienced a shift from collective to privatized forms of social provision.

Summary of section 6.2

While socialized forms of consumption became increasingly dominant during a period of about thirty years after 1945, they have subsequently been subject to a variable degree of erosion and replacement by private forms of provision. However, this process has been far from even, and privatization has proceeded most rapidly in housing where private forms of provision were already dominant. How far this process will go in health and education remains to be seen. But, given the central importance of political support and encouragement for privatization, it seems that the privatization of provision and consumption in education and health are likely to continue expanding under the current Conservative government at least until the early 1990s. To this extent, Saunders is correct. We are witnessing a shift from collective to privatized forms of social consumption. But, they are not all as marked as he suggests and the continued growth of privatized consumption is neither inevitable or inexorable. Although it is possible to identify a series of phases in the forms of consumption, they are all historically specific, and they are susceptible to change if there is a change in general economic, social or political conditions.

6.3   Consumption and class: the empirical evidence

As we saw at the beginning of section 6.2, *Saunders* (1984) suggested that, if we are moving towards a predominantly privatized mode of consumption, the division between the privatized majority and the marginalized minority is 'likely to create an increasingly visible fault line in British society, not along the lines of class but along the basis of the private ownership in the means of consumption' (p. 211). The theoretical validity of this argument is assessed in section 6.4. In this section I want to examine the extent to which existing divisions in consumption are empirically related to occupational class and income. *To the extent that consumption divisions can be shown to be class related rather than independent of class this must cast doubt on Saunders' argument.*

6.3.1 Class differences in education

The post-war years have witnessed major changes in the structure of the British educational system. Universal primary education was introduced in 1870, but most secondary schools were fee-paying until the 1944 Education Act. As a result, access to education before the Second World War was largely determined by ability to pay. Not surprisingly, secondary education was generally restricted to the middle classes, and to the occasional bright, working-class scholarship child. The introduction of free universal secondary education removed this barrier, but the links between occupational class and educational opportunity and attainment have remained in one form or another.

The post-war distinction between grammar schools and secondary modern schools, with access to the former being controlled through the 11+ exam, was reflected in marked social class differences. Banks (1968) has shown (see Table 6.5) that, in the late 1940s and early 1950s, children with a father in a professional or managerial occupation were twice as likely to go to a grammar school as children with fathers in other non-manual occupations, four times as likely as children with fathers in skilled manual jobs, and nine times as likely as children with fathers in unskilled jobs. Where sixth form grammar school education was concerned, the differences were even more marked: children with fathers in professional and managerial occupations were twenty-seven times more likely to stay on until age 17 than children with fathers in unskilled occupations.

Table 6.5 Percentages obtaining education of a grammar-school type among children of different classes born in the late 1930s

Father's occupation	At ages 11–13	At age 17
Professional and managerial	62	41.5
Other non-manual	34	16
Skilled manual	17	5
Semi-skilled manual	12	3
Unskilled	7	1.5
All children	23	10.5

Source: Banks, 1968, p. 55

The abolition of the 11+ and the grammar school/secondary modern distinction in most of Britain (though not in Northern Ireland), and its replacement by non-selective comprehensives, weakened these differences but did not eliminate them. Table 6.6 shows the social class profiles of candidates to universities in 1979 compared with the social class composition of the population as a whole. When the proportion of candidates from each social class is divided by the proportion of the population in that class to produce a ratio of over-, or under-representation, we find that candidates from social class 1 were over-represented by a factor of 4, those from class 2 were over-represented by a factor of 2, and those from class 3 (non-manual) by a factor of 1.4. Conversely, candidates from social class 3 (manual) were under-represented by a factor of 0.4, those from class 4 were under-represented by a factor of 0.3, and those from class 5 by a factor of 0.14. In other words, children from professional and managerial backgrounds were twenty-eight times more likely to go to university than children from unskilled manual backgrounds.

Table 6.6   Social class profiles of candidates and accepted candidates to universities in 1979 (percentages*)

	Social class					
	I	II	III(N)	III(M)	IV	V
Candidates	20	42	14	17	6	1
Accepted candidates	22	42	13	16	5	1
Approx. national population of family heads†	5	20	10	40	18	7

* Of classified candidates only, rounded
† Based on heads of families with children aged 10–14 years in 1971 census, who by time of survey would have been 18–22 years
N = 126 014 candidates, 69 087 accepted candidates
Source: Reid, 1981; derived from UCCA Report, 1980, table E5

The class differences in private education are even more marked. A study by the Public Schools Commission (DES, 1968) of the social class of fathers of children attending public or independent secondary schools on a daily rather than a boarding basis in 1968 revealed that over 80 per cent of pupils were from social classes 1 and 2, although these classes comprised just 18 per cent of the adult male population. Conversely, social classes 4 and 5, which made up 28 per cent of the adult male population, provided just 1 per cent of pupils. The *General Household Survey* reveals similar patterns. In 1976 and 1977, 5 per cent of all children aged 11–15 years went to private schools, but the proportions varied from 26 per cent of children from professional backgrounds, to 12 per cent of children from managerial backgrounds, 6 per cent from other non-manual backgrounds, and just 1 per cent of children from all manual backgrounds.

Tawney commented in 1931 that 'the hereditary curse upon English education is its organization along class lines'. The evidence indicates that these differences still exist. And, while the proportion of children aged 11–15 attending private schools had almost doubled to 10 per cent by 1987, it is highly unlikely that the differences in social background had changed significantly from 1977. On the contrary, the increase may simply reflect an increasing proportion of professional and managerial parents buying their way out of the comprehensive system. The reasons for this are complex, but given the strong relationship between educational achievement and qualifications on the one hand, and occupation and income on the other (60 per cent of members of social class 1 had a degree level education in 1978 compared to 10 per cent in classes 2 and 3 and 1 per cent or less in classes 3, 4 and 5 (Office of Population, Censuses and Surveys, *General Household Survey*, 1980), it is reasonable to assume that parents believe that a private education is more likely to ensure better educational qualifications, and a better job and higher income at the end of the day. Education can thus be seen to be class related in two ways. First, because differences in educational opportunities and attainment commonly reflect parental social class and, secondly, because a child's educational background, level of attainment and qualifications are an important determinant of his or her future occupation and income.

6.3.2   Inequalities in health and health care

Prior to the introduction of the National Health Service in 1947, health care was available according to the ability to pay. Morbidity and mortality were also distinctly class related. Manual workers were more prone to illness and early death than non-manual workers. The NHS was set up to provide health care based on need rather than the ability to pay. It was expected that, as a result, the class differences in mortality and morbidity would be reduced along with the financial fears linked with illness. The NHS successfully reduced these fears, but the marked inequalities in health between different classes and different areas remained. As David Ennals, the Secretary of State for Health pointed out in 1977:

> The crude differences in mortality rates between the various social classes are worrying. To take the extreme example, in 1971 the death rate for adult men in social class V (unskilled workers) was nearly twice that of adult men in social class I (professional workers) . . . when you look at the death rates for specific diseases the gap is even wider. (quoted in Black, 1980)

As a result, in 1977 the DHSS set up a working group chaired by Sir Douglas Black, President of the Royal College of Physicians, to examine inequalities in health in Britain. The Black Report (1980), and the subsequent report by Margaret Whitehead (1987) for the Health Education Authority, provide definitive summaries of health inequalities in Britain. They point to the fact that, while there are differences in the incidence of mortality and morbidity by gender, race and geographical region, the clearest and most unequivocal differences are those associated with occupational class. As the Black Report put it: 'class differences in mortality are a constant feature of the entire human life span. They are found at birth, during the first year of life, in childhood, adolescence and adult life' (p. 51). Nor are these differences a recent phenomenon. As Table 6.7 shows, class differences in mortality have a long history in Britain. And, as the Black Report pointed out, male mortality rates of social classes IV and V deteriorated relative to other classes during the 1950s and '60s.

Table 6.7 Mortality of men by occupational class, 1930s–70s (standardized mortality ratios)

			Men aged 15–64			
Occupational class	1930–32	1949–53*	1959–63 unadjusted	adjusted†	1970–72 unadjusted	adjusted
I Professional	90	86	76	75	77	75
II Managerial	94	92	81	-	81	-
III Skilled manual and non-manual	97	101	100	-	104	-
IV Partly skilled	102	104	103	-	114	-
V Unskilled	111	118	143	127	137	121

* Corrected figures
† Occupations in 1959–63 and 1970–72 have been reclassified according to the 1950 classification
Source: OPCS, *Registrar General's Decennial Supplement England and Wales, 1961*; OPCS, *Occupational Mortality Tables*, 1971, p. 22

There is no space to examine in detail the causes of these differences here; suffice to say that while the Black Report recognized that cultural and psychological factors played a part, it concluded that economic disadvantage (whether directly through variations in occupation, income, unemployment, working conditions or indirectly through poor housing and education) was the most important determinant of health. The important point is that variations in health are strongly class related. And, more importantly where Saunders' thesis is concerned, new class divisions appear to be emerging over access to, and use of, private health care. The Office of Population, Censuses and Surveys (OPCS) found that, in 1982, 24 per cent of professional and 19 per cent of employers and managers were covered by private insurance. The figure dropped to 10 per cent of other non-manual workers and just 3 per cent of manual workers (OPCS, *General Household Survey*, 1984). The *General Household Survey* 1985 revealed similar figures for the proportion of in-patient stays that were private. Whereas 13 per cent of professional and 12 per cent of managers' and employers' in-patient stays were private, this fell to 5 per cent of other non-manual stays, 2 per cent of skilled and semi-skilled stays, and 1 per cent of unskilled stays. While these figures are likely to increase, it is also likely that class variations will remain sharp – not least because of the financial cost of private health care.

6.3.3   Housing tenure, class and income

Sections 6.2.1 and 6.2.2 showed that there has been a radical transformation of the structure of housing tenure in Britain since 1945. The issue I want to look at in this section is the extent to which these changes have been associated with changes in the social composition of different tenures. Until 1919, the overwhelming majority of the population rented privately and home ownership was not class related. As Daunton has observed:

> So far as the well-off were concerned, home ownership was not considered socially necessary, the general attitude being that house purchase for self-occupation was merely another investment and not of any pressing importance. (1977, p. 113)

While housing conditions varied sharply by class and income, with many working-class households living in appalling conditions, private renting was a socially heterogeneous tenure. The rise of owner occupation and council housing changed this. Council housing brought a major improvement in working-class living conditions but, because it was relatively expensive, it became associated with the more highly paid skilled working class. Simultaneously, the white-collar middle class began to move into owner occupation as building society mortgage finance became available on a large scale for the first time. These trends continued until the mid-1950s when the rapid expansion of council housing began to open it up to the poorer, less skilled sections of the working class. From the late 1950s onwards, the rapid growth of owner occupation also began to open up this kind of tenure to the better paid working class.

These developments are agreed. Where the debate starts is over their implications for the social composition of the different housing tenures from the 1960s onwards. There are two principal schools of thought. The first is that the opening up of council housing and owner occupation to a wider clientele widened the social base of both tenures. Donnison and Ungerson argue that at the end of the nineteenth century:

> Housing, income and class were directly related to one another. That has changed. The opening up of owner occupation to more than half the population – many in houses initially built for renting – has enormously diversified the range of people who buy their own homes, and the quality of the houses in this sector of the market. As many houses as before are rented, but most of them are now well equipped and modern, and were built or rebuilt by the local authority. By allocating them according to need, rather than ability to pay, local authorities have brought a lot of the poorest people into good housing. (1981)

The other view is that, as the private rented sector contracted from the early 1960s onwards, there has been a growing *social polarization* between the two major tenures which is leading to the relative concentration of the less skilled, the lower paid, the unemployed and various socially marginalized groups – such as single parent families and some ethnic minorities – in the council sector which is becoming *socially and politically residualized*. (Malpass, 1983; Robinson and O'Sullivan, 1983). It is also argued that this tendency towards the residualization of public housing has intensified since 1979 as a result of the Conservative's commitment to owner occupation, their opposition to council housing for all but the needy, the introduction of the right to buy policy in 1980, and the sharp cuts which have been made in central government spending on public housing (Murie, 1982; *Forrest and Murie*, 1987a).

Activity 6.3

Donnison and Ungerson are correct to argue that the advent of council housing on a large scale has broken the link between low incomes and poor housing. But is it correct that housing tenure, income, and occupational class are no longer directly related? Consider the changes shown in Figures 6.3 and 6.4 and Tables 6.8 and 6.9 and make your own assessment.

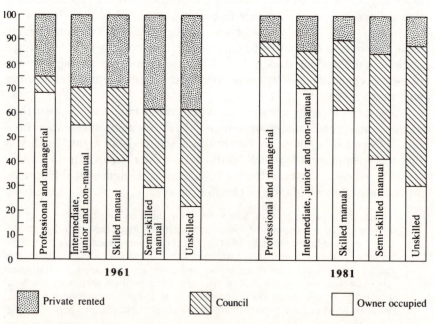

Figure 6.3   Socio-economic groups by tenure of head of household, 1961 and 1981, England and Wales

Sources: Census of Population, 1961 and 1981; Hamnett, 1984

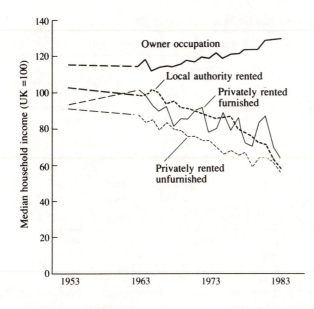

Figure 6.4 Median household income (United Kingdom = 100, by tenure, 1953/4– 83, United Kingdom

Table 6.8 Tenure of supplementary benefit recipients 1967–83

		Proportion of recipients in each tenure		
	Number (thousands)	Owner occupiers %	Council tenants %	Private tenants %
1967	2 154	17	45	38
1968	2 223	17	47	36
1969	2 296	17	49	34
1970	2 329	17	51	32
1971	2 471	17	53	30
1972	2 475	17	55	28
1973	2 292	17	56	27
1974	2 268	17	58	25
1975	2 261	17	57	25
1976	2 328	18	58	24
1977	2 432	19	59	22
1978	2 420	18	60	21
1979	2 342	19	61	20
1980	2 462	19	61	19
1981	2 869	19	61	19
1982	3 208	19	62	18
1983	3 191	21	61	18

Source: Department of Health and Social Security

Table 6.9   Distribution of household income by tenure, 1983

Gross weekly household income (£)	Local authority tenants	Privately rented		Owner-occupiers	
		Unfurnished tenants	Furnished tenants	All	Purchasing
Below 50	15.7	20.0	21.6	2.8	0.5
50–100	37.4	34.7	27.6	13.3	3.2
100–150	18.1	15.0	17.1	13.2	9.2
150–200	12.5	10.9	17.1	16.9	17.8
200–250	8.0	7.8	9.0	16.8	20.4
250 or more	8.2	11.6	7.5	36.9	48.8

Source: Bentham, 1986

My view is that there were sharp differences in the social composition of council housing and owner occupation in 1961, and that these have subsequently widened rather than narrowed. The 1961 figures show that, whereas 67 per cent of professionals and managers were owner occupiers, only 7 per cent were council tenants. Conversely, only 22 per cent of unskilled household heads were owner occupiers while 39 per cent were council tenants. There was distinct social gradation in housing tenure. In 1981, the level of owner occupation had increased across the board to 83 per cent of professional and managerial heads, 58 per cent of skilled manual and self-employed heads, and 42 per cent of unskilled heads. But, while all groups increased their level of owner occupation, the marked differences remained. And, while the proportion of council tenants fell in the top three groups, it increased sharply among the semi-skilled and unskilled to 42 and 56 per cent respectively.

Forrest and Murie (1987b) reach similar conclusions using longitudinal data on the distribution of supplementary benefit recipients by tenure. Table 6.8 shows that the proportion of supplementary benefit recipients in council housing has risen steadily from 45 per cent in 1967 to 61 per cent in 1983, while the proportion in owner occupation only rose from 17 per cent in 1967 to 19 per cent in 1982.

Bentham (1986) found that the median household income of council tenants and owners began to diverge sharply from 1963 onwards and that this trend has accelerated. Owners' incomes have risen steadily compared with the national average, while those of council tenants have fallen steadily (see Figure 6.4). As a result, the distribution of household incomes by tenure in 1983 was markedly divergent, as Table 6.9 shows: 53 per cent of council households had an income of under £100 per week in 1983 compared to just 16 per cent of owner-occupied households and 3.7 per cent of owners with mortgages.

The results all point the same way. They indicate that the semi-skilled, the unskilled, the poor and supplementary benefit recipients have become increasingly concentrated in the council sector relative to the more skilled and better-off. While the increase in owner occupation over the period percolated down to all socio-economic groups, it became increasingly diluted as it reached the lower socio-economic groups. The decline in the private rented sector has been associated with an intensifying degree of polarization between the other two tenures over the last twenty years as a whole, and over the last ten years in particular.

The obvious question is why has this polarization occurred? The answer is complex, but the principal reason is that access to owner occupation is controlled through the mechanisms of price and income while council housing is allocated according to need (Hamnett, 1984a). As a result, as the private rented sector has declined and the other two tenures have grown, the better-off have moved into owner occupation while the less well-off have moved into the council sector.

To the extent that the UK housing market has become increasingly socially differentiated by tenure since the early 1960s, this poses several other questions regarding the relationships between tenure and social class. It is clear that tenure is strongly related to occupation and income, but how far is it *determined* by class position, and how far is it a result of other factors, such as culture or preference? Putting the question another way, is tenure simply a direct reflection of class differences, or can it independently compound or ameliorate class inequalities generated in the labour market? Does tenure comprise a distinct dimension of social stratification in Britain? These questions will be examined in detail in section 6.4.

Activity 6.4

Assess the extent to which differences in access to private health care, education and home ownership in the UK are class-related, and the extent to which such divisions have strengthened or weakened over time.

Summary of section 6.3

Section 6.3 has shown that there have been major changes in the structure of social consumption in education, health and housing since 1945. While the development of the welfare state opened up access on the basis of need rather than ability to pay, this has subsequently been partly eroded by the growth of private provision. And, despite the welfare state, the occupational class differences in educational attainment and access, health and housing remain considerable. These differences have been reinforced by the growth of private provision.

6.4   Consumption, class and social stratification

The post-war period has seen major changes in the structure of the British housing market as council renting and home ownership have replaced private renting as the dominant tenure forms. There have also been smaller-scale changes in the structure of education and health provision. But, section 6.3 showed that the distribution of these inequalities is strongly linked with social class. Put simply, the higher an individual's occupational class and income, the greater the probability of that person being a home owner, healthy and well educated, a member of a private health care scheme, and of sending his or her children to a private school.

These linkages are probabilistic rather than deterministic, but they raise important questions regarding the relationship between the distribution of, and access to, consumption goods and services and social class. Do these consumption inequalities simply reflect social class or do they, as *Saunders* (1984) maintains, constitute distinct and independent forms of class structuration or social stratification, separate from the inequalities founded on relationship to the ownership and control of the means of production and position in the paid labour force? This question can be inverted. Is an individual's social class solely a product of position in the production process, or is it also a product of his or her consumption location? If two individuals occupy the same position in the production process, but different positions in relation to the means of consumption, does this mean that they occupy different class positions?

These questions are important in relation to the contemporary debate about the changes in class structure which are said to have taken place in the UK during the last twenty-five years. It is frequently argued that changes in occupational structure, rising real income, the rise of home ownership, car and share ownership, the growth of private education and membership of private health schemes have served to weaken the traditional working class, and have produced a new middle class, defined as much in terms of consumption as in terms of position in the production process. This debate has been particularly important regarding the reduction of the Labour vote in the 1979, 1983 and 1987 elections. It has been suggested that the Labour vote fell because Labour looked for support to a class which is in terminal decline, and that Labour overlooked the rise of a new class of people who are doing very well and have little or no interest in traditional collectivist policies (Crewe, 1983). This debate is taken up in detail in *Politics in Transition*, (Cochrane and Anderson, 1989), but it should be clear that changes in the structure of consumption may be important, both for class theory and for understanding changes in political alignment. Taking the questions I have raised above in order, section 6.4.1 examines the extent to which consumption differences simply reflect social class or whether they are independent of class.

6.4.1 Class primacy and class determinacy

Given the statistical evidence of the relationships between class, health education and housing, most of it derived from official statistics, we can reject the view that variations in housing tenure, educational attainment and health conditions are primarily a product of culture rather than class. While cultural variations in attitudes, expectations and behaviour certainly exist, many of these are strongly class related or influenced. It is worth pointing out that, while there are strong class variations in housing tenure, a recent survey for the Building Societies Association (1985) showed that preference for owner occupation was strong across all social classes. This suggests that the observable class variations in tenure are not a result of differences in class preferences. On the contrary, the available evidence strongly indicates that they are a product of class differences in income and employment (see Hamnett, 1984a, for a review of the literature).

If differences in consumption locations cannot be explained in terms of cultural variations in attitude, does the evidence that consumption location is strongly related to class mean that class completely determines consumption locations, and that they can be simply read off from class position? The answer to this is clearly 'no', as the empirical evidence in section 6.3 showed, and it is now generally accepted by Marxists and non-Marxists alike that consumption differences are not 'mere reflections or direct consequences of class situation' (Preteceille, 1986). Nor, as previous chapters have shown, is it possible to analyse the inequalities of race and gender solely in class terms. For women, marital status is also very important. Class, in other words, is not totally determinate of other social cleavages and divisions.

But, if class is not completely determinate, to what extent can it be considered primary? It is clear that class locations play a crucial part in structuring consumption (both through constraints imposed by employment and income, and through class attitudes and expectations), but are they *necessarily* the principal influence on consumption.

Saunders (1984) argues that while class location sets limits on consumption location, it does not determine it, and consumption locations bear no *necessary* correspondence to class locations. This is correct in the sense that the relationships between class and consumption are probabilistic rather than deterministic. It is impossible to say that, because an *individual* is an unskilled manual worker, he or she will necessarily be a council tenant, or that, because an individual is a manager, he or she will be invariably healthier or better educated than an unskilled worker. But, as Harloe (1984) points out, to say that class does not determine consumption is one thing; to say that class and consumption are *independently constituted* is quite another. If this were true, we would not find strong links between class and consumption. So, there is a clear correspondence between class and consumption, but it is neither a necessary nor a completely determinate one; consumption is class related, but not class determined.

Saunders, however, goes further than this and suggests that:

> *Class is often a poor guide to a household's consumption location*, for certain forms of private consumption (private cars, superannuation schemes and insurance policies, pre-school and adult education, aspects of health and medication, and, most crucially of all, private housing) are commonly purchased in many capitalist societies by large sections of the population, including many working class families. . . . Consumption location may generate effects which far outweigh those associated with class location. This must force us to reconsider our nineteenth century conceptions of class and inequality as phenomena of the organization of production alone . . . the inheritance factor suggests that consumption location may be every bit as important as class location in determining life chances. Any analysis which insists on asserting the primacy of class is likely to achieve less and less understanding of patterns of power, privilege and inequality as these develop over the next ten or twenty years. (1986, p. 158, emphasis added)

This is a radical claim which, if correct, greatly devalues the importance of class and it is important to examine it in detail. Saunders is correct that certain forms of private consumption are commonly purchased by large sections of the population, but this should not obscure the fact that such things as private health care, private education and home ownership are still strongly class related at the aggregate level, as the evidence in section 6.3 showed. The higher the occupational and income group, the greater the incidence and the probability of owner occupation, higher education, and so on. It is therefore difficult to accept Saunders' argument that class is a poor guide to consumption at the aggregate level. On the contrary it is still a very good guide.

This distinction between individual and aggregate analysis seems to lie at the heart of the argument between the proponents of class primacy and class contingency. While the influence of class on consumption is contingent rather than determinate at the individual level, class appears to be the primary determinant of consumption at the aggregate level. Once this is recognized, it is possible to agree with Saunders that class may be a poor guide to an *individual's* consumption location and simultaneously accept that class is a reasonably good guide to consumption at the *aggregate* level. Accepting this means that it *is* possible for consumption location to have an independent influence and effect over and above that of class, even though consumption is strongly class related. There are some manual workers who belong to private health care schemes and send their children to private schools, even though they are few and far between. Also, a substantial proportion of manual workers now own their own homes and among skilled manual workers, the proportion now exceeds 50 per cent.

The next question, which Saunders does not address very fully, is to ask precisely what these independent effects and influences consist of? The immediate answer is that they may have an effect on individual life chances. Private education and health care *may* bring certain advantages which state education and the NHS (as currently constituted and funded) cannot, such as a different social class mix and achievement level in school, quicker diagnosis and treatment in hospital or, more arguably, better teaching or treatment. Also, owner occupation usually brings greater personal control and choice and better environmental conditions, even though physical standards and conditions may be no better, or even worse in some cases. Being a low-income owner in a decaying inner city house has few, if any, advantages over living in a well-maintained council house.

But putting advantages in life chances or quality of life to one side, what are the effects of the public–private division on the overall structure of class and social stratification? In order to assess this, we need briefly to recap one aspect of the debate on class theory presented in Chapter 3 before looking at housing and class theory in more detail.

6.4.2 Marx and Weber revisited

As Chapter 3 showed, there is a variety of different theories of social class. In many respects, however, they can be reduced to just two major schools of thought: Marxist and Weberian. From the perspective of orthodox Marxist political economy, class relations in the 'pure' capitalist mode of production arise solely from the relationship between wage labour and capital established in the sphere of production. Because labour power is the only commodity which produces value, labour is forced to sell itself to the owners of the means of production in return for wages (which are lower than the value of commodities produced, the surplus value being expropriated by the owners of the means of production), and the exchange of labour power for wages is seen as the *only* form of exchange which produces classes and class conflict. Although there are now several neo-Marxist theories, which have attempted to come to terms with the variety of class positions in modern capitalist societies, they all rest on the view that classes arise from the relations of production.

The other main theory of class formation was formulated by Max Weber. He agreed with Marx that classes were objectively (rather than subjectively) constituted and that they rested on a material economic base. But he differed from Marx in arguing that *classes could arise in a variety of market situations*, not just out of the relationship between capital and wage labour. For Weber, classes arose out of inequalities in economic power, deriving from the ownership of a variety of different forms of property that could realize income in the market. These inequalities could arise in either labour markets or other commodity markets, and Weber distinguished between *property classes*, whose members share common class situations by virtue of their control over marketable resources, and *acquisition classes*, defined in terms of the marketable skills possessed by different sections of the population. His analysis is therefore more concerned with the *distribution* of economic power and resources than with production. It also leads to the conclusion that there is a multiplicity of different classes because there are innumerable differences in market situation.

These distinctions may seem rather abstract but, given the rise of private means of consumption, and the growth of home ownership in particular, they may have major implications for understanding the changing class structure of Britain. Saunders (1979) suggests that three potential implications of the growth of home ownership can be identified which correspond to the three main aspects of class relations: *economic*, *political* and *ideological*. In the rest of this chapter we shall look at the debates which have developed around each of these aspects. First, we look at the economic basis of class formation associated with housing.

6.4.3   The ownership of domestic property and social class

The implications of Weber's approach for analysis of the housing market were first taken up by Rex and Moore (1967) in their study of Birmingham. They argued that the competition for scarce and desirable types of housing could be viewed in terms of a struggle between different *housing classes*, each of which had a different degree of market power. Although they recognized that power in the housing market was in large part a reflection of position in the labour market, income and job security, they argued that it was possible to occupy one class position in relation to production, and another in relation to the distribution of domestic property. In other words, there was no necessary correspondence between an individual's acquisition class and his or her property class position. Rex and Moore identified a variety of different 'housing classes' which they ranked hierarchically on the basis of position in the housing market. These ranged from the outright owners of houses in desirable areas at the top, through mortgaged owners and council tenants, to lodging house tenants living in single rooms at the bottom of the hierarchy.

The many and varied criticisms of Rex and Moore's work have been summarized by Saunders (1978, 1979), but only two concern us here. The first is that they confused the definition of housing classes based on potential power in the system of housing allocation with the empirical identification of housing classes based on current tenure position. In other words, everybody who was currently in the same tenure position was a member of the same housing class, irrespective of their ability to enter other tenures. Secondly, and more importantly, Haddon (1970) argued that Rex and Moore misinterpreted Weber and confused his definition of classes in terms of the power to generate income through the ownership of property, with his notion of status groups which are defined in terms of 'their consumption of goods as represented by styles of life'. Haddon argued that, because housing is an element of consumption which cannot be used to generate income, it cannot provide a basis for class formation, and that Rex and Moore's housing classes were nothing more than housing status groups. As Haddon put it: 'Use of housing is an index of achieved life chances, not primarily a cause'.

This is an important criticism, and it reflects the Marxist view that housing tenure is irrelevant to class formation which, as we have seen, is determined solely in relation to production. While some Marxists accept that some housing conflicts between tenants and landlords may be seen as class conflicts between labour and a specific form of *rentier* capital, this is not seen as relevant to the economic basis of class formation. However, Saunders (1978) argues that, while Haddon provides a convincing refutation of the notion of housing classes, it is based on the *use* of housing rather than its *exchange value*, and that Haddon neglects the key *accumulative potential of home ownership*, which is related to Weber's notion of property classes. Starting from this basis, Saunders attempted to reformulate Rex and Moore's notion of housing classes in such a way that it avoided the confusions identified above and focused on the ownership and exchange value rather than the use of property.

Following Engels – who rejected the notion that home ownership could somehow turn owners into mini-capitalists, but who accepted that it differentiated them from the property-less working class – Saunders suggested that owner occupation provides 'access to a highly significant accumulative form of property ownership which generates specific economic interests which differ from those of the owners of capital and from those of non-owners' (1978, p. 234). To this extent, home ownership can be seen to provide the basis for a distinct class formation in Weber's terms. Saunders (1979) points out that this is not true of other consumption goods, such as washing machines and cars, in that they function for use rather than accumulation and they have no significance for class other than status group formation. Owner-occupied housing is unique in that, like some antiques and art, it functions both for use and accumulation.

Owner occupation and accumulation

There is now general empirical support for the view that owner occupation provides a significant source of accumulation. This is certainly true for almost all of the post-war period. House prices have risen nationally more or less consistently since the early 1950s, and house price inflation has substantially outstripped the general rate of inflation over the same period (see Figure 6.5).

As a result, owner occupation has provided large potential money gains. This has been particularly true of the period since 1970. As a result of the house price booms of 1970–3, 1978–80 and 1984–7, the national average price of houses mortgaged to building societies has risen from £5000 in 1970 to some £55 000 in 1988. This represents an increase of about 1000 per cent (Hamnett, 1988). Some critics have suggested that these gains are illusory in that owners have to live somewhere and cannot realize them unless they move down market or into the rented sector. But, as Ball comments:

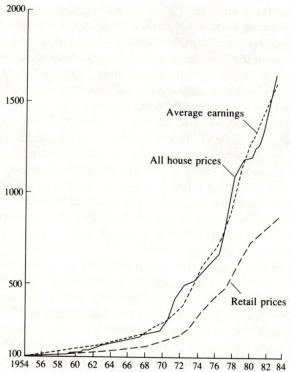

Figure 6.5   Indices of house prices, retail prices and average earnings, 4th quarter 1954 to 4th quarter 1984, United Kingdom

Source: Nationwide Building Society, 1985

> The argument is obviously fallacious; the correct comparison is between owning and not-owning at one point in time. . . . Wealth is created for owners but not non-owners. Whether this wealth is ever realized is immaterial; it still exists, even if it is used only as an inheritance for future generations. (Ball and Kirwan, 1976, p. 25)

Nor is this view confined to academics. Speaking in the debate on the Queen's speech in 1979, Michael Heseltine, then Secretary of State for the Environment, stated that:

> In a way and on a scale that was quite unpredictable, ownership of property has brought financial gain of immense value to millions of our citizens. As house prices rose, the longer one had owned, the larger the gain became. . . . This dramatic change in property values has opened up a division in the nation between those who own their homes and those who do not.

The financial position of owners and tenants is very different. Owners are left with a valuable capital asset, when they have paid off their mortgage. Also, mortgage payments tend to fall over time in real terms as incomes increase. Tenants on the other hand, pay rents in perpetuity and rents usually increase at or above the rate of inflation. When tax relief on mortgage interest payments, the absence of capital gains tax on a main residence, and the relatively low cost of borrowing are taken into account, owners are generally in a very favourable position compared to tenants. As Kit Mahon, ex-Deputy Governor of the Bank of England observed: 'borrowing for house purchase is a cheap, almost risk-free method of financing an appreciating asset with a depreciating debt'.

To the extent that variations in consumption location in health, education and housing are class related, it is reasonable to expect that the effects are also class related. Although owner occupation offers potential for real accumulation compared with renting, the absolute and relative scale of this accumulation is likely to reflect the cost of the housing and, by implication, the occupation and income of the owner. The evidence suggests that a wealthy owner occupier in an expensive house is likely to experience a greater degree of price inflation than a marginal owner in a run-down house in a poor inner city area (Thorns, 1982). Wealthy owners in large, well-equipped and well-maintained houses can also be expected to enjoy greater use values from their houses than low income owners in poor, run-down housing. To this extent, many of the *social effects of differences in consumption locations* (good housing, wealth accumulation, etc.) are likely to reflect, compound and intensify the underlying inequalities of class which shape access to consumption.

The principal exception to this link between occupation, income, accumulation and use values concerns the geographical variations in house price inflation which have characterized the last twenty years. Until recently, these variations have tended to be cyclical in nature and, although the size of the regional house price gap between north and south has fluctuated considerably (see Figure 6.6), the rate of house price inflation has been roughly equal over the period from 1969 to 1981 (Hamnett, 1983, 1988). But, since 1983, house price inflation has been much more rapid in London and the South East than it has been in other parts of the country. In 1985–7, house price inflation was about 25 per cent per year in London and the South East compared with 5–6 per cent in the midlands and the north. This has had a variety of effects, but the one which concerns us here is that these differences in inflation have generally tended to be area-wide, rather than house price and class related. The average house (or flat) price in London in 1987 was £80 000 compared with £30 000 in the north. Although expensive houses in London and the South East may have increased in price more rapidly than cheaper ones, manual owner occupiers in London may have seen the value of their houses increase by 50 per cent. Both the relative and absolute rate of accumulation has been much greater in the South East and this locational effect has arguably overshadowed price and class related effects *within* regions. To this extent, the impact of house price inflation has been independent of social class, and it has created new inequalities which are not directly class related. Many manual or junior white-collar workers in London and the South East may now own houses which are worth more than the houses of higher income professionals or managers living in the north.

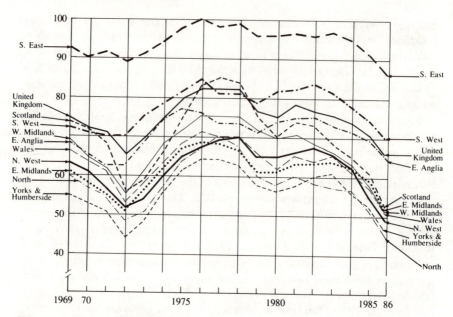

Figure 6.6   Regional house prices as a percentage of London's, 1969–86

One effect of this has been that, even taking regional differences in income into account, it is now easier for a potential buyer in the north to enter owner occupation than it is for a potential buyer in the South East. The ratio of average house prices to the average incomes of buyers in the midlands and the north in 1987 was 2.5 compared with 4.0 in London and the South East (see Figure 6.7). Also, buyers in the north obtain a far higher standard of accommodation for their money. Taking the national average house price of £55 000 in mid-1988, a buyer in the north of the country could get a modern three-bedroom detached house or bungalow, whereas in London the same money might just purchase a one-bedroom older con- verted flat in a cheap area. This points to the existence of an interesting tension between current use value and housing costs and potential accumu- lation in different parts of the UK.

Who is really better off, the buyer of the one-bedroom converted flat paying a very high proportion of income on a mortgage for a property which may be worth £11 000 more in a year's time, or the buyer of a three-bedroom modern detached house which may be worth £2000 more in a year's time? In terms of current use value, there is no contest, but in terms of real accumu- lation, there is no contest the other way. And, in two or three years' time, the London flat owner could move north and put a £20 000–£30 000 deposit on a house. But the northern owner occupier would have a very difficult job moving south. Not surprisingly, few do.

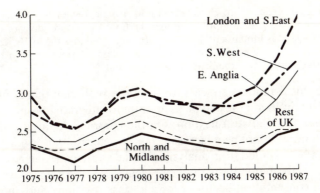

Figure 6.7   Ratio of house prices to incomes: Nationwide borrowers, 1st quarter 1975 to 1st quarter 1987

Source: Nationwide Building Society, 1987

Owner occupation, class and social stratification

We can accept that the considerable accumulative potential of home owner-ship has opened up a major division in society between those who own their own homes and those who do not. But has owner occupation and house price inflation created the basis for a new middle property class as Saunders has claimed?

There have been many criticisms of his thesis. It has been suggested, for instance, that domestic property ownership is not necessarily an enduring source of real accumulation, and that the 1970s and early 1980s have seen a period of exceptional house price inflation which may not last. Also, it has been pointed out that the accumulative potential of owner occupation is far from even and that, while some owners have seen the price of their houses rise dramatically over the past twenty years, those in less prosperous regions of the country or in the inner cities have seen prices rise far more slowly or even fall (Thorns, 1982). It has therefore been argued that, if owner occupiers are a fragmented and not a homogeneous group, they cannot be seen as a middle property class. Bell (1977) also argues that the housing class model is a static one: 'Class ought to be treated as a *relational* concept [but] with a concept of housing class it has not always been clear either who is exploiting whom, or what the relational aspects are'.

These criticisms are important but, paradoxically, the principal critic of Saunders' original thesis is none other than Saunders himself. He argues that *the major problem with the theory is that it fails to show how the notion of property classes meshes with acquisition classes based in production.* It is unclear, says Saunders, how the house-owning factory worker can be classi-fied in the overall class system. As he put it in 1984:

> The problem with a conception of home owners as a property class, whether or not it is seen as internally fragmented, is that it over extends class theory and ultimately fails to relate class relations generated around ownership of

domestic property to those generated around ownership of the means of production. The attempt to integrate housing tenure divisions into class analysis . . . is fundamentally flawed [because] it elides the analytically distinct spheres of consumption and production. Class relations are constituted only through the social organization of production.

In saying this, Saunders appears to reject the Weberian theory of property classes. But this is not the end of his attempt to integrate housing tenure into an analysis of social stratification. On the contrary, he argues that, while housing tenure cannot be a factor in class structuration, this does not mean that it can be excluded from analysis of social stratification in general. Class is not the only major basis of social cleavage in contemporary capitalist societies; consumption sectors crosscut class divisions and represent an increasingly significant form of social cleavage and may – in certain circumstances – outweigh class divisions.

Housing tenure, as one expression of the division between privatized and collectivized means of consumption is analytically distinct from the question of class; it is neither the basis of class formations (as in the neo-Weberian tradition) nor the expression of them (as in the neo-Marxist tradition), but is rather the single most pertinent factor in the determination of consumption sector cleavages. Because such cleavages are in principle no less important than class divisions in understanding contemporary social stratification . . . it follows that the question of home ownership must remain as central to the analysis of social divisions and political conflicts. (*Saunders*, 1984, p. 207)

Housing tenure is dead. Long live housing tenure! What Saunders appears to have done is to have performed a conceptual somersault which gets out of the difficulty of trying to incorporate consumption within class analysis. Instead he argues that class, defined on the basis of production relations, is part of a broader conception of social stratification which includes consumption locations. This is an ingenious way round the problem of trying to integrate consumption cleavages with the Marxist concept of production class. But, by accepting the view that classes are formed solely in relation to production, it implicitly accepts that Weber's view of class formation is too broad and too general to be tenable. Saunders solves one problem by abandoning another, and a potentially more important one. Also, his solution to the problem says nothing about how consumption sector and class position are related in social stratification. What he has done is to displace the problem from the sphere of class formation to the sphere of social stratification. The terms have changed, but the problem remains.

There is also the problem of how consumption cleavages in education and health should be incorporated into class or social stratification theory. Although private ownership of housing has generally functioned as a source of *direct* economic gains, the same is not true of the private consumption of health care and education. Indeed, while houses can be individually owned, health care and education are consumed rather than owned. Although education can be seen, in Weberian terms, as a marketable resource which plays a crucial role in influencing occupation and income, it is not – of itself –

a direct repository of wealth or a source of economic gain in the way in which private housing is. And, although good health is also an important determinant of economic reward in the labour market, it is difficult to put a price on education or health. It is, therefore, difficult to see how education and health care can be easily assimilated into an economic analysis of class or social stratification in the same way as housing. While private housing is a stratification in the same way as housing commodity, education and health care are services, and while they convey distinct *status* attributes, they are not direct economic sources of gain.

Summary of section 6.4

Saunders has attempted to show how housing can be incorporated into an economic analysis of class by virtue of its role as a source of accumulation. This role is indisputable but, as Saunders himself recognizes, there are problems with integrating housing into a strict class analysis based on relations to the means of production. As a result, Saunders has subsequently argued that it is incorrect to attempt to integrate housing into class theory, and he argues that it is an important dimension of social stratification. But this merely serves to displace the problem from class theory to social stratification. It does not provide a simple way of integrating housing tenure, rate of accumulation and position in the paid labour market. This problem remains, as does the problem of whether education and health can be assimilated into an economic analysis of social stratification. That they have economic effects is not in question, but these are not easily quantified.

6.5   The politics and ideology of consumption

So far we have concentrated on the *economic* dimensions of consumption, its role in class formation, and the relative importance of class consumption. But this is only one aspect of the social relations of consumption. There are also the *political* and *ideological* dimensions of consumption cleavages to be considered. The notion that private consumption has political and ideological effects has a long history in the UK, particularly where housing is concerned. In 1927, Harold Bellman, Chairman of the Building Societies Association (BSA), stated:

> The man who has something to protect and improve – a stake of some sort in the country – naturally turns his thoughts in the direction of sane, ordered and perforce economical government. The thrifty man is seldom or never an extremist agitator. To him revolution is anathema; and, as in the earliest days building societies acted as a stabilizing force, so today they stand, in the words of the Right Honorable G. N. Barnes, as a 'bulwark against Bolshevism and all that Bolshevism stands for'.

This statement is not an isolated example or anachronistic. In 1976, the Secretary General of the BSA stated that:

> The point where more than half the houses in the country have become owner occupied was a significant milestone because even a small stake in the country does affect political attitudes. The greater the proportion of owner occupiers the less likely are extreme measures to prevail.

Such views are not confined to the political right. Over one hundred years ago, Engels noted, in *The Housing Question*, that home ownership might weaken labour's struggle with capital and inhibit working class consciousness. More recently, some Marxists have argued that increasing working-class home ownership obscures class divisions, fragments working-class collectivism, aids the ideological integration of the working class in the dominant ideology (Castells, 1975, p. 185), and leads to 'false-consciousness' among the proletariat.

The idea that private ownership can generate different social and political attitudes from public or collective consumption is not confined to housing. The rapid expansion of popular share ownership has formed a key part of the Conservative privatization programme since the mid-1980s, and many Conservatives on the economic right would like to privatize consumption, and create a market economy in which service provision is responsive to consumer demand and the power of the pocket book rather than the ballot box. The argument is that, by reducing taxation and forcing the cost of service provision onto consumers, they will be able to exercise the discipline of the market-place to ensure that they get the kind of services they want, rather than those which central or local government and their agencies deem appropriate.

6.5.1 Consumption cleavages and political alignments

Not surprisingly, the rapid growth of owner occupation and other forms of private ownership over the last few years have prompted a variety of social commentators to examine the political and ideological effects of consumption cleavages in more detail. In a *Sunday Times* report, entitled 'Why the "I'm alright" folk spurn Labour' (19 April 1987), it was argued that the evidence of a MORI opinion poll showed that:

> People who have bought council houses are one-and-a-half times more likely to vote Conservative than council tenants and only two-thirds as likely to vote Labour. Similarly, those who bought shares in the flotations, like British Telecom and British Gas, were one-and-a-half times more likely than average to be Conservative supporters but only half as likely to support labour.

But, academic opinion is divided between those who see private and public consumption differences generating ideological and political effects, and those who argue that there is no direct or necessary link between consumption locations, attitudes and beliefs. The two principal theorists of a consumption-based politics are Saunders and Dunleavy. Saunders (1978) initially argued that domestic property ownership provides 'the basis for the formation of a distinctive political force' in which home owners unite to oppose any threats to their property rights. Such struggles, which could be either local or national, could take place over the possible removal of mortgage tax relief, building in the green belt, or plans to build new council estates in an area.

This argument has been strongly challenged by Gray (1982) and Ball (1983) among others. They argue that while housing tenures *may* affect individual attitudes and beliefs, they do not do so in any automatic or predetermined manner. Housing tenures do not possess inherent qualities which necessarily result in their residents behaving in the same way over the same issue at different times and in different places. It is necessary to examine the potential effects of tenure in a wider social context. Owners and tenants are not distinguished solely by their tenure but by a variety of different attributes. They live and work in different social situations and these may all affect their attitudes and beliefs. The social relations of tenures are not homogeneous or monolithic and 'the link between economic interest, ideology and political demands is a complex and continually changing one' (Gray, 1982). The effects of tenure can only be assessed in terms of a wider social and political context. Also, as Thorns (1982) and others have pointed out, housing tenures are highly differentiated. There is no necessary correspondence of interests between council tenants living in desirable semis and tenants in 'sink estates', or between marginal owners in declining inner city areas and wealthy suburban owners.

A more general argument was advanced by Dunleavy (1979, 1980). He argued that the growth of consumption cleavages between those who are dependent on the state for collective provision and those who are able to afford individual consumption generates a series of specific consumption interests. Because 'voters can be seen as aligned instrumentally towards the party most clearly identified with the interests of their consumption location' (Dunleavy, 1980), these interests are reflected in party political alignments and voting behaviour. This occurs independently of social class, and it is cumulative in that people who are home owners, car owners, members of private health schemes and users of private education are progressively more likely to vote Conservative than Labour, even when differences in social class are controlled for. According to Dunleavy, the growth of consumption sector cleavages goes a long way to explaining the phenomenon of 'class de-alignment', that is, the weakening relationship between occupational class and voting.

What empirical evidence is there to support Dunleavy's views? On the basis of his empirical analysis of voting behaviour in 1974, he found that while middle-class voters were 4.1 times more likely to vote Conservative than Labour, home-owning households with two cars were 4.4 times more likely to vote Conservative than council tenants with no car. Thus he claims 'the independent effect of consumption locations on voting appears to be comparable to, if not slightly greater than, the effects of social grade' (1980, p. 79). This conclusion was supported by Duke and Edgell (1984) on the basis of their reanalysis of national data from the 1979 British Election Study and Survey Research in Manchester. They stated that: 'Political party alignment is influenced more by overall consumption location than by social class' (p. 195).

The evidence is not all one way however, and there are problems with its interpretation. Does the fact that tenant buyers were three times more likely to vote Conservative than Labour mean that the purchase of council houses caused the Conservative voting? It is equally possible that tenant buyers were previously politically predisposed to the Conservatives and that purchase of their homes was one aspect of a more general set of values. These relationships between class, tenure, political attitudes and voting have been explored in detail by Williams (1988; Williams *et al.*, 1987) in his work on Aberdeen.

Dunleavy's methodology has also been questioned by Franklin and Page (1984). They argue that the multivariate statistical technique Dunleavy used focused on the *effects* of particular combinations of characteristics and not on the extent to which these effects succeed in *explaining* voting behaviour. They argue that when a different statistical technique is used, housing and car ownership only explain half as much of the 'variance' in voting behaviour as do the traditional political 'socialization' variables, such as parents' party, parents' class, occupation and trade union membership. They also argue that, because housing tenure is traditionally seen as a 'socialization' variable, as well as a key consumption cleavage, the fact that housing tenure is the best predictor of political allegiance, when the party preference of parents is omitted, cannot be interpreted as supporting the consumption cleavage theory over the socialization theory. Franklin and Page conclude that: 'One test for a new theory is that it explains the world at least as well as the theory it seeks to supplant. When applied as an explanation of electoral behaviour, consumption cleavage theory fails this test' (1984, p. 529).

Needless to say, Dunleavy disputes this conclusion and argues that consumption cleavage theory provides a better explanation of electoral behaviour. The argument seems likely to go on for some time (see Dunleavy and Husbands, 1985). Meanwhile, politicians are trying to come to terms with the new realities of private ownership and are attempting to formulate new policies. At the time of writing, in 1988, Bryan Gould's attempts to get the Labour party to reorientate itself to home and share owners seem to have floundered in the wake of the stock market crash. Whether they will be resuscitated remains to be seen.

6.5.2 The social significance of home and private property ownership

We have examined the political and ideological implications of consumption cleavages, but there is one aspect of consumption we have not looked at – its social and psychological role and significance. It is clear that private consumption has grown very rapidly over the last twenty years. The important question is why? On the one hand, it is argued by suppliers, and by the political right, that they are responding to a growing demand for more choice and personal control, and an increasing dissatisfaction with the quality of the services provided by the state. On the other hand, it is argued by radical critics that such demands are socially created and that, while there may be tendencies to bureaucratic heavy-handedness in dealing with consumers, a decline in the quality and availability of state-provided services reflects under-investment rather than an inherent inability to meet consumer demands. Such critics also point to the fact that 'choice' is generally the prerogative of those with the financial power to exercise it, and that the provision of free and universal health and education services since 1945 dramatically improved choice for the majority of the population.

We do not have the space to consider all these arguments so, in the remainder of this section, I shall focus on the arguments concerning the extent to which the growth of owner occupation can be said to reflect a natural desire for ownership and personal control.

The view that home ownership is normal and natural has a long history, and it is probably now widely accepted by a large majority of the population. It has also been widely propagated by both Conservative and Labour governments over the last thirty years. The 1953 Conservative White Paper 'Houses, the next step', noted that: 'Of all forms of ownership this is one of the most satisfying to the individual and the most beneficial to the nation'. This view was developed in the Conservative White Paper 'Fair deal for housing':

> Home ownership is the most rewarding form of housing tenure. It satisfies a deep and natural desire on the part of the householder to have independent control of the home that shelters him [sic] and his family. It gives him the greatest possible security against the loss of his home, and particularly against the price changes that may threaten his ability to keep it. If the householder buys his house on mortgage he builds up by steady saving a capital asset for himself and his dependents. (1971)

And the Labour government's 1977 Housing Policy Review argued:

> A preference for home ownership is sometimes explained on the grounds that potential home owners believe that it will bring them financial advantage. A far more likely reason for the secular trend towards home ownership is the sense of greater personal independence that it brings. For most people owning one's home is a basic and natural desire. (Department of the Environment, 1977)

Is the desire to own one's home basic and natural or is it socially created? The data on tenure preferences provided by the Building Societies Association indicate that well over 70 per cent of the population would like to own their own home, but this does not provide convincing evidence of a natural desire because it says nothing about why people want to own their own homes.

Some observers argue that, given the rapid decline of private renting and the length of council house waiting lists in many areas, home ownership is often the only option open to people, particularly those with the incomes to buy. It is also argued that, because of the financial advantages of owner occupation (and there can be no doubt that such things as tax relief, the absence of capital gains tax on main residences, and the low composite tax rate on building society deposits are socially created), it is foolish to rent rather than buy, if income permits. It is also possible to ask why, if home ownership is a natural desire, few people were home owners before the war? One response to this is that low income and lack of adequate mortgage finance prohibited many people from buying, but this fails to explain why ownership levels were also low among the middle and upper classes until this century. Some housing historians argue that home ownership had no social cachet in the nineteenth century and that it was viewed by the middle class as tying up capital that could be better used in other ways. There is also some evidence that the building societies deliberately set out to create a demand for owner occupation in the interwar period to expand their business.

Saunders (1984) has argued that home ownership reflects a deep desire for security and control but, while most people may possess such a desire, it is questionable whether these qualities are the prerogatives of owner occupation alone. Kemeny (1980) has argued that there is no inherent reason why they cannot be extended to all tenure forms. To the extent that they are not present in other tenures, it is the result of legal and political decisions, which could be changed. In the Housing Act, 1980, for instance, the Conservatives gave council tenants a statutory right to life-time security of tenure. If such measures were extended, so that there were no differences between tenures in terms of the security, control and financial benefits they offered residents, ownership could cease to seem a natural desire and become just another tenure (see Kemeny, 1980 and Merrett and Gray, 1982 for a fuller discussion).

We can tentatively conclude that, while most people do have a preference for security, control, independence and value for money, these objectives are not necessarily met by owner occupation alone. Indeed, given the current high level of building society repossessions for mortgage arrears, they are not necessarily always met by owner occupation at all. Even owner occupiers can lose their homes. While owner occupation is currently very successful in meeting many of these objectives, this reflects its current legal, financial and social status. The homes themselves are not necessarily any different – witness the one million sitting tenant buyers of council housing. While they may have bought into the financial benefits of owner occupation, they have also bought the home they previously lived in. Changes in the law could give tenants as many rights as owner occupiers currently possess. There is no necessary link between ownership and control, independence and security.

6.6   Conclusion

In this chapter I have attempted to outline and critically assess Saunders' view that consumption cleavages are of growing importance, and that they comprise an independent dimension of social stratification separate from production based divisions. Section 6.2 analysed the extent to which the post-war period has seen the emergence of important consumption divisions between public and private provision. It concluded that, while the private provision and consumption of housing has always been numerically dominant in Britain, this has been sharply reinforced since 1979. But, while private education and health care provision are of growing importance, they are still relatively small scale. While we may be witnessing the beginnings of a market shift away from collective provision towards private provision, this is not yet firmly established outside housing. Section 6.3 examined the extent to which the divisions in housing, education and health, and health care were class related. It concluded that they were strongly class related at the aggregate level, which casts doubt on Saunders' assertion that consumption divisions are independent of class.

Section 6.4 took this discussion further by examining the question of class determinacy and class primacy. It concluded that, while class was not totally determinate of consumption, it was closely associated with consumption at the aggregate level. It also took up the question of the effects of differences in consumption locations. Apart from their influence on individuals' life chances, Saunders has attempted to link differences in housing consumption into a Weberian class analysis, focusing on the role of private housing as a source of wealth accumulation and capital gains. It was argued that, while this is undoubtedly correct where home ownership is concerned, this analysis is far more problematic where health and education are concerned. Saunders has also recently abandoned his attempt to integrate housing into a traditional class analysis, arguing instead that it should be incorporated into an analysis of social stratification more widely defined.

Finally, section 6.5 examined the political and ideological dimensions of different consumption locations. While there is clear empirical evidence that housing tenure and other consumption locations are independently associated with voting differences, there are still considerable arguments over their precise theoretical significance.

So, in conclusion, we can argue that while consumption differences are becoming more important and have independent effects, they are still class related to quite a considerable degree. As yet, class has not been displaced by consumption as the major dimension of social stratification.

7 Spatial differences in modern Britain

Mike Savage

Contents

7.1   Introduction

Earlier chapters have examined the extent to which social relations based around class, race, gender and consumption have been fundamentally changed in the recent past. In this chapter we will examine the extent to which *spatial* differences in Britain have also been subject to major changes. Is it true to say that we are a more spatially divided (or polarized) society, between the 'north' and 'south', or inner cities and suburbs? Can we talk of **spatial polarization** – with rich areas getting richer and poor areas getting poorer – in the way we might talk about class polarization, for instance?

We read accounts of apparently dramatic differences in the fortunes of places in the UK. We know that the unemployment rate in the north is much greater than in the south (according to Department of Employment figures in August 1987 14.2 per cent of the workforce was unemployed in the North, 7.3 per cent in the South East). House prices are also very different. Nationwide Building Society figures show that, in the first quarter of 1988, the average house price in London (£80 100) was almost three times that found in the North (£28 790). When it comes to politics, the 1987 General Election shows a remarkable north-south divide in political allegiance. The Labour Party won only 26 out of 260 parliamentary seats in the south (the South East, East Anglia, and the South West), whilst they won 96 out of 153 in the north (the North West, the North and Yorkshire/Humberside).

However, there are other developments which seem to testify to a growing uniformity in British patterns of life. Virtually every household now has access to a television, allowing the penetration of a predominantly national media into homes in different areas. Most people work for large national or multinational, rather than local, employers. The national state has become far more rigorous in telling local authorities what they can and cannot do. Local shops have been replaced by supermarkets and branch stores in large city centre developments. The products we buy are ever less likely to be made locally. In politics it is the major *national* parties which dominate even local politics.

There are, in fact, quite tricky problems involved in evaluating whether we are living in a society that is now more spatially polarized than in the past, and in this chapter we will start by discussing the conceptual problems of examining spatial change by elaborating three key methodological points. These show how difficult it is to talk about simple patterns of spatial polarization or homogenization. In section 7.2.2, these points are illustrated with reference to two accounts of recent social and spatial change within Britain. The first, by sociologist Alan Warde (1985), tries to assess the strength of the trends towards **spatial homogenization** in the period leading up to the 1980s. The second, by Doreen Massey (1983, 1984), looks at the changing pattern of employment within the UK. We will show how difficult it is to do justice to their arguments by using simple concepts such as polarization or homogenization.

This discussion will take us part of the way towards an understanding of the character of local differences within contemporary Britain. However, we also need to examine the way people themselves think about local differences, and this brings us into the realm of **local cultures**. These are discussed in section 7.3. When we assess the strength of local differences we often think of cultural differences rather than purely economic ones. We think of vague characteristics; for instance, 'northerners are more friendly', or 'Scousers (Liverpudlians) have a dry sense of humour'. One writer even went so far as to say that 'each of the regions of Britain has at bottom a detectable set of interwoven attitudes, a distinctive trend in its underlying psychology, which is long enduring and which imparts a certain look or direction to virtually every kind of human activity carried on by its inhabitants' (Allen, 1968).

How then do we evaluate the strength of these local cultures? Do they really amount to very much? After all, in Chapter 1, we saw that some forms of cultural imagery (concerned with the idealization of the rural) seem to be widely held in Britain. And indeed, to talk of such 'local cultures' goes against many sociological orthodoxies, which maintain that local communities and sentiments are in decline, possibly even terminal decline.

We therefore need to resolve an apparent paradox: people seem to be conscious of the existence of local cultures when meeting and talking to people from different areas, or travelling around the country, yet many social scientists have provided powerful theoretical arguments against their continued viability. Thus, Section 7.3 will examine both the theoretical suppositions involved, as well as a variety of empirical evidence on the salience of these local cultures. Once again, we will see that it is not helpful simply to talk about the strengthening or weakening of local cultures. What is changing is the nature and type of local cultures, and their relationships to national and even global culture.

7.2   Spatial differentiation within Britain?

7.2.1   Methodological issues

Many of the concepts which deal with spatial change are abstract, and they need careful thought before being applied to specific cases: thus, for example, the concept of **uneven development**, which was discussed in *The Economy in Question* (Allen and Massey, 1988, Chapter 2). The basic idea is that different areas do not develop in harmony, but some may grow faster than, and even at the expense of, others, because social processes such as capital accumulation operate on different areas in varying ways. There are, however, three sorts of issue which need to be clarified before the theory can be used to illuminate contemporary change in Britain.

The first type of issue concerns the scale of the places concerned. The theory of uneven development itself tells us nothing about whether there is uneven development between continents, countries, regions, or 'localities'. The second concerns the difference between absolute and relative change. And, finally, it is important to be careful about leaping from observations about the uneven development of particular social phenomena to arguments about the uneven development of places as a whole. I shall call these the problems of *scale*, *absolute change*, and *typicality* respectively. I will discuss these points in some detail to enable us to see how they clarify the nature of spatial differentiation in present day Britain.

The question of 'scale'

If spatially uneven development is taking place we still do not know very much about the precise spatial scale involved. Smith (1983) states that it can take place at an international level (between the First World and the Third World for instance), or at a regional level (between the North and South of Britain), or on an urban–rural scale within any one region (between inner London and the outer South East for instance). The point here is that we cannot say that, because there is uneven development, therefore there must be a growing north–south divide. This is only one form which such uneven development might take, and whether it takes this form will depend on more specific factors; for example, the policies of the nation state, or the structure of regional economies.

In Britain we have, until the recent past, been preoccupied with the *regional* scale of differentiation. This is partly because many types of data are only published for this level, so the regional dimension is enshrined in many official statistics. This is especially true for the large government surveys such as the *General Household Survey*, or the *New Earnings Survey*. Because these are sample surveys, they do not contain many cases for analysis at spatial levels below the regional level, which forces many writers to focus on this level for practical reasons.

Our concern with the regional pattern of differentiation is quite recent, only dating back to the inter-war years. Langton (1984) shows that before the onset of industrial growth in the eighteenth century *counties* were the most important spatial entities, since local government was organized around them. Langton argues that regional cleavages developed in the nineteenth century, but he uses the concept of region in a very loose sense to encompass any form of sub-national spatial unit. Although regional economies developed in the nineteenth century – with each region being based around a particular economic specialism (cotton in the North West, coal and iron in Wales, etc.) – there is no real evidence of systematic inequality on a regional basis, though if anything, wages, especially for agricultural workers, were higher in the north (Hunt, 1973). Contemporaries were preoccupied with the social problems of inner urban slums, or rural poverty, rather than distinct regional problems. An example of this is Booth's survey of poverty in London, which analysed the distribution of poverty on a street by street basis, bringing out the extent of **spatial inequality** on a very small spatial scale. In doing this, he was simply following a long Victorian tradition (see also Jones 1971; Offer 1981; Sutcliffe 1983).

The concern with regional patterns of differentiation only really developed in the inter-war years as the decline of the older industries led to severe unemployment in the industrial heartland regions in the north, Scotland and Wales, while economic growth continued apace in the south and midlands. Hence the regional differences in affluence and prosperity were very marked, and this contributed to the development of a state regional policy in 1934, which has remained with us (in various guises), and which has helped sediment the regional level in our minds as the key level of spatial differentiation. Yet the point is that uneven development only took this regional form because of specific economic conditions in the first part of this century, and there is no reason to suppose that spatial differentiation *generally* takes place on this scale. The Victorians were more concerned with patterns found at a smaller spatial scale, and this is also reviving today: as we will see, despite interest in the north–south divide, some writers see spatial differentiation taking place on a much smaller spatial scale between localities.

The question of absolute change

The issue of absolute change as opposed to relative change can be best illustrated by an example. Supposing a country doubles its Gross National Product (GNP) in twenty years, from, say, £100 per head to £200. It is quite possible that the poorest regions are increasing their GNP faster than the richer ones, so that whereas their GNP per head had been 80 per cent of the national GNP rate per head, it is now 85 per cent; in other words, it increases from £80 to £170 per head. In relative terms differentiation is being reduced, but in absolute terms it is still increasing: formerly their GNP per head was £20 less than the national average, now it is £30.

The conclusions we draw about differentiation depend very much on whether we use an absolute or a relative measure. Consider the example of unemployment; no other measure is more widely quoted as an example of the growing polarization between the prosperous south and the depressed north. In absolute terms there is no doubt that the gap between the numbers unemployed in these areas has dramatically increased. Figure 7.1 shows that the differences between the total numbers of unemployed in the regions were quite small in the 1970s, and that they have now massively widened. The South East has more unemployed than any other region, but since it is by far the most populous region, with almost one third of the British population, this is not surprising. Figure 7.2, however, provides evidence on the relative unemployment rates. These actually narrowed in the mid-1970s, before growing slightly in the early 1980s, and then narrowing again. But certainly there seems no trend which allows us to talk of growing polarization. Because unemployment has increased rapidly since the mid-1970s, the

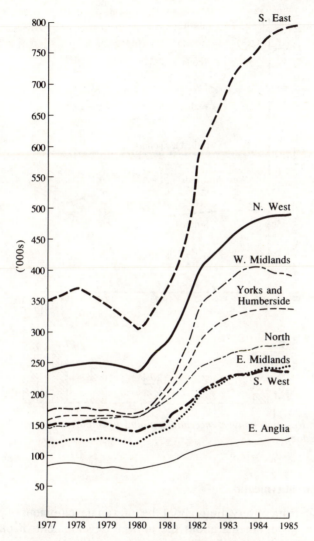

Figure 7.1   Absolute unemployment figures by region, 1976–85, England

absolute differences between the numbers of unemployed in the regions have increased, but the relative differences have declined.

There is also a more general point to consider. In a period when **social polarization** is increasing (as it has been in the recent past), then, given some inequality between areas, it is almost inevitable that absolute differences between these areas will be accentuated. It does not, however, indicate that there is an increase in relative differentiation: this would need to be demonstrated.

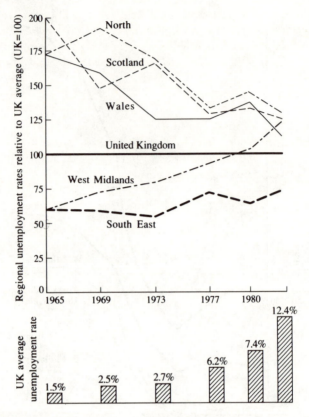

Figure 7.2   Regional convergence and national unemployment growth, 1965–82, United Kingdom

The problem of typicality

Can we leap from observations about the uneven development of particular phenomena to arguments about the uneven development of places as a whole? It might be that the feature under investigation is of only minor importance, even in those areas where it is proportionately well repre-sented. Hence we do not necessarily learn very much about differentiation between regions simply by observing the unequal distribution of one specific feature.

One example of this is the fact that the vast majority of corporate head offices are in the South East of England, and are thus highly differentiated spatially. It has been calculated that in 1976 there were 50 000 people employed in detached head offices in the South East compared with only 13 000 elsewhere. With 33 per cent of total employment, the South East has 80 per cent of the jobs in head offices. But what needs to be recognized is that the 50 000 jobs in the South East are only a tiny proportion of total employment in the area (about 0.6 per cent), so in itself the uneven distribution of head offices *may* not tell us very much about uneven development between the regions as a whole. The concept of uneven development was discussed in *The Economy in Question* (Allen and Massey, 1988, Chapter 2) where we saw that different economic roles or functions were unevenly organized. Control functions (of which the provision of head offices is a clear example) are based in the South East, while production is concentrated elsewhere. Now, the important question is whether the concentration of control functions in the South East has a wider set of implications than employment in head offices alone, in which case we might be able to talk about uneven development between the South East of England and the rest of the country.

7.2.2 Economic restructuring and spatial differentiation

We can now use the points developed above to consider some accounts of spatial change in modern Britain. First, we will consider the arguments of Warde, who, although sympathetic to the concept of uneven development, presents some evidence that Britain has become more homogeneous. Secondly, we will discuss the work of Massey who has argued that there is a new **spatial division of labour** between South East England and the rest of Britain.

Warde (1985) examines long-term changes in Britain during the twentieth century to put more recent changes in perspective. He considers different theoretical accounts of spatial change and concludes that 'spatial inequalities have fluctuated over time, but with little cumulative effect' (p. 49). However, despite this remark, he points to two changes which have led to what he sees as homogenization. First, there has been a decline in regional wage differentials, a finding backed up by other work. In the first decade of this century, agricultural labourers in the highest wage region were paid 27 per cent more than in the lowest paid region (Hunt, 1973, p. 58). Although not strictly comparable, by 1973, male, manual, full-time employees in the highest paid region (the West Midlands) were earning only 13 per cent more than in the lowest paid region (East Anglia), while for women the differential was 12 per cent. Warde argues that this convergence was caused by the expansion of nationally organized trade unions this century, which have been able to demand similar wages for certain sorts of jobs in different parts of the country.

Secondly, Warde points out that the position of women in paid employment has become much more uniform. Until 1914, there were major regional and local differences in the participation of women in the labour market. Many women worked in the Lancashire cotton industry, but virtually none in the South Wales coal industry. After this date, however, there has been a major convergence, especially since 1951, so that by 1979 the percentage of women employed in the formal economy varied between regions by only about 7 percentage points, compared with 15 percentage points in 1921.

Let us consider Warde's account in the light of the methodological points outlined above. With regard to the first – that of *scale* – Warde provides a good example of the fixation with the *regional scale*. Most of his figures (the exception being some evidence on women's position in the labour market in Lancashire) are for the regional level alone, and do not allow us to determine whether there may have been spatial change on a smaller scale. This is not necessarily Warde's fault; particularly when it comes to wage levels, most evidence is only collected on a regional basis.

Secondly, there is the question of *absolute* against relative change. The question of wage differentials is a good example of the problems here. There is no question that relative wage differentials have declined, at least until the 1970s, but in absolute terms it may be that regional wage differentials are greater than ever because real wages have risen. So, if we use absolute wages as a guide, then it might be more accurate to say that regional differences increased, even in a period of the relative narrowing of regional wage differences.

Finally, on the issue of *typicality*, do Warde's indicators bear on the fates of large numbers of individuals in any area and provide a basis for generalization about spatial inequality? Women constitute slightly over half the population; therefore their participation rates clearly affect large numbers of people. However, Warde only focuses on the differences between regions in women's rate of labour market participation. These were only about 15 per cent in 1921, so we are entitled to ask whether these differences really outweigh the similarities in women's position. The implication of Warde's argument is that, on the whole, there has been a long-term trend towards the homogenization of Britain this century. But, his account might be seen in a different light if we consider issues to do with scale, absolute or relative change, and typicality.

Much of Massey's work has demonstrated the emergence, during the past twenty years or so, of a new 'spatial division of labour' whereby many enterprises spatially separate their routine manual processes (such as in assembly work) from their specialist, executive functions concerned with management, marketing, planning and research and development. She has emphasized that many of the latter functions, typically carried out by professional and managerial workers, have become increasingly concentrated in the South East of England, or more precisely, in the 'English sunbelt' which stretches from Cambridge to Bristol. (See, in particular, Massey, 1983, 1984.)

This thesis *seems* to be a straightforward explanation of growing **regional differentiation**, and it could be used to provide a rationale for focusing on the north-south divide. However, there are other aspects of Massey's argument which provide a different emphasis. She points out the declining salience of distinct regional economies within the UK in favour of a simple divide between the South East of England and the rest of the country (see also Lash and Urry, 1987). During Britain's industrial supremacy in the Victorian period, regions were highly differentiated in terms of their economic base. Each region tended to have a specific product which it manufactured in bulk, normally for the export market. Lancashire produced cotton, Clydeside ships, Wales coal, iron and steel, and so forth. Because all these forms of work were highly skilled, different types of manual worker, each with the requisite skills, dominated in each region. Around these distinct industrial bases, highly specific regional working-class cultures developed which were, to a considerable degree, unique to each region. Today, however, these regional economies have declined, and much of the new employment generated this century is less skilled, being based in branch plants of large corporations, all of which only provide low-skilled, routine assembly jobs. As a result, similar types of manual worker are found in different regions.

Therefore, while Massey's argument can be used to emphasize the significance of a growing north-south divide (or more accurately a south-rest divide), she also points to the growing homogenization of the old industrial regions in Britain. As she summarizes, 'the old regional specialisms (cotton, coal, cars) are gone. The main regional contrast . . . is between control and conception on the one hand and execution on the other, between the sunbelt and the rest' (Massey 1984, p. 116). This point is backed up by Martin (1986), who points out that the precipitate decline of manufacturing employment in the old industrial regions has actually led to a situation where similar proportions of workers are engaged in manufacturing in all the regions of Britain.

In some respects then, Massey is arguing for the homogenization of Britain. This point is reinforced when we recall that her argument for the growing differentiation of the South East from the rest of the country is in terms of the increasing proportion of high-level jobs there, which exist to carry out the control functions that dominate in the area. Now, while it is true that the South East does have high proportions of these jobs, it is important to recognize that, even there, these sorts of jobs are only a minority: most of the workforce are employed in routine manual and non-manual jobs. This takes us back to the problem of *typicality*. Can it be demonstrated that the concentration of high-level executive functions in the South East has more general implications for the region as a whole?

Some possible implications might be that the growth of the service sector in the South East is related to this trend. Similarly, while top-level professional workers may be a minority, even in the South East, they may have a considerable impact on social life, for instance in leading to a buoyant housing market with booming house prices for all owner occupiers in the area (see Chapter 6). On the other hand, some work (Buck *et al.*, 1986; Barlow and Savage, 1986) points to increased polarization within the South East, suggesting that not all groups benefit from being in a region with these high-level functions. There are large numbers of long-term unemployed in some parts of the South East (for example, in East Kent, around Margate and Dover, and in inner London).

This, in turn, raises the issue of *scale*. The South East as a whole may appear prosperous, but if we look at a finer spatial level, we find that some parts of the region are in an exceptionally depressed state, especially in inner London. The growing middle class (or service class, as it has been termed elsewhere: see Chapter 3 for a discussion of this) is only a minority of the population, even in the affluent South East.

One implication of these observations is to raise the prospect that spatial differentiation takes place on a far smaller scale than the region, so that, within the South East, there will be buoyant middle-class **localities** set against depressed working-class ones. Massey's work also raises the point about the significance of these small-scale differences. So far, we have only considered her arguments about regional patterns of differentiation, yet she is also partly responsible for drawing attention to a different level of spatial differentiation at the level of the local labour market, an argument which has been taken up by writers such as Urry (1981) and Cooke (1983). Here the focus is on growing differentiation not between regions but between different local labour markets, even in the same region.

The reasoning runs as follows. The key process behind spatial change is capital accumulation. The mobility of capital allows it to invest and disinvest in particular places to maximize its potential to accumulate. Yet investment in the form of a factory or enterprise is not made in a region as a whole, but in a specific local labour market within a region. Hence, when decisions to invest (or disinvest) are being made, what is taken into account is not the nature of the region as a whole, but the precise nature of a specific *local labour market*, particularly with reference to the character of its labour force. Consequently, one might expect to find growing differentiation within regions between local labour markets. Firms crowd into labour markets where local labour forces are amenable, perhaps because wages are low, or the workforce is malleable, or suitably qualified (depending on the particular labour requirements of different employers). They abandon local labour markets where the labour force is in some respects unsuitable: for example, the precipitate decline of employment in Liverpool might be explained by firms moving out because of the existence of a militant workforce. Thus, while regional differences may be less salient, local ones might be becoming more important.

The concept of the local labour market is a potentially important one. It is usually taken to be a travel to work area. This is a spatial unit where a majority of the residents work within the same spatial boundaries as they live. There has been a considerable amount of work recently which points to growing polarization between local labour markets, even within regions.

The work of Champion and Green (1987, 1988) (at the Centre for Urban and Regional Development Studies (CURDS), University of Newcastle), assessed the economic performance of different parts of Britain, identified 280 local labour market areas (LLMAs), and constructed an index of economic performance (the booming towns index). The (1987) index was based on five variables: the percentage of households with two or more cars in 1981; the unemployment rate in May 1985; employment change 1978–81; employment change 1971–8; and population change 1971–81. For each variable each LLMA was ranked on its performance, these were then summed and an overall index of economic performance was produced, ranging from 0.137 at the bottom to 0.764 at the top, with the median value being 0.454. (See Figures 7.3 and 7.4.)

Champion and Green's work shows that, although there seem to be some broad differences between north and south, there is a great deal of diversity within the regions. Thus even in the south there are some very depressed local labour markets, such as Deal in Kent, which ranks 239, out of the total of 280 local labour market areas, in terms of recent economic performance.

Activity 7.1

Look at Figures 7.3 and 7.4, produced by CURDS. Do they provide evidence of a north–south divide, or is there too much variation within regions to justify this? What sorts of area seem to be doing best? Which seem to be doing worst? What reasons might there be for this?

It appears that there has been considerable polarization between different local labour markets, and that this might be a major *new* form of spatial differentiation in modern Britain. Champion and Green's recent work (1988), which included ten variables, with data going up to July 1987, suggests a clearer north–south divide than their earlier work, but, it is nonetheless arguable that inequality on a mainly regional scale has perhaps given way to inequality at this level? Once more we must consider the methodological issues outlined at the start of this section. The CURDS index is based on relative indices. Hence, those rural areas which have an initially low employment base can appear to have high rates of growth, but, in absolute terms, growth might be greater in some urban areas (such as Norwich, or Ipswich), which are starting from a higher absolute level. The CURDS use of relative indices biases their account by emphasizing the growth of rural areas.

In addition, much of the apparent divergence between the fortunes of local labour markets may be best explained by the general trends towards **decentralization** in the British economy (see *The Economy in Question*, Allen and Massey, 1988, Chapter 2). Those local labour markets which have seen the most rapid economic growth are normally in rural or suburban areas, and they have benefited from the movement of employment and people out of central urban locations. Figure 7.4 shows that the most buoyant local labour markets (marked in black) cluster around the London fringes. Many of the new residents of these buoyant local labour markets continue to work in central urban locations. The proportion of workers in inner cities who commuted to work from outside the inner cities rose from

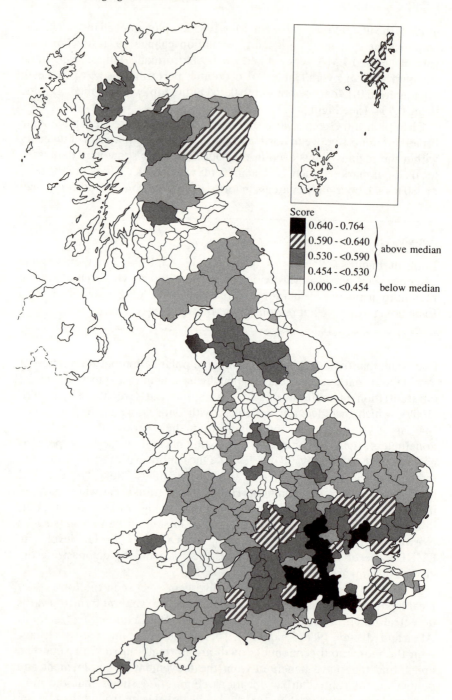

Figure 7.3   Geographical distribution of the booming towns index by local labour market area: above median (0.454)

Source: Champion and Green, 1987

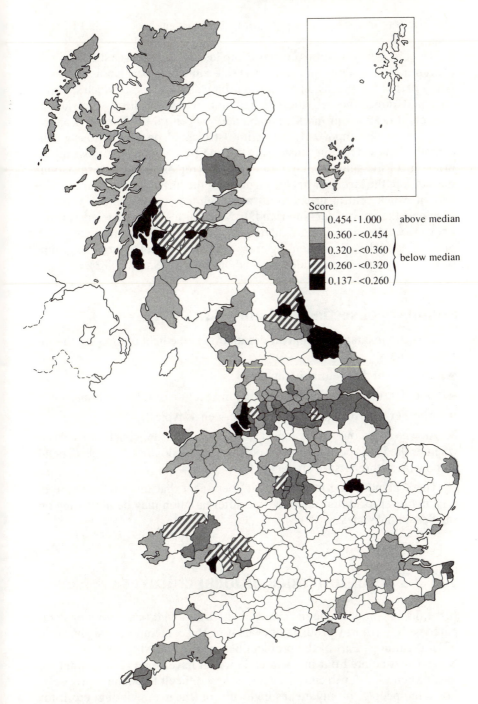

Figure 7.4   Geographical distribution of the booming towns index by local labour market area: below median (0.454)

Source: Champion and Green, 1987

20.7 per cent in 1951 to 38.8 per cent in 1981 (Begg, Mooren, and Rhodes 1986).

The point here is that this evidence implies that the changes should not be conceptualized in terms of (relatively) self-contained local labour markets, but as part of the expansion of central urban labour markets which subordinate and direct the activities carried out in decentralized local labour markets. Local labour markets dominated by central urban sites (London being especially important) are being 'stretched' on to previously self-contained ones. Thus, in considering the question of scale, the most appropriate level for analysis may be neither the region, nor the local labour market, but the level of what we might term the 'urban labour market': the way in which central urban areas and regional service centres come to dominate their particular hinterland. In Neil Smith's terms we might say that uneven development is particularly apparent on the 'urban scale', with growing specialization of housing areas, and growing polarization of groups of workers within an expanded local labour market (Smith, 1983).

Summary of sections 7.1 and 7.2

1   We need to analyse spatial differentiation in the light of three methodological issues:

* the scale of differentiation involved,
* whether differentiation is measured in absolute or relative terms, and
* whether a particular indicator can be seen as typical.

2   As we saw in our discussion of Massey and Warde, conclusions about whether the UK is becoming more or less spatially polarized largely depend on how these three issues are tackled.

3   These points being recognized, it does seem that there is a decline in regional levels of differentiation, but differentiation may be increasing on smaller spatial scales.

7.3   The significance of local cultures

If the discussion of economic change is tricky enough this is nothing compared with the thorny problem of evaluating the contemporary significance of **local cultures**. Part of the problem lies in deciding what 'culture' is. As Nigel Thrift pointed out in Chapter 1, we all have some idea of what we mean when we refer to culture, yet it is very difficult to define it precisely. For some people, it only means **high culture** (theatre, painting, etc.); for others, it is a sort of 'dustbin' concept. Anything which does not fit into nice sharp categories, such as the economic or the political, is consigned to a vague realm of culture. The result is that culture comes to include a variety of disparate phenomena such as language, values, dress, diet, customs, etc., none of which may actually relate to any of the others.

In particular, culture often unhelpfully conflates *practical* and *symbolic* matters. Raymond Williams, for example, argues that culture is 'a whole way of life', which includes practical activities, such as shopping, eating and so on, together with more symbolic feelings about our environment, neighbours, and such like. This division can be seen between those writers who attempt to pinpoint cultural differences in terms of differences in practical ways of living, and those who see culture as an entirely symbolic process, which need not bear much relation to people's actual lives. D.A. Allen is an example of the former. In a book written in 1968, he analyses a number of practices, such as dress, diet and family life, and seeks to show how they vary systematically across the country. He gives an example of Yorkshire culture. People in Yorkshire, he argues, are 'big, muscular and burly'; are prone to commit violent crime; are conservative and scoff at new fashions; do not like tinned food; insist on cleanliness; carry out toilet training early; don't eat much dairy produce; value privacy; wear bonnets (if they are female); extensively decorate their homes; make great efforts in the kitchen (if they are the wives of the family); prefer durable clothes; if they are men, demand that their women treat them as 'lords and masters'; and, last but not least, they have a predilection for cardigans!

The point here is that all these traits are in some way empirically detectable. Indeed, Allen researched his book by looking at market research surveys which actually did reveal regional differences in spending patterns. The cultural differences are bound up with people's actual behaviour. There is, however, a different approach to local culture which puts more stress on the purely symbolic realm. There may be no differences in the actual make up and behaviour of, say, football crowds in Glasgow or London, but the spectator may nonetheless feel very different.

The work of Cohen (1983) has developed this aspect of local culture most forcibly. He has written mainly about rural areas, but we will outline his general arguments before considering whether they may be applied to other places. According to Cohen, we become aware of our local culture only in opposition to other – outside – cultures. Only by perceiving other cultures can we recognize how our culture is different and so gain an understanding of what is specific about it. And, Cohen argues, such a process is a symbolic one, for we generally recognize other cultures, not in terms of what other people do in their everyday lives, but in terms of a few key symbols by which we interpret the other cultures. I suspect that few of you would have known that Yorkshire people wear cardigans or toilet train children early. On the other hand, a list of a few Yorkshire 'symbols' such as Geoff Boycott, cloth caps, Yorkshire pudding, 'trouble at t'mill' or Arthur Scargill, would be much more evocative.

Many of you will be able to think of cultural differences between different parts of Britain. Yet, when you examine these, you will probably find symbolic ideas coming to the fore. We often rely on anecdotes or allusions for our sense of cultural difference. Consider a quote from a novel by Malcom Bradbury where one of his heroes leaves the north and states: 'behind lay decency, plain speaking, good feeling; ahead lay the southern counties, all suede shoes and Babycham'. This may well conjure up an image which we can identify with, but can we honestly say that we see many people in the south drinking Babycham? Probably not!

There is no real link between culture understood in a *practical* sense, and culture as understood in a *symbolic* sense. A good example of this is found in Chapter 1 where we looked at the idealization of the rural. As a symbol the countryside is very important to us, but in practice the rural way of life has more or less entirely disappeared: there are very few farmers left, most villages are full of commuters, and even the 'wilds' of, say, the Lake District have been explored and 'used' as much as any urban area.

There is the possibility that different processes may be at work in the two aspects of culture. What we will discuss below is the idea that while practical culture may be more uniform across places, our symbolic awareness of local differences may, at the same time, be more heightened. We will start by considering those writers associated with 'mass society' theory who assume that local cultures are being eroded by the growth of national organizations and the mass media, before looking at those writers who argue for the persistence of local cultures. Throughout, it is important to keep the distinction between **practical** and **symbolic culture** in mind, because we will see that they may be subject to different sorts of change.

7.3.1   The mass society thesis and the decline of local cultures

Mass society theorists, of which there are several different types, argue that, in modern society, the affective ties which formerly bound people together into social units are being undermined, and that people are being atomized and individualized. For this reason, local context is becoming less significant as a source of social identity, and so the salience of specifically local cultures will be expected to decline.

This line of argument is something of a sociological orthodoxy, stretching back to such eminent sociologists as Emile Durkheim and Max Weber. They argued that as societies modernize, so the character of popular sentiment and belief changes. In primitive society beliefs develop out of the immediate local context, but as **modernization** occurs they become more abstract and less tied to specific locations. Whimster and Lash (1987) argue that Weber's concept of **rationalization**, which refers to the process whereby belief systems become more formalized and internally coherent, is closely related to this change. Thus, in primitive society, 'instead of an ordered cosmology there is a plurality of beliefs, none of which can go beyond the world as it is immediately experienced. And instead of the universality of a religious ethic . . . there is the particularism of village and sib (family)' (p. 6).

The sort of modernization envisaged by such writers is a far-reaching set of changes which have been taking place over a long time period. Four types of change seem of particular importance. First, the development of a 'world economy', where production is not geared to local markets but to worldwide ones, is several centuries old; Wallerstein dates it to the fifteenth century. Secondly, and perhaps more significant, was the development of the modern nation state, which helped undermine local differences in administration, discipline and service provision. Eugene Weber showed how, between 1870 and 1914, the French state created a national system of state schools teaching a common curriculum which successfully eroded local dialects and customs. This occurred over a longer time period in Britain where educational provision has been more decentralized, but the creation of national examination boards clearly ensures some uniformity. Thirdly, changes in the structure of communications have allowed people to travel more, so making the local area less pivotal. The development of the railways in the nineteenth century was especially important here. Before the railway network was built, every town and village ran on its own time. It was the railway's need to standardize times in order to make its timetables comprehensible that finally led to the supremacy of Greenwich Mean Time.

These three structural changes are clearly very important, but we will pay special attention to a fourth change – that of the development of the mass media – because of its particular importance for cultural activities. The mass media (or 'culture industries' in some writers' language) are becoming increasingly dominant, and are helping to manipulate people's values by providing a diet of repetitive, low-brow, hedonistic, meaningless fare. They help implant national (or even 'global') values in people. John Clarke refers to three main aspects of the mass society thesis: the spread of the mass media to large proportions of households; its penetration into the centre of household life; and its content, which tends to undermine traditional standards and values (Clarke, 1984).

To what extent does a national media undermine local cultures? Meyrowitz (1985) argues that it allows us to communicate with people with whom we are not in direct spatial contact. Thus, we get the phenomenon of 'media friends' for instance: people whom we feel close to but are most unlikely to actually meet, and who may have no link with the place where we live. This is very different from relying on people who live alongside us.

An example of a local culture which might have dominated before the advent of the electronic media is provided by the study of a Yorkshire coal mining village in the 1950s, by Dennis *et al.*, (1969). The authors show how some commonly held values, such as that of **masculinity**, arise out of people's contacts in the local setting. The workplace and social forums (notably the Working Men's Clubs) become the crucible in which values are forged. As the authors state: 'the men conversing together have often been lifelong acquaintances, and having been at the same schools and played together as children, they now play as adults, work in the same place, and spend their leisure time together in such places as the club' (p. 144).

Since this account, many sociologists have written about the growth of a privatized, affluent population, whose lives are centred around their homes, and who do not engage in regular contact in the neighbourhood. Goldthorpe and Lockwood's 'Affluent worker' studies (1969) (discussed in Chapter 3) pioneered this approach. They argued that, in Luton, people's lives revolved around the home and the family, and that they had only irregular interaction with other local people. Here the implication is that Meyrowitz's prognosis has come to pass: people take their cues from the TVs anchored in their living rooms and no longer partake in a meaningful local culture.

Before we go on to examine the opposing point of view, it is useful to consider how culture is understood by the proponents of the **mass society theory**. Much of their work focuses on the *practical* dimension of culture. Some reservations need to be made to the picture of a simple growing uniformity which seems to be implicit in such writings. Scotland, for instance, retains certain forms of its own legal and political system, and Northern Ireland also has distinctive patterns of government. Similarly, it is possible to criticize those writers who point to the growth of a privatized population, less atuned to the wider community. The differences between Dennis *et al.*, on the one hand, and Goldthorpe and Lockwood, on the other hand, may simply reflect the research methods used. The former carried out a community study: that is to say, they examined social interaction outside the home, partly by participant observation. The latter relied on individual surveys. These surveys tend to decontextualize individuals, and play down the importance of wider local ties. It is interesting to note that some recent research, which is in some respects repeating the old community studies, has observed that local cultures may indeed be flourishing. Thus recent work on outer Liverpool (part of the CURDS initiative) shows that there is a vibrant local culture orchestrated by churches and other local organizations (Meegan, 1987). And a recent extensive survey of individuals, which took considerable care to provide proper measures for examining **privatism**, concluded that there was no good evidence that it was increasing in modern Britain (Marshall *et al.*, 1988).

Another way of testing the importance of these practical differences between people's lives in different places is to follow the spirit of Allen's work (1968) and use evidence on regional differences in consumption patterns, to see whether regional differences have persisted. Table 7.1 provides evidence on patterns of consumption by region.

Activity 7.2

Do the figures in Table 7.1 reveal a narrowing or widening of regional differences in consumption patterns?

Table 7.1 Spending on selected consumer goods 1972–3/1984–5, Great Britain

	Housing		Alcohol		Tobacco		Fruit		Meat	
	'72	'84	'72	'84	'72	'84	'72	'84	'72	'84
North	86	93	130	127	126	136	84	84	100	109
Yorkshire and Humberside	94	89	111	108	116	104	85	86	100	95
East Midlands	105	98	106	100	97	104	96	97	94	101
East Anglia	106	89	85	85	87	86	119	120	101	98
South East	113	115	87	90	79	79	101	111	97	101
South West	102	102	83	88	82	82	93	82	104	102
West Midlands	102	104	102	104	108	100	89	89	100	108
North West	98	95	113	115	111	118	97	92	106	91
Wales	90	87	100	106	108	118				
Scotland	92	80	117	117	134	136	79	85	90	97

UK = 100

Source: CSO, *Regional Trends*

Mass society theorists put a great deal of emphasis upon the unifying effects of the electronic media. It is possible to examine the extent to which households in different regions do have access to the media to tell whether the spread of the media is uniform across regions.

Table 7.2 gives information on the possession of some consumer durables by region. The figures for possession of televisions are unenlightening because, even in 1973, the market was almost saturated throughout the country. The figures for telephones are, however, much more interesting. In 1973, only a minority of households had telephones, and, interestingly from our point of view, those areas which are often seen as possessing the most durable working-class culture had the fewest telephones (Wales, the North, Yorkshire and Humberside). The South East, though, had a rate of possession much above the national average.

Table 7.2   Percentage of households possessing some consumer goods, 1972–3/ 1984–5, Great Britain

	Telephone		Washing machine		Television	
	'72	'84	'72	'84	'72	'84
North	33	80	66	85	95	98
Yorkshire and Humberside	32	73	79	85	94	98
East Midlands	39	78	77	85	94	98
East Anglia	35	81	77	84	95	99
South East	58	86	57	75	92	97
South West	41	82	65	78	93	97
West Midlands	41	74	65	79	94	99
North West	43	79	70	82	94	98
Scotland	42	76	74	85	95	98
Wales	25	71	66	81	95	98
UK	43	80	67	80	93	98

Source: CSO, *Regional Trends*

Yet, equally striking, is the staggering increase in the rate of possession of telephones by 1984–5 which has eroded these regional differences. In 1973, over twice as many households possessed telephones in the South East compared with Wales. By 1984–5, this differential had fallen to 15 per cent. If we measure local cultures in terms of the sorts of everyday patterns of face-to-face interaction (as in the study by Dennis *et al.*), then it is clear that non-face-to-face communication has dramatically increased, and that previously intense regional variations have been undermined.

The incidence of the possession of washing machines is less dramatic than this, but in some respects surprising. The South East actually had a very low rate of possession in 1973, but this has increased faster than the national rate, and is now only slightly below the national average. By 1984–5, the regional differentials were less than they were in 1973.

Table 7.2 suggests then that regional rates of possession are narrowing as the market for these goods becomes saturated, and this is in line with what mass culture theorists would expect. Virtually everyone has access to the mass media. Telephone access is growing, and fairly uniform across the country.

Activity 7.3

Do the changes shown in Table 7.2 mean that local cultures are actually in decline? Why has the possession of telephones become more uniform? How else might you go about finding out whether the practical dimensions of local cultures are changing?

Tables 7.1 and 7.2 do not tell us very much about the symbolic aspects of culture. This may seem a surprising thing to say, because, after all, the mass culture theorists seem preoccupied with the media, its messages and 'discourses'. But this usually takes the form of examining, for example, the content of television programmes rather than people's perceptions of them. There are actually very few studies which show how people receive media messages, and it may be that people in different localities use the media in symbolically different ways.

7.3.2 The survival of local cultures?

Mass society theorists place great emphasis upon the unifying effects of the mass media and the creation of national (or even global opinion). Yet it might be argued that they fail to demonstrate that the mass media necessarily have the effects they are purported to have. Indeed, it is possible to argue that the mass media may actually help to create a more precise *symbolic* sense of place. This is because the media provide images which allow people to identify with some places and against others, so accentuating their sense of local culture in a symbolic sense. There are two parts to this argument.

First, people are not simply passive recipients of the media. Numerous studies have shown that people's environment affects the way they interpret media messages. In particular, if the TV is watched with other people, the programmes are often understood in very different ways. Television programmes may help to encourage patterns of interaction since they may form the basis of a conversation. Soap operas, for instance, may allow people to discuss emotional issues which they might otherwise find hard to raise. One French writer, Jean Baudrillard, has even argued that a major form of popular resistance today is to treat media images and signs as a spectacle to be observed and 'consumed' rather than as a portrayal of 'reality' (see Lash and Urry, 1987, Chapter 9). Hence, although the media may try to present a national perspective on life, people in specific places may nonetheless interpret their messages according to their own situations.

Secondly, the mass media do not, in fact, simply present 'place-less messages'. Many television programmes refer to different places, either explicitly (news stories about a particular place, regional news programmes, etc.), or implicitly. Soap operas, such as *Dallas*, *Coronation Street*, *Brookside* and *East Enders*, take place in a particular place (though sometimes an artificial one developed by TV producers). The use of specialist, local programmes partly relates to a general economic development discussed in *The Economy in Question* (Allen and Massey, 1988): the way in which firms target particular market niches more effectively. In these cases the niches are people in particular areas.

Since television presents a series of spatial images, people have the opportunity to gain a greater sense of how their own place might relate to the images of other places, and develop a form of symbolic local culture. People could become more sensitive to spatial imagery by watching a variety of television programmes, which could provide the symbols that Cohen (1983) sees as being a very important part of developing a local culture.

Activity 7.4

Think of programmes such as *Boys from the Blackstuff*, *Minder*, *Only Fools and Horses*, *Till Death Us Do Part*, *The Gaffer*, etc. Do you think they provide an imagery of place? Is the imagery 'imaginary', in that it does not correspond to people's actual behaviour? Does this mean that it is less effective?

Finally, it is worth mentioning one other form of social change which may also enhance the creation of a sense of symbolic local culture, namely the recent growth of people's spatial mobility. The growth of mass tourism is a good example. Holiday-making goes back a long way, with seaside resorts such as Blackpool and Brighton developing quickly from the Victorian period onwards. Yet, for many years, resorts such as these attempted to be similar to the home towns of the holiday-makers, even to the extent that people from a particular town would stay with a landlady originating from the same town. Today, writers such as Urry (1987) point out that tourism involves the development of specific facilities such as museums, theme parks, and such like, which mark out that particular place as different from others, and hence worth visiting. Chapter 1 showed how images of rural Britain are sustained by the heritage movement. There are strong pressures for localities actively to cultivate an image in order to boost the potential revenue from tourism. The dramatic change in Glasgow is a case in point: by an aggressive 'Glasgow's miles better' campaign, and the redevelopment of the Merchant City in the centre of Glasgow, Glasgow has succeeded in presenting an 'image' of itself to a variety of people, so adding to people's symbolic repertoire by which they can mark out the distinctiveness of their own place. These developments also relate to the growing salience of *consumption*-based issues, which was discussed in Chapter 6.

7.4 Conclusion

In this chapter we have discussed how to go about understanding **spatial differentiation** within contemporary Britain. We have seen that it is too glib to use terms such as spatial homogenization or polarization. Once one begins to talk of spatial polarization, for instance, it is necessary to specify the scale of polarization (region, local labour market, etc.), whether it is to be measured in absolute or relative terms, and the appropriate type of social indicator. Hence it is possible to have polarization at a local level but not at a regional level, polarization in absolute but not relative terms, and polarization of some social features but not others. So the lesson is that we need to be cautious in analysing patterns of spatial differentiation.

Having noted this, however, what can we say about general trends in the spatial organization of Britain? Three general conclusions stand out. First, that when we look at patterns of economic change, it is not obvious that they should be seen in regional terms. This might have been adequate in the inter-war years but today it can be argued that the major patterns of differentiation are between declining inner urban locations and prosperous outer urban and semi-rural ones. On this interpretation, spatial differentiation is taking place on a fairly small scale rather than in terms of north-south divides, and this shows that, although it may still be possible to detect broad regional differences, these could be the product of a myriad of smaller-scale changes taking place. (However, for a contrary view, see Lewis and Townsend, 1988.)

Secondly, people's actual lives may well be becoming more uniform across the country – though this is the subject of some controversy. Perhaps people tend to have more similar leisure pursuits, more similar types of work and more similar types of upbringing than they did a century ago, though this is a highly uneven trend with plenty of exceptions. Nonetheless – and this is the third point – people may think that their place is very different from others because of the growth of spatial images in the media. While people's *actual* community identification may have declined, their *imagined* community identification may have increased. And this, in a sense, is the issue with which we began: it *is* possible for there to be growing spatial uniformity in some areas (people's leisure, for instance), without there being growing uniformity in others, such as people's perception of local differences.

Further reading

A number of books have recently appeared which look at patterns of spatial differentiation in Britain. See especially Doreen Massey's *Spatial Divisions of Labour* (London, 1984), where she elaborates the ideas briefly introduced in this chapter. In the same vein R. Martin and B. Rowthorn's *The Geography of De-industrialisation* (Basingstoke, 1985) considers how the geography of the UK has been affected by industrial decline. Peter Dickens's *One Nation: Social Change and the Politics of Locality* (London, 1988) examines how economic change in different areas of Britain is related to social and political change. J. Anderson, S. Duncan and R. Hudson's *Redundant Spaces in Cities and Regions* (London, 1983) is a collection of articles showing how spatial patterns are related to different historical periods. More generally, the Lancaster Regionalism Group's *Localities, Class and Gender* (London, 1985) explains why social processes based around class and gender need to be analysed in a local context. For a key article arguing that localities are of increasing importance in modern society, see J. Urry, 'Regions, localities and social class', *International Journal of Urban and Regional Research*, 1981.

A number of recent research projects have examined the question of patterns of spatial change. For a general overview, see M. Savage, J. Barlow, S. Duncan and P. Saunders, 'Doing locality research: the Sussex programme on "Economic restructuring, social change and the locality"', *Quarterly Journal of Social Affairs*, 1987. For a book summarizing the research undertaken by a group of workers examining the inner city problem, see V. Hausner (ed.) *Urban Economic Change* (Oxford, 1987). See also the earlier book of P. Hall, *The Inner City in Context* (London, 1981). For research carried out as part of the Changing Urban and Regional Research Initiative see P. Cooke (ed.), *Localities* (London, 1988).

The question of local cultures is taken up by the collection of work in A. P. Cohen (ed.), *Belonging* (Manchester, 1983). See also the older literature on the meaning of community life and recent changes to it. R. Frankenburg, *Communities in Britain* (London, 1966), remains a useful summary of this older literature. J. Clarke, C. Critcher and R. Johnson, *Working Class Culture* (London, 1978), is a useful discussion of how working-class culture is affected by economic change in different periods, while Clarke's article in J. Allen and D. Massey (eds), *Geography Matters!* (Cambridge, 1984), shows the limitations of mass culture theory.

References

ABERCROMBIE, N. and URRY, J. (1983) *Capital, Labour and the Middle Classes*, London, George Allen and Unwin.

ADAIR, G. (1986) *Myths and Memories*, London, Fontana.

ALDRICH, H., JONES, T. and McEVOY, D. (1984) 'Ethnic advantage and minority business', in Ward, R. and Jenkins, R. (eds).

ALLATT, P. and YEANDLE, S. (1986) ' "It's not fair, is it?" Youth unemployment, family relations and the social contract', in Allen, S. *et al.* (eds) pp. 98–115.

ALLEN, J. and MASSEY, D. (eds) (1988) *The Economy in Question* (Restructuring Britain), London, Sage/The Open University.

ALLEN, D.A. (1968) *British Tastes*, London, Hutchinson.

ALLEN, S., WATON, A., PURCELL, K. and WOOD, S. (eds) (1986) *The Experience of Unemployment*, London and Basingstoke, Macmillan.

ANDERSON, J. and COCHRANE, A. (eds) (1989) *A State of Crisis: The Changing Face of British Politics* (Restructuring Britain Reader), London, Hodder and Stoughton/The Open University.

ANDERSON, B. (1983) *Imagined Communities: Reflections on the Origin and Spread of Nationalism*, London, Verso.

ANTHIAS, F. (1980) 'Women and the reserve army of labour: a critique of Veronica Beechey', *Capital and Class*, No. 10, pp. 50–63.

ARCHBISHOP OF CANTERBURY'S COMMISSION ON URBAN PRIORITY AREAS (1985) *Faith in the City: A Call for Action*, London, Church House Publications.

ATKINSON, A.B. (1972) *Unequal Shares: Wealth in Britain*, London, Allen Lane.

ATKINSON, A.B. (1980) 'On the measurement of inequality', in Atkinson, A.B. (ed.) *Wealth, Income and Inequality* (2nd edition), Oxford, Oxford University Press.

ATKINSON, A.B. (1983) *Economics of Inequality* (2nd edition), Oxford, Oxford University Press.

ATKINSON, A.B. and HARRISON, A.J. (1978) *Distribution of Personal Wealth in Britain*, Cambridge, Cambridge University Press.

ATKINSON, J. and GREGORY, D. (1986) 'A flexible future: Britain's dual labour force', *Marxism Today*, April, pp. 12–17.

BALL, M. and KIRWAN, R.M. (1976) *The Economics of an Urban Housing Market*, Bristol Area Study, Research Paper 15, London, Centre for Environmental Studies.

BALL, M. (1982) 'Housing provision and the economic crisis', *Capital and Class*, No. 17, pp. 60–77.

BALL, M. (1983) *Housing Policy and Economic Power*, London, Methuen.

BALLARD, R. and HOLDEN, B. (1975) 'Racial discrimination: no room at the top', *New Society*, 17 April, pp. 133–5.

BANKS, O. (1968) *The Sociology of Education*, London, Batsford.

BANTON, M. (1987) *Racial Theories*, Cambridge, Cambridge University Press.

BARBALET, J.M. (1986) 'Limitations of class theory and the disappearance of status: the problem of the new middle class', *Sociology*, Vol. 20, No. 4, pp. 557–75.

BARKER, M. (1981) *The New Racism: Conservatives and the Ideology of the Tribe*, London, Junction Books.

BARLOW, J. and SAVAGE, M. (1986) 'Conflict and cleavage in a Tory heartland', *Capital and Class*, No. 31.

BARRATT-BROWN, M. (1988) 'Away with all the great arches: Anderson's history of British capitalism', *New Left Review*, No. 167, pp. 22–52.

BEACHAM, R. (1984) 'Economic activity: Britain's workforce', *Population Trends*, No. 37, pp. 6–14.

BECKER, G.S. (1965) 'A theory of the allocation of time', *Economic Journal*, Vol. 75, pp. 493–517.

BECKER, G.S. (1975) *Human Capital*, Princeton, National Bureau of Economic Research, Princeton University.

BEECHEY, V. (1978) 'Women and production: a critical analysis of some sociological theories of women's work', in Kuhn, A. and Wolpe, A.M. (eds) *Feminism and Materialism: Women and Modes of Production*, London, Routledge & Kegan Paul.

BEGG, I., MOOREN, B. and RHODES, J. (1986) 'Economic and social change in urban Britain and the inner cities', in Hausner, V. (ed.) *Critical Issues in Urban Economic Development*, Oxford, Clarendon.

BELL, C. (1977) 'On housing classes', *Australian and New Zealand Journal of Sociology*, Vol. 13, pp. 36–40.

BEN-TOVIM, G. and GABRIEL, J. (1982) 'The politics of race in Britain: a review of the major trends and recent debates', in Husband, C. (ed.) *'Race' in Britain: Continuity and Change*, London, Hutchinson, pp. 145–74.

BENNETT, T., MERCER, C. and WOOLLACOTT, J. (eds) (1986) *Popular Culture and Social Relations*, Milton Keynes, Open University Press.

BENTHAM, G. (1986) 'Socio-tenurial polarization in the United Kingdom, 1953–83: the income evidence', *Urban Studies*, Vol. 1, pp. 57–62.

BEURET, K. and MAKINGS, L. (1987) ' "I've got used to being independent now": women and courtship in a recession', in Allatt, P., Keil, T., Bryman, A. and Bytheway, B. (eds) *Women and the Life Cycle*, London and Basingstoke, Macmillan, pp. 64–76.

BEVERIDGE, SIR W. (1943) *Pillars of Security*, London, Allen & Unwin.

BLACK, SIR D. (1980) *Inequalities in Health: Report of a Research Working Group*, London, DHSS. Subsequently published as: Townsend, P. (1982) *Inequalities in Health: the Black Report*, Harmondsworth, Penguin.

BOAL, F.W. and DOUGLAS, J.N.H. (eds) (1982) *Integration and Division: Geographical Perspectives on the Northern Ireland Problem*, London, Academic Press.

BODDY, M. (1980) *The Building Societies*, London and Basingstoke, Macmillan.

BOURDIEU, P. (1984) *Distinction: A Social Critique of the Judgement of Taste*, London, Routledge and Kegan Paul.

BOWLEY, M. (1937) 'Some regional aspects of the building boom', *Review of Economic Studies*, pp. 172–86.

BOHNING, W.R. (1972) *The Migration of Workers in the United Kingdom and the European Community*, London, Oxford University Press for the Institute of Race Relations.

BRAH, A. (1986) 'Unemployment and racism: Asian youth on the dole', in Allen, S. *et al.* (eds) pp. 61–78.

BRAVERMAN, H. (1974) *Labour and Monopoly Capital: The Degradation of Work in the Twentieth Century*, New York, Monthly Review Press.

BREUGEL, I. (1979) 'Women as a reserve army of labour: a note on recent British experience', *Feminist Review*, Vol. 3, pp. 12–23.

BRIAR, C. (1987) 'Part-time employment and the State in Britain, 1941–87', paper given at the Women and Employment Conference 'Part-time work – whose flexibility?', West Yorkshire Centre for Research on Women (WYCROW), University of Bradford, 18–19 September.

BROWN, C. (1985) *Black and White Britain: the Third PSI Survey*, Aldershot, Gower. Originally published 1984, London, Policy Studies Institute.

BUCK, N., GORDON, I. and YOUNG, K. (eds) (1986) *The London Employment Problem*, Oxford, Clarendon.

BUILDING SOCIETIES ASSOCIATION (1985) *Housing Tenure*, London, Building Societies Association.

BUTLER, D. (1988) *The British General Election of 1987*, London and Basingstoke, Macmillan.

CAMPBELL, B. (1984) *Wigan Pier Revisited*, London, Virago.

CANNADINE, D. (1983) 'The context, performance and meaning of ritual: the British monarchy and "the invention of tradition" c. 1820–1977', in Hobsbawm, E. and Ranger, T. (eds) *The Invention of Tradition*, Cambridge, Cambridge University Press, pp. 101–64.

CANNADINE, D. and PRICE, S. (eds) (1987) *Rituals of Royalty: Power and Ceremonial in Traditional Societies*, Cambridge, Cambridge University Press.

CARCHEDI, G. (1977) *On the Economic Identification of Social Classes*, London, Routledge and Kegan Paul.

CARCHEDI, G. (1986) 'Two models of class analysis', *Capital and Class*, No. 29, pp. 195–215.

CARTER, R. (1985) *Capitalism, Class Conflict and the New Middle Class*, London, Routledge and Kegan Paul.

CASTELLS, M. (1975) *The Urban Question*, London, Edward Arnold. (Second edition, 1977.)

CASTLES, S. (1984) *Here for Good*, London, Pluto Press.

CASTLES, S. and KOSACK, G. (1973) *Immigrant Workers and Class Structure in Western Europe*, London, Oxford University Press.

CENTRAL STATISTICAL OFFICE (CSO) (annual) *Economic Trends*, London, HMSO.

CENTRAL STATISTICAL OFFICE (CSO) (annual) *Regional Trends*, London, HMSO.

CENTRAL STATISTICAL OFFICE (CSO) (annual) *Social Trends*, London, HMSO.

CENTRE FOR CONTEMPORARY CULTURAL STUDIES (CCCS) (1982) *The Empire Strikes Back: Race and Racism in 70s Britain*, London, Hutchinson.

CHAMPION, A.G. and GREEN, A.E. (1987) 'The booming towns of Britain: the geography of economic performance in the 1980s', *Geography*, Vol. 72, pp. 97–108.

CHAMPION, A.G. and GREEN, A.E. (1988) *Local Prosperity and the North-South Divide: Winners and Losers in 1980s Britain*, University of Warwick, Institute of Employment Research.

CHESSHYRE, R. (1987) *The Return of a Native Reporter*, London, Viking.

CLARKE, J. (1984) ' "There is no place like . . .": cultures of difference', in Allen, J. and Massey, D. (eds) *Geography Matters!*, Cambridge, Cambridge University Press.

COCHRANE, A. and ANDERSON, J. (eds) (1989) *Politics in Transition* (Restructuring Britain), London, Sage/The Open University.

COCKBURN, C. (1983) *Brothers*, London, Pluto Press.

COCKBURN, C. (1986) *Machinery of Dominance*, London, Pluto Press.

COHEN, A.P. (1982) 'A polyethnic London carnival as a contested cultural performance', *Ethnic and Racial Studies*, Vol. 5, No. 1, pp. 23–41.

COHEN, A.P. (1983) *Belonging*, Manchester, Manchester University Press.

COHEN, S. (1972) *Folk Devils and Moral Panics: The Creation of the Mods and Rockers*, London, MacGibbon and Kee.

COLES, B. (1986) 'School leaver, jobseeker, dolereaper: young and unemployed in rural England', in Allen, S. *et al.* (eds) pp. 79–97.

COLLS, R. and DODD, P. (eds) (1986) *Englishness: Politics and Culture 1880–1920*, London, Croom Helm.

COMMISSION OF THE EUROPEAN COMMUNITIES (1984) *Women and Men of Europe in 1983*, Brussels, CEC.

CONNELL, R.W. (1987) *Gender and Power*, Cambridge, Polity Press.

COOKE, K. (1987) 'The withdrawal from paid work of the wives of unemployed men: a review of research', *Journal of Social Policy*, Vol. 16, No. 3, pp. 371–82.

COOKE, P. (1983) *Theories of Planning and Spatial Development*, London, Hutchinson.

CORRIGAN, P. and SAYER, D. (1985) *The Great Arch*, Oxford, Blackwell.

COSGROVE, D. and DANIELS, S. (eds) (1988) *The Iconography of Landscape: Essays on the Symbolic Representation, Design and Use of Past Environments*, Cambridge, Cambridge University Press.

COUNTRYSIDE COMMISSION (1987) *Countryside Recreation Survey*, London, Countryside Commission.

COYLE, A. (1982) 'Sex and skill in the organization of the clothing industry', in West, J. (ed.) *Women Work and the Labour Market*, London, Routledge and Kegan Paul, pp. 10–26.

CREWE, I. (1983) 'The disturbing truth behind Labour's rout', *The Guardian*, 13 June, p. 6.

CROFT, S. (1986) 'Women, caring and the recasting of need – a feminist reappraisal', *Critical Social Policy*, Vol. 16, pp. 23–39.

CROMPTON, R. and JONES, G. (1982) 'Clerical "proletarianisation": myth or reality?', in Day, G. (ed.) *Diversity and Decomposition in the Labour Market*, Aldershot, Gower, pp. 125–45. Reprinted in McDowell, L. *et al.* (eds) (1989) (associated Reader).

CROMPTON, R. and JONES, G. (1984) *White Collar Proletariat*, London and Basingstoke, Macmillan.

CROSS, M. (1987) 'The black economy', *New Society*, 24 July, pp. 16–19.

CURRAN, J. and BURROWS, R. (1986) 'The sociology of petit capitalism: a trend report', *Sociology*, Vol. 20, No. 2, pp. 265–79.

DAHRENDORF, R. (1959) *Class and Class Conflict in Industrial Society*, London, Routledge.

DAHRENDORF, R. (1969) 'The service class', in Burns, T. (ed.) *Industrial Man*, Harmondsworth, Penguin, pp. 140–50.

DAHRENDORF, R. (1987) 'The erosion of citizenship', *New Statesman*, 12 June, pp. 12–15.

DANIEL, W.W. (1968) *Racial Discrimination in England*, Harmondsworth, Penguin.

DANIELS, S. (1988) 'The duplicity of landscape' in Peet, R.J. and Thrift, N.J. (eds) *The New Models in Geography*, London, Unwin Hyman.

DAUNTON, M.J. (1977) *Coal Metropolis: Cardiff, 1870–1914*, Leicester, Leicester University Press.

DAVID, M. (1986) 'Morality and maternity: towards a better union than the moral right's family policy', *Critical Social Policy*, Vol. 16, pp. 40–56.

DAVIDOFF, L. (1973) *The Best Circles: Society, Etiquette and the Season*, London, Croom Helm.

DAVIDOFF, L. and HALL, C. (1987) *Family Fortunes: Men and Women of the English Middle Class, 1750–1850*, London, Hutchinson.

DAY, L. and POND, C. (1982) 'The political economy of taxation', Socialist Economic Review.

DENNIS, N., HENRIQUES, F. and SLAUGHTER, C. (1969) *Coal is Our Life*, London, Tavistock.

DEPARTMENT OF EDUCATION AND SCIENCE (1968) *Public Schools Commission: First Report*, London, HMSO.

DEPARTMENT OF EMPLOYMENT (DE) (annual) *Family Expenditure Survey*, London, HMSO.

DEPARTMENT OF EMPLOYMENT (DE) (annual) *Labour Force Survey*, London, HMSO.

DEPARTMENT OF EMPLOYMENT (DE) (annual) *New Earnings Survey*, London, HMSO.

DEPARTMENT OF EMPLOYMENT (DE) (1986) *Building Businesses Not Barriers*, Cmnd 9794, London, HMSO.

DEPARTMENT OF THE ENVIRONMENT (DoE) (1977) *Housing Policy: A Consultative Document*, London, HMSO, Cmnd 6851 (plus three Technical Volumes).

DEPARTMENT OF THE ENVIRONMENT (DoE) (quarterly) *Housing and Construction Statistics*, London, HMSO.

DEX, S. (1985) *The Sexual Division of Work*, Brighton, Wheatsheaf.

DEX, S. and PERRY, S.M. (1984) 'Women's employment changes in the 1970s', *Employment Gazette*, Vol. 92, No. 4, pp. 151–64.

DICKENS, P., DUNCAN, S.S., GOODWIN, M. and GRAY, F. (1985) *Housing, States and Localities*, London, Methuen.

DODD, P. (1986) 'Englishness and the national culture' in Colls, R. and Dodd, P. (eds).

DONNISON, D. and UNGERSON, C. (1981) *Housing Policy*, Harmondsworth, Penguin.

DUKE, V. and EDGELL, S. (1984) 'Public expenditure cuts in Britain and consumption sectoral cleavages', *International Journal of Urban and Regional Research*, Vol. 8, No. 2, pp. 177–201.

DUNLEAVY, P. (1979) 'The Urban basis of political alignment: social class, domestic property ownership, and state intervention in consumption processes', *British Journal of Political Science*, Vol. 9, pp. 409–43.

DUNLEAVY, P. (1980) *Urban Political Analysis: The Politics of Collective Consumption*, London and Basingstoke, Macmillan.

DUNLEAVY, P. and HUSBANDS, C. (1985) *British Democracy at the Crossroads: Voting and Party Competition in the 1980s*, London, Allen and Unwin.

DUNN, R., FORREST, R. and MURIE, A. (1987) 'The geography of council house sales in England, 1975–85', *Urban Studies*, Vol. 24, No. 1, pp. 47–59.

FIELD, F. (ed.) (1983) *The Wealth Report 2*, London, Routledge and Kegan Paul.

FIELD, F., MEACHER, M., and POND, C. (1977) *To Him Who Hath: A Study of Poverty and Taxation*, Harmondsworth, Penguin.

FINCH, J. and GROVES, D. (1984) *A Labour of Love*, London, Routledge and Kegan Paul.

FISKE, J. (1987) 'British cultural studies and television', in Allen, R.C. (ed.) *Channelsat Discourse*, Methuen, London, pp. 254–89.

FORREST, R. and MURIE, A. (1987a) 'Fiscal reorientation, centralization and the privatization of council housing', in van Vliet, W. (ed.) *Housing Markets and Policies under Conditions of Fiscal Austerity*, Westport, Conn., Greenwood Press. Reprinted in McDowell, L. *et al.* (eds) (1989) (associated Reader).

FORREST, R. and MURIE, A. (1987b) 'The pauperisation of council housing', *Roof*, Jan/Feb., pp. 20–22.

FRANKLIN, M.N. and PAGE, E.C. (1984) 'A critique of the consumption cleavage approach in British voting studies', *Political Studies*, Vol. 32.

FRIEND, A. and METCALF, A. (1981) *Slump City: The Politics of Mass Unemployment*, London, Pluto Press.

GAME, A. and PRINGLE, R. (1984) *Gender at Work*, London, Pluto Press.

GELLNER, E. (1983) *Nations and Nationalism*, Oxford, Blackwell.

GENTLEMAN, D. (1982) *David Gentleman's Britain*, London, Weidenfeld and Nicolson.

GERSHUNY, J. and MILES, I. (1983) *The New Service Economy*, London, Frances Pinter.

GIDDENS, A. (1973) *The Class Structure of the Advanced Societies*, London, Hutchinson.

GILROY, P. (1987) *There Ain't No Black in the Union Jack: The Cultural Politics of Race and Nation*, Hutchinson, London. Extract (Chapter 4) reprinted in McDowell, L. *et al.* (eds) (1989) (associated Reader).

GLASS, R. (1968) 'Anti-urbanism' in Pahl, R.E. (ed.) *Readings in Urban Sociology*, Oxford, Pergamon, pp. 63–73.

GOLDBLATT, P. (1983) 'Changes in social class between 1971 and 1981: could these affect mortality differences among men of working ages?' *Population Trends*, No. 51, pp. 9–17.

GOLDTHORPE, J.H. and PAYNE, C. (1986) 'Trends in intergenerational class mobility in England and Wales, 1972–1983', *Sociology*, Vol. 20, No. 1, pp. 1–24.

GOLDTHORPE, J.H., LOCKWOOD, D., BECHHOFER, F. and PLATT, J. (1969) *The Affluent Worker in the Class Structure*, Cambridge, Cambridge University Press.

GOUGH, I. (1979) *The Political Economy of the Welfare State*, London and Basingstoke, Macmillan.

GOVERNMENT CERTIFICATION OFFICER (1988) *Annual Report for 1987*, London, HMSO.

GRAHAM, H. (1984) *Women, Health and Family*, Brighton, Wheatsheaf.

GRAY, F. (1982) 'Owner occupation and social relations', in Merrett, S. and Gray, F. (eds) Chapter 15.

HADDON, R. (1970) 'A minority in a welfare state society', *New Atlantis*, Vol. 2, pp. 80–133.

HALL, S. and JEFFERSON, T. (eds) (1976) *Resistance through Rituals: Youth Subcultures in Post-war Britain*, London, Hutchinson.

HALL, S., CRITCHER, C., JEFFERSON, T., CLARKE, J. and ROBERTS, B. (eds) (1978) *Policing the Crisis: Mugging, the State and Law and Order*, London and Basingstoke, Macmillan.

HALL, S. (1977) 'Culture, the media and the "ideological effect" ', in Curran, J. (ed.) *Mass Communication and Society*, London, Edward Arnold.

HALL, S. (1980) 'Encoding/decoding', in Hall, S., Hobson, D. and Willis, P. (eds) *Culture, Media, Language*, London, Hutchinson.

HALSEY, A.H. (1978) 'Class Ridden Prosperity', *The Listener*, 19 January.

HALSEY, A.H. (1987) 'Social trends since World War II', *Social Trends*, Vol. 17, pp. 11–19. Reprinted in McDowell, L. *et al.* (eds) (1989) (associated Reader).

HAMNETT, C. (1983) 'Regional variations in house prices and house price inflation, 1969–81', *Area*, Vol. 15, No. 2, pp. 97–109.

HAMNETT, C. (1984a) 'Housing the two nations: socio-tenurial polarization in England and Wales, 1961–81', *Urban Studies*, Vol. 21, No. 3, pp. 389–405.

HAMNETT, C. (1984b) 'Life in the cocktail belt', *Geographical Magazine*, October, pp. 534–8.

HAMNETT, C. (1987) 'Conservative government housing policy in Britain, 1979–85: economics or ideology', in van Vliet, W. (ed.) *Housing Markets and Policies under Fiscal Austerity*, Westport, Conn., Greenwood Press.

HAMNETT, C. (1988) 'The owner occupied housing market in Britain: a north-south divide?', in Lewis, J. and Townsend, A. (eds) *North-versus-South: Industrial and Social Change in Britain*, London, Paul Chapman.

HARBURY, C. and HITCHINS, G. (1980) 'The myth of the self-made man', *New Statesman*, 15 February.

HARLOE, M. (1984) 'Sector and class: a critical comment', *International Journal of Urban and Regional Research*, Vol. 8, No. 2, pp. 228–37.

HARLOE, M. and PARIS, C. (1984) 'The decollectivisation of consumption: housing and local government finance in England and Wales, 1979–81', in Szelenyi, I. (ed.) *Cities in Recession*, London, Sage. Reprinted in McDowell, L. *et al.* (eds) (1989) (associated Reader).

HARRISON, P. (1983) *Inside the Inner City*, Harmondsworth, Penguin.

HARTMANN, H. (1981) 'The unhappy marriage of Marxism and feminism: towards a more progressive union', in Sargent, L. (ed.) *Women and Revolution*, London, Pluto Press.

HAUG, W.F. (1986) *Critique of Commodity Aesthetics: Appearance, Sexuality and Advertising in Capitalist Society*, Cambridge, Polity Press.

HAUG, W.F. (1987) *Commodity Aesthetics, Ideology and Culture*, New York, International General.

HAYDEN, I. (1987) *Symbol and Privilege: The Ritual Context of British Royalty*, Tucson, University of Arizona Press.

HEATH, A. and McDONALD, S.K. (1987) 'Social change and the future of the left', *Political Quarterly*, Vol. 58, No. 4, pp. 364–77. Reprinted in McDowell, L. *et al.* (eds) (1989) (associated Reader).

HEBDIGE, D. (1979) *Subculture: The Meaning of Style*, London, Methuen.

HEWISON, R. (1987) *The Heritage Industry: Britain in a Climate of Decline*, London, Methuen. Extract (Chapter 3) reprinted in McDowell, L. *et al.* (eds) (1989) (associated Reader).

HIRD, C. (1979) 'The poverty of wealth statistics', in Irvine and Evans (eds), *Demystifying Social Statistics*, London, Pluto Press.

HIRO, D. (1973) *Black British, White British*, Harmondsworth, Penguin.

HMSO (1971) *British Labour Statistics Historical Abstract: 1886–1968*, London, HMSO.

HMSO (1981), *The Brixton Disorders 10–12 April 1981: Report of an inquiry by the Rt Hon Lord Scarman, OBE*, Cmnd 8427, London, HMSO.

HOBSBAWM, E. (1978) 'The forward march of Labour halted?', *Marxism Today*, September, pp. 279–86.

HOBSBAWM, E. (1983) 'Labour's lost millions', *Marxism Today*, Oct., pp. 7–13.

HOBSBAWM, E. (1987) 'Out of the wilderness', *Marxism Today*, Oct., pp. 12–19.

HOBSBAWM, E. and RANGER, T. (eds) (1983) *The Invention of Tradition*, Cambridge, Cambridge University Press.

HORNE, D. (1984) *The Great Museum: the Re-presentation of History*, London Pluto Press.

HOWKINS, A. (1986) 'The discovery of rural England', in Colls, R. and Dodd, P. (eds).

HUNT, E. (1973) *Regional Wage Variations in Britain*, Oxford, Clarendon.

HURSTFIELD, J. (1987) *Part-timers Under Pressure*, London, Low Pay Unit.

HUWS, U. (1985) 'Challenging commoditisation', in Collective Design, *Very Nice Work If You Can Get It*, Nottingham, Spokesman, Chapter 13.

INGHAM, G. (1984) *Capitalism Divided? The City and Industry in British Social Development*, London and Basingstoke, Macmillan.

INLAND REVENUE (1986) *Statistics*, London, HMSO.

INSTITUTE OF DIRECTORS (1984) *Wages Councils: The Case for Abolition*, London, Institute of Directors.

INSTITUTE OF HEALTH SERVICE MANAGEMENT (1988) *The Potential Role of Private Health Insurance*, London, ISHM.

JACKSON, P. (1987) 'The idea of "race" and the geography of racism', in Jackson, P. (ed.) *Race and Racism: Essays in Social Geography*, London, Allen and Unwin, pp. 3–12.

JAQUES, M. (1987) *The Guardian*, 1 September.

JENKINS, R. (1982) *Hightown Rules: Growing up in a Belfast Housing Estate*, Leicester, Youth Bureau.

JENKINS, R. (1983) *Lads, Citizens and Ordinary Kids: Working-class Youth Life-styles in Belfast*, London, Routledge and Kegan Paul.

JENNINGS, J.H. (1971) 'Geographical implications of the municipal housing pro-gramme in England and Wales, 1919–1939', *Urban Studies*, Vol. 8, No. 2, pp. 121–38.

JHALLY, S. (1987) *The Codes of Advertising: Fetishism and the Political Economy of Meaning in the Consumer Society*, London, Frances Pinter.

JONES, G.S. (1971) *Outcast London*, London, Allen Lane.

JOSHI, H.E. (1984) *Women's Participation in Paid Work: Further Analysis of the Women and Employment Survey*, Department of Employment Research Paper 45.

JOURNAL OF SOCIAL POLICY (1987) *Special Issue on Poverty*, Vol. 16

KEMENY, J. (1980) *Home Ownership and Family Life Cycles*, Birmingham, University of Birmingham, Centre for Urban and Regional Studies, Working Paper 70.

KERR, C. *et al*. (1962) *Industrialism and Industrial Man*, London, Heinemann.

KLEINMAN, M. and WHITEHEAD, C. (1987) 'Local variations in the sale of council houses in England, 1979–84', *Regional Studies*, Vol. 21, No. 1, pp. 1–12.

LAING, S. (1986) *Representations of Working-class Life, 1957–1964*. London and Basingstoke, Macmillan.

LAING, S. (1988) 'A review of private health care', *New Society*, 15 April.

LAND, H. (1983) 'Who still cares for the family? Recent developments in income maintenance, taxation and family law', in Lewis, J. (ed.) *Women's Welfare, Women's Rights*, London, Croom Helm.

LAND, H. (1986) *Women and Economic Dependency*, Manchester, Equal Opportunities Commission.

LANGTON, J. (1984) 'The industrial revolution and the regional geography of England', *Transactions of the Institute of British Geographers*.

LASH, S. and URRY, J. (1987) *The End of Organised Capitalism*, Cambridge, Polity Press.

LAYARD, R. PIACHAUD, D. and STEWART, M. (1978) *The Causes of Poverty*, Royal Commission on the Distribution of Income and Wealth, Background Paper No. 5, London, HMSO.

LEADBEATER, C. (1987) 'In the land of the dispossessed', *Marxism Today*, April, pp. 18–25. Reprinted in McDowell, L. *et al*. (eds) (1989) (associated Reader).

LEGRAND, J. (1982) *The Strategy of Equality, Redistribution and the Social Services*, London, Allen and Unwin.

LEISS, W., KLINE, S. and JHALLY, S. (1986) *Social Communication in Advertising: Persons, Products and Images of Well-being*, London, Methuen.

LEONARD, D. (1981) *Sex and Generation*, London, Tavistock.

LEWIS, J. and TOWNSEND, A. (eds) (1988) *North-versus-South: Industrial and Social Change in Britain*, London, Paul Chapman.

LOCKWOOD, D. (1958) *The Blackcoated Worker*, London, Unwin.

GREATER LONDON COUNCIL (GLC) (1985) *London Industrial Strategy*, London, Greater London Council.

LOW PAY UNIT (1987) *Mortgage Interest Tax Relief: An Unequal Subsidy*, Review 31, London, Low Pay Unit.

LOW PAY UNIT (1988) *The Poor Decade: Wage Inequalities in the 1980s*, London, Low Pay Unit.

LOW PAY UNIT/CPAG (1988) *An Abundance of Poverty*, London, Low Pay Unit.

LUMLEY, T. (1988) *The Museum Time Machine: Putting Cultures on Display*, London, Comedia.

MALPASS, P. (1983) 'Residualisation and the restructuring of housing provision', *Housing Review*, March/April, pp. 1–2.

MANN, M. (1987) 'Ruling class strategies and citizenship', *Sociology*, Vol. 21, No. 3, pp. 339–54.

MARCUSE, H. (1964) *One-dimensional Man*, London, Routledge and Kegan Paul.

MARSDEN, D. (1982) *Workless*, London, Croom Helm.

MARSHALL, G., NEWBY, H., ROSE, D. and VOGLER, C. (1988) *Social Class in Modern Britain*, London, Hutchinson.

MARSHALL, J. (1968) 'The pattern of housebuilding in the interwar period in England and Wales', *Scottish Journal of Political Economy*, pp. 184–205.

MARSHALL, T.H. (1953) *Class, Citizenship and Social Development*, New York, Doubleday.

MARTIN, R. (1986) 'Thatcherism and Britain's industrial landscape', in Martin, R. and Rowthorn, B. (eds) *The Geography of De-industrialisation*, London and Basingstoke. Macmillan.

MASSEY, D. (1983) 'The shape of things to come', *Marxism Today*, April, pp. 18–27.

MASSEY, D. (1984) *Spatial Divisions of Labour*, London and Basingstoke. Macmillan.

MASSEY, D. and ALLEN, J. (eds) (1988) *Uneven Re-Development: Cities and Regions in Transition* (Restructuring Britain Reader), London, Hodder and Stoughton/The Open University.

McDOWELL, L., SARRE, P., and HAMNETT, C. (eds) (1989) *Divided Nation: Social and Cultural Change in Britain* (Restructuring Britain Reader), London, Hodder and Stoughton/The Open University.

McGHIE, C. (1988) 'Lure of the village piles on the pressure' *Sunday Times*, 15 May, p. C13.

McKEE, L. and BELL, C. (1986) 'His unemployment; her problem: the domestic consequences of male unemployment', in Allen, S. *et al.* (eds) pp. 134–149.

McKENDRICK, N., BREWER, J. and PLUMB, J.H. (1982) *The Birth of a Consumer Society: The Commercialisation of Eighteenth Century England*, London, Hutchinson.

MacNICOL, J. (1987) 'In pursuit of the underclass', *Journal of Social Policy*, Vol. 16, No. 3, pp. 293–318.

MEEGAN, R. (1987) 'Local culture in outer Liverpool', paper given at LSE seminar.

MERRETT, S. (1979) *State Housing in Britain*, London, Routledge.

MERRETT, S. and GRAY, F. (eds) (1982) *Owner Occupation in Britain*, London, Routledge and Kegan Paul.

MEYROWITZ, J. (1985), *No Sense of Place: the Impact of Electronic Media on Social Behaviour*, New York, Oxford University Press.

MILES, R. (1982) *Racism and Migrant Labour*, London, Routledge. Extract (Chapter 7) reprinted in McDowell, L. *et al.* (eds) (1989) (associated Reader).

MILES, R. (1984) 'Marxism versus the sociology of "race relations"', *Ethnic and Racial Studies*, Vol. 7, No. 2, pp. 217–37.

MILES, R. (1987) 'Recent marxist theories of nationalism and the issue of racism', *British Journal of Sociology*, Vol. 38, pp. 24–43.

MILLER, F.A.B. and TRANTER, E.B. (eds) (1988) *Public Perception of the Countryside*, Reading, Centre for Agricultural Strategy, University of Reading.

MINCER, J. (1962) 'Labour force participation of married women: a study of labour supply', in National Bureau of Economic Research, *Aspects of Labour Economics*, Princeton, Princeton University Press.

MINISTRY OF LABOUR (1942) *Mobilization of Woman-power: Planning for Part-time Work*.

MINISTRY OF LABOUR (1955/6) *The Employment of Older Men and Women*, Cmnd 9629, London, HMSO.

MONEY MAGAZINE (1988) 'Britain's Richest 200', March.

MORLEY, D. (1986) *Family Television: Cultural Power and Domestic Leisure*, London, Comedia.

MORT, F. (1988) 'Perfect lifestyle, ideal home', *Marxism Today*, March, pp. 49–50.

MURIE, A. (1982) 'A new era for council housing', in English, J. (ed.) *The Future of Council Housing*, London, Croom Helm.

MURPHY, R. (1986) 'The concept of class in closure theory: learning from rather than falling into the problems encountered by neo-Marxism', *Sociology*, Vol. 20, No. 2, pp. 247–64.

NAIRN, T. (1988) *The Enchanted Glass*, London, Radius.

NATIONWIDE BUILDING SOCIETY (1985) *House Prices over the Past Thirty Years*, London, Nationwide Building Society.

NATIONWIDE BUILDING SOCIETY (1987) *House Prices: The North/South Divide*, London, Nationwide Building Society.

NEALE, R.S. (1972) *Class and Ideology in the Nineteenth Century*, London, Routledge and Kegan Paul.

NEWBY, H. (1982) *Green and Pleasant Land? Social Change in Rural England* (2nd Edition), London, Hutchinson.

O'CONNOR, J. (1973) *The Fiscal Crisis of the State*, New York, St Martins Press.

OAKLEY, A. (1974) *The Sociology of Housework*, Oxford, Martin Robertson.

OFFER, A. (1981) *Property and Politics*, 1870–1914, Cambridge, Cambridge University Press.

OFFICE OF POPULATION CENSUSES AND SURVEYS (OPCS) (1980) *Classification of Occupations*, London, HMSO.

OFFICE OF POPULATION CENSUSES AND SURVEYS (annual) *General Household Survey*, London, HMSO.

OFFICE OF POPULATION CENSUSES AND SURVEYS (OPCS) (1971) *Occupational Mortality Tables*, London, HMSO.

OFFICE OF POPULATION CENSUSES AND SURVEYS (OPCS) (1961) *Census of Population, 1961*, London, HMSO.

OFFICE OF POPULATION CENSUSES AND SURVEYS (OPCS) (1981) *Census of Population, 1981*, London, HMSO.

OFFICE OF POPULATION CENSUSES AND SURVEYS (OPCS) (1961) *Registrar General's Decennial Supplement England and Wales, 1961*, London, HMSO.

PAHL, J. (1983) 'The allocation of money and the structuring of inequality within marriage', *Sociological Review*, Vol. 31, pp. 237–62.

PARKIN, F. (1979) *Marxism and Class Theory: A Bourgeois Critique*, London, Tavistock.

PATEL, S. (1988) 'Asian retailing in Britain', unpublished thesis, The Open University.

PEACH, G.C.K. (1965) 'West Indian migration to Britain: the economic factors', *Race*, Vol. 7, No. 1.

PEACH, G.C.K. (1966) 'Factors affecting the distribution of West Indians in Britain', *Transactions and Papers of the Institute of British Geographers*, No. 38, pp. 151–63.

PEACH, G.C.K. (1968) *West Indian Migration to Britain*, London, Oxford University Press for Institute of Race Relations.

PEACH, G.C.K. (1978) 'British unemployment cycles and West Indian immigration, 1955–1974', *New Community*, Vol. 7, No. 1.

PEACOCK, A. and WISEMAN, D. (1966) *The Growth of Public Expenditure in the UK*, 2nd edn, London, Allen and Unwin.

PHIZACKLEA, A. and MILES, R. (1980) *Labour and Racism*, London, Routledge.

PIACHAUD, D. (1987) 'The distribution of income and work', *Oxford Review of Economic Policy*, Vol. 3, No. 3.

PLAYFORD, C. and POND, C. (1983) 'The right to be unequal: inequality in incomes', in Field, F. (ed.).

POND, C. (1983) 'Wealth and the Two Nations', in Field, F. (ed.). Reprinted in McDowell, L. *et al.* (eds) (1989) (associated Reader).

POTTER, J. and WETHERALL, M. (1987) *Discourse and Social Psychology: Beyond Attitudes and Behaviour*, London, Sage.

POTTER, L. (1987) 'Country style', *Country Living*, September, pp. 46–51.

POULANTZAS, N. (1975) *Classes in Contemporary Capitalism*, London, New Left Books.

POWER, J. (1972) *The New Proletarians*, London, British Council of Churches.

POWER, M. (1983) 'From home production to wage labour: women as a reserve army of labour', *Review of Radical Political Economics*, Vol. XV, No. 1, pp. 71–91.

PRETECEILLE, E. (1986) 'Collective consumption, urban segregation, and social classes', *Society and Space*, Vol. 4, pp. 145–54.

QUICK, P. (1977) 'The class nature of women's oppression', *Review of Radical Political Economics*, Vol. 9, No. 3, pp. 42–53.

RABAN, J. (1986) *Coasting*, London, Picador.

RATTANSI, A. (1985) 'End of an orthodoxy? The critique of sociology's view of Marx on class', *Sociological Review*, Vol. 33, No. 4, pp. 641–69.

REID, I. (1981) *Social Class Differences in Britain*, London, Grant McIntyre.

RENNER, K. (1978) 'The service class', in Bottomore, T. and Goode, P. (eds) *Austro-Marxism*, London, Oxford University Press, pp. 249–52.

REX, J. and TOMLINSON, S. (1979) *Colonial Immigrants in a British City: A Class Analysis*, London, Routledge and Kegan Paul.

REX, J. and MOORE, R. (1967) *Race, Community and Conflict*, Oxford, Oxford University Press.

ROBINSON, J.M. (1984) *The Latest Country Houses*, London, Bodley Head.

ROBINSON, R. (1986) 'Restructuring the welfare state: an analysis of public expenditure, 1979/80–1984/5', *Journal of Social Policy*, Vol. 15, No. 1, pp. 1–21.

ROBINSON, R. and O'SULLIVAN, T. (1983) 'Housing tenure polarisation', *Housing Review*, July/August, pp. 116–17.

ROEMER, J.E. (1982) *A General Theory of Exploitation and Class*, Cambridge, Mass., Harvard University Press.

ROSE, D. and MARSHALL, G. (1986) 'Constructing the (W)right classes', *Sociology* Vol. 20, No. 3, pp. 440–55.

ROSE, E.J.B. (1969) *Colour and Citizenship: A Report on British Race Relations*. London, Oxford University Press for the Institute of Race Relations.

ROSE, S. and LEWONTIN, R. (1983) *Not in Our Genes*, Harmondsworth, Penguin.

ROYAL COMMISSION ON THE DISTRIBUTION OF INCOME AND WEALTH (1979) Report No. 7, Cmnd 7595, London, HMSO.

ROYAL COMMISSION ON THE DISTRIBUTION OF INCOME AND WEALTH (1979) Report No. 8, Cmnd 7679, London, HMSO.

RUBERY, J. (1978) 'Structured labour markets, worker organisation and low pay', *Cambridge Journal of Economics*, Vol. 2, March.

SAMUEL, R. (1988a) 'Little Dickens' *The Guardian*, 19 February, p. 23.

SAMUEL, R. (1988b) *Theatres of Memory*, London, Verso.

SAUNDERS, P. (1978) 'Domestic property and social class', *International Journal of Urban and Regional Research*, Vol. 2, pp. 233–51.

SAUNDERS, P. (1979) *Urban Politics*, London, Hutchinson.

SAUNDERS, P. (1984) 'Beyond housing classes: the sociological significance of private property rights in means of consumption', *International Journal of Urban and Regional Research*, Vol. 8, No. 2, pp. 202–27. Reprinted in McDowell, L. *et al.* (eds) (1989) (associated Reader).

SAUNDERS, P. (1986) 'Comment on Dunleavy and Preteceille', *Society and Space*, Vol. 4, pp. 155–63.

SCASE, R. and GOFFEE, R. (1982) *The Entrepreneurial Middle Class*, London, Croom Helm.

SCOTT, J. (1979) *Corporations, Classes and Capitalism*, Hutchinson, London. Extract (Chapter 5) reprinted in McDowell, L. *et al.* (eds) (1989) (associated Reader).

SCOTT, J. and GRIFF, C. (1984) *Directors of Industry: The British Corporate Network, 1904–76*, Cambridge, Polity Press.

SHAW, C. (1988) 'Latest estimates of ethnic minority populations', *Population Trends*, No. 51, pp. 5–8.

SHIELDS, R. (1988) *Reading the Built Environment: 150 Years of the Shopping Arcade*, University of Sussex Urban and Regional Studies Working Paper No. 61.

SHOARD, M. (1987) *This Land is Our Land: The Struggle for Britain's Countryside*, London, Paladin.

SIBLEY, D. (1981) *Outsiders in Urban Societies*, Oxford, Blackwell.

SINFIELD, A. (1981) *What Unemployment Means*, Oxford, Martin Robertson.

SMITH, D.J. (1977) *Racial Disadvantage in Britain*, Harmondsworth, Penguin.

SMITH, G. (1987) *The English Season*, London, Pavilion.

SMITH, N. (1983) *Uneven Development*, London, Methuen.

SMITH, S.J. (1987) 'Residential segregation: a geography of English racism', in Jackson, P. (ed.) *Race and Racism: Essays in Social Geography*, London, Allen and Unwin, pp. 25–49.

SMITH, W. (1988) 'Live-in kitchens' *Savills Magazine*, Spring, pp. 17–19.

STARK, T.A. (1988) *New A-Z of Income and Wealth*, London, Fabian Society.

SUTCLIFFE, A. (1983) 'In search of the urban variable: Britain in the later nineteenth century', in Fraser, D. and Sutcliffe, A. (eds) *The Pursuit of Urban History*, London, Edward Arnold.

SWEENEY, J. (1988) 'The thin black line', *Observer Magazine*, 24 January.

TAWNEY, R.H. (1931) *Equality*, London, Unwin.

THATCHER, M. (1977) *Let Our Children Grow Tall: Selected Speeches, 1975–1977*, London, Centre for Policy Studies.

THOMAS, D.E. (1987) 'Don't lie back and just think of England', *The Guardian*, 21 December, p. 17.

THOMAS, K. (1983) *Man and the Natural World: Changing Attitudes in England 1500–1800*, London, Allen Lane.

THORNS, D. (1982) 'Industrial restructuring and change in labour and property markets in Britain', *Environment and Planning*, A. 14, pp. 745–63.

THRIFT, N.J. (1987) 'An introduction to the geography of late twentieth century class formation', in Thrift, N.J. and Williams, P. (eds) *Class and Space*, London, Routledge and Kegan Paul.

THUROW, L. (1969) *Poverty and Discrimination*, Washington, DC, Brookings Institution.

THUROW, L. (1970) *Investment in Human Capital*, Belmont, Calif., Wadsworth.

TOWNSEND, P. (1979) *Poverty in the United Kingdom*, Harmondsworth, Penguin.

URRY, J. (1981) 'Localities, regions and social class', *International Journal of Urban and Regional Research*, Vol. 5, No. 2.

URRY, J. (1987) *Holidaymaking, Cultural Change and the Seaside*, Lancaster Regionalism Group Working Paper No. 22.

URRY, J. (1988) 'Cultural change and contemporary holiday-making', *Theory, Culture and Society*, Vol. 5, pp. 35–55. Reprinted in McDowell, L. *et al*. (eds) (1989) (associated Reader).

VANLAER, J. (1984) '200 Millions de voix: une geographie des familles politiques européennes', Société Royal Belge de Géographie.

VOGEL, L. (1983) *Marxism and the Oppression of Women*, London, Pluto Press.

WALDINGER, R., WARD, R. and ALDRICH, H. (1985) 'Ethnic business and occupational mobility in advanced societies', *Sociology*, Vol. 19, No. 4, pp. 586–97.

WALLERSTEIN, I. (1974) *The Modern World System*, 2 vols, New York, Academic Press.

WARD, R. (1985) 'Minority settlement and the local economy', in Roberts, B., Finnegan, R. and Gallie, D. (eds) *New Approaches to Economic Life*, Manchester, ESRC and Manchester University Press, pp. 198–212. Reprinted in McDowell, L. *et al*. (eds) (1989) (associated Reader).

WARD, R. and JENKINS, R. (eds) (1984) *Ethnic Communities in Business: Strategies for Economic Survival*, Cambridge, Cambridge University Press.

WARDE, A. (1985) 'The homogenization of space? Trends in the spatial division of labour in twentieth century Britain', in Newley, H. *et al*. (eds) *Restructuring Capital*, London and Basingstoke, Macmillan, pp. 41–62.

WEBER, E. (1977) *Peasants into Frenchmen*, London, Chatto and Windus.

WEBER, M. (1948), 'Class, status and party', in Gerth, H. and Mills, C.W. (eds) *From Max Weber: Essays in Sociology*, Routledge and Kegan Paul, London, pp. 180–95. Reproduced from *Wirtschaft und Gesellschaft (Economy and Society), Part III*, Chapter 4, pp. 631–40.

WEBSTER, J. (1986) 'Word processing and the secretarial labour process', in Purcell, K. *et al*. (eds) *The Changing Experience of Employment*, London and Basingstoke, Macmillan, pp. 114–131. Reprinted in McDowell, L. *et al*. (eds) (1989) (associated Reader).

WEDDERBURN, D. (1980) 'Inequalities in pay', in Routh, G., Wedderburn, D. and Wootton, B. *The Roots of Pay Inequalities*, London, Low Pay Unit.

WERBNER, P. (1980) 'From rags to riches: Manchester Pakistanis in the textile trade', *New Community*, Vol. 8, No. 1, pp. 84–95.

WESTERGAARD, J. and RESLER, H. (1975) *Class in a Capitalist Society*, London, Heinemann.

WESTWOOD, S. (1984) *All Day, Every Day*, London, Pluto Press. Extracts reprinted in McDowell, L. *et al.* (eds) (1989) (associated Reader).

WHIMSTER, S. and LASH, S. (1987) *Max Weber: Rationality and Modernity*, London, Allen and Unwin.

WHITEHEAD, M. (1987) *The Health Divide: Inequalities in Health in the 1980s*, London, The Health Education Authority.

WIENER, M. (1981) *English Culture and the Decline of the Industrial Spirit*, 1850–1980, Cambridge, Cambridge University Press.

WILLIAMS, N. (1988) 'Housing tenure, political attitudes and voting behaviour' *Area* (forthcoming).

WILLIAMS, N., SEWEL, J. and TWINE, F. (1987) 'Council house sales and the electorate: voting behaviour and ideological implications', *Housing Studies*, Vol. 2, No. 4, pp. 274–82.

WILLIAMS, R. (1981) *Culture*, London, Fontana.

WILLIAMS, R. (1973) *The Country and the City*, London, Paladin.

WILLIAMS, R. (1977) *Marxism and Literature*, Oxford, Oxford University Press.

WILLIAMS, R. (1979) *Politics and Letters*, London, New Left Books.

WILLIAMSON, J. (1986) *Consuming Passions: The Dynamics of Popular Culture*, Edinburgh, Marion Boyars.

WILLIS, P. (1977) *Learning to Labour: How Working Class Kids Get Working Class Jobs*, Fouborgh, Saxon House.

WILLIS, P. (1978) *Profane Culture*, London and Basingstoke, Macmillan.

WILSON, E. (1977) *Women and the Welfare State*, Tavistock, London.

WRIGHT, E.O. (1978) *Class, Crisis and the State*, London, New Left Books.

WRIGHT, E.O. (1985) *Classes*, London and New York, Verso.

WRIGHT, P. (1985) *On Living in an Old Country: The National Past in Contemporary Britain*, London, Verso. Extract (Chapter 7) reprinted in McDowell, L. *et al.* (eds) (1989) (associated Reader).

WUTHNOW, R. (1987) *Meaning and Moral Order: Explorations in Cultural Analysis*, Berkeley, University of California Press.

Acknowledgements

Grateful acknowledgement is made to the following sources for permission to use material in this textbook:

Text

Extracts 1 and 2: Game, A. and Pringle, R. *Gender at Work*, 1984, Pluto Press.

Figures

Figure 1.1: Austin Rover Group Ltd.; *Figure 1.2*: Laing Homes Limited; *Figure 1.3*: BMW Limited; *Figure 1.4*: Yorkshire Television Limited; *Figure 1.5*: National Countryside Recreation Survey, Countryside Commission, 1987; *Figure 1.7*: Conservative Central Office; *Figure 2.1*: Fabian Society; *Figures 3.1, 3.2 and 3.3*: Wright, E.O. *Classes*, 2nd Edn. 1987, Verso Books; *Figure 3.4*: Grail, J. and Rowthorn, R. 'Dodging the taxing questions' in *Marxism Today*, November 1986; *Figure 4.2*: Jones, P.N. 'The distribution and diffusion of the coloured population in England and Wales 1961–71', in *Transactions*, Institute of British Geographers, 3, (4), 1978; *Figure 5.1*: Women and Geography Study Group of the Institute of British Geographers, in *Geography and Gender* 1984; *Figure 5.4*: Huws, U. *Very Nice Work if You Can Get It*, 1985, Spokesman; *Figure 5.5*: OPCS, *General Household Survey, 1985*, (HMSO), 1987; *Figure 6.1*: Redrawn from Ball, M. *Housing Policy and Economic Power*, 1983, Methuen & Co. Ltd.; *Figure 6.2*: Laing, *Review of Private Healthcare*, 1988; *Figure 6.5*: *House Prices Over the Past 30 Years*, April 1985, National Building Society; *Figure 6.6*: *House Prices, the North/South Divide*, August 1987, Nationwide Building Society; *Figure 7.2*: Short, J.R. and Kirby, A. (eds.) *The Human Geography of Contemporary Britain*, 1984, Macmillan Publishers Limited; *Figures 7.3 and 7.4*: Champion, A.G. and Green, A.E. 'In search of Britain's booming towns: an index of local economic performance for Britain', *Discussion Paper 72*, Centre for Urban and Regional Studies, University of Newcastle Upon Tyne, 1985.

Tables

Table 3.2: Goldblatt, P. 'Changes in social class between 1971–1981: could these affect mortality differences among men of working ages?', *Population Trends*, 51, 1983; *Table 3.3*: Heath, A. and McDonald, S.K. 'Social change and the future of the left', *Political Quarterly*, 1987; *Table 3.4*: Goldthorpe, J.H. and Payne, C. 'Trends in intergenerational class mobility in England and Wales 1972–1983', *Sociology*, Vol. 20, No. 1, February 1986; *Table 3.5*: Wright, E.O. *Classes*, p. 83 and p. 89, 1987, Verso; *Table 3.6*: Royal Commission on the Distribution of Income and Wealth, Report No. 8, Cmnd 7679, Table 213; *Tables 4.2 and 4.3*: Brown, C. *Black and White Britain – the PSI Survey*, 1985, Gower, Aldershot; *Table 5.1*: Jowell, R. and Airey, C. (eds.) *British Social Attitudes*, 1984, Gower, Aldershot (Survey year 1983); *Table 6.1*: Boddy, M. *The Building Societies*, 1980, Macmillan, London, Ltd.; *Table 6.3*: D.O.E. *Housing and Construction Statistics*, June 1987; *Table 6.4*: Gough, I. *The Political Economy of the Welfare State*, 1982, The Macmillan Press Ltd.; *Table 6.5*: Banks, O. *Sociology of Education*, 1976, B.T. Batsford Limited; *Table 6.6*: Reid, I. *Social Class Differences in Britain*, 1981, Basil Blackwell Limited; *Table 6.9*: Bentham, G. 'Socio-tenurial polarization in the United Kingdom, 1953–83: the income evidence', *Urban Studies*, Vol. 2, 1986; *Table 6.10*: OPCS, *Census 1981: Housing and Households, England and Wales*, (HMSO), 1983.

Author index

Subject index

Key concepts are printed in bold and the page number in bold indicates where this concept is defined.